Shakespeare's Authentic Performance Texts

Shakespeare's Authentic Performance Texts

The Case for Staging from the First Folio

Graham Watts

McFarland & Company, Inc., Publishers
Jefferson, North Carolina

LIBRARY OF CONGRESS CATALOGUING-IN-PUBLICATION DATA

Watts, Graham, 1959–
Shakespeare's authentic performance texts : the case for staging from the first folio / Graham Watts.
    p.   cm.
Includes bibliographical references and index.

ISBN 978-0-7864-9720-1 (softcover : acid free paper) ♾
ISBN 978-1-4766-1872-2 (ebook)

1. Shakespeare, William, 1564–1616—Dramatic production—Methodology. 2. Shakespeare, William, 1564–1616—Criticism, Textual. 3. Shakespeare, William, 1564–1616—Stage history. I. Title.

PR3091.W388 2015   792.9'5—dc23   2014046484

BRITISH LIBRARY CATALOGUING DATA ARE AVAILABLE

© 2015 Graham Watts. All rights reserved

No part of this book may be reproduced or transmitted in any form or by any means, electronic or mechanical, including photocopying or recording, or by any information storage and retrieval system, without permission in writing from the publisher.

On the cover: artwork *Actors' Changing Room*, 1635, Pieter Codde (© 2015 PicturesNow)

Printed in the United States of America

*McFarland & Company, Inc., Publishers
Box 611, Jefferson, North Carolina 28640
www.mcfarlandpub.com*

To my mother and father,
Patricia Watts *née* Sims and William Watts,
both scholars of history.
They inspired my curiosity and
surrounded me with love.

Acknowledgments

I owe a huge debt of gratitude to Fairbanks Shakespeare Theatre, Alaska, and in particular their extraordinary artistic director Bruce Rogers, who allowed me to direct nine different Shakespeare productions that formed the ideas present in this book. Jo Ryman Scott at the Fairbanks Summer Arts Festival, University of Alaska Fairbanks, and Professor Stephen Crosby of Alfred University, New York, provided intelligent and enthusiastic students who challenged my thinking and tested it in the classroom. Trinity College London supported me throughout the writing process and sent me to work with students from different cultures around the world. John Gardyne, head of Drama and Performance at Trinity, was an invaluable guide in the early stages of this book. I first became aware of the importance of the First Folio by watching productions at Drama Studio London, particularly those directed by Crispin Harris. Two theatre companies in Germany—the English Theatre of Hamburg and White Horse Theatre—engaged me to direct several Shakespeare plays which provided a German perspective. Without Terry Hands, former artistic director of the Royal Shakespeare Company, I wouldn't be a director today. His wisdom, kindness, and generosity were both life-changing and humbling. The same may be said of my friend and accountant Keith Dixon who has not only kept me afloat financially in the precarious world of the theatre but has sponsored my productions and encouraged me over a 25-year period. Finally, I must thank the hundreds of actors I've worked with throughout my career—too many to mention by name—who had the courage and creativity to experiment in rehearsal and who also bore my insistence on speaking the text using First Folio punctuation with patience and good humor.

Table of Contents

Acknowledgments vi
Preface 1
Introduction. How Did This Argument Begin? 3

1. The Heavy Hand of the Editors: "Oh pardon me ... that I am meek and gentle with these butchers" 15
2. The Shaman at Work: "Words, words, words" 30
3. Bungling Printers: "You strike like the blind man" 51
4. Creating a Role from the Folio Text: "Know you the character?" 67
5. Shakespeare's Rogues and Vagabonds: "Unperfect actors"? 108
6. Character as Actor: "I can counterfeit the deep tragedian" 121
7. Ambiguity: "Faire is foule, and foule is faire" 147
8. A Director's Approach: "The rich advantage of good exercise" 173
9. Weighing Up the Options: "Measure for Measure" 199

Conclusion. "I'll to my book, for yet ere supper-time I must perform" 213
Chapter Notes 219
Bibliography 241
Index 247

Preface

When we pick up a copy of a Shakespeare play there is an assumption that we will be reading—or performing—the words he wrote. We won't. What is set out on the page is not Shakespeare's text but an editor's version of the script. In some cases this script differs so greatly from the First Folio (printed by Shakespeare's friends and colleagues after his death) that it should rightly be called an adaptation. I've been directing Shakespeare for over 30 years and have lost count of the number of times when an edited text proved to be unplayable. Arguments for revisions seemed persuasive on the page, but when we tried to stage them it was quite a different matter. Actors would spend hours pondering a passage before finally admitting in exasperation, "I don't know why Shakespeare wrote that." A quick look at the First Folio often revealed that, actually, he didn't.

I took these experiences as my theme for a talk I gave to the Bergren Forum at Alfred University, New York. The positive response I received convinced me that there was need for a book on the subject of the (in)stability of modern published Shakespeare. Many months of research in the British Library followed, examining the original printings of the plays and comparing the texts to how they appear in the present day. As a professional director I was then able to place these findings in a rehearsal context. What I discovered is that, with few exceptions, the First Folio copies of Shakespeare's plays are the ones which are most effective dramatically. Neil Freeman and Patrick Tucker reached this conclusion some years ago and have written about it in detail, but until now no one has attempted an in-depth study of the damage modern editors can do to the plays. It is not my intention to advocate a kind of Shakespeare Talibanism, where everything must be understood and presented in one "correct" way. My objective is simply an attempt to free actors and students from the yoke of Shakespeare's editors and encourage them to make their own selections based on the folio text. Hamlet (Shakespeare?) was very clear in his advice: "Let your own discretion be your tutor."

Editors can accidentally limit options and, because they are unaware that an alternative exists, the reader and actor can be left in confusion. In seeking to outline the range of these options, this book is divided into a number of complementary chapters. Firstly, it looks at the editors themselves and the substantial changes they make to individual words, characters, line assignments, the meter of the verse and the structure of the prose, as well their refusal to recognize performance cuts and additions probably made by Shakespeare or at least his company. The work of the printers of the First Folio is examined, as well as how they preserved acting indicators such as speech prefixes, capital letters, italics, spellings/pronunciations, and punctuation that helped Shakespeare's players to perform a role. There is a close study of the texts, including an in-depth analysis of a short ambiguous passage from *Henry V* and a consideration of the character of Iago as actor, a director's approach to rehearsing a Shakespeare play with various exercises useful for both professional and student actors, and finally a chapter on *Measure for Measure* where all of the findings are applied to one play. Throughout the book the texts most referred to are generally the better-known works. The objective is to provide the reader/actor/director with a common starting point that can then be applied when tackling other plays in the canon. Similarly, the editions often quoted are the Arden ("texts for performance") and New Penguin ("prepared from the original texts") since they are the most popular volumes used in contemporary professional theatre. Act, scene, and line numbers follow the latest Arden publications. All quotes from the First Folio are taken from Charlton Hinman, *The First Folio of Shakespeare: The Norton Facsimile*, 2nd edition (New York: W. W. Norton, 1996).

Introduction

How Did This Argument Begin?

The popular image of anyone who works professionally producing Shakespeare is that they are an irrelevant group of "artistes" who are lazy, pampered, self-indulgent, often neurotic, a drain on the public purse, snobs who perform to other snobs, and people who should get a "proper job." That was certainly the type of view shared by the British Prime Minister Margaret Thatcher, who made it a priority in her first term in government to investigate the Royal Shakespeare Company. She sent Clive Priestley and a team from the "Efficiency Unit" (i.e., Cuts Unit) to the company headquarters in Stratford to discover how much money was being wastefully floated down the Avon in the name of "art." The resulting Priestley Report became known as the "love letter on white paper" as not only did he find sound financial management but concluded that the RSC was "palpably under funded" and recommended an increase rather than a reduction in subsidy. One of the things Priestley highlighted was the "devotion" of the staff. Simply put, he couldn't believe that people were working so hard, with such dedication, producing such quality, for so small a financial return.[1]

Clive Priestley was right, of course. An incredible amount of time and energy is expended before an audience sees a Shakespeare play performed. This not only includes the heavy contribution of the production departments but long hours of rehearsal which might incorporate stage fighting, acrobatics, vocal coaching, movement classes, singing, dance, historical research, and close study of the text. It's no exaggeration to say that actors will invest their whole being into creating a role and their scrupulous endeavors to "get it right" continue throughout the run of a play. Every area is examined and reexamined down to the smallest detail—apart from one. Modern professional theatre doesn't question the text they are working from. Everything else comes in for scrutiny but the actual words that are said (apart from cuts and some minor word alterations) are left unchallenged in the hands of the producers of the plays. This book seeks to address that.

Editors alter words, punctuation, the structure of both verse and prose, assign lines to different characters, and even change the characters in scenes. A more correct term for them would be editor/adaptors—they adapt the text and therefore the meaning. Here's a small example from *Henry IV, Part 1*, Act 3, scene 3, line 196. The First Folio printing of 1623 sets Hal's dialogue as:

> Go *Peto,* to horse: for thou, and I,
> Have thirtie miles to ride yet ere dinner time.[2]

That seems simple enough. Most modern editions, however, follow the first two (probably unauthorized) quarto publications and add an extra "to horse" even though quartos 3–5 and all four folios have only one "to horse." They alter a 9-beat line (perhaps indicating a hesitation from Peto so that the Prince has to qualify his instruction?) to one of 11 beats. Not too much of a difficulty to cope with, one might think, but the single word "Peto" has caused controversy among editor/adaptors. It is crucial that the director and the actor playing Peto should at the very least know who is actually in the scene. Not Peto, says the *New Cambridge Shakespeare*, and changes the character to Poins. Citing previous editor/adaptors Dr. Johnson and Edmond Malone, the New Cambridge edition argues:

> Poins suits the metre.... I may also add that it would be strange for Poins to disappear altogether after *l.* 146 and yet turn up later in *2 Hen. IV* with all his old vivacity.[3]

The third Arden version of the play differs and prints "Peto," although it still adds the extra "to horse." The editor/adaptor, David Scott Kastan, remarks that to change "Peto" to "Poins" "seems editorially inappropriate, correcting Shakespeare, rather than trying merely to recover what he wrote."[4] The Warwick Shakespeare[5] agrees with him and places Peto in the scene, although the lines are set as prose, not verse, leaving one to speculate why the extra "to horse" is also included since there is no "problem" with the meter to justify it. Perhaps the most schizophrenic volume when it comes to this passage is the well-regarded Oxford Shakespeare. An early "Complete Works" edited by the noted scholar W. J. Craig follows Dr. Johnson by printing "Go Poins."[6] Incorrect, proclaims the current Oxford Shakespeare individual publication of *Henry IV, Part 1*, who returns it to "Peto."[7] The more recent Oxford "Complete Works"[8] contradicts both colleagues and sets something entirely different: "Go Harvey." The editor/adaptors argue that this was Shakespeare's original intention before Elizabethan politics caused a name change, but although "Harvey" can be found as a stage direction in the first quarto it is not printed within the body of the dialogue. The same character reappears in *Henry IV, Part 2* but, in the Oxford "Complete Works," not as "Harvey"—he suddenly becomes "Peto" again.

Confused? It's no wonder. And this is just one word, in one scene, of the 36–40 plays that Shakespeare wrote or had a hand in. As the pressure from the "Shakespeare Industry" increases to come up with new angles, pruning the language has become the norm so that each fresh edition has become almost like a new play. As an example, the Oxford "Complete Works" alters Iago's military title of "Ancient" to "Ensign." One of its editors, the highly respected Stanley Wells, explains, "'Ancient' could be seriously misleading, so we prefer 'Ensign.'"[9]

His view is that the audience and reader might mistakenly think Iago is old. This type of alteration is the start of a slippery slope. Should the Apothecary in *Romeo and Juliet* be called a Pharmacist? The Soothsayer in *Julius Caesar* be referred to as an Astrologer? Or Dr. Pinch in *The Comedy of Errors* have his title "Conjurer" reassigned to Exorcist? This is not editing the plays but translating them. An actor and director will search in vain to find a consistent and secure text that supports them in performance. Shakespearean academics appear unconcerned with how the words might play on the stage.

The relatively insular world of academia is not something that has gone unnoticed by the scholars themselves. M. R. Ridley, editor of the second edition of the Arden *Othello*, wrote, "A good deal of Shakespearean textual criticism is an elaborate game, entertaining to the players ... but not very profitable."[10] An example of this can be found in *Shakespeare the Thinker* by the critic/commenter A. D. Nuttall. In a chapter on *Anthony and Cleopatra*, Professor Nuttall confidently writes:

> The union of Anthony & Cleopatra, meanwhile, is childless. Here Shakespeare departs from Plutarch—I believe deliberately. He wanted—not sterility—but a certain blankness to surround this spectacular case of *egoisme a deux*.[11]

Professor Nuttall seems more concerned with scoring points over his colleagues by proposing a fresh idea than watching or reading the play itself. "My theme can lick your theme" is how Richard Levin puts it.[12] In Act 3, scene 6, line 7, of *Anthony and Cleopatra* (set here as in the First Folio), Octavius Caesar describes the two protagonists:

> And all the unlawfull issue, that their Lust
> Since then hath made betweene them
> ...
> His Sonnes hither proclaimed the King of Kings,
> Great Media, Parthia, and Armenia
> He gave to *Alexander*. To *Ptolomy* he assign'd,
> Syria, Silicia, and Phoenetia: she
> In th' abiliments of the Goddesse *Isis*
> That day appeer'd, and oft before gave audience,
> As 'tis reported so.

Alexander and Ptolomy are of course, in Shakespeare as well as Plutarch, the sons of Anthony and Cleopatra; their union is not childless, as Nuttall proclaims. For an actor playing Octavius Caesar, this is vital information. Not only is Anthony raising his children by another woman while married to Octavius's own sister, but he is dividing up the Roman Empire—the theme of the consequences of such divisions can also be seen in *King Lear*. The actor playing Octavius has a strong motivation to invade Egypt and sever the Anthony/Cleopatra knot. "A certain blankness," to quote Professor Nuttall, is totally irrelevant to *actors* in this play and could very well guide them towards a passionless performance.

Editors change the folio line "His Sonnes hither proclaimed the King of Kings" to "His Sonnes he there[13] proclaimed the Kings of Kings." Octavius mentions the plural "sonnes" so the grammatically minded editors adjust the singular "King" to "Kings." This gives a completely different meaning, and the idea conveyed is that they, like Banquo, will be father to a line of kings. However, the honorific "The King of Kings" not only means "emperor" but is one conferred on Jesus Christ, born during the period the play is set. To further underline this allusion, "Herod of Jewry" is mentioned four times in the play. The passage goes on to paint a picture of Cleopatra as a goddess. Anthony and Cleopatra are becoming not just a political threat but a spiritual one too. The stakes for the actors are thus raised higher. This is backed up by history. Octavius became the first emperor of Rome and was given the name Augustus—"the revered one." On his death he was proclaimed a god. It was his adopted son, Tiberius, who succeeded him and ruled the Roman Empire when Christ was killed.

When actors and directors become part of Ridley's "elaborate game," they can produce work that lacks immediacy and vitality as the text is not discovered moment by moment in performance but rather repeated out of pages written, often long ago, in the confines of the study. It leads to the "Deadly Theatre" described by Peter Brook in his groundbreaking book *The Empty Space*: "The Deadly Theatre approaches the classics from the viewpoint that somewhere, someone has found out and defined how the play should be done."[14] As Jonathan Miller puts it, work appears "quoted rather than produced."[15] Miller very astutely labels this "cloning" and it's easy to see why. If you asked a random group of people to think of Juliet and describe what she looks like, most of them would answer "She's small, white, with flowing, straight, dark hair, wearing a long dress." It's difficult not to agree with Jonathan Miller that it's as if there's a contract with Actors Equity demanding Shakespearean characters should always be presented in the same way. And so onstage we see Cleopatra wearing a headband (often of a snake), an abundance of fur in productions of *King Lear* and, even in a modern-dress film of *Hamlet*, Claudius ripping up a paper on the line "So much for him."[16] A favorite scenic staging is to have passive women sitting sewing with a tapestry ring, for no particular reason. From an actor and director's point of view a character's *actions,* in the latter case sewing, are vitally important. Take Mariana in *Measure for Measure* as an example. If she's given an action in a scene where she's stitching her own clothes because of poverty, it tells one story. If she's lovingly embroidering a shirt that once belonged to Angelo, it tells another. A sewing ring tells us nothing and stands in the way of conveying the narrative. It is my belief, born out of a 30-plus year career spent in the rehearsal room grappling with 28 Shakespeare productions, that not only can editors and critics fail to enlighten the actor but they can often be harmful and dam the flow of creative juices. Rather than deferring to scholarly editions prepared by editor/adaptors, actors and directors will find most help and inspiration in the pages of the First Folio text.

It's worth recapping the circumstances of the publication of Shakespeare's plays. As far as we know, none were published *with his authority* during his lifetime.[17] Then, seven years after his death,[18] his two close friends and actor/business partners, John Heminge and Henry Condell, printed them in what has become known as the First Folio. We have a lot to thank Heminge and Condell for and yet, apart from a small bust of Shakespeare near the Barbican in London, there is no lasting monument to these two great men. These two great *actors*. And perhaps that's the reason why. Philip Edwards, in his 1985 New Cambridge edition of *Hamlet*, expresses the commonly held view that Shakespeare's plays were ruined by actors: "It is sadly true that the nearer we get to the stage, the further we are getting from Shakespeare."[19] Edwards's speculation completely ignores the fact that Shakespeare himself was part of the "stage" he speaks so disparagingly of. Shakespeare is named in the First Folio as one of the "Principal Actors" of his own plays. He was there when they were first performed; alongside Heminge and Condell. Surely Bernice Kliman, a pioneer in making Shakespeare texts available online with *The Enfolded Hamlets*, is right when she says:

> The main argument against the Folio—that it is a text contaminated by theatrical experience—was for me the principal argument in its favor, for the contaminating actors were Shakespeare's colleagues.[20]

Without Heminge and Condell, half of Shakespeare's plays would have been lost to us; plays we all enjoy, such as *The Tempest, Twelfth Night, As You Like It, Macbeth*, and *Julius Caesar*. Their publication caused a scandal as they were lovingly printed on the same quality paper as the Bible, which seriously upset the Puritans of the time. Place a copy of the "Authorized" King James Bible alongside Shakespeare's First Folio and they look fairly similar, although the Bible was printed in a larger format than a folio so that it fitted on a church lectern. The plays were billed as "Published according to the true original copies":

> He, not having the fate, common with some, to be executor to his own writings.... We have but collected them, and done an office to the dead, to procure his Orphans, Guardians; without ambition either of self-profit, or fame; only to keep the memory of so worthy a friend and fellow alive, as was our SHAKESPEARE ... it hath been the height of our care, who are the presenters, to make the present worthy of your Highnesses by the perfection ... by a pair so careful to show their gratitude both to the living, and the dead."[21]

In short they are saying it was a careful labor of love to keep their friend's memory alive, not undertaken out of motive for profit (in fact printing them could have caused their company a considerable loss of income),[22] but to be *guardians* of his plays, the *executor* of them. Unlike Ben Jonson's *Works*[23] they did not include Shakespeare's poems but stuck to what they knew best—the plays.

If the Dedicatory Epistle to the First Folio didn't spell it out enough, Heminge and Condell are even clearer in their introduction:

> We pray you do not envy his friends, the office of their care, and pain, ... and so to have published them, as where before you were abused with diverse stolen, and surreptious copies, maimed, and deformed by the frauds and stealthes of injurious imposters, that exposed them: even those are now offered to your view cured, and perfect of their limbs, and all the rest, absolute in their numbers,[24] as he conceived them.[25]

Were his friends lying? "Cured and perfect of their limbs ... as he conceived them." Here is the *only* direct link between Shakespeare and not one but *two* people who had worked with him for over 20 years and knew the plays intimately. Many of the characters were written especially for them, they'd performed in the premieres, and without doubt they would have spent many hours talking directly to Shakespeare about his work. Yet the editor/adaptors ignore this very clear and unambiguous statement and make extensive alterations to the texts. And who do they blame for having to make these changes? Heminge and Condell. As an example, here's M. R. Ridley talking about them in his introduction to an Arden *Othello*:

> They were not hampered by modern notions of scholarship.... They conceived it to be their business to present to their contemporaries and to posterity the work of their beloved and admired fellow in the "best" shape that they could manage. If, therefore, Shakespeare had written what they considered he should not have written, they thought it laudable, and not, as we think it, reprehensible, to put him right.[26]

There is not a single shred of evidence to support Ridley's condescending view. Indeed, the prefaces to the folio point to the contrary. What seems to have escaped Ridley is the irony of his conjecture. The "modern notions of scholarship" he describes in the first half of his statement are *exactly* that of the second. It is the present-day editor/adaptors who believe that, if Shakespeare has written something they consider he should not have written, it is laudable to put him right. Sometimes they do this through leaps of imagination but most often by reference to the quarto editions of Shakespeare's plays that were published during and after his life. The quartos *do* have authority over the folio in many places and it would be foolish to completely discard them. However, it doesn't seem fully credible that the folio printers—under instruction from Shakespeare's fellows to set the text faithfully—should be less able in their work than the pirating printers of the quartos who were out to turn a quick profit.

In referring to the plays published in quarto, editor/adaptors sometimes show little systematic methodology other than personal taste. *Othello*, like *King Lear*, exists in a very different version in the folio, probably a rewrite, and as such represents an opportunity for editor/adaptors to prove "what Shakespeare really meant" by cherry-picking material from the two quartos that were published to create a completely new text. In the first scene of *Othello* alone—just 230 lines—editor/adaptors make 59 changes; that is, they alter about a quarter of the lines that Shakespeare wrote. This is by no means unusual. In some plays and scenes the percentage is even higher. And many of the things they change from the folio are vital to actors in performance. In fact, it might be said that the First Folio text is Shakespeare's blueprint for helping actors to perform his plays. It is this text, free from the hands of editor/adaptors, to which performers should (at least initially) refer when creating their roles.

There are three basic arguments against the folio. First, that some of the plays and passages were constructed from actors' bad memories. An example of this view was expressed by Harold Jenkins, editor/adaptor of the Arden *Hamlet*, who comments on one section: "It seems more likely the confusion arose in the memory of the actors and that F [folio] here reproduces what was actually spoken on the stage."[27]

Shakespeare's actors performed several different plays each week, so they must have had phenomenal memories or the plays would have been hooted off the stage.[28] As Leo Kirchbaum writes:

> Did the Elizabethan actor customarily jumble his own lines, borrow phrases and lines from other actors ... jump ten or more lines because of a similar phraseology in two passages, sometimes with the consequent omission of other actors' speeches?[29]

The second argument is that some of the text in the folio was prepared from Shakespeare's "Foul Papers"[30]—copy that was in his own handwriting, full of changes, cuts, and additions. There is a false assumption that because the plays were handwritten they were unclear. This is a modern view of handwriting. In fact, the first thing most people do when looking at an old document is marvel at the "copperplate" handwriting. At the British Library, there is a volume of Chaucer with notes made by Gabriel Harvey in 1598, and his writing is not only fully legible but almost a work of art. Displayed alongside this book is what is thought to be the prompt copy of Massinger's "Believe as You List" from 1631, and although the handwriting is not as accomplished as Harvey's, it is perfectly readable. This was not the age of typewriters and computers; to be understood, people had to make sure their handwriting was clear.

Leaving aside Heminge and Condell's claim that they "have scarce received from him a blot in his papers" (were they lying again?), the plays were subject to an intense state censorship. Shakespeare's company, before performance, had to submit a clean copy of the script to the Master of the Revels *by law* or they couldn't perform the play. There was even a man, "the Book Keeper"[31] (Edward Knight[32]/Thomas Vincent in Shakespeare's troupe), whose special job was to look after this text—what is still in theatre called "the book," that is, the prompt copy. When the book for *The Winter's Tale* was lost, Heminge had to submit another copy to the Master of the Revels before any subsequent performances could take place.[33] If the text couldn't be clearly read by the Master of the Revels, then he would simply send it back. Henry Herbert, for example, wrote to a theatre company before licensing a play, "I command your Bookeeper to present me with a fairer Copy hereafter."[34]

The fee charged by the Master of the Revels wasn't cheap—£1 for a reading and license but £2 if the text required cutting or a further read. If you consider that Henslowe paid writers around £5–8 per script and £1 was an artisan worker's monthly salary, then the vital importance for a playhouse to keep an accurate copy of the play can be seen. Edmund Tilney, the Master of the Revels, even threatened the actors that unless they made changes to *The Book of Thomas More* it would be "at their peril."[35] As far as we know it was never performed. Given the sadistic range of Elizabethan punishments that Tilney's "peril" might have entailed, we can be pretty certain the company kept a close hand on their scripts.

The folio often inserts actors' names in place of characters, which is an indication that a performance prompt book was sometimes used as proof for the printers.[36] That is not to say that the prompt book was used to set *all* of the texts; we know that isn't the case, and it was, of course, written out by hand. While it's certainly true that half of the plays in the folio had to have been set from handwritten pages since they had never been previously printed, the handwriting would have been that of a professional scribe. And if the actors could read what was on the page, so could a printer, whose job it was every single day to set texts from handwritten copy. All of the plays had been performed before printing[37] so there would have been prompt books for them, although it's possible they might have perished when the Globe Theatre burned down in 1613. The script, remember, was the property of the theatre company and not the author. Some scholars believe that copy for some of the late plays came from Shakespeare's own papers, and they label this group the "Stratford Texts," as they imagine Shakespeare wrote these plays in retirement in Stratford and sent his scripts to the King's Men down in London. He was therefore not on hand to check and adjust the transposition and supervise the performance. Of course, there's no actual evidence for this speculation. We know from public records that Shakespeare was in London in 1612, 1613,[38] and 1614, and the retirement of people in their late 40s was very uncommon at this time. What is factually true is that there is no play in the folio that Shakespeare didn't at least contribute to and no play excluded that was wholly written by him. So these two actor/editors did a pretty good job. A manuscript from the period from which a play was printed has not survived, let alone Shakespeare's plays or the folio, so *any* alterations made on the basis of faulty printer's copy must remain conjecture.[39] However, common sense would suggest that, in undertaking such a huge and important project as the printing of the First Folio (a task that took at least two years), there must have been a much more ordered approach than the scraps of paper, old and poorly written out actor play scripts, corrupt quartos, and much altered prompt books that the editor/adaptors would have us believe Heminge and Condell worked from.

The third (related) argument against the folio is that the text suffered at the hands of negligent compositors, the general attitude being best expressed by W. J. Craig that the printers "introduced much that is unintelligible into the original editions of Shakespeare's works."[40]

There is a case to support this view, as there are undoubtedly printing errors in the First Folio. However, many of the plays underwent a thorough proofreading process prior to publication. We know this as pages with corrected copy survive and they adjust the smallest detail. Can it really be conceivable that Shakespeare's two close friends (who had both named their sons William), turning the pages to read the folio and seeing on their fingers the ring that Shakespeare had left them in his will, would have allowed the enormous numbers of "mistakes" that modern editor/adaptors propose?[41] It seems inescapable not to support the conclusion reached by Charlotte Porter and Helen Clarke[42] in the preface to the Pembroke Shakespeare Edition of the *Complete Works* (1903): "The First Folio remains, as a matter of fact, the text nearest to Shakespeare's stage, to Shakespeare's ownership, to Shakespeare's authority."[43]

If we accept Porter and Clarke, why has a whole industry developed that seeks to "correct" the folio and find Shakespeare's "true meaning"? The root of the problem is the view that Shakespeare was an *actor,* worked in the theatre with other actors, and collectively this has destroyed his true poetical intent. Even in his own lifetime he was spoken of in derogatory terms for being a mere actor—"Shakespeare Ye Player"—[44] and Alexander Pope, the second editor of the *Collected Works* in 1725, took up this theme with gusto:

> Players are just such judges of what is *right* as Tailors are of what is *graceful*. And in this view it will be but fair to allow that most of our Author's faults are less to be ascribed to his wrong judgement as a Poet than to his right judgement as a Player.[45]

He goes on to blame "the ignorance of the Players" for "innumerable errors" when printing Shakespeare's work. Despite the fact that, as actors, Heminge and Condell spoke the language onstage every day of their working lives, Pope absurdly states, "Prose from verse they did not know." He proposed that a new edited volume of the plays was needed to save Shakespeare's genius from "the Impertinence of his first Editors."[46]

Pope, of course, was himself a poet, and the idea of Shakespeare as primarily a poet ruined by contact with the acting world is an ignoble tradition that persists to this day. In *Shakespeare's Language*, Frank Kermode, writing on the sonnets, speculates:

> It seems reasonable to suggest that he arrived in London intending to make his way as a poet not of the theatre but of the page.... Perhaps 1593 was the year when Shakespeare thought he could free himself from the drudgery of the theatre; he could even have welcomed the opportunity offered him by the long intermission of the plague.[47]

It begs the question that if this were true, why didn't Shakespeare produce any poetry when, according to Kermode, he stopped writing plays and lived in comfortable retirement?[48] Frank Kermode is perhaps the type of person Jonathan Bate had in mind when he wrote of "bookish scholars ... who (like everyone who writes about Shakespeare) have a subliminal desire to make him more like themselves than he really was."[49]

The major difference between an academic and a performer's approach to the text is that where an academic will propose an *explanation* of a line, an actor will seek its *motivation*. The former's purpose is to provide a solution to the overall meaning of the play, but the latter will attempt to discover exactly why and how the characters have created the circumstances in the script. For example, it's interesting to note, as the "Cambridge Student Guide" does, that Richard III might be the "Scourge of God"[50] chosen to punish a sinful people. An actor, in the character of Richard, would be unaware of this. In the play he has no dialogue with God in the same way Faustus does with Mephistopheles in Marlowe's *Dr. Faustus*. Both the director producing *Richard III* and the actor playing the title role will want to answer just one simple question: *Why* does Richard behave in the way he does? A performer will be uninterested to learn *The Comedy of Errors* observes the classic unity of time, but modern editor/adaptors devote thousands of words to this concept. What the time scheme indicates to an actor is pace and that their character should be concerned the clock is counting down to Egeon's death. Hal has a soliloquy in *Henry IV, Part 1* that is crucial not only to his character but to how he behaves in the two plays that come after it (if performed as part of a cycle). It comes at the very end of Act 1, scene 2, line 206, and concludes:

> Ile so offend, to make offence a skill,
> Redeeming time, when men thinke least I will.

It's a complex speech in which Hal seems to be saying that he is only feigning his raucous antics so that his later "reformation" might place him in a better light. But he also states, "I will imitate the Sun (Son)," so could he be playacting when addressing his father too? This will raise all sorts of questions for the actor: "Is Hal manipulative and selfish?" "Is this a prepared plan or an instinctive reaction to events in the scene?" "In behaving in this way does he mirror his father's shifty personality?" "Is he jealous of, and vindictive towards, his father?" and so on. What won't assist a performer is to read an editor/adaptor's assessment of the passage such as this from G. L. Kittredge: "This is, in effect, the author's explanation—a kind of chorus—and should be so understood."[51]

For a director to tell an actor playing Hamlet that he has an "Oedipus complex" is not helpful since, if true, he would be unaware of it. Following the editor/adaptor's commentary could lead to what is referred to as "faculty thinking."[52] The actor will wish to respond spontaneously to events[53] in scenes with his mother moment by moment and create an imagined back story of Hamlet's childhood. This may or may not add up to the onstage portrayal of an "Oedipus complex." Where Shakespearean directors can often go off course is that they read a theory on the play put forward by an academic and then try to make their production fit that view, sometimes with disastrous results.[54]

The focus of this book is on the editor/adaptors, but it's worth pausing for a moment and recording some of the more bizarre assessments of Shakespeare's plays and characters published recently in the world of academia. Richard Levin charted a few of their declarations in his excellent book *New Readings vs. Old Plays*.[55] Levin displays good manners by not naming and shaming the scholars who wrote the following statements so they remain anonymous:

Of *Romeo & Juliet*: "The tragedy is not primarily concerned with love."[56]
Of Romeo, comparing him to Richard III and calling Juliet his "victim": "Like Richard, also, Romeo is a catalyst for disaster, and something close to a mass murderer."[57]

The idea that many much-loved Shakespearean characters are in reality psychopaths appears to be a popular one with critical commentators, as in the following descriptions of Henry V and Brutus quoted by Levin:

"Whatever Shakespeare may say about Henry, in his heart he regarded him as a murderer."[58]
"Brutus commits unmitigated acts of savagery as a result of his having broken all ties with humanity."[59]

Hamlet, Shakespeare's most famous character, doesn't escape without censure either. He's apparently "a profane fool ... a fellow celebrant with Claudius in a black mass."[60] Nor are the character criticisms gender specific. Desdemona, the woman described by Cassio as "perfection," has, in a commentator's mind, a previously unseen fatal flaw: "She cannot face her own feminine fraility ... [and] shrinks from the reality of the whore within her."[61] Imagine the consequences if an actor or director were to attempt to incorporate these views in performance.

It is to the "ouija board of the surviving texts," as David Scott Kastan puts it,[62] that we must turn if we are to discover "Shakespeare's meanings." As published in the First Folio, they contain many directorial notes: scene intentions, clues to character and mood, how to deliver individual lines and words, and overall purpose and intention. Heminge and Condell urged: "Read him, therefore; and again, and again."[63] It was the First Folio volume of Shakespeare's plays they meant when they wrote this and not any other, including previously published quartos. Editor/adaptors, commentators and critics, often seem to set themselves up as Shakespeare's shaman; they are in a privileged position to unlock the meaning of the text and full understanding will only come through the conduit of their unique intelligences.[64] It is a position they are not bashful in proclaiming, as in the following advice from Frank Kermode to actors: "The meaning is best left to editors and commentators." He adds (seemingly unaware of the irony), "I myself, when editing *The Tempest*, wrote a note of about a thousand words on the passage, to nobody's great benefit."[65]

The encroachment of the editor/adaptor into the world of the stage is rapidly increasing. As recently as 2003, a series of published essays called *In Arden* gave an overview of contemporary editorial practices in the widely used Arden series. From within its pages R. A. Foakes declares, "Editors should be encouraged to take more liberties in suggesting possible action."[66]

It is precisely this "taking of liberties" that actors and directors should beware of. Foakes is backed by his colleague George Walton Williams who in the same volume writes, "Every editor should be a director whose page is his stage."[67]

Williams encourages editors to rewrite stage directions. The example he gives is from *Richard III* Act 1, scene 1, line 41, where the folio has "Enter Clarence, and Brakenbury, guarded." Williams thinks it would make better sense if it read "Enter Clarence guarded, and Brakenbury" since Brakenbury is not under arrest. All published editions print something along those lines. For the actor playing Brakenbury, the folio stage direction is important. To feel he is also under guard while simultaneously guarding Clarence gives a wonderful frisson to this scene, explains his actions and motivation, and shows the audience what a police state England has become under Edward.[68] This is a very small detail but one which performers will grasp with relish. What Williams proposes denies them that opportunity. Moreover it runs contrary to the text. Brackenbury is a person who does not like to get directly involved, which is why a probable Shakespeare rewrite substitutes "Brackenbury the Lieutenant" (as the folio calls him elsewhere) attending on Clarence in his cell with an undefined "Keeper." This label of "Keeper" has led modern editions to place Brackenbury as the man who has custody of the princes in the Tower in Act 4, scene 1 (despite the fact that all the quartos and folios specify a plain "Lieutenant"), but this is not the type of responsibility he would undertake. Seeing clearly how events are unfolding around him Brackenbury disappears, his attitude being:

> I will not reason what is meant heereby,
> Because I will be guiltlesse from the meaning.[69]

He's the perfect example of Edmund Burke's famous warning: "All that is necessary for evil to triumph is for good men to do nothing." Perhaps it is fitting that he is one of those named as dying in the Battle of Bosworth.[70] With a simple changing of a stage direction, not only is a character reduced but a level of the play's meaning is stripped away.

Williams goes further: "The editor must decide how the actor should speak one particular group of speeches—specifically the 'aside.'"[71] Let's take a short passage from *Julius Caesar* to demonstrate this. In Act 2, scene 2, line 123, there is an exchange between Caesar and the Conspirators who are attempting to lure him to the Senate in order to commit their act of assassination. In the folio the passage reads as follows, with Caesar first talking to Trebonius:

Caesar.
Be neere me, that I may remember you.

Trebonius.
Caesar I will: and so neere will I be,
That your best Friends shall wish I had beene further.

Caesar.
Good Friends go in, and taste some wine with me
And we (like Friends) will straight way go together.

Brutus.
That every like is not the same, O *Caesar,*
The heart of *Brutus* earnes to thinke upon.

Almost all published modern editions mark the speeches of Trebonius and Brutus as "asides" and in doing so destroy the wonderful complexity of the situation. If they are not asides, as in the folio, then Trebonius's response to Caesar is laden with irony. He is apparently innocently saying that Caesar's friends will be jealous, but there is an obvious subtext. Does Caesar realize this and dare Trebonius to do his worst, all of it couched as humorous remarks among "friends"? He is, after all, the "immortal" Caesar. His reply picks up on Trebonius's words and is likewise ironic; they will go to the Senate *like* friends—he knows they actually aren't. And what of Brutus? Does Caesar recognize his words are a warning in the same way Calphurnia has just attempted to prevent his journey to the Capitol that day? If so, he will be even more shocked to discover Brutus is actually part of the conspiracy and prompts Caesar's famous words "Et tu Brute?" Is this the moment Brutus's careful logic gives way to emotion? Has he suddenly got "cold feet"? After all, there is no Cassius in the scene to support him. This is the stuff of drama and yet the most recent Arden volume, edited by David Daniell, doesn't even record that Brutus's words are not marked as an aside in the folio and instead gives the desperately unhelpful actor note "The Latin proverb *Omne simile non est idem*" with no translation.[72] There are four ways to approach this short exchange:

1. Trebonius's and Brutus's lines are both asides.
2. Only Trebonius's lines are an aside.
3. Only Brutus's lines are an aside.
4. Neither Brutus's nor Trebonius's lines are asides.

In only printing option number 1, editor/adaptors provide just 25 percent of the potential of this scene, and yet George Walton Williams would have this become a universal practice.

The final word should go to George Bernard Shaw:

> The simple thing to do with a Shakespeare play is to perform it. The alternative is to let it alone. If Shakespeare made a mess of it, it is not likely that Smith or Robinson will succeed where he failed.[73]

1

The Heavy Hand of the Editors

*"Oh pardon me ... that I am meek
and gentle with these butchers"*

In beginning this chapter on some of the changes editor/adaptors make to the First Folio text, it should be very clearly stressed that *not all of their departures are misguided.* There are undoubtedly flaws in the folio printing of one kind or another, for a variety of reasons. Hero in *Much Ado About Nothing*, for example, has three folio speeches where her prefix is marked as "Bero,"[1] but it would absurd to insist that this must be slavishly followed and characters should refer to her as "Bero." Nor is it likely that Shakespeare intended Hamlet to speak of "the dreadfull Sonnet of the Cliffe," which is the First Folio setting for "the dreadful summit of the cliff." In fact, some of the quarto printings of both *Much Ado About Nothing* and *Hamlet* are arguably less error-strewn than the folio. The problem arises when ever-increasing volumes of alterations are made on much less secure ground so that the plays stray further and further away from their author's original performance intentions. Many of these changes are made but not noted by the editor, so that textual impositions become accepted as fact.

As an example, in the New Penguin edition of *King John*, a fairly consistent and worthy volume, the editor R. L. Smallwood explains, "Obvious misprints in Folio have been silently corrected, as have the very few instances of obvious mislineation."[2] The Arden version of the same play, edited by E. A. J. Honigmann, employs much the same tone, stating that some changes "are passed over silently."[3]

"Obvious" to whom? And why "silently"? This is the very crux of the problem an actor and director face when using an edited copy of a play. They hit a scene, passage, line, word, or character detail that doesn't make sense, and it's often because Shakespeare's original has been hidden from them. Both Smallwood and Honigmann express noble aims. Honigmann writes, "the present edition follows the Folio as closely as possible,"[4] and gives warning of the apparent textual problems in *King John* highlighted by other editors: "Some of the 'inconsistencies' are actually subtleties, and the editors and not Shakespeare himself must be blamed for working too hurriedly."[5] Similarly, Smallwood states, "The Folio text seems to have been set up from an authorial manuscript ... the Folio text presents few problems."[6] He goes on to praise Honigmann for his "exceptional conservatism in handling the Folio text."[7] One wonders why, with this "exceptional conservatism," both Smallwood and Honigmann, along with the majority of the editors of *King John*, including the much respected

Riverside edition, completely remove the character of the Citizen of Angiers from the play and give his lines to a totally different character, Hubert?

At first glance, and examining the text in the study, the reasons for this can seem persuasive, and it's entirely to do with one of the errors in the folio mentioned earlier. In Act 2, scene 1, a character appears on the walls of the besieged city of Angiers who for his first four speeches in the folio (beginning line 201) is called "Citizen." He exits in the scene[8] but when he returns at line 325 he now has the prefix "Hubert." Obviously a mistake has been made—but is the character Citizen or Hubert? Most editors, no doubt because "Hubert" appears more times in the text prefixes than "Citizen," assign the role to Hubert. Apart from the excellent Royal Shakespeare Company *Complete Works*, which gives all the lines to the Citizen but notes the character may be Hubert, this change is often passed over without much comment. Might not the role in Act 2 be equally assigned to the Citizen? The BBC Shakespeare, normally conservative in following modern editors, does exactly that in the 1984 TV film of *King John* and there is no noticeable loss to the narrative, meaning, or the character of Hubert. In performance, it works. Shakespeare's probable sources "The Troublesome Reign of King John" and Holinshed's "Chronicles" make no mention whatsoever of Hubert being a Citizen of Angiers. In fact, Holinshed says the English "slue manie of the citizens" and left "the wals of the citie beaten flat to the ground,"[9] so, historically at least, the Citizen would have been unlikely to survive. Later, Holinshed calls Hubert "a man of notable prowesse and valiancie,"[10] which the Citizen of Angiers is clearly not.

Why was the word "Hubert" substituted for "Citizen" in this scene? Possibly because the two roles were doubled so the actor playing Hubert also played the part of Citizen, hence the use of two character names for one actor's part. T. J. King, in his landmark study of the distribution of Shakespeare's roles, has a single actor playing both the Citizen and Hubert.[11] It was Shakespeare's practice to sometimes write an actor's name and not the character as a speech prefix, and the folio retains several examples of this.[12] Honigmann is correct in saying that there is "no comparable parallel in the canon"[13] for a character name being inserted to denote an actor's doubling of roles, but this, of course, is no proof that it didn't happen on this occasion.[14]

King John is a frustrating play to date. Academics generally agree it was probably written around 1596, but it has examples of fine writing that suggest maturity and experience, and clumsiness that points to it being from the early period of Shakespeare's career. There is an argument that the text printed in the folio is a rewrite of an earlier play, *The Troublesome Reign of King John*. If this is true—and there is no concrete evidence that supports this theory—Shakespeare at the time of writing *Troublesome Reign* was unattached to any particular theatre. Perhaps, not yet the famous author he was to become, he was writing a play that could be performed by *any* company, so it's possible he used the character and not the actor name for the doubling in *Troublesome Reign* and it found its way into the rewrite and printing of *King John*.[15] In other words, Shakespeare is indicating that the actor who played Hubert in performance should also double the separate part of Citizen of Angiers. Later, when he was a shareholder, he could assign roles to his fellows and insert their name in the text. This theory is speculative to say the least, but it's certainly possible. The title page of the first quarto of another early Shakespeare play, *Titus Andronicus*, states that it was acted by three separate companies: Pembroke's Men, Derby's Men, and Sussex's Men.

The circumstances that caused one role to be called both Citizen and Hubert will never be known with any certainty until, as David Crystal puts it, "séance science takes a huge leap forward,"[16] but we *can* look at the text to examine the differences in the characters of the Citizen and Hubert. What divides them is their loyalty to King John. The Citizen of Angiers's attitude is that he will follow whoever wins the battle between France and England. Hubert, on the other hand, is King John's trusted "enforcer," to whom he gives the highly secret and pivotal task of killing Arthur (as well as the prophet Peter of Pomfret.) The Dukes recognize him in this role. If the Citizen of Angiers was also Hubert, he'd have to undergo a 180-degree turn from indifference to fierce allegiance to the English throne. And if Hubert was the Citizen of Angiers, why doesn't he join the rebellion of the nobles when they go over to France? In fact, he urges John to "arme you against your other enemies."[17] It's also unlikely that the Bastard, who has said of the Citizen: "Here's a large mouth indeede ... not a word of his/But buffets better than a fist of France,"[18] would greet the same character with the trust and friendship he shows Hubert in Act 5. King John says to Hubert (Act 3, scene 2, line 29):

> O my gentle *Hubert,*
> We owe thee much: within this wall of flesh
> There is a soule counts thee her Creditor,
> And with advantage meanes to pay thy love:
> And my good friend, thy voluntary oath
> Lives in this bosome, deerely cherished.

There is an intimacy in these words that suggests Hubert has been with the king for quite a length of time. King John tells him "I love thee"[19]—he has no reason to love the stubborn Citizen of Angiers. To make the "Citizen as Hubert" theory work, Dover Wilson suggests there was originally a scene in the play where Hubert of Angiers gave a "voluntary oath" to King John but it was later cut.[20] Rather than rely on such imaginative guesswork, it's better to look for a solution to this difficulty in the text.

If he is assigned the lines of the Citizen, an actor playing Hubert will struggle to find a motivation for his transition from impudent defier of King John to one who is his "good friend" and confidant. In performance it is very clear that the Citizen and Hubert are two separate characters.[21] Editor/adaptors in making this change not only hinder the work of the actor playing Hubert but also forget the fundamental principle set out by Ernst Honigmann that it is "an Editor's worst offence to campaign against any reading that might be Shakespeare's."[22]

This is the same Ernst Honigmann who edited the Citizen of Angiers from the pages of *King John*. For good measure he also removes Lewis from most of the first two speeches of Act 2, scene 1, and gives the lines to King Philip,[23] while at line 368 of the same scene King Philip's speech in the folio is reassigned by Honigmann to Hubert. Shakespeare was very particular about the speech prefixes in *King John* and Chapter 4 examines this more closely.

In the third Arden edition of *Henry IV, Part 1*—an excellent and thorough volume and one of the best modern publications of the play—David Scott Kastan shares Honigmann's views on the role of the editor:

> We too often think of editing as an activity that is mechanical and objective; it is neither.... The attractive solidarity of the modern published editions on a bookshelf or open on a desk asserts

far more certainty about what is on the page than its editor can possibly feel. Our editions inevitably belie the provisional nature of the edited text, overstating the authority of what is set forth in the impressive physical form in which they appear.[24]

Refreshing and humble words from an enlightened editor ... who promptly changes the character name Bardolph to Bardoll, which is how it is spelled in the quartos but not in the folios or in any of the three other plays that include Bardolph in the cast. Not to be outdone, the editors of *Henry IV, Part 1* in the Oxford *Complete Works* alter the famous Falstaff to his supposed original name of Oldcastle.[25] It's difficult to comprehend the value of this latter change beyond gimmickry, especially since the earliest printed copy advertises "the humorous conceits of Sir John Falstaff." In the other three plays where the character name appears (*Henry IV, Part 2*, *Henry V*, and *The Merry Wives of Windsor*), the Oxford series prints "Falstaff"; indeed, the single-volume Oxford edition of *Henry IV, Part 1* contradicts the *Complete Works* by printing "Falstaff" too. The pressure for editors to come up with a new twist (similar to directors who feel they need to present a new "concept") takes the plays further and further towards adaptations.

As well as changing the cast, published texts often reassign lines to other characters. Sometimes this is because, as with the Hubert/Citizen problem, the folio speech prefix is ambiguous. In *Love's Labour's Lost* there are characters called Boyet, commonly identified by the prefix "Boy," and Mote, who is a young boy and a page to Don Armado. The speech prefix used for Mote is generally "Page," but he is also sometimes called "Boy." In the last act, both Boyet and Mote are onstage together and there is a passage in the folio marked "Boy":

> True, and it was injoyned him in *Rome* for want of Linnen: since when, Ile be sworne he wore none, but a dishclout of *Jaquenettas*, and that hee weares next his heart for a favor.[26]

So are these lines said by Mote or Boyet? A quick reading of the folio printing provides the answer. Mote's previous speech has the prefix "Page," and he is helping Don Armado to undress and urging him to fight Costard. A "dishclout" was another name for a sanitary napkin.[27] Why would Mote suddenly speak against his master and employ such bawdy language? Boyet, on the other hand, has been mocking Don Armado and others, often in very obscene terms. Clearly these lines were meant for Boyet and are very much in his character. Nonetheless, the *New Penguin Shakespeare* editor/adaptor, John Kerrigan, assigns the speech to Mote with the explanation "Mote is the one likely to know about his master's underclothes."[28] Leaving aside that this supposes the content of the passage to be true and not an exaggerated put-down, an actor will be completely unconcerned with irrelevant details such as laundry arrangements. He will, however, wish to know *why* he says the lines—what his motivation is.

The closing speech of *King Lear* has no speech prefix confusion in the folio; it is spoken by Edgar. However, in the quarto it is assigned to Albany. Some editor/adaptors prefer the quarto version so that it is Albany who says:

> The waight of this sad time we must obey,
> Speake what we feele, not what we ought to say:
> The oldest have borne most, we that are yong,
> Shall never see so much, nor live so long.[29]

In changing the character assignment from the folio, they change the whole meaning of the play. There's a world of difference between the steady Albany saying these lines, which indicate an acceptance of authority over Britain, and Edgar—a man who has spent most of the play "feigning" madness and is so immersed in his role it's difficult not to believe he still retains elements of unbalance. Edgar will now "speak what he feels," a wonderfully rich ambiguity that offers a far from positive conclusion to the story—Britain is ruled by another madman.[30] Theobald, in his 1733 edition of Shakespeare's plays, has Albany deliver the final speech of *King Lear*, and his justification for this encapsulates the speculative reasoning an editor/adaptor can sometimes adopt:

> This speech from the authority of the Old Quarto is rightly placed to *Albany;* in the Edition by the players it is given to *Edgar,* by whom, I doubt not, it was of Custom spoken. And the Case was this: he who play'd *Edgar,* being a more favorite Actor, than he who personated *Albany,* in Spight of Decorum, it was thought proper he should have the last word.[31]

Where's the evidence?

A much more secure instance of line reassignment by editor/adaptors occurs in Act 2, scene 2, of *Romeo and Juliet*—what has come to be universally known as "The Balcony Scene." It ends with this well-known exchange, set out in the following way in the First Folio:

Romeo.
I would I were thy Bird.

Juliet.
Sweet so would I,
Yet I should kill thee with much cherishing:
Good night, good night.

Romeo.
Parting is such sweete sorrow,
That I shall say goodnight, till it be morrow.

Juliet.
Sleepe dwell upon thine eyes, peace in thy brest.

Romeo.
Would I were sleepe and peace so sweet to rest.

It will be immediately noticed that the lines have different character assignments to modern editions of the play. Using the folio alignment it might be said that, as Romeo and Juliet seal their love, they begin to share one voice. As a performance choice it's interesting, would certainly work, and could prove more effective than the editor/adaptor version:

Romeo.
I would I were thy Bird.

Juliet.
      Sweet so would I,
Yet I should kill thee with much cherishing:
Good night, good night. Parting is such sweet sorrow,
That I shall say goodnight, till it be morrow.

Romeo.
Sleep dwell upon thine eyes, peace in thy breast.
Would I were sleep and peace so sweet to rest.

The ending here is more formal, the lovers exchanging a final pair of rhyming couplets. Which version is correct? And how has the discrepancy come about? For an actor or director, neither is "correct," and they will choose what they feel works for the characters they have created—if they are aware an alternative exists. The editor/adaptor has other concerns and will wish to print what they believe is closest to Shakespeare's intentions. The difference in the two passages has arisen because the folio version seems to have been printed using quarto 3 as copy and this *might* be said to be one of the "diverse stolen, and surreptious copies" that Heminge and Condell write about in their introduction to the folio. A slight variation appears in quarto 2 where "Sleep dwell upon thine eyes, peace in thy breast" is given to Juliet along with the couplet before it, but editor/adaptors, in this instance, reasonably print the speeches as found in four out of the six quartos that were published (one was a variant of quarto 4.) An argument can be made for both alignments of this passage, but once it is acknowledged that the quartos, in this section, appear to have more authority, it gives the green light for editor/adaptors to make wholesale changes on much shakier ground.

A section of Act 5, scene 1, line 42, of *A Midsummer Night's Dream* exists in a very different format in the four folios than it does in the two quartos. Theseus is considering a list of possible entertainments for his wedding celebration and all the folios set the passage as follows:

Egeus.
There is a breefe how many sports are rife:
Make choise of which your Highnesse will see first.

Lysander.
The battell with the Centaurs to be sung
By an Athenian Eunuch, to the Harpe.

Theseus.
Wee'l none of that. That have I told my Love
In glory of my kinsman Hercules.

Lysander.
The riot of the tipsie Bachanals,
Tearing the Thracian singer, in their rage?

Theseus.
That is an old device, and it was plaid
When I from *Thebes* came last a Conqueror.

Lysander.
The thrice three Muses, mourning for the death
of learning, late deceast in beggerie.

Theseus.
That is some Satire keene and criticall,
Not sorting with a nuptiall ceremonie.

Lysander.
A tedious breefe Scene of yong *Piramus,*
And his love *Thisby;* very tragicall mirth.

Theseus.
Merry and tragicall? Tedious, and briefe? That
is, hot ice, and wondrous strange snow. How shall wee
finde the concord of this discord?

Most modern texts prefer to print the quarto version, which has Philostrate rather than Egeus deliver the first two lines—he is, after all, the man in charge of such events—and then the whole of the rest is given to Theseus, with no interruptions from Lysander. He reads out each prospective performer on the bill of "Athens's Got Talent" and, Simon Cowell–like, delivers his verdict on each of them. Here is what the Arden edition prints.[32] (The stage directions and much of the punctuation, including the directorial use of question marks, are the editor's addition.)

Philostrate.
There is a brief how many sports are rife:
Make choice of which your Highness will see first.
(*Giving him a paper.*)
Theseus.
(*Reads*) "The battle with the Centaurs, to be sung
By an Athenian Eunuch, to the Harpe"?
We'll none of that; that have I told my love
In glory of my kinsman Hercules.
(*Reads*) "The riot of the tipsy Bacchanals,
Tearing the Thracian singer in their rage"?
That is an old device, and it was play'd
When I from Thebes came last a Conqueror.
(*Reads*) "The thrice three Muses mourning for the death
of learning, late deceas'd in beggary"?
That is some satire, keen and critical,
Not sorting with a nuptial ceremony.
(*Reads*) "A tedious brief scene of young Pyramus,
And his love Thisbe, very tragical mirth"?
Merry and tragical? Tedious and brief?
That is hot ice, and wondrous strange snow!
How shall we find the concord of this discord?

Harold F. Brooks, editor/adaptor of the Arden edition, explains his choice to use the quarto rather than the folio setting:

> The actors, like some editors, may have seen theatrical advantage in breaking up Theseus' longish speech; but Q1 testifies that this was not Shakespeare's original intention, and F can yield no assurance that he changed his mind.[33]

Once again it should be remembered that one of the actors Brooks blames for this tinkering with the text was Shakespeare himself. Brooks also fails to mention that the Q1 setting of the lines was repeated by Q2. This is important. The Second Quarto was printed by William Jaggard in 1619 although he passed it off as having been published in 1604 by James Roberts, selling it as an old copy. William Jaggard, of course, also printed the First Folio. If he already had the Q2 version of "Dream" in his presses and it was the correct copy, why didn't he simply use that and not bother with a whole new setting for the First Folio? Why did Brooks omit the detail that the passage as laid out in the First Quarto was repeated in the Second Quarto? After all, he acknowledges that Q2 "was set up from Q1, of which, except for the first five leaves of Sheet G, it is a page-for-page reprint."[34] As is typical of the practices of the editor/adaptors, the reader is left to guess at what the contents of "the first five leaves of Sheet G" might be. Harold Brooks seems to be deliberately opaque. Brooks's theory is that the most authoritative text for *A Midsummer Night's Dream* is the First Quarto and not the First Folio, the Second Quarto being an apparently inferior copy of the First Quarto. However, the folio setting of the lines above clearly shows that, at least for this scene, with its major reassignment of lines and characters, the Second Quarto *couldn't* have been used as the source text for the folio. This casts doubt on the authority of Brooks's cherished First Quarto and all his theories that go along with it. If that happens, then his standing among fellow academics is much diminished.

What the folio demonstrates is that Shakespeare rewrote this scene—and editor/adaptors generally disregard the concept of Shakespearean afterthoughts.[35] Although Brooks may dismiss the idea, it seems clear that Shakespeare did indeed change his mind (if we make the big assumption that Q1 is his original script). Why would he do this? Some commentators suggest that the actor who played Philostrate also doubled as one of the Mechanicals acting in "Piramus and Thisby" and so was unable to be in two places at once. However, this could equally be true of the actor playing Egeus. There are too many alterations for the setting to be considered a printing house error. The other folios correct small details but not this large passage, so the adjustments would appear to be deliberate. Having Egeus in the scene completes an appropriate reconciliation with his daughter Hermia; the play, after all, is a comedy. Splitting the lines up between Theseus and Lysander is more effective dramatically. The duke's reading of a long list of entertainers is pretty uninteresting, but add Lysander and an element of conflict and drama is introduced. The lines move from a mere description from Theseus to an interaction with Lysander, who is desperately trying to choose selected items among many (not just the ones mentioned) that Theseus might enjoy, but each of his suggestions is shot down. A director will give the actor a note such as "search for something that suits Theseus's mood," but the obstacle is that it is difficult to gauge Theseus's tastes. There are other characters in the scene too and they need to be engaged in the action. Demetrius and Helena might enjoy their friend squirming, Hermia be trying to support him, Egeus either seeing his new son-in-law in a fresh light or confirming how useless he is. Egeus might disapprove of a singing eunuch being present at his daughter's wedding, but on the other hand, old as it is and probably out of fashion, a Thracian singer could be just the thing. Perhaps a position at court depends on the outcome of Lysander's recommended choice? He would certainly be keenly aware of the watching eyes of his new wife, father-in-law, and erstwhile rival. The play that really interests the duke is "Piramus and Thisby," and this is marked in all the quartos and folios by Theseus speaking in an excitable outburst of prose. Editor/adaptors remove this moment by changing the lines to verse even though the last line, "How shall we find the concord of this discord?," is irregular and doesn't have a feminine ending, although it has 11 beats.

The speech that precedes the scene demonstrates the difference between an actor's approach to the script and an academic's. Modern scholarly texts, based on the quarto version, print:

Theseus.
Where is our usual manager of mirth?
What revels are in hand? Is there no play
To ease the anguish of a torturing hour?
Call Philostrate.[36]

With this reading Theseus calls for Philostrate, the person who is usually in charge of festivities, to ask what the night's entertainment will be. Here's the First Folio version:

Theseus.
Where is our usuall manager of mirth?

What Revels are in hand? Is there no play,[37]
To ease the anguish of a torturing houre?
Call *Egeus*.

Philostrate is not present and Theseus wonders where he is—"Where is our usual manager of mirth?" Not finding him, the duke summons Egeus instead. The actor playing Theseus could stress the word "usual" in the line "Where is our *usual* manager of mirth?" in order to convey this thought. The folio setting of these sections of *A Midsummer Night's Dream* provides the performers with both comic potential and dramatic conflict, involving all of the six actors on stage. The editor/adaptor version is simple narration which, no doubt, is why it was changed in the First Folio.

Not all line reassignments from the editor/adaptors are based on earlier quartos. Some are made from nothing more than subjective opinion; a personal whim, one might say. The 1997 Arden edition of *Othello* is a good example, edited by the popular E. A. J. Honigmann. With fragile reasoning it reassigns Desdemona's line, Act 4, scene 3, line 34: "This Lodovico is a proper man" to her maid (and Iago's wife) Emilia.[38] The explanation the editor/adaptor gives for this is: "For Desdemona to praise Lodovico at this point seems out of character."[39] Had he looked at the previous scene where Othello has hit Desdemona in public and only Lodovico comes to her aid, he might have discovered Lodovico is indeed a "proper man." The men in Desdemona's life are decidedly improper: Othello, Iago, Rodorigo, Brabantio—even Cassio, it might be argued. Honigmann appears to be suffering from the same type of problems as Othello and Iago, reading into an innocent remark a hint of infidelity. For an actress playing Desdemona, the line provides ambiguity and therefore depth (this scene was probably added by Shakespeare) and makes Desdemona a more fully rounded character—a "modern woman" whom an audience can relate to rather than the weak cipher she can sometimes be in performance. Even if you accept Honigmann's gloss of "proper" as "handsome" why shouldn't she, despite loving Othello, find other men attractive? It also, of course, changes the character of Emilia, but the editor/adaptor (no doubt daydreaming of Desdemona as his ideal woman, his mouth watering like the Spaniard in *Pericles*) hadn't given any thought to that.[40]

The somewhat Victorian attitude to Desdemona is shared by some other male editors of *Othello* who cannot bear to print Othello's words in the First Folio, "She gave me for my pains a world of kisses," and prefer instead the quarto's "She gave me for my pains a world of sighs."[41] Is there a hint of racism present in this reassignment? Kenneth Muir in the New Penguin edition bluntly comments, "The F reading, 'kisses,' is obviously impossible,"[42] while M. R. Ridley in the second Arden edition thinks if kisses were true "Desdemona would surely have blushed at herself."[43] Ridley puzzles further over the line: "It is hard to imagine anyone making the alteration deliberately" (Shakespeare?) and concludes with one of the crazy lapses of logic editors are prone to in attempting to support their adaptations of a play: "Perhaps the compositor had recently been setting a passage in which "world of kisses" occurred, and it stuck in his mind." Ridley's speculation might be more secure if he had examined other books Jaggard's printing house was setting alongside the First Folio in which the phrase "world of kisses" could be found and provide proof. Of course he hadn't, and Jaggard had no such book in his presses.

In the opening scene of *Henry IV, Part 1* (line 70), the newly installed king is praising Hotspur's feats in battle to Westmorland. Here is the text as set in the First Folio:

King.
     Of Prisoners, *Hotspurre* tooke
Mordake Earle of Fife, and eldest sonne
To beaten *Dowglas,* and the Earle of *Atholl,*
Of *Murry, Angus,* and *Menteith.*
And is not this an honourable spoyle?
A gallant prize? Ha Cosin, is it not? Infaith it is.
Westmorland.
A Conquest for a Prince to boast of.

Animated by his wayward son's lack of similar achievement, Henry's verse becomes irregular and he finishes with one long line of 14 beats or perhaps prose. Behaving like a king, he answers his own questions with "Infaith it is," leaving Westmorland to feed him the (9 beat) line (indicating a slight hesitation?) that Henry wants to hear: "A Conquest for a Prince to boast of." There were eight quarto versions of *Henry IV, Part 1* published between 1599 and 1639—more than any other of Shakespeare's plays. In all of them, as well as the folios, the lines are set out as above. Nonetheless, editor/adaptors attempt to make the verse more regular, reassign "In faith it is" to Westmorland, and generally print the conclusion as:

King.
A gallant prize? Ha Cousin, is it not?
Westmorland.
          In faith,
It is a conquest for a prince to boast of.

If anything, this change makes the lines less regular. In the recent Arden edition of the play, David Scott Kastan seems to support the text as it appears in the quartos and folios, writing of Shakespeare that:

> Part of his development as a theatre poet can be seen in the increasingly varied and complex metrical structuring of character thought.... Shakespeare's versification not only allows a far more various set of rhythmical possibilities than a strict understanding of blank verse might suggest, but also demands to be understood as being rooted in dramatic necessities and based less upon syllable counts.[44]

Despite these views and his insistence on the authority of the quartos, Kastan bows to editorial convention and replaces the long line from Henry with a long line from Westmorland, printing:

Westmorland.
In faith, it is: a conquest for a prince to boast of.

  Not only do editor/adaptors reassign lines and alter the verse structure, they often do so without comment. It would be a very sharp and diligent actor or director who could decipher the confusing information on various quartos, folios, and editor glosses printed in small writing at the bottom of the page in the Arden editions or consult almost the last page of the New Penguin edition to examine the "collations." It's almost a feat of archaeology to retrieve Henry's lost line "In faith it is," and it is rarely heard in performance. The editor's adaptation has taken precedence. Editor/adaptors have become so obsessed with "discovering new meanings" in the text that, as John Russell Brown astutely observes, "It has become easier to join the critical debate than to experience the play freshly and imaginatively for oneself."[45]

1. The Heavy Hand of the Editors

There is a scene in *King Lear* (Act 1, scene 4, line 278) where the retinue requested by the king is reduced from 100 knights to 50. Not knowing the detail of this information, although it has been suggested that he cut down the number of his followers, Lear curses Goneril and exits, leaving her onstage with her husband Albany. This is the dialogue in the folio:

Lear.
Turn all her Mothers paines, and benefits
To laughter, and contempt: That she may feele,
How sharper then a Serpents tooth it is,
To have a thanklesse Childe. Away, Away.
Exit Lear

Albany.
Now Gods that we adore,
Whereof comes this?
Goneril.
Never afflict your selfe to know more of it:
But let his disposition have that scope
As dotage gives it.
Enter Lear

Lear.
What fiftie of my Followers at a clap?
Within a fortnight?

G. K. Hunter, editor of the New Penguin *King Lear*, writes of this passage:

> Editors have usually sought to explain this by realistic means: fifty followers must have been removed, without comment, at some earlier stage. I think we should rather praise the bold foreshortening that makes the loss of fifty followers seem the consequence of an absence during which only four lines are spoken.[46]

He glosses "Within a fortnight" as "The length of time he has been staying with Goneril."[47] In other words, during King Lear's four-line absence, two weeks have passed. It's an interesting theory to add to the "critical debate" and one that puts Hunter one-up on his editorial competitors in their search for the new; but how on earth is a director to stage this? How could it be practically conveyed to the audience without interrupting the flow and speed of the dialogue and events? "Within a fortnight" can, of course, be explained in the sense that Lear has been informed he has two weeks to reduce his followers from 100 to 50 and this affects Goneril's character. In her mind she is being not unreasonable but fair, allowing time for preparations to be made in the same way Lear gave Kent 10 days to leave the country. A two-week intermission also robs the actress playing Goneril of the immediacy of her father's statement that he wishes her sterile, and it's the sting from these words that governs her later actions in the scene.[48]

The most common action taken by editor/adaptors in dealing with a textual crux is that if a rival has printed one opinion, they will simply take the opposite view. There is a short exchange at Act 2, scene 1, line 113, of *Love's Labour's Lost* between Berowne and Rosaline that begins, "Did not I dance with you in *Brabant* once?" The quarto version of this passage assigns the lines to Katherine. Some editions, such as the Riverside, go with the quarto and print Katherine while others, such as the Arden, give the lines to Rosaline as in the folio. Other editions choose one or the other. It might be thought that beyond personal preference there would be nothing new to add about these fifteen lines until John Kerrigan produced his version of *Love's Labour's Lost* for the New Penguin series. His solution is to cut the exchange entirely. Kerrigan proudly writes of this obliteration of Shakespeare's text, "This edition is the first to alter Q and F by reorganisation and excision."[49]

If actors and directors join the "critical debate," they can lose sight of the principal objective of any theatrical performance, which is simply to tell a story. Frank Kermode may salivate, in discovering in a Polonius speech to Ophelia, words that are "venturing on what may be a zeugma, possibly a hendiadys,"[50] but what assistance can that provide to an actor in the rehearsal room? The language used seems deliberately constructed to mystify rather than to enlighten. The concerns of critical commentators and editor/adaptors are completely different from those of actors and directors; like oil and water, they simply don't mix. Peter Brook sums up the difference neatly: "The actor's task is not to think of words as part of a text, but of words as part of a person whom we believe actually minted them in the heat of the moment."[51]

The "critical debate" with its pressure for the new has led to editor/adaptors proposing assessments of the plays and the characters that can range from the misguided to the bizarre. Othello, in Act 1, scene 2, line 28, says, "But look, what lights come yond?" It's a pretty common Shakespearean device for introducing characters, especially as the actors didn't have the full text and were working from cue scripts.[52] Lines such as "Who comes here?" or "Who's there?" pepper all of the canon. And yet E. A. J. Honigmann, writing in the Arden edition of *Othello*, spies something more in this innocent remark: "Here and elsewhere Othello seems to be suffering from failing eyesight."[53] While it may be true that Othello, like King Lear, lacks insight and does not see the fact of Desdemona's fidelity, the practical application of an Othello who has "failing eyesight" would result in a performance that is comical and absurd, and in no way enlightens the text or develops the character. Othello's vision appears sound enough in his detailed descriptions of Desdemona before her death—or perhaps he's just suffering from myopia? But then how has he become the leading general in Venice if he cannot physically see? Why send a partially sighted man to defend Cyprus at this critical time? What has caused his developing blindness? Syphilis, perhaps? And now the story and character branch off at a tangent that takes us away from the play. If every character in Shakespeare who said "What lights come yond?" or something similar was assumed to have "failing eyesight," the stage would resemble a collection of Keystone Kops–type scenes of misunderstandings, wrongful identities, collisions, and mistakes. Shakespeare could write someone with "sand blindness" if he wanted to—and he did, in the character of Old Gobo in Act 2, scene 2, of *The Merchant of Venice*.

A favorite game of Shakespearean scholars is to attribute the subject matter of a play to events in Shakespeare's life—events that have no documentary proof to support them. E. K. Chambers, for example, proposed that Shakespeare wrote *Timon of Athens*: "under conditions of mental and perhaps physical stress, which led to his breakdown."[54] Taking this to its logical conclusion, Shakespeare would have recently taken part in a war prior to writing *Henry V* and visited an enchanted island before embarking on *The Tempest*. Henry Cuningham, the first Arden editor/adaptor of *Macbeth*, is even more remarkable in displaying his psychic powers. Without any evidence whatsoever, he is able to state of *Macbeth* that "the first act, as we find it in the Folio, was begun by Shakespeare drunk and continued by Shakespeare sober."⁵⁵ These are just a few of the more outlandish claims editor/adaptors make in playing what M. R. Ridley confessed is "an elaborate game." The objective of the game is something like Joyce describes in *Ulysses*—"He proves by algebra that Hamlet's grandson is Shakespeare's grandfather and that he himself is the ghost of his own father."⁵⁶ If an actor or director tries to participate in this game, "O, that way madness lies."⁵⁷

Anyone who has attempted to stage or act in a Shakespeare production that uses an edited text will have experienced a common frustration. That is, complex words and phrases that are vitally important to a scene or character have an obscure or unhelpful note while the blindingly obvious is patronizingly "explained."⁵⁸ Often an editor/adaptor will brazenly write something like, "There is no explanation of this line,"⁵⁹ leaving performers tearing their hair out and flinging their scripts at an unsuspecting stage manager. A good example of this can be found in the Arden *Measure for Measure* edited by J. W. Lever. In Act 1, scene 3, lines 34–48, the duke says to Friar Thomas (in the folio text):

> I doe feare: too dreadfull:
> Sith 'twas my fault, to give the people scope,
> 'T would be my tirrany to strike and gall them,
> For what I bid them doe: For, we bid this be done
> When evill deedes have permissive passe,
> And not the punishment: therefore indeede (my father)
> I have on *Angelo* impos'd the office,
> Who may in th' ambush of my name, strike home,
> And yet, my nature never in the fight⁶⁰
> To do in slander: And to behold his sway
> I will, as 'twere a brother of your Order,
> Visit both Prince, and People: Therefore I pre'thee
> Supply me with the habit, and instruct me
> How I may formally in person bear
> Like a true Frier:

The key phrase an actor will need guidance on is "When evil deeds have their permissive pass,/And not the punishment," but no comment is offered. The preceding, very simple line, "For, we bid this be done," is complicated by the note "Cf. Seneca, *Troades,* 291: "*Qui non vetat peccare cum posit, iubet.*"⁶¹ "Habit," however, we are told is the "attire of a friar." Only in the topsy-turvy world of the editor/adaptor could it be imagined that there is a reader or actor who understands Latin, is familiar with Seneca in the original, and yet can't work out a friar's clothes might be his "habit."⁶²

Using untranslated Latin is a common distancing device employed by the editorial shaman. It's as if they're saying, "If you don't understand Latin then you can't have access to the texts." As an appendix to the Arden *King John*, for example, E. A. J. Honigmann provides a useful two-page extract from Coggeshall which may have been a source for the story of Arthur's blinding.⁶³ It's entirely in Latin with no translation, but a note on the word "remembrance," he explains, means "memory."⁶⁴ The conclusion to Act 4, scene 2, of *All's Well That Ends Well* (line 74) is Diana's easy-to-understand intention: "I think't no sinne,/To cosen him that would unjustly winne" but in a show of editorial brilliance the Arden editor G. K. Hunter gives the following note: "Cf. Terence, *Eunuch,* 385: Nunc referam gratium atque eas itidem fallam, u tab illis fallimur"—but fails to translate it.⁶⁵ In the previous scene, he glosses "plausive" as "plausible."⁶⁶ Similarly, in Act 2, scene 3, line 72, of *Henry IV, Part*

1, Hotspur exclaims "O Esperance!"[67] to which the Arden editor/adaptor A. R. Humphreys adds the note "'Esperance ma comforte' was the Percy motto."[68] This is very interesting—but what does the motto actually mean? Humphreys doesn't tell us. All an actor portraying Hotspur needs to know is that "Esperance" is "hope"—he can play that.[69]

Often editors/adaptors will display a somewhat casual attitude to the text, leaving one wondering why they bothered to edit the script in the first place. On the very first page of his Arden version of *Troilus and Cressida*, Kenneth Palmer runs up the white flag and admits that "the edition should be better than it is."[70] Likewise, J. M. Nosworthy, editor/adaptor of the most recent Arden *Cymbeline*, uses his opening paragraph to explain that while he has generally printed the dialogue as he found it in the First Folio, "I have also aired a few suggestions of my own, for what they are worth."[71] Act 3, scene 1, of *The Taming of the Shrew* begins with:

> *Enter Lucentio, Hortentsio, and Bianca.*
>
> **Lucentio.**
> Fidler forbeare, you grow too forward Sir,
> Have you so soone forgot the entertainment
> Her sister *Katherine* welcom'd you withall.
>
> **Hortentsio.**
> But wrangling pedant, this is
> The patronesse of heavenly harmony:

The lines make perfect sense, except that "But wrangling pedant, this is" is not regular blank verse so editor/adaptors like to think there's a line missing before it. Brian Morris, editor of the Arden volume, appears bored by the task of having to consider this question:

> The line is in some way incomplete. Various attempts have been made to expand it, but none is more than guesswork. Theobald's "She is a shrew" at the beginning of the line is as good as any.[72]

This "guesswork" may be "as good as any" ("It'll do," the editor seems to be saying), but Theobald's addition still doesn't provide a regular line, or rather it provides one with a feminine ending which seems to go against the energy of the scene. The line that follows this passage—"Then give me leave to have prerogative"—is pretty self-evident in its meaning, but Morris provides the gloss "*prerogative*) precedence (OED)."[73] If a word can be explained by the *Oxford English Dictionary* then why is it necessary to consult the Arden script?

There is little benefit for an actor or director in using an editor's adapted copy of one of Shakespeare's plays. The text is prepared for an entirely different purpose and there's not much in them for a performer to find beyond what the First Folio, a decent dictionary, and the Internet can give them. As the experienced and noted actor Simon Callow realizes, "Unless ideas become translated into sensations, they're of no use whatever to acting."[74] Editors on the other hand, might well profit from having the humility to listen to actors—the men and women who inhabit the characters and deliver the play night after night to audiences all over the world. What may seem on the page to be a textual difficulty is given a truth by the actor in performance that makes it work.

One of the principal "crimes" of the editor/adaptors is that they change individual words and therefore meaning, generally because they believe there's been a printing error but sometimes because they think they have a "better" word that Shakespeare probably would have used. And only the shaman, of course, can grasp, as Shakespeare puts it in *Troilus and Cressida*, "the author's drift."[75] An example of this can be found in the Oxford Shakespeare version of *Richard III*[76] which alters young Prince Edward's couplet in Act 3, scene 1, line 22, from:

> Fie, what a Slug is *Hastings,* that he comes not
> To tell us, whether they will come, or no.

to:

> Fie, what a slug is Hastings, that he hastes not
> To tell us whether they will come or no.

"Comes" in the first line is emended to "hastes" so that it avoids repeating "come" in the second[77] and puns on the name of Hastings. All of the quartos and folios print "comes." This is a brilliant piece of writing by the editor/adaptor—unfortunately, it's not Shakespeare's brilliant writing. This type of practice deserves a chapter all its own.

2

The Shaman at Work

"Words, words, words"

Act 1, scene 7, of *Macbeth* starts with a soliloquy from the would-be king in which he apparently ponders the "bank and shoal of time." He's still undecided about killing Duncan and it requires a further scene of persuasion from his wife to push him onwards. Here's the passage, beginning at line 5, as it is set in almost every modern printed edition:

> ...here,
> But here, upon this bank and shoal of time,
> We'd jump the life to come.—But in these cases,
> We still have judgement here; that we but teach
> Bloody instructions, which, being taught, return
> To plague th'inventor: this even-handed Justice
> Commends th'ingredience of our poison'd chalice
> To our own lips.

This is a classic example of a key word change, since the folio prints "Schoole" rather than "shoal"; a shoal being a large group of fish, connecting with the image of a river "bank." Kenneth Muir, editor of the second Arden edition, calls this a "brilliant emendation for Schoole."[1] An actor playing the role of Macbeth, in deep terror at the thought of how carrying out a regicide will affect him in the afterlife, might justifiably ask: why, in the heat of this passion, am I talking about fish? The complete phrase in the First Folio (there was no version published in quarto) is the "Banke and Schoole of time." Bank (banquette)[2] is a term for a seat of judgment, still used by the judiciary today (think of "the bench"), and to *school* someone is to chide or to teach them. Shakespeare uses the latter word in this context *in the same play*. In Act 4, scene 2, line 14, Rosse upbraids the understandably emotional Macduff's Wife, urging her to pull herself together: "My dearest Coz,/I pray you Schoole yourself." Stephen Gosson wrote *The Schoole of Abuse* (1579) as a treatise against Players and uses the word "schoole" "To teach about" and "To warn" of the evils committed by actors.

Here is the speech with the words linking "school" to justice and instruction marked in capital letters. (The folio doesn't set the individual words in this way.)

> ...Heere,
> But heere, upon this BANKE and SCHOOLE of time,
> Wee'ld jumpe the life to come. But in these CASES,
> We still have JUDGEMENT heere, that we but TEACH

> Bloody INSTRUCTIONS, which being TAUGHT, returne
> To plague th'Inventer, This even-handed JUSTICE
> Commends th'Ingredience of our poyson'd Challice
> To our owne lips.

He's clearly talking about a lesson learned from time and a reckoning in the future. Or, as Rosalind says in *As You Like It*: "Time is the old justice that examines all such offenders."[3] And yet the imposed word "Shoal," which never appears in any of Shakespeare's other plays, still remains in most texts as if it were original. In fact, "schoole" is printed in all 4 folios and in the later editions is spelled "school," with the "e," removed, so the printers had worked on resetting the word and could have corrected it, had it been wrong. An actor or director might decide to go with the fish/riverbank imagery (it's a choice for them) and if they do there is an alternate word to use instead of "Schoal" that means the same thing: "school"—"a school of fish." We wouldn't change the words of Jane Austen, Charles Dickens, Leo Tolstoy, or Virginia Woolf—we wouldn't even change the words of Dan Brown—and yet, for the greatest writer that has ever lived, it seems that anything goes.

Many of the word changes are not changes for the better and have no justification to support them. Take Falstaff's wonderful pun in Act 5, scene 3, of *Henry IV, Part 1* where at line 36 he calls his pitiful band of recruits "my rag of Muffins." This is found in all of the quarto versions of the play as well as the folios, but editor/adaptors alter it to the much less effective "my ragamuffins." The word "ragamuffin" was current in Shakespeare's time whereas "muffin" was probably not. However, Shakespeare uses the phrase "rag of money" in *The Comedy of Errors*, Act 4, scene 4, line 84, to mean something worthless, of little value, and the etymology of "muffin" is variously described as being from the German for "little cakes" or "musty" or "stupid clumsy person." Which ever version of the word you use there's no doubt that the phrase "my rag of muffins" contributes to Falstaff's witty character. After all, he has begun the speech with another pun—"Though I could scape shot-free at London, I feare the shot here"—but no editor changes "shot-free" to "scot-free." (A "shot" can also mean a bill, i.e., debt free.) Earlier Falstaff has dubbed the Warwickshire town of Sutton Coldfield "Sutton Cop Hill"—to "cop" is to steal. (A phrase still used in Britain today is "not a lot of cop" to describe something that is inferior in quality. Whether this is coincidental or not, modern British audiences would get the joke—if allowed to by the editor/adaptors.) The name is spelled this way in all of the quartos and folios but the humorless modern editors—who have little idea of character development—print "Sutton Coldfield."[4]

In the first scene of *King Lear*, Act 1, scene 1, line 179, Lear banishes Kent with the following speech in the folio:

> Five[5] dayes we do allot thee for provision,
> To shield thee from disasters of the world,
> And on the sixt to turne thy hated backe
> Upon our kingdome; if on the tenth day following,
> Thy banisht trunke be found in our Dominions,
> The moment is thy death, away. By Jupiter,
> This shall not be revok'd[6]

The 1997 Arden *King Lear*, edited by R. A. Foakes, alters the word "tenth" to "next" despite the fact that the folio and the single quarto both print "tenth." Foakes reasons, "This is

Blayney's ingenious suggestion, assuming the word was misread as 'tenth' (Q and F) which makes no sense."[7] According to the "assuming" Foakes and friend, two separate printers, at two different times, misread a four-letter word as a five-letter word, although neither would look in the least bit similar written in any hand. And why shouldn't it make sense that, certainly in Shakespeare's time, a journey might be started in which it would take four days (from the sixth to the ninth) before the person actually left the shores of Britain?

Further evidence to support the word "tenth" is supplied by reading one of Shakespeare's other plays. In Act 1, scene 3, line 43 of *As You Like It*, Duke Frederick banishes Rosalind with the words:

> Within these ten daies if that thou beest found
> So neere our publike Court as twentie miles,
> Thou diest for it.

Continuing with *King Lear*, at the end of Act 1, scene 1, line 304, Goneril says to her sister Regan, in the folio, "Pray you let us sit together." This suggests a considered and balanced response to Lear's ravings—the "poor judgment" she has spoken of a few lines earlier. She is urging a unified approach and the word "sit" paints a picture of the two sisters sitting calmly to discuss the situation but also a hint of sitting on a throne and ruling Britain jointly. Nearly all modern texts prefer the phrase "hit together," which is published in the quarto, with the senses of "agree," "hitting back," or possible violence against King Lear. Why change it? Foakes simply says the word "sit" "is weaker"—a pretty weak argument.[8] The folio *King Lear* is probably a rewrite from the quarto as can be seen earlier with the word change of "four days" to "five." A Shakespearean rethink—it is certainly not uncommon for authors to revisit their plays once they have been performed. And it's also very possible, unlike the words "tenth" and "next," for the quarto printer to read "sit" as "hit" in a scribal copy, a long "*s*" appearing to be an "*h*." It was the usual practice at this time that an "*f*" was often used in place of "*s*," Cassio's name, for example, being spelled *Caffio* in print. Or perhaps it was a simple compositor error, "s" and "h" being fairly close together in his box containing the type?

Not all changes of words are based on the "evidence" found in quarto versions of a play. In *Measure for Measure*, Act 3, scene 1, line 92, the condemned Claudio is told by his sister Isabella that he will be saved from death if she has sex with Angelo, newly deputized as head of state. The First Folio setting of the passage reads:

Isabella.
His filth within being cast, he would appeare
A pond, as deepe as hell.

Claudio.
The prenzie, *Angelo*?

Isabella.
Oh 'tis the cunning Liverie of hell,
The damnest bodie to invest, and cover
In prenzie gardes; dost thou thinke *Claudio*,
If I would yeeld him my virginitie
Thou might'st be freed?

The Second Folio alters both uses of "Prenzie" to "Princely." Elizabethan/Jacobean spelling was often phonetic and "Prenzie" would sound and read very similar to "princely" in the dialect of the time. There are many references to dress in the play, as there are in "Macbeth," and in particular the inappropriate garb adopted by characters such as Angelo. Isabella in an earlier exchange, for example, has spoken of "proud man/Dress'd in a little brief authority."[9] Her reply to Claudio in this scene takes up the same theme with the idea that the robes the princely Angelo wears are the "cunning Liverie of hell" (the capital letter on Liverie in the folio underlining this thought more strongly). Isabella repeats the word "prenzie/princely" with deep sarcasm, joining it with the word "guards," which means the border of clothing, but also has the sense that it is only the clothes Angelo wears by virtue of his position that guard and protect him. Nearly all modern copies of *Measure for Measure* change the two times "princely" is spoken to "precise"—a word used to define Angelo in other parts of the play. Editors such as J. M. Nosworthy in the New Penguin reason "the two words looked so much alike in the manuscript that the printer took them to be identical."[10] Another apparently remarkable occurrence of a Jacobean printer reading a six letter word as seven—twice. No original manuscript that formed the basis of a published text survives, so how can this theory be presented as if it were a fact? Apart from sharing the first two letters, the words 'Prenzie/Princely' and 'precise' hardly look alike even if written with poor hand writing. And to print "Prenzie" meant the compositor had to reach across for the unfamiliar and underused "unnecessary letter"[11] zed. J. W. Lever in the Arden edition comments on "Prenzie": "The word was certainly obscure, or it would not have been changed in F2."[12] And yet he doesn't accept the Second Folio clarification of the word to "Princely." Other words editor/adaptors replace "Prenzie/Princely" with include priestly, precious, proxy, and even frenzied. As *Measure for Measure* was only published in the First Folio, there are no quarto versions to refer to. This represents a great opportunity for the editor/adaptors who, seeing an obscure word, can use their imaginations to reveal Shakespeare's "true intention" that a "bungling printer" has denied the world. And there are no unhelpful quarto printings to contradict their views. Patrick Tucker is onto to this game and points out:

> I have found that comparing Editors with the Folio, the more famous the play, the more changes they make, whereas the less well known plays are printed in much closer versions to the "original." Do we really believe that the original compositors were meticulous with, say, the *Henry the Sixth* plays, but needed to be corrected on almost every line for a famous play like *Hamlet*?[13]

One of the best-known phrases in all Shakespeare appears at line 145 in Act 2, scene 5 of *Twelfth Night*—another play that is only printed in the folio—when Malvolio reads from a letter supposedly written to him by Olivia: "Some are born great, some achieve greatness, and some have greatness thrust upon them." Well, that's what all the modern published texts print. The folio version is: "Some are become[14] great, some atcheeves greatnesse, and some have greatnesse thrust upon em." The meaning is clear; certain circumstances might combine for a person to become great, or they might achieve it through their own actions, or through the actions of another. All three have the objective of goading on Malvolio to woo Olivia. The line that follows confirms this purpose: "Thy fates open theyr hands, let thy blood and spirit embrace them"—Malvolio is about to "become great" if he embraces his fate and acts accordingly. Even before he finds the letter this is clearly his ambition: "'Tis but Fortune, all is fortune.... There is example for't. The Lady of the *Strachy*,[15] married the yeoman of the wardrobe."[16] Editor/adaptors alter the folio "become" to "born" because that is what is said at two other points in the play. In Act 3, scene 4, line 40, Malvolio quotes Olivia's supposed letter back to her: "Some are borne great.... Some atcheeve greatnesse.... And some have greatnesse thrust upon them."[17] The character of Malvolio alters the letter to suit his purposes, changing "become" to "born" at this point because it highlights the difference in social status between himself and Olivia. He almost seems close to quoting Juliet's "What's in a name?" as he paints a picture of love conquering all despite mere accidents of birth. Malvolio makes a further alteration to the original letter in this scene that editor/adaptors rarely comment on, or for consistency's sake, change too. "If not, let me see thee a steward still" in his words is now "If not, let me see thee a servant still" (line 54.) This again emphasizes the class divide, with Olivia apparently urging Malvolio not to just leave his job as steward but to move from servant to master. In Malvolio's mind he and Olivia are playing out a reverse gender scene from *King Cophetua and the Beggar Maid*. Act 5, scene 1, line 369 has Feste repeat the phrase from the letter a third and final time but again with a twist to the language: "Why some are borne great, some atchieve greatnesse, and some have greatnesse throwne upon them." This is mockingly aimed at Malvolio, who Olivia has just called a "poor fool," and is a quote back to him of his own words. The use of "thrown"[18] rather than "thrust" tells Malvolio exactly what happened: he has been "thrown over" or duped, the letter literally thrown into his path so he could find it.

Three different versions of the same line, spoken in three different sets of circumstances, with three different objectives, and yet editor/adaptors make each line more or less the same, closing down performance and character options. M. M. Mahood in the New Penguin edition of *Twelfth Night* repeats the familiar story that the printer mistook "borne" for "become" despite the words only sharing the first and last letters. Once again a printer, apparently as blind as Honigmann's Othello, has seen a 5-letter word as 6 and managed to somehow misread "borne" on this one occasion but spotted it correctly in a further two instances. To support his point, Mahood claims that the letter, rather than being a separate stage property, was inserted into the pages of the prompt book and used as print copy: "A property letter would be less legible than the prompt book, either because of rough handling or because it was a piece of the author's manuscript, and this might explain 'become' as a misreading of 'borne.'"[19] Of course, there's no evidence for this, and if the letter was so badly damaged it conjures up an image of an actor performing onstage and struggling to read the words. This is why in professional theatre, property letters are *more* legible, written in larger type and so forth. They also tend to go missing at an alarming rate, so any stage manager will make several clean copies and replace them regularly.

The problem with making changes such as these is that they quickly become established as fact and Shakespeare's intentions, as well as options for an actor, are lost. As an example of this, Maynard Mack in his book *King Lear in Our Time* quotes Iago telling Rodorigo in *Othello* to "defeat thy favor with a false beard,"[20] whereas the actual line is "defeate thy favor, with a usurp'd beard."[21] It doesn't necessarily mean that Rodorigo should wear a false beard, but the gloss of "usurped" as "false" has become so current that Mack gets the line wrong. Alternative readings are discarded and in production Rodorigo often appears in later scenes sporting a beard. Any other interpretation of "usurped beard," such as a general disguise, different personality, Rodorigo usurping another's appearance as he plans to usurp Othello's bed, are not available to the actor and the cliché of a literal beard is focused on and repeated.

However, it mustn't be thought that the folio *always* gets it right and the editor/adaptors *always* get it wrong. A final example is from Act 1, scene 2, of *The Winter's Tale*, in which Leontes, King of Sicilia, claims his wife is having an affair with Polixenes, the king of Bohemia. At line 276 Leontes tells his trusted aide Camillo, in the folio, "My Wife's a Holy-Horse." In all modern printed editions of the play this is changed to "My wife's a hobby-horse." Bohemia was a country of comparative religious freedom when *The Winter's Tale* was written but was also part of the Catholic Holy Roman Empire, which had Prague as its capital. Unrest was underlying at this time, and after Emperor Ferdinand II began oppressing the rights of Protestants in 1618 the Thirty Years' War broke out. The Holy Roman Emperor kept a stud farm in Stuttgart established to supply his cavalry. Holy horses? In this context Leontes is saying his wife has committed not only adultery but treason too, being on the side of the Catholic emperor, and this could lead to bloody religious wars. A potent reason for Camillo to commit his own act of treason, warn Polixenes, and flee the country he has served so loyally. Numerous images of Catholicism throughout the play—the resurrection of the statue of Hermione/Mary being one of them—might be said to support this view. Although seductive, this is not an interpretation which can be strongly supported, particularly by the dates. It's probable "My wife's a hobby-horse" was written and there was a printing error in the folio. In the compositor's box of typeface, the letter "l" was directly below the letter "b." Moreover, "hobby-horse" is mentioned in four other Shakespeare plays. In *Love's Labour's Lost* Don Armado says, "Call'st thou my love Hobby Horse?"[22] while Bianca tells Cassio in *Othello* to take Desdemona's handkerchief and "Give it to your Hobbey-horse,"[23] Benedick in *Much Ado* refers to his teasing friends as "these hobby-horses"[24] and Hamlet exclaims in a passion, "By'r lady, he must build churches, then; or else shall he suffer not thinking on, with the hobby-horse, whose epitaph is, 'For, O, for, O, the hobby-horse is forgot.'"[25] In all these cases "hobby" is printed with 2 *b*'s so perhaps there might have been a misreading of the scribal text, two *b*'s together looking like *l*'s? We don't know.[26]

There are numerous moments in the folio where it certainly veers away from Shakespeare's original text, but while it would be foolish to follow the folios slavishly[27] it might also be wise to observe Bernard Shaw's words: "A glance through any of the facsimiles already published will discover points at which changes made by modern editors are changes for the worse."[28] So what are these "changes for the worse"? Here is a very small sample using ten instances in each of five plays, with the changed word marked in bold. When reading these examples, keep in mind Ernst Honigmann's maxim that it is "An Editor's worst offence to campaign against any reading that *might* be Shakespeare's."[29] First, here's a play found only in the folio:

Measure for Measure

Scene	EDITOR'S VERSION	
1/1 *l.*51	Duke: "We have with **leavened** and prepared choice/ Proceeded to you; therefore take your honours."	The New Penguin Editor, J. M. Nosworthy, comments: "The F line in unmetrical and somewhat un–Shakespearian: and removes "a."[30]
	FOLIO VERSION Duke: "We have with **a leaven'd**, and prepared choice/ Proceeded to you; therefore take your Honors"	The majority of the speech has 11 beat lines—including the line after this, which Nosworthy doesn't change to regular verse. These feminine endings perhaps indicate that the Duke is not quite as sure of his action as he appears.

Scene 1/2 *l.*125	EDITOR'S VERSION Lucio: "I had as lief have the foppery of freedom as the **morality** of imprisonment." FOLIO VERSION Lucio: "I has as liefe the foppery of freedome, as the **mortality** of imprisonment."	The two words are very close in spelling, so it's certainly possible there was a folio printing error. However, the word "morality" does not appear in any of Shakespeare's plays whereas "mortality" does; see, for example, the Duke's "Mortality Mercy in Vienna/Live in thy tongue" (1/1 *l.*44). The folio sense is clear: Lucio would prefer to live life as a fool than waste it away in prison. The Arden editor, J. W. Lever, writes that "F 'mortality' has never been convincingly defended."[31] Does it need to be?
Scene 2/1 *l.*12	EDITOR'S VERSION Escalus: "...the resolute acting of **your** blood..." FOLIO VERSION Escalus: "... the resolute acting of **our** blood..."	Another example of a possible folio printing error, although if it is, none of the subsequent folios spotted it. "Our" is important since it suggests Escalus has been guilty of sexual indiscretion at some point in his life and also that it is something the whole male gender suffers from. This paints the character of Angelo as someone who displays human weakness rather than being a crazed rapist; a crucial detail if his later marriage to Mariana is to be convincing.
Scene 2/1 *l.*35	EDITOR'S VERSION Angelo: "See that Claudio/Be executed **by** tomorrow morning,/Bring **his** Confessor, let him be prepared." FOLIO VERSION Angelo: "See that Claudio/Be executed **by nine** to morrow morning;/Bring **him his** confessor, let him be prepar'd."	A double deletion from J. M. Nosworthy. Of the first he says: "F's 'by nine and to morrow' renders the line hypermetrical and suggest an undeleted alteration."[32] Of the second: "F's 'him' is unmetrical and unnecessary."[33] Despute Nosworthy's efforts the first line is still hypermetrical. Irregular verse at this point suits the character and situation; Angelo is nervous, perhaps excited, and his words spill out. He is far from being controlled. "Nine" is important to the plot as time is running out for Claudio. It could be the moment Escalus discovers that the execution now has a fixed date and time.
Scene 2/4 *l.*93	EDITOR'S VERSION Angelo: "Could fetch your brother from the manacles/Of the **all-binding** law." FOLIO VERSION Angelo: "Could fetch your Brother from the Manacles/Of the **all-building-Law**."	Although connecting "manacle" and "binding" is persuasive, the folio suggests Angelo is saying all of society is built upon the law, something many current politicians would agree with. Notice the folio connects 3 words with a hyphen and puts a capital letter on "Law." Care was obviously taken by the compositor when setting this phrase.
Scene 3/2 *l.*176	EDITOR'S VERSION Lucio: "The Duke, I say to thee again, would eat mutton on Fridays. He's **not** past it yet, and I say to thee, he would mouth with a beggar, though she smelt brown bread and garlic."	Nosworthy makes no comment about changing "now" to "not" and you have to search hard to the end of the New Penguin edition in order to discover his amendment. To make the alteration work, Nosworthy places a comma after "yet" rather than before it. The line is addressed the the duke, who

2. The Shaman at Work

	FOLIO VERSION Lucio: "The Duke (I say to thee again) would eat Mutton on Fridays. He's **now** past it, yet (and I say to thee) he would mouth with a beggar though she smelt brown-bread and Garlic;"	cannot respond to the insult since he is in disguise—one of the funniest moments in the play. At this point he may already have designs on marrying young Isabella so would not be pleased to hear that he's thought to be "now past it." Nosworthy's alteration conveys completely the opposite meaning.
Scene 4/1 *l.*53	EDITOR'S VERSION Duke: "Do you persuade yourself that I respect you?" Mariana: "Good Friar, I know you do, **and** have found it." FOLIO VERSION Duke: "Do you persuade your self that I respect you?" Mariana: "Good Friar, I know you do, **and so** have found it."	Both Lever and Nosworthy add the word "so" after "and," although there is no evidence to base this on apart from guesswork (amazing that they both guessed the same word). Lever explains that "some monosyllabic word like 'so' or 'oft' seems to have dropped out in F."[34] What? In all 4 printings stretching over 62 years? Nosworthy makes no comment, but the change is usually made on metrical grounds, creating a feminine ending followed by an alexandrine. In doing so they disrupt the rhythm of two 11-beat lines that mirror each other as the characters come together but are still in doubt.
Scene 4/3 *l.*91	EDITOR'S VERSION Duke: "Quick, dispatch, and send the head to *Angelo*/Angelo./Now will I write letters to **Varrius**." FOLIO VERSION Duke: "Quick, dispatch, and send the head to Now will I write Letters to *Angelo*."	It's difficult to defend this alteration from Nosworthy since "Varrius" does not appear in any of the published folios. There is a repeat of "Angelo" and confusion about who should meet whom and where. However, the next scene concerns Angelo discussing a letter he has received from the duke.
Scene 5/1 *l.*34	EDITOR'S VERSION Isabella: "Hear me! O hear me, **hear**!" FOLIO VERSION Isabella: "Heare me: Oh heare me, **heere**."	Lever calls this a "weak conclusion" while Nosworthy makes no comment at all. Notice the addition of the directorial exclamation points that rarely appear in the folios. It may seem petty to quibble about the spelling of a word since it will sound the same when said in performance. For an actor it's important since they need to know exactly what it is they are saying. Isabella is pleading to be heard immediately, in public, and not behind closed doors. This, of course, is part of the duke's plan.
Scene 5/1 *l.*256	EDITOR'S VERSION Duke: "Do with your injuries as seems you best,/In any chastisement. I for a while/Will **leave**." FOLIO VERSION Duke: "Doe with your injuries as seems you best/In chastisement; I for a while/Will **leave you**."	Nosworthy cuts the word "you," which he explains is "oitiose and results in misleneation."[35] Lever "corrects" this apparent mislineation by setting the lines: "Do with your injuries as seems you leave you"; but this doesn't create regular verse and is actually less regular than the folio setting. The actor won't worry about the numbers of syllables: "leave you" flows better. Both these changes made by the editor/adaptors are otiose.

With the following two plays the editor/adaptors have the quartos to refer to in addition to the folios:

King Lear

Scene 1/1 *l.*282	EDITOR'S VERSION Cordelia: "Time shall unfold what plighted cunning hides/Who **covert** faults at last with shame derides." FOLIO VERSION Cordelia: "Time shall unfold what plighted cunning hides/Who **covers** faults, at last with shame derides."	"Covers" is also found in the quarto and links to the word "hides" in the previous line.
Scene 1/4 *l.*233	EDITOR'S VERSION Goneril: "Men so disordered, so **debauched** and bold" FOLIO VERSION Goneril: "Men so disordered, so **debosh'd**, and bold"	"Debosh'd" means "debauched" but an actor will relish the onomatopoeic drunken sound of the word and still convey the meaning.[36] For further evidence, see *The Tempest* Act 3, scene 2, line 25, where Trinculo calls Caliban "thou debosh'd fish."
Scene 2/2 *l.*336	EDITOR'S VERSION Regan: "Nature in you stands on the very verge/Of **her** confine." FOLIO VERSION Regan: "Nature in you stands on the very Verge/Of **his** confine."	"Her" appears in the quarto. "His" points the line away from nature and towards King Lear.
Scene 4/2 *l.*17	EDITOR'S VERSION Goneril: "I must change **armes** at home and give the distaff/Into my husband's hands." FOLIO VERSION Goneril: "I must change **names** at home and give the Distaff/Into my Husbands hand."	"Armes" is found in the quarto and follows the idea of changing a domestic weapon, a distaff, for a military one. "Names" is much more powerful, turning Albany into a woman and Goneril into a man (see Macbeth's Wife, "unsex me," etc.).
Scene 4/2 *l.*28	EDITOR'S VERSION Goneril: "**A** fool usurps my **bed**" FOLIO VERSION Goneril: "**My** Fool usurps my **body**"	Editors follow corrutp quartos, which also have "My foot usurps my head." Goneril is either talking about the person she loves as "My fool" (Lear says of Cordelia "And my poor Fool is hanged") or that love, her "fool," has taken over her actions.
Scene 4/4 *l.*17	EDITOR'S VERSION Cordelia: "Be aidant and remediate/In the good man's distress"	Another example of following the quarto, with "distress" preferred over the folio "desires." R. A. Foakes justifies the change by commenting that "desires" "is less appropriate to Lear's con-

	FOLIO VERSION Cordelia: whatever he desires,	dition."[37] The line is Cordelia's and should be appropriate to her. She is now giving Lear having earlier denied him.
Scene 4/6 *l*. 83	EDITOR'S VERSION Lear: "No, they cannot touch me for **coining**. I am the King himself." FOLIO VERSION Lear: "No, they cannot touch me for **crying**. I am the King himself."	Quarto's "coining" is about counterfeiting the ing's money—a capital offense. Trying not to cry is something Lear has attempted to do on a number of occasions. "Crying" gives the actor playing Lear an action whereas "coining" relies on the audience having an in-depth knowledge of Jacobean history.
Scene 4/6 *l*. 161	EDITOR'S VERSION Lear: "**Plate** sin with gold,/And the strong lance of justice hurtless breaks." FOLIO VERSION Lear: "**Place** sin with gold,/And the strong lance of justice hurtless breaks."	"Plate" as a substitute for "place" was first used by Theobald in 1726 and has remained in printed copies ever since. "Place" gives the sense of placing people (sinners) in office through bribery and Shakespeare uses it that was in *Timon of Athens*, Act 4, scene 3, lines 34–38, when Timon finds a hoard of gold while digging in the woods: "This yellow slave/Will knit and break Religions, bless th'accurs'd,/ Make the hoare leprosy ador'd, **place thieves**,/ and give them title." Lear and Timon share many character similarities and it's possible the two plays were written around the same date.
Scene 4/6 *l*. 246	EDITOR'S VERSION Oswald: "Seek him out/Upon the **British** party." FOLIO VERSION Oswald: "Seek him out/Upon the **English** party."	Another editor preference from the quarto. There is no longer a Britain since Lear divided the land. As Goneril's servant, Oswald urges Edmond be sought in the English part of the land, i.e., that belonging to Regan. Foakes believes "English" may be "a casual equivalent put in by [an] actor."[38]
Scene 5/3 *l*. 291	EDITOR'S VERSION Albany says of Lear: "He knows not what he **sees**." FOLIO VERSION Albany says of Lear: "He knows not what he **says**."	"Sees" is from the quarto. As Lear recognizes Kent just a few lines earlier, his sight appears not to be a problem at this point. Lear's reply to "All's cheerless, dark, and deadly" and the news of his daughters' deaths is "Ay, so I think," which may well prompt Albany to say, "He knows not what he says." Lear is still king and the scene is in public.

Othello

Scene 1/1 *l*. 24	EDITOR'S VERSION Iago: "Wherein the **togued** consuls can propose" FOLIO VERSION	Editors follow the First Quarto in printing the word "togued"—the Consuls wear togas as befits their position of authority. "Tongued" suggests Consuls who are all talk and no action, which is how we first see them in the

	Iago: "Wherein the **Tongued** Consuls can propose"	play. Othello later says of Brabantio, a Consul as well as Desdemona's father, that he "shall out-tongue his complaints."[39]
Scene 1/1 *l.*29	EDITOR'S VERSION Iago: "At Rhodes, at Cyprus and on **other** grounds,/**Christian** and heathen" FOLIO VERSION Iago: "At Rhodes, at Cyprus, and on **others** grounds,/**Christian'd**, and Heathen"were	Editors follow the First Quarto in printing the word "Christian" and use "other" rather than "others." But "Christian'd" means the people "others" means it was their own land, belonging to them and not to Venice. Both invoke a picture of Venice as a state with imperialistic ambitions of colonization and help explain the later uprising in Cyprus.
Scene 1/1 *l.*32	EDITOR'S VERSION Iago: "And I, God bless the mark, his **worship's** ancient!" FOLIO VERSION Iago: "And I, (bless the mark) his **Mooreship's** Ancient"	Editors follow the First Quarto in printing "worship's." An actor would find an opportunity for a play on words that would convey both meanings as well as an early insult towards Othello from Iago.
Scene 1/1 *l.*63	EDITOR'S VERSION Iago: "But I will wear my heart upon my sleeve/For **Doves** to peck at." FOLIO VERSION Iago: "But I will wear my heart upon my sleeve/For **Dawes** to peck at."	Editors follow the First Quarto in printing the word "doves," but a jackdaw, with its dark feathers and opportunistic thieving, is a much more potent image. In effect Iago is saying that no one can steal his heart.
Scene 1/1 *l.*99	EDITOR'S VERSION Brabantio: "Upon malicious **bravery** dost thou come" FOLIO VERSION Brabantio: "Upon malicious **knaverie** dost thou come"	Editors follow both quartos in printing the word "bravery," but knaverie underlines Brabantio's contempt of Rodorigo. M. R. Ridley comments that "knaverie" "is slightly redundant after malicious,"[40] but the repeat of two such strong words is surely the point?
Scene 1/1 *l.*180	EDITOR'S VERSION Brabantio: "And raise some special officers of **night**" FOLIO VERSION Brabantio: "And raise some special Officers of **might**"	Editors follow the First Quarto in printing the word "night," but "might" gives a suggestion of Brabantio's power and the lengths he might go to in order to "save" his daughter. The audience doesn't need to be reminded that the scene takes place at night, given the amount of times Brabantio has called for "light."
Scene 1/3 *l.*43	EDITOR'S VERSION Messenger (of Montano): "And prays you to **relieve** him"	Both the quartos and the folio print "beleeve" so there is no justification for this change. The latest Arden edition comments "Believe is feeble, in such a situation, and relief is sent

	FOLIO VERSION Messenger (of Montano): "And prays you to **beleeve** him"	immediately."[41] Actually relief isn't sent immediately, that's still up for debate, and the Consuls have been receiving conflicting reports that suggest an attack on Rhodes. Montano asks them to believe him that the real target is Cyprus. Truth, reality, and who to believe are, of course, major themes in the play.
Scene 3/3 *l.*324	EDITOR'S VERSION Iago: "I will in Cassio's lodging **lose** this napkin" FOLIO VERSION Iago: "I will in *Cassio's* Lodging **loose** this napkin"	NB: "lose" is commonly spelled "loose" in the folio The Arden edition, which supposedly catalogs differences between the quartos and folios, doesn't even acknowledge this subtle difference. An actor will be able to convey the sense of losing the handkerchief in Cassio's lodging but also that this act will let loose a whole series of events that will have dire circumstances. In *Hamlet* Polonius tells the King "Ile loose my Daughter to him."[42]
Scene 3/3 *l.*477	EDITOR'S VERSION Iago: "'Tis done **as you** request." FOLIO VERSION Iago: "'Tis done **at your** request."	Editors follow both quartos in printing "as you request." This suggests a willingness from Iago to help a "friend." "At your request" puts the blame squarely on Othello for Cassio's murder; Iago is only carrying out orders.
Scene 4/3 *l.*21	EDITOR'S VERSION Desdemona: "Good **faith**, how foolish are our minds" FOLIO VERSION Desdemona: "Good **Father**, how foolish are our minds?"	Editors follow both quartos in printing the word "faith," but using the word "father" at this moment is crucial for the actress playing Desdemona. She is speaking to her distant father, unaware that he is dead, and possibly with some momentary regret for her hasty action in marrying Othello. Perhaps she might also be pleading to God the Father?

The next example is from one of Shakespeare's lesser-known plays, published only in the First Folio. *King John* is the classic example of Patrick Tucker's view that editor/adaptors make the most changes to the more famous plays. A comparatively smaller number of alterations (although still significant) appear in the modern printings of *King John*—until we reach the famous scene of the attempted blinding of young Arthur and then textual interference increases:

King John

Scene 1/1 *l.*19	EDITOR'S VERSION King John: "Here have we war for war, and blood for blood,/Controlment for **control**: so answer France."	Despite the obvious intention to use a set of repeated words some Editors such as Dover Wilson[43] shorten "Controlment" to "Control" so that the meter becomes regular.

FOLIO VERSION
King John:
"Heere we have war for war, & bloud for bloud,/Contrement for **controlment**: so answer France."

Scene 2/1 *l.*8	EDITOR'S VERSION Lewis: "**Ah**, noble boy, who would not do thee right?" FOLIO VERSION Lewis: "**A** noble boy, who would not doe thee right?"	This is E.A.J. Honigmann's emendation made "since Arthur is being addressed."[44] It's unnecessary, the line making perfect sense in the folio, and is a good example of an editor playing director. If this is a printing error then none of the other folios picked it up and corrected it.
Scene 2/1 *l.*215	EDITOR'S VERSION King John: "**Confronts** your city's eyes, your winking gates." FOLIO VERSION John: "**Comfort** your Citties eies, your winking gates."	R. L. Smallwood, in the New Penguin edition, makes no comment about this change and you have to search hard to the end of the volume (p. 361) in order to discover his amendment. Notice how the folio speech prefix drops the "King"—he is being mischievous and ironic. The First Folio actually prints "Comfort yours," which folio's 3 and 4 correct to "your." It seems odd that they would make this small adjustment and not notice the word alongside it was also "wrong."
Scene 2/1 *l.*423	EDITOR'S VERSION Hubert: "That daughter there of Spain, the Lady Blanche,/Is **niece** to England." FOLIO VERSION Hubert: "That daughter there of Spaine, the Lady Blanch/Is **neere** to England."	Another literal reading of a line from the editor/adaptors, since Blanch is King John's niece. The folio's "neere" more importantly tells the French that she is close in line to the throne. The New Penguin's Smallword changes the text to "niece" but grudgingly admits that the folio setting "is possible."[45]
Scene 3/1 *l.*147	EDITOR'S VERSION King John: "What earthy name to interrogatories/Can **task** the free breath of a sacred King?" FOLIO VERSION King John: "What earthie name to Interrogatories/Can **tast** the free breath of a sacred King?"	(Some editions print "**tax**.") Smallwood notes the folio alternative word but gives no reason for not retaining it—presumably it was a matter of personal taste. A skilled actor will be able to pick out the play on words of "taste/test." Although it might initially seem that printing a *t* instead of a *k* is an easy mistake to make, elsewhere in the folio the word "taste" is spelled "tast." For example, in Act 2, scene 3, line 67 of "Romeo and Juliet" where the Friar's words are set: "How much salt water throwne away in wast,/To season Love that of it doth not tast." (Notice the rhyme with "wast/waste.")
Scene 3/1 *l.*259	EDITOR'S VERSION Cardinal Panulph: "A **chafed** lion by the mortal paw,"	(Some editions print "**caged**" or "**chased**.") It's true that the *f* may easily have been mistaken by the printer as standing for an *s*, but

	Panulph: "A **cased** Lion by the mortall paw,"	the folio "cased" has the double meaning of a lion in a cage, angry and ruthless if let loose, as well as a reference to Austria, who is wearing the "case" of a lion's skin.
Scene 3/2 *l.* 37	EDITOR'S VERSION King John: "If the midnight bell/Did, with his iron tongue and brazen mouth,/Sound on into the drowsy **ear** of night"; FOLIO VERSION John: "If the mid-night bell/Did, with his yron tongue, and brazen mouth,/Sound on into the drowzie **race** of night";	A double example of editors (although neither Smallword nor Honigmann) substituting the word "ear" since it conforms with the imagery and sense. To support the first example (3/2) from the folio, Honigmann references Edmund Spenser's Night "who must run her timely race." Spenser had helped to familiarize the cliché *drowsy night*."[46] In the second example (4/2), seeking a "Mother's care" is a return to childhood: a desperate and rather pathetic attempt at survival from John, (as the folio speech prefix calls him), now facing death and defeat.
Scene 4/2 *l.* 118	EDITOR'S VERSION King John: Where is my mother's **ear**,/That such an army could be drawn in France,/And she not hear of it?" FOLIO VERSION John: "Where is my Mothers **care**?/That such an Army could be drawne in France,/And she not heare of it?"	
Scene 3/3 *l.* 110 "	EDITOR'S VERSION Lewis: And bitter shame hath spoil'd the sweet **world's** taste," FOLIO VERSION Dolphin: "And bitter shame hath spoyl'd the sweet **words** taste,"	Smallwood again concedes that the folio "might be right" but prints "world's" on the grounds that "world" appears 3 lines earlier—which is actually a good enough reason not to repeat it here.[47] The image in the speech is of "a twice-told tale," so "words" would be an appropriate choice. Alexander Dyce, writing in the 19th century, thought that the preference for "words" was "sheer foolishness."[48]
Scene 5/7 *l.* 15	EDITOR'S VERSION Prince Henry: "Death, having preyed upon the outward parts,/Leaves them **invincible**, and his siege is now/Against the **mind**," FOLIO VERSION Henry: "Death having praide upon the outward parts/Leaves them **invisible**, and his siege is now/Against the **winde**,"	Prince Henry is talking about his father's descent into death. Smallwood notes the first word change but not the second, although his explanation relies on "mind," which the folio doesn't print. He explains that Henry describes "the mind, like the body, going beyond sensibility to suffering to incoherence … the idea of the body being *invincible* to the suffering which death tries to impose, though paradoxical, is perfectly coherent."[49] Honigmann retains the folio's "invisible" but not "winde," and like Smallwood alters it to "mind." Shakespeare calls Death the "invisible commander" in his poem "Venus and Adonis"[50] and there's an argument that it is Death Hamlet is referring to when he sees Fortinbras's army which "Makes mouths at the invis-

ible event."⁵¹ The folio's "winde" works in the sense that King John is raving against thin air—a "siege" can be an attack as well as a defense. It is also in keeping with Prince Henry's final thought on the king's behavior: "'Tis strange that death should sing."⁵²

The final examples are from Shakespeare's most famous play, *Hamlet*. The emendations made to *Hamlet* by editor/adaptors would fill a very large volume. It was printed four times in quarto with Q2 thought to have the most authority. Past editorial practice has been to create a hybrid text from the First Folio and Second quarto, but many word alterations appear in neither and are simply speculation.⁵³

Hamlet

Scene 1/2 *l.*79	EDITOR'S VERSION Hamlet: "O that this too too **sullied** flesh would melt," FOLIO VERSION Hamlet: "O that this too too **solid** Flesh would melt,"	The quartos print "sallied" ('troubled') and some modern editions do too. Both the Arden and New Penguin choose "sullied"—a word first proposed by Dover Wilson that does not appear in either quarto or folio. An actor, of course, will be able to indicate the pun of "Solid/Sullied," so the change is completely unnecessary.
Scene 1/3 *l.*21	EDITOR'S VERSION Laertes: "The **sanity** and health of **this** whole state"; (Arden) The **safety** and health of **this** whole state"; (New Penguin) FOLIO VERSION Laertes: "The **sanctity** and health of **the** whole State";	The New Penguin follows Q2 in printing "safety." Arden's "sanity" is conjecture, but the editor, Harold Jenkins, gives no reason for including the word, despite it being absent from both the folio and the quartos. However, he explains (presumably for readers who are insane enough not to understand) that "sanity" means "well-being."⁵⁴ The First Folio's "sanctity" makes the point that Hamlet's choice of queen affects not just the physical welfare of the state but its spirituality too—a potent image when one considers the succession problems of Henry VIII and Elizabeth I and the religious strife that attended it. The subtle change of the quarto's "this" to "the" in the folio underlines the point. The problem is not just confined to "this" state of Denmark but countries in general, including England.
Scene 1/5 *l.*22	EDITOR'S VERSION Ghost: "List, **list,** O list!/If thou didst ever they dear father love—" FOLIO VERSION Ghost: "list **Hamlet,** oh list,/If thou didst ever they deare Father love—"	Most modern volumes print the line as found in Q2 and add their own punctuation, creating a pretty hammy stage ghost. The folio marks the moment when the Ghost first calls Hamlet by his name. No wonder Hamlet's response to this is "Oh God!" ("Oh Heaven!" in the folio due to a Jacobean government act). This is one of the rare uses of an exclamation point in the folio. In the next line the Ghost tells Hamlet he has been murdered. The shocks are coming quickly and obviously affect the actor playing this role.

2. The Shaman at Work

Scene 1/5 *l.*175	EDITOR'S VERSION Hamlet: "There are more things in heaven and earth, Horatio,/Than are dreamt of in **your** philosophy." FOLIO VERSION Hamlet: "There are more things in Heaven and Earth, Horatio,/Than are dream't of in **our** Philosophy."	This is one of Shakespeare's most famous and oft-quoted lines and nearly all modern texts print the quarto "your," explaining the sense is philosophy in general. Using the word in this way is common in Shakespeare—see, for example, Act 5, scene 1, line 165, when the Gravedigger says, "And your water, is a sore Decayer of your horson dead body." The folio "our" suggests a joint outlook on life shared by Hamlet and Horatio. This is supported by a later exchange between them at Act 5, scene 2, line 10. Hamlet: "There's a Divinity that shapes our ends,/Rough-hew them how we will." Horatio: "That is most certaine." None of the other three folios change "our" to "your," although 26 lines earlier the Second Folio correctly adjusts "Come one" to "Come on."
Scene 2/1 *l.*1	EDITOR'S VERSION Polonius: "Give him **this** money and these notes, Reynaldo." FOLIO VERSION Polonius: "Give him **his** money, and these notes Reynaldo."	On the face of it this is a printing mistake and editors seem right in following the quarto's "this." However, all of the folios set "his," and it's certainly more actable. The modern version of the line is just a simple instruction, while the folio—especially with the comma after "money"—portrays a father grudgingly giving money to a son whom he suspects is frittering away his allowance. No doubt he sets Reynaldo to spy on him to see if he is spending Polonius's hard-earned cash on "gaming," "drinking," "fencing," and "drabbing."⁵⁵ The folio shows us a different side to Polonius. Instances such as this are why actors generally prefer to perform the folio text.
Scene 2/2 *l.*548	EDITOR'S VERSION Hamlet (of the Player): "All his visage **wann'd**,/Tears in his eyes, distraction in his aspect," FOLIO VERSION Hamlet (of the Player): "All his visage **warm'd**,/Tears in his eyes, distraction in his aspect,"	Modern editions print Q2's "wann'd/wand," meaning the actor's face turned pale. They point out that earlier (line 515) Polonius has observed, "Looke whe're (where) he ha's not turn'd his color." Hamlet and Polonius are unlikely to agree about acting, or indeed anything else. In the theatre we talk of "warming up"—getting the voice and body ready for performance. Marcius in Act 1, scene 5, line 19 of *Coriolanus* says, "My work hath yet not warm'd me." Literally he isn't warm, but he's also only just started and is not yet fully warmed up. In this context Hamlet *could* be saying that the Player's face, rather than being shocked and consequently tight, is warm and full of expression.
Scene 3/2 *l.*225	EDITOR'S VERSION Gertrude: "The lady **doth protest too** much, methinks."	Another famous line where modern editors follow the Second Quarto. The quarto sense is that the Player Queen overdoes her promising—she does it "too much." First Folio's

	FOLIO VERSION Gertrude: "The Lady **protests** to much methinkes."	"Protests to" gives the meaning of vowing several things, such as "If once a Widdow, ever I be Wife" and "never come mischance betweene us twaine."⁵⁶ (N.B. "Protests to" in this folio line does not have the contemporary meaning of "objects to" but means "avows to" or "proclaims.") The folio setting is shorter and curt, expressing the rising anger in Gertrude as she sees herself portrayed onstage.
Scene 4/2 *l.* 16	EDITOR'S VERSION Hamlet: "He keeps them, **like an ape an apple,** in the corner of his jaw," FOLIO VERSION Hamlet: "He keeps them, **like an Ape** in the corner of his jaw,"	This is a good example of editors constructing a completely new line from various printings of the play. Q1 has "as an ape doth nuts in the corner," Q2 "like an apple in the corner," and the folio "like an Ape in the corner." Stitch bits of them together and the modern "like an ape an apple, in the corner" is produced even though the line is not found in any of the quarto or folio versions. New Penguin's T.J.B. Spencer is worth quoting on this. He believes that Q2 and folio "each give only a very strained meaning ... it seems most likely that the Q2 and F readings are each a confusion of *like an ape an apple.*"⁵⁷ Refuting this opinion, the Arden's Harold Jenkins prints the First Folio version with the sound logic that to change it "is both unnecessary and improbable since it would imply that the two good texts each made a separate error."⁵⁸
Scene 4/7 *l.* 182	EDITOR'S VERSION Laertes: "Alas, then **she is** drown'd." FOLIO VERSION Laertes: "Alas then, **is she** drown'd**?**"	Another editor preference for the Second Quarto. The folio's question is in keeping with Laertes's confusion at the news of his sister's death, perhaps even a moment of desperate hope that what he has heard isn't true and he needs it confirmed. The folio's setting is active for an actor, the modern printing of the line passive; actors always seek actions. Laertes has previously asked (line 164), "Drowned! Of where?" Modern editions remove the folio exclamation point after "Drowned" and replace it with a question mark, removing Laertes's total shock and disbelief (what does it matter where?) when he is told what has happened.
Scene 5/2 *l.* 317	EDITOR'S VERSION Hamlet: "O villainy! **Ho!** Let the door be lock'd." FOLIO VERSION Hamlet: "Oh Villany! **How?** Let the doore be lock'd."	This is very similar to the example above, with editors printing Q2's "Ho!" explaining it is, as Harold Jenkins writes, "A call to stop the combat."⁵⁹ But the combat has finished 4 lines earlier, when Laertes says, "I am justly kill'd with mine owne treacherie"? The "Ho!" is unnecessary as an order, since the line after it, "Let the doore be lock'd," does the same thing. Hamlet has spent the play asking questions but not acting on them. He now wonders how someone has killed his mother and is immediate in his revenge.

These charts will give some slight indication of the literally thousands of changes editor/adaptors make to Shakespeare's words. A comprehensive catalog of all of the alterations in the canon would take years to complete and run to a large number of volumes. However ... A WORD OF WARNING! Although it might be wise for theatre professionals to approach edited texts with skepticism and begin their work using the folio, it is very dangerous to do so unquestioningly. Here's an example of how a too-rigorous adherence to the First Folio is actually counterproductive. Probably the most famous editor emendation in all of Shakespeare occurs in Act 2, scene 3 of *Henry V* when Mistress Quickly, speaking of the dying Falstaff, at line 16 says, "and 'a babbled of green fields." This is a phrase that doesn't appear in the three quartos[60]; in fact, it doesn't appear in the folio either, at least not in that form. The folio version is: "and a Table of greene fields." The word "babble" (but not "babbled") is used in *Twelfth Night*, *The Two Gentleman of Verona*, and *Much Ado*, and there's "babling" in *Richard III* and *Twelfth Night*,[61] but "babbled" hardly looks like "Table" when written in any hand, especially as one has 7 letters and the other only 5. The folio compositor has also taken pains to print "Table" with a capital letter and sets no apostrophe after "a." An error in printing should probably be ruled out since "b" and "T" were at the opposite ends of the different boxes that contained the compositor's letters. None of the three later folios correct the word "Table," despite adjusting hundreds of other small mistakes.

It's seductive to believe that "Table" *could* be the correct word. Hamlet speaks of "the Table of my Memory,"[62] a "table book" being where stories, words, phrases, and such were set down to be remembered later. In using "Table," Sir John could be recalling the green fields of his youth when he "lay all night in the windmill in Saint George's field" with Master Shallow and "heard the chimes at midnight."[63] In the phrase prior to "Table of green fields," Mistress Quickly describes Falstaff's nose as being "as sharp as a Pen," so perhaps the two images—table book and pen—are connected? Alternatively an actor might follow John Southworth's explanation:

> Table was the Tudor term for small, alabaster plaques depicting devotional subjects, including the decapitated head of St. John the Baptist on a salver ... surviving examples of which some traces of paint remain show a green field in the lower background.... John the Baptist was of course Sir John's name saint, and he dies calling on God.[64]

When spoken "Sir John" sounds very like "St. John," especially as it is commonly pronounced "Sin-Jen"—an apt term for Falstaff. Keeping with religion, it's also possible the dying Falstaff, confused in his mind and attempting the reconciliation with God he speaks of many times in the plays, is trying to recite Psalm 23 and either he gets it wrong or Mistress Quickly fails to understand the reference:

> The Lord is my shepherd; I shall not want. He maketh me to lie down in green pastures: he leadeth me beside the still waters.... Thou preparest a table before me in the presence of mine enemies...[65]

Nonetheless, Theobald's emendation of "Table" to "babbled," made almost 300 years ago, now stands in the canon as the correct word. It is such an accepted change to the lines that if a modern actor were to say "Table" instead of "babbled" it would strike a contemporary audience as very odd, perhaps even perverse—for a good reason.

To take the possible connection to Psalm 23 first, it wasn't published in the above form until the King James Bible in 1611, about 13 years after *Henry V* was originally performed. Shakespeare would probably know the psalm from the Thomas Sternhold translation of 1549:

> My shepherd is the living Lord,
>   nothing therefore I need;
> In pastures fair, near pleasant streams,
>   he setteth me to feed.
> And in the presence of my foes
>   my table thou shalt spread :
> Thou wilt fill full my cup, and thou
>   anointed hast my head.[66]

There is no mention of "green" in Sternhold's version and both translations use the word "pastures" rather than "fields," although they both include "table." What First Folio advocates omit in their analysis of a single phrase is the full passage, and in this context the word "Table" in Mistress Quickly's description of Falstaff's death sounds very much like nonsense:

> A parted ev'n just betweene Twelve and One, ev'n
> at the turning o'th' Tyde: for after I saw him fumble with
> the Sheets, and play with Flowers, and smile upon his fingers
> end, I knew there was but one way: for his Nose was
> as sharpe as a Pen, and a Table of greene fields.

Clearly "Table" in the speech doesn't make sense; why would Falstaff's nose be as sharp as a table, for example? It's easy to see how it's possible to be seduced into believing the First Folio is inerrant and attempt to twist the text when common sense will tell you otherwise. If there were a misreading of poorly written copy then perhaps "Talk'd" was thought to be "Table"—"and 'a Talk'd of green fields." Nonetheless, for the actor playing Mistress Quickly and a colorful description of the death of Falstaff, "babbled" is the strong theatrical choice. Generally the First Folio supports the work of the actor and director, but it is wise to hold to Shakespeare's rule and "Let your own discretion be your tutor."[67] However, I can honestly state that my experience as a professional director has been that when actors are given the option between a word found in the First Folio and a version that has been speculatively edited, they have always seized on the folio. It works better for their characters.

Many of the word alterations that editor/adaptors make are corrections from supposed printing house errors and, as demonstrated, there were indeed numerous places in the First Folio that signify lapses in the printing process. A considerable amount (although by no means all) of these were adjusted when the Second Folio was published in 1632.[68] Cross-referencing the First and Second Folios when finding a moment of confusion in the text can often prove profitable to the actor and director in attaining clarity. An example of the degree of scrutiny and the range of corrections the Second Folio employed when making amendments might be imagined from the following chart that plots just a few of the changes the Second Folio made to the First Folio printing of *Romeo and Juliet*:

FIRST FOLIO	SECOND FOLIO
There are a number of examples of split words such as trans gression, wisewe : sely, so are, movethn ot, gloriou s, O rif, Pl ants, t he, ha ve, itli ht, whi ch, sol emne, Bri dall, s ounding,—and appropriately—sep arated.	The Second Folio corrects these split words to transgression, wise wisely, soare, moveth not, glorious, Or if, Plants, the, have, light it, which, solemne, Bridall, sounding, separated.

2. The Shaman at Work

There are also numbers of examples of words joined together such as asmall, asute, oflath, alittle, dogsname, Icharge, Iam, Butnot, isthis, shallbe, thinglike, thebones, flagis, notaway, and ofbreath.

The Second Folio corrects these joined words o a small, a suit, of lath, a little, dogs name, I tcharge, I am, But not, is this, shall be, thing like, the bones, flag is, not away, and of breath.

others	other
open	ope
Fennell	Female
lauguish	languish
a eleven	eleven[69]
speeh	speech
learne	learnd
agaaine	againe
Fries	Friers
yet ringing	yet ring
wits faints	wit faints
hid	hide
cirustance	circumstance
climde	climbe
alove	alone
names	name
not	but
It	I
And	Second Folio omits the word so that the meter is regular.
dimne	damned
him	him so
which	with
Philosohpie	Philosophie
of	or
ir	it
strave	starve
It is	Is it
Benig	Being
his	this
stay	slay
my	his
some	fond
Mo	No
persent	present
Vallaine	Villaine
thon	thou
Match	Watch
wth	with
out	our
ontrage	outrage

Some of this might seem fairly obvious to the eye, but often a Second Folio correction can reveal vital plot information, as in *Richard III* (Act 4, scene 2, line 89), where Buckingham's request in the First Folio to be given the "Th'Earledome of Hertford" is clarified to "Th'Earledome of Hereford" in the second. The seat of Hereford was once occupied by Henry IV—in fact it was specially created for him by the king he usurped, Richard II—and demonstrates a mark of Buckingham's ambition. The next section will look at the printers more closely—the men who, unlike editor/adaptors, actually had Shakespeare's text or his company's performance prompt book[70] in their hands when making their judgments.

3

Bungling Printers

"You strike like the blind man"

Anyone who has used a computer to compose an article, letter, or email will recognize the following scenario. Everything is carefully typed, the text is proofread and spellings are corrected, some phrases are altered or cut, and sections moved to different places. Satisfied that everything is in order, a final spell check is run … where the writer is horrified to discover the number of mistakes they have missed. Even worse is the realization that the computer's "auto correct" has changed words it thinks you really meant, leaving some of the text incomprehensible. This is the modern version of Shakespeare's printers, who were thorough but not infallible. Despite modern technology, it's remarkable how many times we read a published book or article and discover an apparently glaringly obvious error has been missed by the printers. The Elizabethan/Jacobean era was no different, which is why Thomas Middleton could wittily write in his preface to *The Ant and the Nightengale* in 1604: "I never wisht this book better fortune, than to fall into the hands of a true spelling Pritter."[1] Take this phrase from Act 2, scene 3, line 20 of *Othello* where Cassio's observation of Desdemona that "Indeed she's a most fresh, and delicate creature" is printed in the First Folio as "Indeed she s a m ost fresh, anddelicate creature." Or the famous Crispin's Day speech in *Henry V*, Act 3, scene 3, line 47, when Henry declaims the memorable words:

> Then will he strip his sleeve, and show his scars,
> And say, these wounds I had on Crispin's Day.

In the First Folio "And say, these wounds I had on Crispin's Day" is missing, but luckily the quarto versions of the play have preserved it for posterity. The copy the compositors worked from indicates that it wasn't always secure. There are a number of characters printed in the folio who don't appear in the plays; Innogen, supposedly Leonato's wife/Hero's Mother in *Much Ado About Nothing*, for example. This combination of some faulty copy and supposedly erratic printing procedures is what spurs on editors in adapting the plays.

An apparently common mistake made in the First Folio is not just omitting lines but repeating them. In the folio version of *Richard III*, Queene Elisabeth (wrongly given the speech prefix "Queene Mother") repeats the same phrase twice:

Queene.
If he were dead, what would betide on me?
If he were dead, what would betide on me?[2]

This isn't because she wishes to emphasize her own fragile state of mind but rather that the line was set at the bottom of a page by the printer and then reset again at the top of the next. There's a good example of repeated text in Act 2, scene 2, line 186 of *Romeo and Juliet* when Romeo concludes the scene with:

Romeo.
Would I were sleepe and peace so sweet to rest,
The gray ey'd morne smiles on the frowning night,
Checkring the Easterne Clouds with streakes of light,
And darkenesse fleckel'd like a drunkard reeles,
From forth dayes pathway, made by Titans wheeles.
Hence will I to my ghostly Fries close Cell,
His helpe to crave, and my deare hap to tell. *Exit. Enter Friar alone with a basket.*

The Friar then begins Act 2, scene 3 with a passage that is remarkably similar, and seems out of place:

Friar.
The gray ey'd morne smiles on the frowning night,
Checkring the Easterne Clouds with streakes of light,
And fleckled darkenesse like a drunkard reeles,
From forth dayes path, and Titans burning wheeles:

The Second Folio corrects this mistake and omits these lines from the Friar's speech.[3]

Some of these obvious folio errors are seized upon, with a kind of missionary zeal, as "truth" by staunch First Folio advocates who, in their inflexibility and conviction that the folio is inerrant, can sometimes be as harmful to an actor/director as an editor/adaptor. An example of this is what we would today call a "Freudian slip." In Act 1, scene 3, line 386 of *Othello*, Iago says, in the folio, "I hate the Moore,/And it is thought abroad, that 'twixt my sheets/She ha's done my office" rather than the accepted emendation "*He* ha's done my Office." In other words, using the folio version, Iago hates Othello for sleeping with Emilia rather than him: having sex with Othello is Iago's "office," not Emilia's. This is in tune with the theory that Iago's actions are prompted through jealousy since he has a latent homosexual passion for Othello. As seductive as this reading might be, the Second Folio corrects the line to "He"; Othello is doing Iago's office of sleeping with his wife Emilia. So there *are* mistakes in the folio. With such a massive volume, which has about 860,000 words, it would be naïve to think that there wouldn't be errors in the publication. The print run was 500–750 copies, of which 232 survive. Critics of the First Folio point out that of these 232, none are identical. This is true but there are no substantial differences such as content, and the discrepancies might be thought to demonstrate an attention to detail and a desire to get things right than a slapdash approach to the printing. Legend has it the mistakes were principally caused by the twin evils of the rogue printer, William Jaggard, being blind while working on the folio publication and the incompetence of his employees, one of whom, known to the world as "Compositor E," was an apprentice. But that is far from the full story.

Jaggard and the publishers will be looked at later in this chapter, but it's worth pausing for a moment to consider poor old "Compositor E," a 17-year-old by the name of John Leason. The picture that's painted of him is a rebellious teenager, in a dead-end job for which he has no aptitude or enthusiasm, spending his nights cruising his horse around the streets of London drunk on sack, stopping off for a quick galliard and the seduction of a willing wench before, stuffing himself with cates, he winds his way home in the early hours. If he were nursing a hangover and bored with his employment, it's no wonder he made so many errors. This is an exaggeration, of course, but it's not far from the kind of imagined scenario many would have us believe. As with so much scholarship surrounding Shakespeare, it doesn't make sense. Age 17 would not be, at these times, the same as a teenager today. Shakespeare himself was 18 when he got married. An apprentice was little more than the property of his master, so was very much under control—there was even a law detailing the type of clothes apprentices could wear. Make a mistake and they would be severely punished; John Leason must have lived in fear of retribution if he made a slip-up. And stop for a moment to think of your own experiences as a young newcomer to a job, or perhaps you've hired someone who lacks skill and you had to train them? In these circumstances it's likely the person is carefully monitored in the work they do. The idea that someone like Leason would be let loose without supervision on the printing of such an important book as the First Folio—a book on which the whole future of the business depended—is illogical. If anything, it is probable his work was *more* scrutinized than any of the other compositors.'[4] Yes, as an apprentice, Leason did make many mistakes (he is believed to have set much of *Romeo and Juliet* and made the error quoted earlier), and they found their way into the final printing of the folio. In fact, he made a bit of a mess of *Romeo and Juliet* and it's left to the Second Folio to set the play more or less correctly. Examples of Leason's slip-ups when setting the First Folio *Romeo and Juliet* include Capulet pleading for Romeo's life rather than death, Peter joining Romeo in the churchyard as they seek to find Juliet's corpse,[5] and Romeo saying "Thus with a kiss I die" twice, giving the impression that he dies, comes back to life to speak 13 lines, then dies again. Still, there are large sections that he accurately reproduced, but these are still changed by editor/adaptors. It's well to remember, incompetent or not, Leason worked from original copy which no one writing today has sight of.[6] The problem is, because there were some undoubted errors in the folio printing, editor/adaptors take this as evidence for a whole lot more. The argument would be that if a mistake was made with a certain passage, then surely the same kind of error must have occurred in other places too? And this has led modern editors to propose as many convoluted arguments to justify "mistakes" made in printing the First Folio as anti–Stratfordians to deny the very existence of the Warwickshire-born playwright William Shakespeare.

To illustrate this, the three acknowledged instances of errors mentioned earlier—repeated text, omitted lines, and the fortuitous "Freudian slips"—need to be carefully scrutinized. All are clearly mistakes in printing, but this does not necessarily mean the same thing happened elsewhere. An example of repeated text in the folio occurs in *Love's Labour's Lost* when Berowne in Act 4, scene 3, line 298 says:

> From womens eyes this doctrine I derive,
> They are the Ground, the Bookes, the Achadems,
> From whence doth spring the true *Promethean* fire.

He then more or less replicates this a little later at line 347:

> From womens eyes this doctrine I derive.
> They sparcle still the right promethean fire,

> They are the Bookes, the Arts, the Achademes,
> That shew, containe, and nourish all the world.

But is it a mistake? The two passages are similar, but *not* identical, and it would be suitable to the situation for Berowne to rerun and sum up his argument in attempting to persuade his friends to woo the women they love despite the vows against this they have made. John Kerrigan, in the New Penguin Shakespeare edition of the play, omits not only the section at line 298 but a whole passage of 23 lines that contains them. Kerrigan gets out his Ouija Board to write of "Shakespeare's declining confidence in the speech." He explains it was a "false start": "Dis-satisfied, he picked up the threads from line 293 (though writing on the manuscript) and remodelled the argument in the form that is shown in this text."[7] Kerrigan makes this cut to the script despite the passage also appearing in the quarto and all four folio printings of *Love's Labour's Lost*. And in doing so an opportunity for character and scene development falls by the wayside. This type of practice has led to the present situation where even a much respected volume such as the Riverside Shakespeare makes, in Don Weingust's estimation, 2,000–3,000 alterations from the folio *per play*. And this, as Weingust puts it, "deprives makers of theatre of some of the basic textual material of their trade."[8]

Even with "Freudian slips" it's sometimes possible to argue that these were deliberately placed by Shakespeare rather than a printing error. In Act 4, scene 1, line 95 of *Henry V* the young king apparently makes a mistake in calling Sir Thomas Erpingham—his old and trusted advisor—Sir John Erpingham. Nearly all printed copies correct the folio's "Sir John" to "Sir Thomas."[9] But could Henry be thinking at that moment of the other father figure in his life, Sir John Falstaff, and have made a Freudian slip? His real father is dead, along with Bardolph and Nym, so on the eve of battle the king may well wish he could turn back time and wish himself "in an alehouse in London"[10] with Falstaff.

Reintroducing "omitted" lines from the quartos is a favorite pastime among editors when preparing their adapted copies of the plays. It seems likely that the First Folio is a record of the plays in performance, *not* after their writing. In fact many Elizabethan/Jacobean publishers made use of this when issuing plays, advertising them as "proved" on the stage and "As it was acted" before printing. By the time the folio was published, all of Shakespeare's plays (with the probable exception of *Timon of Athens*) would have been "proved" on the stage, and that's precisely what Heminge and Condell tell us: "These Plays have had their trial already, and stood out all Appeals; and do now come forth quitted rather by a Decree of Court."[11]

What is thought by the editor/adaptors to be omissions by negligent printers are much more likely to be cuts made in performance. There is an interesting introduction to Beaumont and Fletcher's works of 1647 that appears to support this idea. The Stationer Humphrey Mosley writes:

> When these Comedies and Tragedies were presented on the Stage, the actors omitted some scenes and Passages (with the Author's consent) as occasion led them; and when private friends desir'd a copy, they then (and justly too) transcribed what they acted. But now you have both. All that was Acted, and all that was not; even the perfect full Originals without the least mutilation.[12]

Mosley's words sound a little like present-day marketing of movies as "the director's cut" or DVDs that contain extras such as deleted scenes. As with Heminge and Condell, there is a claim that the plays are the "originals," but he also describes one possible working method in assembling Shakespeare's plays. Not having the author's own text, as Mosley claims to have access to with Beaumont and Fletcher, perhaps for some of their copy Heminge and Condell approached their fellows in the King's Men who "justly" "transcribed what they acted"? Of course we have no direct evidence that it was Shakespeare himself who struck out the lines that are not in the folio, but if he didn't, then it's probable it was done, as Mosley puts it, "with the author's consent." However, the fact that he was a shareholder and actor in his company as well as a writer pushes the balance of probability towards Shakespeare making the cuts. If we are to believe Heminge and Condell that the plays are "as he conceived them"—who else would it be? And yet editor/adaptors persist with the idea that anything they find unfavorable or missing in the folio text couldn't be Shakespeare at work.

The easy route some editors take is to pass off textual problems as not coming from Shakespeare's hand. Take Kenneth Muir, editor/adaptor of the New Penguin *Othello*, who confidently writes, "The text clearly contains some 'improvements' for which Shakespeare was not responsible."[13] Or M. R. Ridley in an Arden edition of *Othello* who, commenting on the "blunders of honest but not always skilful transcriber and compositor" believes the folio text shows "a good deal of divergence from the original for which he (Shakespeare) was not responsible."[14] J. M. Nosworthy, also an editor/adaptor for the New Penguin Shakespeare, in this case *Measure for Measure*, is even more forthright: "Metrically defective lines may be readily attributed to Crane or the compositors, but, under no circumstances, to Shakespeare."[15] Nosworthy is writing specifically about the meter[16] but these editors present as fact something they cannot possibly prove to be true. Editor/adaptors dislike contradiction and ambiguity, but an actor will warmly embrace them and actively seek them out. They provide a character with depth and richness; they are the stuff of an actor's trade. In presenting conjecture as fact, the editor/adaptors stand in opposition to a performer's craft.

Any Shakespeare play was a new play when first performed. Think of a present-day theatre dedicated to new writing. It is often possible to buy a copy of the script you are about to see, and then afterwards notice, because the text was printed before rehearsals began, that there have been a number of cuts, rewrites, additions, and other changes made before performance. It appears the King's Men adopted a similar approach to their plays. Nine copies of Thomas Middleton's *A Game at Chess* (1624) have survived—6 in manuscript and 3 in quarto—and none of them are identical. In modern theatre a play is written and then adjusted according to a wide range of considerations and practicalities; the personnel available, staging requirements, audience reaction, discoveries made in rehearsal, the need to shorten the text perhaps for a tour and, crucially, an author's own reflections after seeing what they have written actually performed. This working method would be recognizable to anyone working in contemporary theatre. What always surprises those who aren't theatre practitioners is just how much of a collaboration any production is. Writer, director, designer, actors, and many others will work together until a consensus is reached on what will work in performance. Rehearsal isn't a matter of taking a text and simply copying the written instructions but a journey of discovery where things are constantly tried out and rejected. A play is shaped on the rehearsal room floor rather than in the study. In short, a modern rehearsal is a process of constant alteration and amendment, which continues throughout the run. Tom Stoppard wrote about this when his play *Jumpers* was printed in 1972:

In preparing previous plays for publication I have tried with some difficulty to arrive at something called a "definitive text," but I now believe that in the case of plays there is no such animal. Each production will throw up its own problems and very often the solution will lie in some minor changes to the text, either in the dialogue or in the author's directions, or both.[17]

That is not to say that Shakespeare rehearsed his plays as a present-day theatre company would. Some fine research has been undertaken into the rehearsal practices of the King's Men, and it seems "rehearsal" was another word for "repeat"; the actors would copy their instructor. Launce asks Speed in *Two Gentlemen of Verona* to "Rehearse that once more" when he wants him to repeat a phrase in a letter.[18] Quince in *A Midsummer Night's Dream* is both writer and director and appears to follow the pattern of instructing his actors to copy his phrasing—with an important difference. Quince makes changes to the script from rehearsal to performance.[19]

When Hamlet asks the Players if he can add some lines to their already learned dialogue, they react in a nonchalant fashion that suggests that script alterations are a common occurrence in their job:

Hamlet.
You could for a need study a speech of some dosen or sixteene lines, which I would set downe, and insert in't? Could ye not?
Player.
I my Lord.[20]

Ben Jonson includes a joke about people other than the playwright "putting in" the script in his Induction to *Bartholomew Fair*, which is an indication that such things happened. The stage-keeper (what we would today call a stagehand) has suffered the wrath of the writer for making suggestions for improvements: "He has, sir reverence, kicked me three or four times about the tiring-house, I thank him, for but offering to put in, with my experience."[21]

The very word "Sharer" in a theatre company points to collaboration. In fact, many plays written at this time were collaborations between two or more people in a way that is rarely seen today—the work of Beaumont and Fletcher is perhaps the prime example. Shakespeare collaborated with other authors on three to five of his plays, maybe more. He allowed Fletcher to write *The Woman's Prize or The Tamer Tamed* as a sequel to *The Taming of the Shrew*. It worked the other way too. The "Hecate" scenes in *Macbeth*[22] are certainly an interpolation from Middleton's *The Witch*, and *The Two Noble Kinsmen* draws on material from Beaumont's 1613 *A Masque at the Inner Temple and Grays Inn*.[23] We know that some of the plays were commissions for a special place or event, which is a kind of collaboration in that the initial writing impulse probably wasn't Shakespeare's. The first recorded mention of Shakespeare is the famous diatribe by Robert Greene, who called him a "Johannes Fac Totem"—a "Jack of all Trades." If, as Greene thought, Shakespeare had his fingers in many pies, he can only have done so collaboratively.

One of Hamlet's instructions to the Players is to "speake no more than is set downe for them,"[24] and Olivia chides Cesario/Viola for being "out of your text."[25] Such comments have been taken as indicators that Shakespeare required actors to strictly observe what he had written, but evidence from the plays themselves suggest this was not the case. *Henry IV, Part 1* has an unusually high number of stage directions that call for input from the actors: *"Here they both call for him, the Drawer stands amazed, not knowing which way to go," "Glendower speaks to her in Welsh, and she answers him in the same"* and *"Here the Lady sings a Welsh song."* Similarly—and assuming that, unlike Sir Charles Chaplin, Shakespeare didn't write the music included in his scripts—we find in *The Tempest* directions such as: *"Solemn and strange music; and Prosper on the top (invisible). Enter several strange Shapes, bringing in a banquet; and dance about it with gentle actions of salutations; and inviting the King, etc, to eat, they depart," "Enter certain Reapers, properly habited: They join with the Nymphs in a graceful dance; towards the end whereof Prospero starts suddenly, and speaks; after which, to a strange, hollow, and confused noise, they heavily vanish"* and *"A noise of hunters heard. Enter divers Spirits, in shape of dogs and hounds, hunting them about; Prospero and Ariel setting them on."* Whole scenes are sometimes indicated but not scripted, such as this in *Henry VI, Part 2*: *"Here do the ceremonies belonging, and make the circle; Bolingbroke or Southwell reads, CONJURO te, etc. It thunders and lightens terribly; then the Spirit riseth."* Timon's first entry in Act 1, scene 1 of *Timon of Athens* requires the actor to improvise: *"Enter Lord Timon, addressing himselfe curteously to every Sutor."*

It is reasonable to propose that Shakespeare, at least on occasion, worked with others in both writing and producing and allowed his actors flexibility in performance. When some of his plays were printed in quarto, the publisher advertised them (perhaps fraudulently, although we have no way of knowing) as "Newly corrected and amended" and "Newly corrected, augmented, and amended." It seems to have been accepted that once the script was written or produced, changes would be made. So it is fair to conjecture that Shakespeare, for whatever reason, made cuts and other adjustments to his texts. There could be a contradiction in this claim, because if we believe Heminge and Condell's declaration that they printed Shakespeare's plays "as he conceived them," what are we to make of their later statement?: "His mind and hand went together: And what he thought, he uttered with that easiness, that we have scarce received from him a blot in his papers."[26] This appears to indicate that a clean copy was given to them by Shakespeare, without any alterations at all. The key word is "received." This is how they *first* encountered the text. There were no blots, second thoughts, or messy crossing-outs at this stage; what he wrote, worked. The word "blot" can also mean "cut," and it is used in this context by Shakespeare in *Henry VI, Part 3* Act 2, scene 2, line 90 when Edward says:

> You that are King, though he do weare the Crowne,
> Have caus'd him by new Act of Parliament,
> To blot out me, and put his owne sonne in.

It's possible that Shakespeare initially delivered to his company a clean script, without any blotting-outs, and cuts were made in rehearsal or after early performances. This view is backed up by Ben Jonson. His poem in praise of Shakespeare is the first in the folio and contains the famous line: "He was not of an age, but for all time!" What isn't often quoted is Jonson's subtitle to his poem: "What he hath left us." In other words, it was an evaluation of Shakespeare as a writer, and one of the things Jonson mentions is Shakespeare's ability to rewrite his plays:

> *Yet must I not give Nature all: Thy Art,*
> *My gentle* Shakespeare, *must enjoy a part.*
> *For though the* Poets *matter, Nature be,*
> *His Art doth give the fashion. And, that he,*
> *Who casts to write a living line, must sweat,*

> *(Such as thine are) and strike the second heat*
> *Upon the* Muses *anvil: Turn the same,*
> *(And himself with it) that he thinks to frame;*
> *Or for the laurel, he may gain a scorn,*
> *For a good* Poet's *made, as well as born.*
> *And such wert thou.*[27]

"and strike the second heat/Upon the Muses anvil" and "a good Poet's made, as well as born" suggest that Shakespeare revised his plays.[28] There is further evidence of Ben Jonson's involvement in a Shakespearean rewrite. In his book *Timber*, Jonson says of Shakespeare:

> Many times he fell into those things, could not escape laughter: as when he said in the person of Caesar, one speaking to him, Caesar thou dost me wrong; he replied, Caesar never did wrong, but with just cause; and such like, which were ridiculous.[29]

Just to rub it in, Jonson included the line satirically in the Induction to his play *The Staple of News* and has the Prologue remark to Expectation: "Cry you mercy, you never did wrong, but with just cause."[30] There is no quarto version of *Julius Caesar* to refer to, but it seems that someone, and we can only assume it was Shakespeare, rewrote the line about "just cause" so that, 24 years after the first performance, in the folio version of *Julius Caesar* it is missing and the phrase, at Act 3, scene 1, line 47, reads:

> Know, *Caesar* doth not wrong, nor without cause
> Will he be satisfied.

Notice the short verse line at the end: "Will he be satisfied." Does this indicate a dramatic pause after these words or a cut? If Shakespeare wanted to build the action to a swift climax, a stop would not be appropriate. In this case two iambic lines would be needed so the original words, the ones that Jonson complained about, were probably something like:

> *Caesar* never did wrong but with just cause,
> Nor without cause will he be satisfied.

Often the quarto version of a play, generally thought to be based on an early performance, can indicate changes that were made throughout its production life, with the final copy printed in the folio. For example, *Richard II*, Act 5, scene 6, line 8 names the rebels against the new Henry IV as "Oxford, Salisbury, Blunt, and Kent," which is historically inaccurate. The First Folio duly amends the list to "Salsbury, Spencer, Blunt, and Kent." Perhaps a more indicative amendment, useful for an actor, was made to *Henry IV, Part 1*. Much ink has been spilled in academic circles either supporting or refuting the charge that Falstaff is a coward. When Hal and Poines rob Falstaff of the money he's recently stolen, the quarto stage direction (printed in nearly all modern editions) is "*They all run away, and Falstaff after a blow or two runs away too, leaving the booty behind them.*" In this version Falstaff fights before retreating. The First Folio prints something significantly different: "*They all run away, leaving the booty behind them.*" Falstaff doesn't fight, he retreats immediately. Aware that the comedy of Falstaff is the glue that holds the whole play together, the folio/performance script emphasizes the humor of him running away in contradiction to his later description of putting up a fight. The quarto script might in some way support Falstaff's lies while the folio is less ambiguous. It was probably the experience of performance that led to this change.

A very good example of omissions made for performance can be found in the last act of *Hamlet* and they are very similar to the type of cuts a modern director would suggest. There's a famous exchange with Osric that reveals the king's wager in a fight between Hamlet and Laertes.[31] It's a memorable comic scene but perhaps comes at the wrong moment when the dramatic need at this point might be to move the story along. The folio shortens the text by cutting Osric's description of Laertes's return (both Hamlet and the audience already know that), removes some of Osric's affected wordplay (we've seen that too), and a line from Horatio, so the interplay is between Hamlet and Osric alone. About 30 lines are cut in total. The folio also omits a later section where a lord returns to tell Hamlet to go to the hall to prepare for his bout. This never happens—the king and court come to Hamlet—and the lord provides no information that hasn't already been given by Osric. Another 15 lines are thus removed as well as the need for an extra actor/costume. More importantly the folio cuts tighten the scene so that events move swiftly, and both the character of Hamlet and the actor playing him have no time to reflect on events before they unfold. However, immediately before Osric's entry, the folio *adds* 12 lines that are not in any of the six (including a variant) copies of *Hamlet* published in quarto. All the quartos and the folio print:

Hamlet.
Does it not, thinkst thee, stand me now upon
He that hath kill'd my King, and whor'd my Mother,
Popt in between th' election and my hopes,
Thrown out his Angle for my proper life,
And with such cozenage; is't not perfect conscience,

But only the folio has Hamlet continue with (Act 5, scene 2, line 69):

Hamlet.
To quit him with this arme? And is't not to be damn'd
To let this Canker of our nature come
In further evil.
Horatio.
It must be shortly knowne to him from England
What is the issue of the business there.
Hamlet.
It will be shorre, (short)
The *interim's* mine, and a mans life's no more
Then to say one: but I am very sorry good *Horatio*,
That to *Laertes* I forgot my selfe;
For by the image of my Cause, I see
The Portraiture of his; Ile count his favours:
But sure the bravery of his griefe did put me
Into a Towering passion.
Horatio.
Peace, who comes heere?
Enter young Osrick.

The folio makes clear the moment Hamlet decides to kill Claudius personally—"is't not perfect conscience,/To quit him with this arme?" Hamlet had previously thought he would be damned if he assassinated the king while he was at prayer but now believes he would be damned if he *doesn't* kill him. The additional text stresses the need for speed and urgency, which the cuts in the next scene provide, and has Hamlet reflect on what he has done to Laertes. After all, Hamlet did kill Laertes's father. Crucially, the inserted lines have Hamlet draw a parallel between Laertes's situation and his own: "For by the image of my Cause, I see/The Portraiture of his"; Laertes, like Hamlet, has also lost a father and Ophelia. One can almost imagine Laertes also thinking in his doubt about murdering Hamlet: "By the image of my Cause, I see/The Portraiture of his." This section alone should leave us in no doubt that Shakespeare revised his plays.[32]

The sharp-eyed will have noticed that Hamlet in the folio-added speech says, "I'll count his favours," while modern texts print "I'll court his favours" on the very reasonable grounds that "court" could easily be mistaken for "count" when handwritten. This is an emendation made by Nicholas Rowe, the first acknowledged editor of Shakespeare, writing 86 years after the First Folio was published, and it has stood for over 300 years.[33] He's probably right, and the lines tend to point in the direction of "court." However, an actor might wish to consider the option of "count" as it could provide a wonderful dramatic opportunity for the character of Hamlet and the play. If Hamlet believes he can "count" on Laertes's support or "favors," he has made a terrible mistake, although there is a moment of doubt when he recalls "the bravery of his griefe." Before he can think it through and consider it further Osric enters. Events are moving fast. The suspense is built in the next scene as Laertes tells the audience he is on the verge of changing his mind and not going along with Claudius's plans. Will Laertes turn on the king and Hamlet be saved to rule in Denmark? For the actors in the scene, the simple word "count" provides high drama with Hamlet expecting Laertes to be on his side[34] and Laertes wavering. Of course it comes to nothing and Hamlet dies, perhaps surprised that he has misjudged the situation. He is not altogether misguided in his judgment that he can count on Laertes. They exchange forgiveness after Laertes realizes "I am justly kill'd with mine owne Treacherie."[35] All this potential drama has been obliterated by the editor/adaptors with the stroke of a pen.

When considering if Shakespeare revised his plays it's difficult to argue with Stanley Wells's conclusion:

> It is clear from the available evidence that Shakespeare wrote, not as a dramatist whose work would be completed at the moment he delivered his script to the company for which it was written, but as one who knew that he would be involved in the production process.[36]

Despite the evidence for this, editor/adaptors still cannot resist tinkering. The quartos of the plays provide them with a double-edged sword to cut through Shakespeare's texts. If there is a quarto version they prefer, they will use it and cite it as Shakespeare's "original intention." However, if there is *not* a quarto version it represents an opportunity to blame a printing error and adjust words and passages as their imagination suits them. If there is no quarto to support the folio, who can dispute them, especially given the undoubted flaws in the folio? On other occasions they will simply create their own text by using bits of both the quarto and folio. Patrick Tucker identifies one such instance in *Romeo and Juliet* Act 5, scene 1, line 24, when Romeo hears of Juliet's supposed death. In the First Folio, Romeo says, "Then I denie you stars," while the first "bad" quarto prints his line as "then I defie my stars." Editor/adaptors take elements from both and construct a completely new line: "Then I defy you, stars!," adding their own punctuation to boot. It's a line that will be found in nearly all modern published copies, but it was never printed and never played.[37]

Not just words, phrases, and speeches were rewritten before they reached the folio printers. It is now generally accepted among scholars that there was at least one whole play that Shakespeare revised: *King Lear*. The differences between the quarto and folio versions are so great that the Oxford Shakespeare publishes them separately under the titles *The History of King Lear* (quarto) and *The Tragedy of King Lear* (folio). Until the editors of the Oxford Shakespeare (Gary Taylor and Stanley Wells) took this step, it was common editorial practice to conflate both versions into one huge and unwieldy play. Unfortunately this approach to *King Lear* still persists, so that most of the current published versions of the play are actually something Shakespeare never wrote or saw performed but has been invented by editor/adaptors. Imagine how a modern writer would feel if all their cuts, rewrites, and additions were assembled into one unplayable whole? Tennessee Williams is a good example of an author who wrote several versions of the same script over many years. Thankfully, we wouldn't paste all of Williams's revisions into a single volume, or try to combine Chekhov's *Uncle Vanya* with *The Wood Demon* (his earlier attempt on the same story), but that is precisely what happens to Shakespeare, particularly with *King Lear*. No wonder audiences often complain that *Lear* is too long. The folio version seeks to address this problem and the major difference to the quarto is extensive cuts. Probably the most noticeable cut is the scene in the hovel where Lear imagines putting his daughters on trial.[38] This is undoubtedly a good scene but it holds the action up, has no bearing on the narrative, and tells us nothing about Lear that we don't already know. ("OK, OK. We get it. He's gone crazy.") Anyone working in theatre will have come across this situation many times: we like a scene, speech, or character, but for the sake of the overall production it has to go. It's usually the playwright who first notices this and suggests the cut.

Act 3, scene 1 of *King Lear* is an example of this. Kent meets a knight who tells him that Lear has gone out into the storm. Both the quarto and the folio retain most of their dialogue. However, the folio adds some extra lines to explain the division between Albany and Cornwall in more detail and cuts the extraneous instruction telling the knight to go to Dover. Again, anyone working in present-day professional theatre will recognize this type of compensatory cut. In fact it wouldn't be unusual for a director to say to an actor, "You can add (or keep) that line, but you have to omit something from one of your other speeches." Having directed a *King Lear* that used the folio text, I can offer the experience that it plays remarkably well and none of the cuts are missed or remarked on by the audience. Yet editor/adaptors of *King Lear* attempt an amateur dramaturgy and blame negligent compositors for what are positive amendments, probably based on how the play was first received in performance. The latest Arden edition continues the tradition of conflating the folio and quarto texts, and the editor, R. A. Foakes, comments on the passage mentioned above, where Kent urges the knight to make for Dover: "These lines, from Q, are not in F, where they may have been accidentally omitted."[39]

Of course, the cuts made to *King Lear* should not be obliterated from the canon. Probably the most sensible solution is what Taylor and Wells have done in printing the quarto and folio texts separately so there is a choice. However, it is misleading to present a manufactured version of *King Lear* as Shakespeare's play with any cutting blamed on omissions by blundering printers. As R. W. David writes, for an editor to cite Jaggard's printing shop for textual anomalies is the "easy cutting of every Gordian knot."[40]

Just how sloppy were Jaggard and his workers when they set the First Folio?[41] In one aspect they were fairly consistent, the excision of what were then regarded as blasphemous oaths. The 17th century "C-word" was "Christ" and anything related to his name such as "zounds" ("by

Christ's wounds") and "'sblood" ("by Christ's blood"). Since the 1606 "Act to Restrain the Abuses of Players," any mention of God or other religious utterings in *performance* was met with a £10 fine for each occurrence, which is certainly the reason why the later plays make reference to classical gods such as Jove. It's true to say that it wasn't against the law to *print* any perceived profanities, although it would, no doubt, have been frowned upon. The omittance of oaths could therefore be an indication that Jaggard was printing a performance text. In *Measure for Measure*, only published in the folio, Angelo says (Act 2, scene 4, line 2):

> : heaven hath my empty words,
> Whilst my Invention, hearing not my Tongue,
> Anchors on *Isabell:* heaven in my mouth,
> As if I did but onely chew his name,
> And in my heart the strong and swelling evill
> Of my conception:

The third line, "Anchors on *Isabell:* heaven in my mouth," is extra metrical and was probably changed in performance to comply with the law. It possibly originally read, especially with the word "his" in the next line and the repeat of "heaven," "God in my mouth," which would provide a regular iambic line. This seems to be an example of Jaggard following his copy closely. He had good reason to. Some printing errors could also attract severe punishment. Robert Farrier was fined the enormous amount of £200 for leaving out the word "not" in the Seventh Commandment when he published the Bible. His version read: "Thou shalt commit adultery."[42] After taking care with religious oaths, why would Jaggard accidentally omit the prologue to *Romeo and Juliet* the beginning to one of Shakespeare's most famous plays?[43] Or add the prologue to *Troilus and Cressida* which is not found in the quarto? The answer, of course, is that he probably didn't; he printed his copy as faithfully as he could. The mere fact that there were corrections made to the folio during the printing process indicates at least some degree of conscientiousness. It profited Jaggard's workers to do so as printers were paid per page and only if the work was correct. Consider, too, Patrick Tucker's simple but highly persuasive logic:

> If the Folio were so full of errors, then just sometimes an actor would give an inferior performance when made to do what the Folio has set down rather than a careful Editor, but I have yet to have that experience.[44]

So how have Jaggard and his colleagues attracted such bad press? Swinburne called Jaggard an "infamous pirate, liar, and thief,"[45] and this is the general view that still prevails. Much of this negative publicity draws on the words of the playwright Thomas Heywood, who claimed in his prologue, to *If You Know Not Me, You Know Nobody, Part One* about a previous publication of the script Jaggard had issued: "Some by stenography drew The plot; put it in print: (scarce one word true:)."[46] He wrote on the same theme in his 1608 play *The Rape of Lucrece*, and states in the introduction "To The Reader":

> Some of my plays have (unknown to me, and without any of my direction) accidentally come into the printer's hands, and therefore so corrupt and mangled, (copied only by the ear) that I have been unable to know them, as ashamed to challenge them.[47]

Jaggard was a subject Heywood seems obsessed with, and his book *An Apology for Actors*, written in 1612, comments on "Mr. Jaggard (that altogether unknown to him) presumed to make so bold with his name."[48]

It wasn't just Thomas Heywood who suffered from Jaggard's dubious working methods.

When Heminge and Condell wrote, and William Jaggard printed, that Shakespeare's plays had been "abused with diverse stolen, and surreptious copies, maimed, and deformed by the frauds and stealthes of injurious imposters, that exposed them,"[49] the principal offender was William Jaggard! Heywood's assertion that Jaggard "presumed to make so bold with his name" refers not to himself but to Shakespeare, and he tells us that Shakespeare was "much offended." From the early years of Shakespeare's career, Jaggard had been pirating his work and using Shakespeare's name to promote writing of inferior quality. He began with a collection of 20 poems supposedly by Shakespeare called *The Passionate Pilgrim*. In fact only five of the pieces can be attributed to Shakespeare, and most of those are extracts from deliberately bad poetry in *Love's Labour's Lost*. Jaggard padded the pages with poems, and extracts of poems, by Marlowe, Sir Walter Raleigh, and Thomas Heywood, among others. In 1619 he illegally issued 10 of Shakespeare's plays in what has become known as the "False Folio"[50] as he had no authority to do so. They were published with incorrect dates to make it appear they were earlier volumes. Ironically, it's possible this action prompted Heminge and Condell to gather Shakespeare's plays and print them "as he conceived them." So why did they choose Jaggard for this task? A more obvious candidate would have been Richard Field, printer of accurate volumes of Shakespeare's poetry and his childhood friend from Stratford. Field had also worked with Edward Blount, one of the publishers of the First Folio, on *The Phoenix and the Turtle* and didn't die until 1624, although his printing shop continued to thrive long after his death. But Field wasn't chosen. Jaggard was.

Most of the objections against Jaggard concern his shady working methods rather than the quality of his output.[51] It's true that Heywood also writes of "the negligence of the printer, as the misquotations, mis-taking of syllables, misplacing halfe-lines, coining of strange and never heard of words, these being without number,"[52] but this was about *Britaines Troy*, printed by Jaggard back in 1609, 14 years before the First Folio. One would have thought he had grown more experienced and proved himself more reliable during the interim. There was no copyright law at this time and, although there were regulations that could shut down a business that infringed them, Jaggard generally behaved lawfully while taking advantage of gray areas in legislation. For such an important task as the printing of Shakespeare's First Folio—the folio format being used only for books of prestige—there was only one man who had the staff, equipment, premises, and diligence to do the job, and that man was William Jaggard. His track record was excellent. He had printed Raleigh's *History of the World*, *Don Quixote*, Boccaccio, a list of the Ten Commandments that went to every parish in the land, an English dictionary, and Bacon's *Essays*. In 1611, around the time Heywood was accusing him of sloppy workmanship, Jaggard became the official printer to the City of London. His publication of Edward Topsell's *The History of Four-Footed Beasts* is a fine example of quality printing, which is why it is a much-sought-after volume by present-day bibliophiles. There is documentary evidence of his skill. Thomas Wilson had his work issued by Jaggard in 1612 and remarked on "the printer's very great care and diligence."[53] Wilson followed this with a further statement in 1614 and informed readers that if they found faults in his text Jaggard was not to blame: "There would have been far more if the great diligence of the printer had not prevented it."[54]

In the preface to Augustine Vincent's[55] 1622 *Discoverie of Errors* called *The Printer*, Jaggard makes a defense against an attack from Ralph Brooke and indignantly points out that no printer would allow mistakes such as setting "chancellor" instead of "treasurer" or confuse "The Tower of London" for "Hampton Court."[56] And yet these are precisely the sort of errors Shakespeare's editor/adaptors accuse him of.

William Jaggard never lived to see the folio hit the bookshelves as he died in 1623. Like Shakespeare, Jaggard worked in collaboration with others, principally his son Isaac. In fact it is Isaac whose name appears as the printer on the title page of the folio—probably because he had taken over the business by the time of publication. Unlike today, the printing process was very slow, 2–4 years, and during that period William Jaggard became blind. He was probably suffering from the syphilis that eventually killed him. This didn't mean he stopped working or was less efficient. In *The Printer* he mentions that he proofread pages from other work from his sickbed. Jaggard's workers seem to have been a close-knit bunch and eventually the business passed from Isaac to the former apprentice Thomas Cotes. It is Cotes who is responsible for the Second Folio publication of 1632. The Second Folio includes some "clarifications" that are clearly mistakes and further muddy the water in the quest for Shakespeare's text, but generally it tidies up a lot of First Folio printing errors. However, these Second Folio adjustments number just 1,700 to around 860,000 words—a sure sign that the First Folio printing is basically correct. In contrast, remember Don Weingust's estimation that the respected Riverside edition of Shakespeare's works makes 2,000–3,000 adjustments *per play*.

In addition to being the printers of the First Folio, the Jaggards were part of the consortium of publishers that included Edward Blount, John Smethwick, and William Aspley. Not much is known of Smethwick apart from the fact he was associated with William Jaggard's brother John. He might have regretted the connection. It appears they misjudged their elite market. Far from being the success they'd hoped for, the publication of the First Folio was a *Heaven's Gate* for these united artists. Aspley published nothing else for 6 years after its release while Blount, who published around 3 or 4 volumes a year until 1623, didn't produce a single volume for four and a half years, lost his bookshop, and was forced to take out loans. Edward Blount is a very important figure in the history of the First Folio. Unlike the Jaggard's he doesn't appear to have been motivated by money. He was a connoisseur who relied on his taste and good judgment. He published Florio, Montaigne, Cervantes, Ben Jonson, John Lyly, and Marlowe, all of whom have important associations with Shakespeare. Blount appears to have been the ideal publisher, someone who, like Heminge and Condell, issued works not out of a motive for profit but in admiration of the work. He liked the writers he published. This is borne out by his relationship with the dangerous figure of Christopher Marlowe, and he was one of the few mourners who dared attend Marlowe's funeral. According to Charles Nicholl, Blount sheltered Thomas Nashe and prevented his arrest after the *Isle of Dogs* controversy.[57] While Thomas Kyd was prepared to disown Marlowe and speak against him (admittedly under severe torture), Blount did not desert his friend. At great risk to his personal safety, he published Marlowe's *Hero and Leander* in 1598 and wrote in the preface:

> I suppose my self executor to the unhappy deceased author of this Poem.... At this time seeing that this unfinished tragedy happens under my hands to be imprinted; of a double duty, the one to your self, the other to the deceased, I present the same to your most favorable allowance.[58]

These words are very similar to the Dedicatory Epistle to Shakespeare's plays by Heminge and Condell. He is the "executor" of Marlowe and has a "duty" to the deceased. He *cared*.

There is an interesting side character in the story of the First Folio's publication—William Heminge, son of John and possibly named after Shakespeare. In 1626 William Heminge wrote a play called *The Jewes Tragedy*[59] which is remarkable in that it draws on many of Shakespeare's plays. Heminge clearly knew the work backwards. Carol A. Morley quotes John William Hebel's 1920 doctoral thesis *The Plays of William Heminges*[60] in which Hebel lists 15 verbal parallels in *The Jewes Tragedy* with *Hamlet*, 8 with *King Lear*, 4 with *Macbeth*, 2 with *The Merchant of Venice* and *Henry IV, Part 1*, 1 with *Coriolanus*, *Othello*, and *Julius Caesar*, as well as the Watch from *Much Ado About Nothing*. Perhaps the most famous *homage,* sampling, or plagiarism Heminge included in *The Jewes Tragedy* is:

> To be, or not to be, Ay there's the doubt,
> For to be Sovereign by unlawful means,
> Is but to be slave to base desire,
> And where's the honour then?[61]

Interestingly, Heminge repeats the folio comma after the first "To be," which most modern editor/adaptors remove from Shakespeare's version. It's a huge leap of imagination but perhaps Carol Morley is right to speculate:

> Heminge did not matriculate at Oxford until 1624. Given that this interim was precisely the period when the First Folio was being prepared, it is reasonable to wonder whether William was involved, helping with that massive volume's planning and proofreading.[62]

There's no direct evidence for this but it's certainly possible. It's equally possible William Heminge was involved in the publication of the Second Folio. By the time it was issued in 1632, the major players in the printing of the First Folio—the Jaggards, Henry Condell, and John Heminge—were all dead. Blount had transferred his rights in the volume in 1630 and was to die in 1632. William Aspley and John Smethwick were still listed as publishers, and the old Book Keeper of the King's Men, Edward Knight, was still alive. William Heminge inherited his father's shares of the Globe, but appeared to be profligate with his money and sold them in 1633. In need of cash, and close to the text, it's credible to suggest he had some hand in checking and correcting the Second Folio, although he is not listed as a contributor. An interesting thought, perhaps, but one that takes us away from the facts and into the speculative world of the editor/adaptors and critical commentators.

A more pertinent consideration might be why, with such a large cast of characters involved in and around the printing of the First Folio, one of them didn't cry out "Wait! You got it wrong!" There was Ben Jonson,[63] who knew and commented on the smallest detail in the plays and wrote the introductory poem to the folio (two poems in fact), Shakespeare's intimate colleagues Heminge and Condell, the Jaggards—best printers in London, Edward Blount, who regarded himself as executor of an author's work, John Fletcher, who collaborated with Shakespeare on a number of plays, Edward Knight the Book Keeper, Cuthbert Burbage, older brother of Richard Burbage, who didn't die until 1636 and was also an actor in the King's Men, as well as the thousands of audience members at the Globe, at Court, at Blackfriars, and on tour. If there were huge errors such as missing text, faulty meter, added lines, wrongly assigned characters and the like, surely *one* of them would have stepped forward to challenge the veracity of the First Folio? Or at the very least ensure these mistakes were corrected in the Second Folio printing? If you take Weingust's estimate of modern changes in the authoritative Riverside edition conservatively, it still adds up to 72,000 First Folio flaws that modern editors identify where the Second Folio corrects only 1,700 (about 2 per page) and these are mainly spelling, punctuation, and typographical errors.

Apart from the quarto publications (and some of the First Folio was indeed set from quartos) there is not a single piece of documentary evidence to justify editor/adaptor manipulations of Shakespeare's texts.[64] But Heminge and Condell, remember, published the folio to discredit the quartos and over half of the works were never printed in quarto form. The logic that the First Folio is principally a close record of Shakespeare's plays as he left them is overwhelming. These are the scripts that worked in performance and if they worked for Shakespeare and the King's Men it's the obvious starting point for any present-day actor or director. When tinkering with this performer's text, editor/adaptors have a very different audience in mind, but they might do well to remember John Jones's maxim: "The declared rule should hold: print the Folio unless you have good reason not to."[65]

Does any of this really matter? This game of "He said, she said"? An actor, after all, will just want a script they can play and won't much care if the lines are quarto, folio, emendation, or speculation. The answer is, of course, that it matters very much indeed, as the folio printing provides a huge amount of information to help actors to create their role—as we shall see in the next chapter.

4

Creating a Role from the Folio Text

"Know you the character?"

Reading a play is a very different experience from watching one. Some things only become apparent once they are staged. When we read Brutus's final speech in Act 5, scene 5, line 33 of *Julius Caesar* it appears dignified:

> ...Countrymen:
> My heart doth joy, that yet in all my life,
> I found no man, but he was true to me.
> I shall have glory by this loosing day
> More then *Octavius*, and *Marke Antony*,
> By this vile Conquest shall attaine unto.
> So fare you well at once, for *Brutus* tongue
> Hath almost ended his lives History:
> Night hangs upon mine eyes, my Bones would rest,
> That have but labour'd, to attaine this houre.

In performance it can be seen that Brutus is surrounded by a field of dead Romans when delivering these lines, with just four living friends of low status who remain true to him. The "Countrymen" at the beginning of the speech reminds the audience of the crowd of thousands Brutus had previously addressed in the Capitol at the height of his fame and power. When staged, the passage looks and sounds rather pathetic and Brutus, making a speech to a few soldiers and many silent corpses, seems pompous and out of touch. Given the context, his words "I shall have glory by this losing day" become ironic. It's difficult to read irony but actors can convey irony if they choose. (The use of irony/ambiguity is more closely examined in Chapter 7.)

Act 4, scene 8 of *Henry V* has the king receive a list of the French dead from the French Herald, Montjoy.[1] At line 81 Henry reads out the long and detailed losses that include the High Constable of France, the man who had sent Montjoy to ask for Henry's ransom before the battle began. Ten thousand French have been slaughtered, and the ending of the king's speech is darkly ironic as the final verse line is finished by Exeter—"'Tis wonderfull." The thrust of the meaning is clear enough when read, but in performance it is conveyed not so much by Henry's words as by the French Herald's reaction to them. Montjoy is still onstage, hearing of the deaths of people he knew, and he would be grief-stricken, shocked, angry, and ashamed. In a solo reading of the scene, that important detail would almost certainly be missed. The quarto versions of the play omit the French Herald's return with the numbers of the slain and have Exeter deliver the information instead. Giving Henry the list to read, as the folio does, allows him the opportunity to reflect on what he has done. No doubt some of the French he calls out had their throats cut on his orders. This seems to be another example of a change made for performance and further evidence that at least part of the First Folio is a record of the plays when staged.

The General Introduction to the Third Arden Shakespeare series claims their publications are "designed to present the plays as texts for performance."[2] Although a laudable aim, it falls short in two ways. Firstly, in seeking to re-create the plays in performance, the editor/adaptors stray into the world of the director, but a director, it must be emphasized, presents a production of a play for a certain time, place, and audience. Directors never seek to establish a definitive version of the text as the editor/adaptors do but one that works within certain circumstances and will change according to other circumstances. Which is why a great director like Max Reinhardt could produce several different versions of *A Midsummer Night's Dream* throughout his career, including one on film, starring Jimmy Cagney. And why an audience can watch the same play many times, over a number of years, and still enjoy it. On screen the least successful offerings of Shakespeare's plays are those, like the BBC Shakespeare, that seek to establish a "base" production to which all others can refer. To audiences they can appear neutral and conservative, while the most successful (although still faithful to the text) are more radical movies such as Baz Luhrmann's *Romeo + Juliet* or Polanski's *Macbeth*. In an effort to make the plays closer to performance, the editor/adaptor might often add—although this practice is thankfully dying out—extraneous detail that obscures the text rather than enlightens. The Cambridge New Shakespeare editions, whose versions of Shakespeare's plays are still widely read, is a major culprit in adding novelistic or directorial detail such as the following from *The Two Gentlemen of Verona*: "A wall, with a postern, behind the Duke's palace: inside a strip of garden dividing the wall from a lofty turret; outside, a narrow lane with bushes: a moonlit night," "LAUNCE, with his dog at his heels, comes forth from the postern, and casts himself under a bush, groaning," "She snatches at the letter; Lucetta hastily hides it behind her back, and runs."[3] Full marks for imagination, but this is not what Shakespeare wrote or probably intended. As Samuel Schoenbaum has noticed, "The industry of editors, with their sometimes superfluous scene divisions and literary stage directions, has sometimes obscured the exhilarating freedom of Shakespeare's art."[4] As an example of this, editor/adaptors make the exchange in the orchard between Romeo and Juliet (the "balcony scene") stand alone, whereas Shakespeare writes one complete scene that balances the lovers' romantic feelings for each other with the obscene words and views of Mercutio.

The idea of the Arden Shakespeare as "texts for performance" is inadequate because it often doesn't print a performance text. *King Lear*, as previously mentioned, is a classic case of publishing a version of the play that was never actually performed. In fact the Arden series, along with other modern versions, removes or adjusts the very things the folio provides, and actors need, when using a script for creating a role: original spellings and pronunciations, capital letters, italics, speech prefixes, punctuation, and verse/prose lineation. Not only do modern actors need them but their counterparts in the King's Men needed them too—which is why it is probable Shakespeare took the trouble to include them in his text.

Folio Spellings

The folio dialogue, written for actors, was meant to be spoken[5] and some of the spellings are therefore phonetic: "Wensday" instead of "Wednesday," "shoo" rather than "shoe," and "cizers" in place of "scissors" can all be found in the folio *Comedy of Errors*. This was common practice at the time—think of "Shaxbeard" (one written spelling of "Shakespeare"), which works when pronounced with the Elizabethan burr. In fact some of the folio spellings are close to modern "street" or SMS spellings—"has" printed as "haz" for instance. Often spellings can help with age-old problems of how to pronounce certain words such as "bade" and "abhore." The folio generally spells them "bad" and "abhorre" (not "baid" and "a-bore.")

There are two scenes in *All's Well That Ends Well* (Act 4, scenes 1 and 3) when whole lines are spelled entirely phonetically. This is because the French Lords are trying to fool the braggart soldier Parolles into believing they are Russian soldiers, as here at Act 4, scene 1, line 62:

Lord.
Throca movousus, cargo, cargo, cargo.
All.
Cargo, cargo, cargo, villianda par corbo, cargo.
Parolles.
O ransome, ransome,
Do not hide mine eyes.[6]
Interpreter.[7]
Boskos thromuldo boskos.

This is a clear example of Shakespeare writing for his players in order to help them convey a semblance of the "Choughs language"[8] the situation requires.

Similarly, in Act 2, scene 7, line 124 of *Anthony and Cleopatra*, Octavius has a spelling of a word that conveys his professed drunkenness and allows him to display a rare moment of humor (an attempt to be "one of the boys"?) when he remarks, "Mine owne tongue/Spleet's what it speaks": The literary minded editor/adaptor of the most recent Arden edition,[9] John Wilders, prefers to print the Fourth Folio version (only found in the Fourth Folio), "Mine own tongue/Splits what it speaks," despite the fact that this was published 62 years after the First Folio and contains plays that clearly aren't written by Shakespeare. Most modern editor/adaptors choose the word "spleets" but just a few lines later they alter the drunken Enobarbus's folio statement:

> Take heed you fall not *Menas:* Ile not on shore,

to:

> Take heed you fall not. Menas, I'll not on shore,[10]

The folio setting is funnier—an intoxicated man telling someone who is in a much more composed condition than him to take care. There is also an obvious opportunity for comedy if Enobarbus were to fall over after "Take heed you fall not *Menas,*" realize the state he is in, and then decide "Ile not on shore." It's difficult to understand why a printer would carefully reproduce the unusual word "spleets" but then get the punctuation wrong just 7 lines after that.

Actors will often rely on the *sound* of a word to convey meaning and, because they are vocally trained and verbally dexterous, can achieve two meanings on a single word. The First Folio (Shakespeare?) appears to recognize this and the choice of spelling sometimes seems to be deliberate. Where an editor/adaptor will spy a mistake in the text, an actor will see an opportunity for a pun: "There's a double meaning in that,"[11] as Benedick puts it. Sir Peter Hall, founder of the Royal Shakespeare Company, writes about this problem: "With few exceptions, scholarship *reads* the text, it does not *hear* it."[12]

The story of *The Winter's Tale* begins when Leontes suspects his wife Hermione is having an affair with his best friend, Polixenes. In the second scene, unable to persuade Polixenes to prolong his stay with them, Leontes asks Hermione to plead with him instead. After an exchange between Polixenes and Hermione, in which Leontes is distant and silent, he approaches them and asks "Is he won yet?"[13] The folio text misspells "woon," which editor/adaptors correct to "won." In doing so they delete a wonderful ambiguity which an actor can bring out in speaking the phrase: "Is he Woon yet?"—"Has he been both woo'd and won?" For an actor creating the role of Leontes, the crux of this scene is: when does Leontes suspect they are having an affair? Is it immediately after Hermione has left on the arm of Polixenes—"Too hot, Too hot"[14]—or earlier? "Woon" seems to point to the seeds of jealousy being present in Leontes's mind early in the scene.

In *King Lear* Goneril has betrothed herself to Edmund even though she is already married to Albany. Albany understandably objects to this and reprimands Edmund with the words "I her husband contradict your banns"[15]—that is, the wedding banns called prior to a marriage. Well, that's what editor/adaptors would have us believe. The folio spells the word "banes"—banes, poison. So Albany contradicts both the wedding and Goneril's poisonous intentions. And they are literally poisonous since she's just poisoned her sister. An actor, in delivering the text, can make the word sound like both "banns" and "banes." There are many examples of this in the First Folio printing, but are they coincidental? Iago vows to "make the Net/That shall en-mash them all."[16] He will capture them in the mesh of his net but also beat them down, mash them. Macbeth realizes, "This push/Will cheere me ever."[17] If he wins the battle, the throne (chair) will be his forever and the people cheer him as king. The duke's plan in *Measure for Measure* is to judge Angelo with "weale-balanced form."[18] His procedures are both "well-balanced" and for the good of the country, weale, or commonweale. Constance in *King John* has lost her son Arthur's claim to the throne of England when the French Dauphin marries King John's niece Blanche. On hearing the news, Constance is naturally furious about the turn of events and responds in the folio by calling Blanche "Blaunch"—the phonetic spelling of the French for "half note" or "minim"[19] and, of course, "white." Constance cannot believe they have placed such a nonentity in a position of power and is referring to Blanche with sarcasm as "Blaunch."[20] This is the only time in the play the spelling occurs, and only in the mouth of Constance. Compositor B is thought to have set the text (scholars label the compositors from A to E depending on their level of competence) and he doesn't repeat his "mistake" elsewhere. Coincidental or not, the actress playing Constance will no doubt be delighted to deliver the word "Blaunch." The same can be said of Hotspur in *Henry IV, Part 1*, who in the folio dubs his humorless Welsh ally "Owen Glendour"[21] and refers to the libertine Prince of Wales as having "cumrades."[22]

Shakespeare relished the English language and loved to use puns, often for comic effect and often for obscene comic effect. There is a famous set piece in *Henry V* (Act 3, scene 4) where Alice gives Princess Katherine an apparently innocent language lesson and she learns the English names for various parts of the body.[23] In Katherine's ears, some of the words have bawdy associations. "Foot" sounds like the French "foutre"—to fuck—while "la robe" is translated as "gown" but mispronounced by Alice as "coun"; French for "cunt." The beauty of the scene is that it works on two levels, the French pronunciation of English words also giving them obscene meanings to the English audience. "Neck" becomes "nick"—vagina in colloquial English; "elbow" is pronounced "bilbow"—knob/penis; and "chin," "sin"—sexual intercourse. The folio spells "coun" as "count" so that both the French character and the English audience simultaneously hear "cunt" in their respective languages. Most modern editions drop the *T* on "count"; the somewhat puritanical Arden editor T. W. Craik explains, "That Alice adds a final *t* is improbable."[24]

However, the same joke of "count" sounding like "cunt" when spoken is used in *Twelfth Night*, too, with Malvolio referring to himself as "Count Malvolio."[25] Never one to let a good obscenity die, Shakespeare repeats it later in the scene (Act 2, scene 5, line 87)—twice:

Malvolio.
By my life this is my Ladies hand: these bee her
very C's, her U's, and her T's, and thus makes shee her
great P's. It is in contempt of question her hand.

Andrew.
Her C's, her U's, and her T's: why that?

The word "and" is often abbreviated in English to "n" and pronounced that way—think of rock "n" roll, fish "n" chips, or salt "n" pepper—and with this in mind the word, with the folio use of capital letters, is spelled out clearly: "Her C's, her U's, 'N her T's." The line "thus makes she her great P's," with a possible squatting action from Malvolio—"pees" being an English colloquialism for pisses—underlines the running verbal joke still further.

The spelling of names in the folio can be revealing. In *Richard II* and the *Henry IV* plays, Shakespeare follows Holinshed and spells the usurper to the throne "Bullingbrooke" rather than the version found in most modern editions, "Bolingbroke." A "bully" in Shakespeare's times was the opposite of the modern word—although it fortuitously works in that context—but meant "friend/brother," or "good fellow." Bottom is referred to as "Bully Bottom" and Pistol says of Henry V, "I love the lovely Bully."[26] To be "bullish" still retains the meaning of obstinate courage, and Alencon in *Henry VI, Part 1* refers to the English as lacking this: "They want their courage and their fat bull beeves."[27] "Bull beef" was also the term for a big, blustering man. A brook, of course, is a small stream of water, so King Henry IV's name, when translated literally, is something like "Friendly and courageous, but sometimes obstinate and blustering, brother from across the water," which is a pretty accurate summary of Bullingbrooke's character.[28] This is particularly true when his public persona is contrasted with his attitude to his son. A statement such as this would not hold water in academic circles (although Henry's name does in fact derive from his place of birth, "Bulla's Brook"), but for an actor it could be useful. And that's the difference between editor/adaptors and theatre practitioners. John Barton, longtime director of the Royal Shakespeare Company, describes a modern director's working process when he says:

> I have never worried over-much about the precise accuracy of what I may say in the rehearsal room. The test there is not whether a particular statement is objectively true but whether it helps, stimulates and releases an actor at a particular rehearsal.[29]

Whether the spelling of Bullingbrooke/Bolingbroke is significant or not, one must wonder—why change it? Would we alter *Death of a Salesman*'s Willy Loman to William Loman, prefer the name Jimmy in *Long Day's Journey into Night* to James, or recast Big Daddy in *Cat on a Hot Tin Roof* as Mr. Pollitt?[30]

No matter if you believe the folio spellings are coincidental, fortuitous, or by design—and there's an argument that at the very least they can be helpful to an actor and shouldn't be ignored—we can be certain that Shakespeare, Heminge, and Condell were all aware of spelling and pronunciation. In *Romeo and Juliet* the Friar chides Romeo with the words, "Thy Love did read by rote, that could not spell."[31] The very first line of the First Folio introduction "To the Great Variety of Readers" has Heminge and Condell write: "From the most able, to him that can but spell."[32]

Shakespeare used differences in spelling to comic effect when he put the following satirical speech in the mouth of Holofernes, the Pedant, in Act 5, scene 1, line 17 of *Love's Labour's Lost*. This is the folio printing, which modern editions more or less follow:

> He draweth out the thred of his verbositie, finer
> then the staple of his argument. I abhor such phanaticall
> phantasims, such insociable and poynt devise
> companions, such rackers of ortagriphie, as to speake
> dout fine, when he should say doubt; det, when he shold
> pronounce debt; debt, not det: he clepeth a Calf, Caufe:
> halfe, haufe: neighbour vocatur nebour; neigh abreviated
> ne: this is abhominable, which he would call abhominable.

In the passage Holofernes argues that each word should be pronounced as it is written for reading; the "b" in "debt," for example, and the "h" in "Abhominable." Notice how the "i" in "point" is replaced with a "y" and spelled "poynt," although it is still pronounced the same. The "y" in Shakespeare's time generally, although not always, gave the "i" sound (think of the current day British and American spellings of tyre/tire). There are a number of examples of phonetic spelling in this speech that help an actor with pronunciation, including "thred" for "thread," "verbositie" for "verbosity," "ortagriphie" for "orthography" and "phanaticall" for "fanatical." The folio spelling of "phanaticall" identifies for the actor a play on words with "phantasims." However, although Jaggard's compositors carefully set words like "dout" and "det" to convey the meaning they were not 100 percent accurate, the final two abhominable's are spelled exactly the same. For the joke to work, the last "abhominable" needed to be printed something like "abomnable" or "abominable."

As well as the original spellings, the original pronunciations of words (known as OP) can be enlightening too. David Crystal has undertaken some superb work in this area and readers should refer to his excellent books,[33] pronunciation not being particularly relevant to an examination of the First Folio. However, actors should note it. A good example of this is Mistress Quickly's name, which would have been originally pronounced "Quick-lie" and describes her occupation as a prostitute. ("Having a quick one" is still a slang British phrase for illicit or surreptitious sex.) The names of the lead characters in *Much Ado About Nothing*, Beatrice and Benedick, would have originally been pronounced something like "Bare-trice" and "Bare-ne-dick." With this in mind, Claudio's comment that "the two bears will not bite one another when they meet"[34] makes sense. A similar play on words is used in a later scene: "if you husband have stables enough, you'll look he shall lack no barns"[35]—"barns" being pronounced like "bairns," children. As Macbeth begins to lose everything he has been given at the hands of dark powers, he calls on Seyton—pronounced Satan.[36] Leontes, thinking he has been cuckolded, believes himself to be "ore head and eares a fork'd one."[37] The forks are the cuckold's horns, but spoken with an original accent the phrase has more depth—a "fuck'd one." *Troilus and Cressida* employs a play on words with the name "Ajax"/a-Jax—a "jacks" is a toilet (the slang is still in current usage in Ireland), and Kent uses the word in this context in *King Lear*.[38] Iago asks Rodorigo in the first few lines of *Othello* whether he should be "affin'd to love the Moor."[39] "Affin'd" means "bound" but is pronounced "a fiend." When the Nurse says of Juliet, "Faith I can tell her age unto an houre,"[40] the pronunciation would have been: "Faith I can tell her age unto a Whore"—a moment of comedy at her expense. David Crystal identifies the same hour/whore joke at work in *As You Like It*, Act 2, scene 7, line 26.[41] Jacques reports Touchstone talking about the hours of time but when pronounced originally, he has said things like "And so from whore to whore, we ripe, and ripe/And then from whore to whore, we rot, and rot." Crystal finds a similar subtlety of meaning in the pronunciation of the first chorus of *Romeo and Juliet* with the famous "From forth the fatall loynes of these two foes." The word "loins" (as it is spelled in modern times) would have been pronounced as "lines," so there's a pun on the birth of the protagonists but also their genealogical lines; perhaps even the lines the actors say.[42] There are hundreds of examples of the use of original accent throughout the canon, an indication that employing a sometimes anemic English accent in Shakespeare's plays can often be reductive.[43]

Capital Letters

A useful tool for performance found in the folio, helpful to actors but ignored by all published texts, is the extensive use of capital letters, and not just for nouns. David Crystal quite rightly warns against too rigid a reliance on their significance:

> We need to exercise a great deal of deal of caution when considering the role of capitalization in relation to textual interpretation and dramatic performance

but he partially concedes, "it is possible to suspect an intention behind a use of capitals."[44]

It appears to depend on what copy was referred to by the compositors when setting the script. Sometimes, it must be admitted, the copy was probably the supposedly corrupt quartos Heminge and Condell sought to override, and in some plays the use of capitals isn't always consistent. Nonetheless, capital letters in the First Folio generally appear to be an indicator to the actors of important words that need to be marked. Stanley Wells recalls a story that when the legendary actor Charles Laughton performed at Stratford he had his wife sit in the stalls with a copy of the First Folio and shout out when a word had a capital letter so that he could remember to give it an extra stress.[45] My own experience in preparing a play for rehearsal, and having to replace the capital letters an editor/adaptor has removed, is that a pattern emerges and it's possible to predict where the next capital letter will come. Many times in rehearsal I've heard an actor swallow or rush an important word and when I've looked at the folio it has a capital letter. It's difficult to imagine the inclusion of capital letters to have been a printing error since it meant more work for the compositor to set them. A printer would reach for letters in one box that contained capital letters and into another box that had the other letters. In fact, so there was no mix-up, the capitals were in an upper case, and the non-capitals in a lower case—phrases we still use today. A professional compositor is unlikely to keep placing his hand in the wrong case by mistake with such regularity. There can be little doubt that the printers of the folio used capital letters deliberately—but does this have any meaning?

Here's Hotspur in *Henry IV, Part 1*, Act 1, scene 3, line 29 explaining to the new King Henry that he didn't keep his Scottish prisoners wilfully. The words in capital letters have been placed in bold for easy identification (they were not printed like this in the folio, of course):

Hot.
My **Liege**, I did deny no **Prisoners.**
But, I remember when the fight was done,
When I was dry with **Rage**, and extreame **Toyle**,
Breathlesse, and **Faint**, leaning upon my **Sword**,
Came there a certaine **Lord**, neat and trimly drest;
Fresh as a **Bride-groome**, and his **Chin** new reapt,
Shew'd like a stubble **Land** at **Harvest** home.
He was perfumed like a **Milliner**,
And 'twixt his **Finger** and his **Thumb**e, he held
A **Pouncet**-box: which ever and anon
He gave his **Nose**, and took't away againe:
Who therewith angry, when it next came there,
Tooke it in **Snuffe**. And still he smil'd and talk'd:
And as the **Souldiers** bare dead bodies by,
He call'd them untaught **Knaves**, **Unmannerly**,
To bring a slovenly unhandsome **Coarse**
Betwixt the **Winde**, and his **Nobility**.
With many **Holiday** and **Lady** tearme
He question'd me: **Among** the rest, demanded
My Prisoners, in your **Majesties** behalfe.
I then, all-smarting, with my wounds being cold,
(To be so pestered with a **Popingay**)
Out of my **Greefe**, and my **Impatience,**
Answer'd (neglectingly) I know not what,
He should, or should not: **For** he made me mad,
To see him shine so briske, and smell so sweet,
And talke so like a **Waiting-Gentlewoman,**
Of **Guns**, & **Drums**, and **Wounds**: **God** save the marke;
And telling me, the **Soveraign'st** thing on earth
Was **Parmacity**, for an inward bruise:

And that it was great pitty, so it was,
That villanous **Salt-peter** should be digg'd
Out of the **Bowels** of the harmlesse **Earth**,
Which many a good **Tall Fellow** had destroy'd
So **Cowardly**. And but for these vile **Gunnes**,
He would himselfe have beene a **Souldier**.
This bald, unjoynted **Chat** of his (my **Lord**)
Made me to answer indirectly (as I said.)
And I beseech you, let not this report
Come currant for an **Accusation**,
Betwixt my **Love**, and your high **Majesty**.

The words in capital letters give a pretty neat summary for the actor of this long speech, helping to keep the narrative on track. Hotspur begins with his subject "Prisoners" and contrasts his own feats as a "Soldier"—"Rage," "Toil," "Breathless," "Faint," "Sword"—with the effeminate "Popingay" sent by the king; "Bridegroom," "Milliner," "Lady," "Waiting Gentlewoman." He's at pains to show his "Love" for Henry and begins with "My Liege" and ends with "high Majesty"—although interestingly not "High Majesty." There is no capital letter in "high." Perhaps he is hinting that Henry is not appointed by God on High? There's a conflict within Hotspur as he clearly doesn't like the men of this new regime and uses words marked in capitals such as "Lord," "Nobility," "Cowardly" and "Chat" to criticize them. On the other hand he knows he mustn't allow his famed temper[46] to overcome the justice and logic of his argument. It's equally illuminating to note the words that are *not* in capitals, the words the actor shouldn't overmark, the words Hotspur doesn't want Henry to be overly aware of: "fight," "angry," "all-smarting," "pestered," and the phrase "he made me mad." Once Henry has left the scene, Hotspur's opinion of him has hardened to the view that he is, in initial capitals, an "Unthankful King."[47]

Perhaps the most complex use of capital letters in the folio is Mark Anthony's Forum speech in *Julius Caesar* when Anthony is speaking to the Plebeians over the body of the dead Caesar. He wants the people to allow him to read Caesar's will (in fact, it doesn't exist). Mark Anthony employs the same system the folio uses to highlight to actors the stress needed on important words—capital letters—in order to manipulate his onstage audience into doing what he wants them to do. It's much like the technique used today by entertainer "mentalists" such as Derren Brown to force people to make decisions by linguistic suggestion. Notice how many times the word "will" is used in the following speech (Act 3, scene 2, line 122):

Anthony.
O Maisters! If I were dispos'd to stirre
Your hearts and mindes to Mutiny and Rage,
I should do *Brutus* wrong, and *Cassius* wrong:
Who (you all know) are Honourable men.
I will not do them wrong: I rather choose
To wrong the dead, to wrong my selfe and you,
Then I will wrong such Honourable men.
But heere's a Parchment, with the Seal of *Caesar*,
I found it in his Closset, 'tis his Will:
Let but the Commons heae this Testament:
(Which pardon me) I do not meane to read,

And they would go and kisse dead *Caesars* wounds,
And dip their Napkins in his Sacred Blood;
Yea, begge a haire of him for Memory,
And dying, mention it within their Willes,
Bequeathing it as a rich Legacy
Unto their issue.

Have patience gentle Friends, I must not read it.
It is not meete you know how *Caesar* lov'd you:
You are not Wood, you are not Stones, but men:
And being men, hearing the Will of *Caesar*,
It will inflame you, it will make you mad:
'Tis good you know not that you are his Heires,
For if you should, O what would come of it?

Will you be Patient? Will you stay a-while?
I have o're-shot my selfe to tell you of it,
I feare I wrong the Honourable men,
Whose Daggers have stabb'd *Caesar:* I do feare it.

Plebeian 4
They were Traitors: Honourable men?

All.
The Will, the Testament.

Plebeian 2
They were Villaines, Murderers: the Will, read the Will.

Anthony.
You will compell me then to read the Will:
Then make a Ring about the Corpes of *Caesar,*
And let me shew you him that made the Will.

Although it doesn't primarily concern us here, the folio phonetic spelling of "Corpes" and "Shew," the original pronunciations of "Maisters" and "Stay a While" ("Stay a Will,") the italics that juxtapose one mention of Brutus and Cassius to the six mentions of Caesar, and the rare use of a folio exclamation point to begin the section should all be noted. Anthony begins with the Will, which, because it is his subject and a specific object, he naturally capitalizes and repeats it a further 4 times. The other 8 mentions of "will," once the point has been made, are not in capitals and have no need to be stressed. Mark Anthony uses the word "will" 13 times in just 31 lines; about a third of the dialogue. The genius of the speech is that "will" becomes like the beat in a piece of music and establishes a rhythm. On top of this are words placed in capitals designed to incite the crowd: Mutiny, Rage, Honourable, Commons, Sacred Blood, Memory, Legacy, Friends, Wood, Stones, Heirs, Patient, Daggers, and Corpse. These are the words for an actor to choose, the words that will have the most impact on the onstage audience.[48] So we have a speech in which the word "will" is constantly repeated as an underlying pulse while the key words, marked with a capital letter, are carefully chosen to punch the message home.

The folio (Shakespeare?) puts a capital letter on important words and these words, as they begin with a capital letter, naturally stand out to the actors when they learn the script and remind them that they shouldn't be ignored. In fact, if you point out an important word to actors they will usually underline it. The use of capital letters in the folio generally does the job for them. Take the capital letters away from the text and you take away yet another possible instruction to an actor.

Italics

The use of italics for proper names can have a similar function to capital letters in creating ease of identification, but this practice is only found in the folio, not in modern texts.[49] A director will often suggest to an actor that names are crucial in telling the story and making the narrative clear. They're like signposts leading the audience, and if they are missed those watching can be left confused. The italics indicate a specific person or place which the character will have an attitude to, and reminds the actor to be particular in choosing them rather than generalized. Here's a difficult speech from Act 1, scene 1, line 28 of one of Shakespeare's more complex plays, *Cymbeline*, as it is printed in the First Folio. It's an example of one of those notorious Shakespearean passages where the plot and background are explained very early in the tale. If the actor gets it wrong, the audience will find the rest of the play hard to follow:

1st Gentleman.
I cannot delve him to the roote: His Father
Was call'd *Sicillius,* who did joyne his Honor
Against the Romanes, with *Cassibulan,*
But had his Titles by *Tenantius,* whom
He serv'd with Glory, and admir'd Successe:
So gain'd the Sur-addition, *Leonatus.*
And had (besides this Gentleman in question)
Two other Sonnes, who in the Warres o'th' time
Dy'de with their Swords in hand. For which, their Father
Then old, and fond of yssue,[50] tooke such sorrow
That he quit Being; and his gentle Lady
Bigge of this Gentleman (our Theame) deceast
As he was borne. The King he takes the Babe
To his protection, calls him *Posthumus Leonatus,*
Breedes him, and makes him of his Bed-chamber,
Puts to him all the Learnings that his time
Could make him the receiver of, which he tooke
As we do ayre, fast as 'twas ministred,
And in's Spring, became a Harvest: Liv'd in Court
(Which rare it is to do) most prais'd, most lov'd,
A sample to the yongest: to th' more Mature,
A glasse that feated them: and to the graver,
A Childe that guided Dotards. To his Mistris,
(For whom he now is banish'd) her owne price
Proclaimes how she esteem'd him; and his Vertue
By her election may be truly read, what kind of man he is.

Good advice to an actor with a passage like this is: trust the folio and use it as a guide. The names stand out clearly in italics so they are not missed, the verse structure helps the actor to take breath and to phrase the speech correctly, while what might seem to be over-punctuation (there are only 5 sentences) in fact defines the detail of the story step by step. The capital letters identify key words that provide the overall tone of the speech—Honour, Titles, Glory, Sur-addition, Wars, Harvest, Court, Childe (which can also mean "Knight"), Mistress, and Virtue. These capitalized words summarize the noble character of Posthumus ("our Theame") and establish his love for Innogen. If the words in capital letters "may be truly read," they tell an audience immediately "what kind of man he is."[51] The latest Arden edition of *Cymbeline*,[52] apart from some minor punctuation changes, modernizing the spellings, and dropping the capital letters and italics, leaves this speech intact. The verse structure, the words, and most of the punctuation remain as they are found in the First Folio—the only published copy of the play. This is further evidence of Patrick Tucker's view that the more popular the play, the more alterations the editor/adaptors make, while the more obscure plays remain relatively untouched. Can it really be possible that the compositors and Heminge and Condell only screwed up on the plays they knew best?

The folio convention of printing names in italics is a useful guide to actors in making the narrative clear. But was it Shakespeare's or the compositor's choice to use them? David Crystal, whose study of the printing of early texts is comprehensive, is clear in his view: "The use of italics for proper names ... was an extremely systematic practice, with only occasional inconsistencies."[53]

Shakespeare's sonnets were first issued in 1609 (they are not included in the First Folio) and it's thought he supervised their publication, although there is no direct evidence of this. He was certainly alive in 1609, and the usual practice with printers was to consult the author for proofreading. The verses are unlikely to have been pirated, as the printing house of Shakespeare's friend from Stratford, Richard Field, published them. In the sonnets we can see how the careful choice of italics is used to establish the sense. Did Field receive his instructions to do this straight from Shakespeare? Sonnet 135, for example, is probably Shakespeare writing about himself since the word "will" is repeated many times in different contexts. Notice the use of italics on the word "will" when it is used as a name and, perhaps more importantly, where italics are *not* employed. How would the printer know the correct word to italicize unless he received instructions from the writer?

> Whoever hath her wish, thou hast thy *Will*,
> And *Will* to boot, and *Will* in overplus;
> More than enough am I that vex thee still,
> To thy sweet will making addition thus.
> Wilt thou whose will is large and spacious,
> Not once vouchsafe to hide my will in thine,
> Shall will in others seem right gracious,
> And in my will no fair acceptance shine:
> The sea all water, yet receives rain still
> And in abundance addeth to his store;
> So thou being rich in *Will* add to thy *Will*,
> One will of mine to make thy large *Will* more.
> Let no unkind, no fair beseechers kill;
> Think all but one, and me in that one *Will*.

There's further tantalizing "evidence" suggested by Sonia Massai that in some way supports the idea that italics and other marks of punctuation were placed there by the author.

4. Creating a Role from the Folio Text

She quotes Joseph Moxon in a book from 1683 called *The Art of Printing*. In it Moxon instructs:

> It behoves an author to examine his copy very well e're he deliver it to the printer, and to point[54] it, and mark it so as the compositor may well know what words to set in italics, English, Capitals etc.[55]

As seductive as this statement might be, it unfortunately falls down in two ways. Moxon was writing 60 years after the publication of the First Folio, and printing practices may have changed in that time. Although Moxon's guidelines might suggest that Shakespeare supervised the publication of his sonnets, they can't effectively be used to argue that the folio punctuation was Shakespeare's since he couldn't have "pointed" his lines for the printers—he was dead.[56] On the other hand, it serves as a reminder that if Shakespeare included things like italics in his copy, he did so exclusively to help his actors. The plays were not for publication when he wrote them, so what other reason could he have?

The folio places proper names, letters, songs, foreign languages, maxims, proverbs, and quotes from other sources all in italics. The editor/adaptor may find this practice a little fussy, but for an actor in rehearsal, looking down at the page, it assists them. Seeing a passage in italics, the words are clearly separated from the rest of the dialogue and the actor's voice spontaneously adjusts in tone when delivering the text. There's no need for a director to guide the actor and the context can be instantly grasped and conveyed. Modern editions do now generally print songs, other languages, and letters in italics, but not always. The Arden *Macbeth* has no italics for the first words Macbeth's wife utters in the play[57]—a letter. Instead it inserts a stage direction that she is "reading a letter." The First Folio direction is "alone with a letter"—she hasn't read it yet. No mention of this distinction is made in the Arden notes, but there's a big difference between the actor discovering the contents of a letter for the first time and analyzing something that has been previously read.

In *Othello*, Act 2, scene 1, Iago's witty (and obscene) banter towards Desdemona on the Cypriot quay side is printed in italics in the First Folio but not in modern editions. This cannot have been the compositor's error, since the responses in between Iago's lines aren't set in the same way. Clearly the choice of using italics is deliberate and indicate Iago's humor isn't something made up on the spot—he is *quoting* from other sources. Iago is not the sparkling and quick-witted fellow delivering extempore remarks that he attempts to portray, and Desdemona sees behind his mask: "These are old fond paradoxes to make fools laugh I'th'alehouse."[58] This is crucial to the development of the plot and also to Iago's character. He is belittled in front of his wife, Cassio, and (probably) Rodorigo. Desdemona judges Iago's carefully prepared punch line a "most lame and impotent conclusion."[59] "Impotent" is an unfortunate choice of words for her to use, since it suggests sexual inadequacy. Iago's immediate response is to set a plan in motion beginning with the Cyprus mutiny. Whereas his original motivation was "I hate the Moor,"[60] this scene causes that hatred to grow into a much more sinister objective: "Nothing can, or shall content my Soul/Till I am even'd with him, wife, for wife."[61] For Iago and the characters around him, the folio use of italics is a key indicator of this change.[62]

Sometimes the folio use of italics can unlock moments in the plays that have puzzled editor/adaptors for centuries. Act 4, scene 4, line 174 of *Richard III* portrays the new king meeting his mother, the Duchess of York. The duchess tells him, in most modern editions:

> What comfortable hour canst thou name
> That ever graced me with thy company?

and Richard replies:

> Faith, none but humphrey hour, that call'd your grace
> To breakfast once,[63] forth of my company.

The editor of the New Penguin edition, E. A. Honigmann, simply writes "unexplained" as his note to Richard's bitter response.[64] A director cannot say to his/her actor, "Speak these lines but no one knows what they mean," since the actor must still deliver the words, and deliver them with intention. Through a combination of research, positive assumption, and imagination, the director needs to assist the actor not only with this line and its impact on the scene but how it affects the other characters and the overall narrative of the play. In the folio, "humphrey hour" is placed in italics, has capital letters, and is spelled "Humphrey Hower" ("Hour" is generally spelled "houre" in the First Folio). Notice, too, how the folio lineation of the meter depicts a Richard trying to control his emotions as he recalls an event or series of events from his past that have left him emotionally scarred:

> Faith none, but *Humphrey Hower,*
> That call'd your Grace
> To Breakefast once, forth of my company.

Since *Humphrey Hower* is set in italics, perhaps it is fair to assume it is the name of a person? Is Richard saying that his mother was happiest when she left his company to be called away to have sex outside of her marriage? Her hour with Master Humphrey?[65] That is, with her husband absent, did she abstain from sex until the hour Humphrey arrived and then break her sexual fast? (The meaning of the word "breakfast" is to break your fast.) If the original pronunciation is applied to the word "hour," as we have seen, there's a play on words for "hour/whore." With this in mind, the words become "Humphrey Whore"—Humphrey is a male whore—or perhaps Richard's mother is, in his opinion, "Humphrey's Whore." The only time Richard shows any sign of remorse or pulling back from his acts is when, after telling Buckingham to infer Edward was not his father's son, he says, "Yet touch this sparingly, as 'twere farre off;/Because, my lord, you know my mother lives."[66] If there are any softer feelings to be found in Richard, they are solely towards his mother. It is a complex psychological relationship, since he also blames her for his failure to receive love: "Love foreswore me in my Mothers Wombe."[67] The *Humprey Hower* scene picks up a few moments later at line 183, Act 4, scene 4, when Richard's mother tells her only surviving son, "I shall never speake to thee againe." Richard's response, all on its own, and only found in the folio, is just one word. He simply says, "So." There is a pause in the meter while Richard reflects on his mother's words.

So who was Master Humphrey? And who is the father of Edward IV and the supposed lover of Richard's mother? The obvious candidate is Humphrey Stafford, Duke of Buckingham—the current Duke of Buckingham's father.[68] Which would mean that Buckingham's father was having sexual relations—at least in Richard's mind—with Richard's mother. Perhaps that is why Richard uses Buckingham and then discards him, in the same way Buckingham's father had treated Richard's mother. And perhaps it might be why the "High-reaching Buckingham" says the ambiguous phrase of apparent ambition which is an immediate reply to Richard's suggestion that his mother was adulterous:

> Ile play the Orator
> As if the Golden Fee, for which I plead,
> Were for my selfe.[69]

Taking this approach, the audience would see an obvious tension in the Buckingham/Richard relationship and one of the possible motivations for Richard's acts—his mother's abandonment leading to a distaste of women. Why does he mention Mistress Shore so much when she doesn't even appear in the play? Did she reject his advances? Or is it jealousy/disgust of her perhaps? The circumstances of his mother's affair might even establish a degree of sympathy and understanding for Richard. After all, the play is called *The TRAGEDY of Richard the Third*. None of this can be offered as *fact;* it's certainly not historically accurate, but then much of Shakespeare's history is not true history. However, for an actor attempting the role of Richard and a director trying to tease out the subtle layers of the story, it's a lot more helpful than "unexplained."

As well as noting where the First Folio sets italics, it's equally important to mark passages that the folio doesn't set in italics, as it can sometimes help to establish the mood. The witches' spells in *Macbeth* are a good example of this as they don't have italics. These are not old and well-tried-out curses quoted from dusty books but new and created especially for Macbeth. They may not work, and this affects the witches' attitude to the spells and Macbeth's response. If they are successful—and nobody knows if they will be—Lucifer has moved one step further in his battle against the forces of good. This creates a tension throughout the play.

Curiously, although editor/adaptors are swift to remove italics from passages—erasing meaning and acting notes in one swoop—they are equally quick to add italics of their own, or sometimes the modern typographical equivalent, inverted commas. Act 1, scene 2, line 15 of *Henry IV, Part 1* has Falstaff exclaim, in the First Folio, "We that take Purses, go by the Moon and the seven Starres, and not by Phoebus he, that wand'ring Knight so faire." There are no italics. Modern editor/adaptors add either italics or inverted commas around the last part of Falstaff's words and print them as "*by Phoebus, he, that wand'ring knight so fair.*" The reason they give for doing this is that the phrase is, as P. H. Davison notes in the New Penguin edition, "Possibly a line from a ballad at the time."[70] The problem is that none of the editor/adaptors can actually find any ballad that contains this phrase. Perhaps it's because none existed? If it was a ballad, the compositors would surely have known it and set the line in italics as was their practice. There were 7 quarto versions of *Henry IV, Part 1* published between 1598 and 1632, the year of the reissue of the folio. None of them set the "wand'ring Knight" passage in italics (nor do any of the other folios), and the quartos follow the folio punctuation exactly. On the other hand, in all of the quartos, and from the Third Folio onwards, "Phoebus" is in italics.[71] It seems very strange indeed that at least 7 separate printers would set "Phoebus" in italics but not bother to configure the rest of the line in the same way. Later in the same scene, at line 116, Hal quotes a proverb, "He will give the divell his due," and the folio printers take care to place this in italics. Editor/adaptors print neither inverted commas nor italics on this phrase; another example of their editorial inconsistency and "chopped logic."[72]

It may seem pedantic to require modern play copies to print the First Folio italics exactly, and it's certainly difficult to explain the difference to nonactors. However, they undoubtedly have a practical application and anything that might help an actor should be included in a performance text.

Speech Prefixes

One of the other things editor/adaptors alter from the folio is the speech prefixes. This was pointed out earlier with Boyet and Mote in *Love's Labour's Lost*. Mote is called Page, Boy, and Mote in the folio text, so editor/adaptors, to avoid confusion when reading, give him and other characters just one common speech prefix throughout the play. All very well, but in doing so they remove a possible clue from Shakespeare to his actors on how to approach the scene and the characters. Shakespeare never refers to Juliet's mother by the name she has traditionally come to be known through modern editions of *Romeo and Juliet*—Lady Capulet. She is not a member of the aristocracy and the folio refers to her most often as "Lady of the House."[73] Instead she is given a variety of speech prefixes that are appropriate to the situation. As Neil Freeman astutely observes,[74] when she enters to tell Juliet of the arranged marriage to Paris she has the speech prefix "Wife"—she is carrying out her duties on behalf of her husband. At the end of the Nurse's long speech in the same scene,[75] perhaps affected by the tedium of listening to the same story (yet again), she becomes "Old Lady." Her final lines—"We follow thee, *Juliet,* the Countie staies"—have the prefix "Mother." As a mother she is no doubt happy to have secured her child's future. In a later scene (Act 3, scene 5), she has to inform Juliet of the quick change in the timing of the marriage to Paris. When she first enters in the folio she is called "Lady"—the female head of the household. When she speaks intimately to Juliet, the speech prefix calls her "Mother." This changes when Capulet comes in and begins his verbal assault on Juliet. Supporting her husband, the speech prefix changes back to "Lady," but in her final fatal words to Juliet it alters yet again so that it is her "Mother" that Juliet hears say "I have done with thee." This is a terrible thing for a young girl to be told and has the effect of totally isolating her. There are other examples in the folio *Romeo and Juliet*. Capulet is referred to as "1st Capulet" at his party, as if he were head of the clan, "Father" in his obscene flurry of words at Juliet's refusal to marry, but "Father Capulet" when he makes the marriage arrangements as he is acting on both his daughter's and his family's behalf. When the "dead" Juliet is discovered in her bed, it is appropriately "Father," "Mother," and "Nurse" who mourn for her. The Friar has the prefix "Friar Lawrence" throughout the folio, with the one exception being when he meets Friar John. In this private scene of friendly equals, they are referred to as "Lawrence" and "John." These are very good acting notes from Shakespeare. A director will soon learn that simple and clear instructions are much more effective than a lengthy and complex explanation.

Neil Freeman finds extensive use of different character prefixes in the folio version of *King John*. He writes of Queen Eleanor:

"Eleanor" seems to cover her more relaxed-with-family-and-comfortable court situations; "Queen" is applied when she verbally fights Constance and the French; "Queen Mother" is used when she attempts to woo young Arthur away from his mother, Constance; "Old Queen" is applied as she advises John to accept the proposed marriage for his niece Blanche and the French Dolphin as a peaceful conclusion to what could be a devastating war.[76]

Freeman highlights other characters in the play whose speech prefixes change depending on the situation they find themselves in. "Philip" becomes "Bastard" immediately when he gives up his claim to the Faulconbridge Estate, while the Dolphin, who has been known as "Lewis" throughout, changes to his official title of Dolphin when making the political match with Blanche. King Philip of France is called "King" but then "France" when he speaks on behalf of his country, King John is "John" in private moments with his mother, Hubert, and the Bastard, but after his second crowning becomes "King John." Both kings are given the speech prefix "Philip" and "John" when they are allies, but revert to "France" and "England" when the peace between them breaks down.

Similarly, *Henry V* assigns Captains Jamy, Fluellen, and Mackmorrice the speech prefixes "Scot," "Welch," and "Irish" only in the scene when they argue about their "Nation."[77] They are representing their countries at that point. In the peace negotiations in the final act of *Henry V*, the French king has the prefix "France" while Henry becomes "England." However, when Henry attempts to woo Katherine, the prefix reverts to "King Henry" and stays that way until the blunt question "Shall Kate be my Wife?"[78] when he again has the prefix "England." This is a clear indication that the proposed marriage to Katherine is a political rather than a love match.

There are numerous other examples in the folio. Angelo the Goldsmith in *The Comedy of Errors* is referred to as Angelo in the first scene with Antipholus of Ephesus. He is supposedly Antipholus's friend and, as with similar characters in *Timon of Athens*, he is happy to dine with him and take his money. When Antipholus apparently refuses to pay him money that he owes, the speech prefix changes to the more formal professional title of "Goldsmith." Similarly, Egeon never has the speech prefix of his name, (although he is referred to that way by other characters), and is "Merchant" when first arrested, suitable for his nonpersona status in Ephesus. At the moment he first sees his son, he is called "Marchant. Father," which mirrors his confusion and his growing, but tentative, hope.[79] When he is certain he has found his long-lost child, the prefix changes once again to "Father."[80] Like his twin boys and their servants, Egeon, too, discovers his identity in the play.[81] Richard III is labeled "King" after he takes the throne, but when the ghosts of his victims visit him before Bosworth this alters to "Richard," indicating his vulnerability as simply a man. His final soliloquy—"O coward Conscience! How does thou afflict me?"[82]—is delivered by "Richard," but as soon as Ratcliffe enters he composes himself and the prefix once again becomes "King." Interestingly, although he is "King" throughout the battle, his last two speeches as his power wanes (including the famous "A Horse, a Horse, my Kingdom for a Horse") are spoken by "Richard." Shylock in *The Merchant of Venice* appears to have been given the speech prefix "Shylock" for his "reasonable" exchanges with the Christians, but at other moments, such as his early aside "How like a fawning publican he lookes,"[83] it is as if the script becomes racist by telling us he is "reverting to type" and he is assigned the prefix "Jew." Revealingly, he has the prefix "Shylock" when talking to his friend Tubal, but for most of the court scene, when he is bent on vengeance, he is "Jew." This changes back to "Shylock" when he loses the legal argument, so it is Shylock the man whom the court strips of everything. There are two exceptions to this: "Shylock" says "My deeds upon my head, I crave the Law/The penaltie and forfeite of my bond"[84] and "An oath, an oath, I have an oath in heaven:/Shall I lay perjurie upon my soule?/No not for Venice."[85] This appears to indicate it is Shylock rather than a representative of his religion who brings destruction upon himself. Perhaps it might also be an instruction for the actor to behave more coolly at these points as he quotes the Christian law back to the assembled court? The use of speech prefixes seems to reinforce the anti-Semitism that is present in *The Merchant of Venice*—a challenge that actors and directors will approach with enthusiasm.[86]

The folio printing of different speech prefixes—and we have no evidence that Shakespeare wrote them (although as a shareholder in the business of the King's Men he would want to get the best out of his actors)—can often help with knotty problems in rehearsal. For example, Don Pedro in *Much Ado About Nothing* appears to ask Beatrice to marry him. The question actor and director will ask themselves is: does he mean it? Throughout the party scene (Act 2, scene 1)—indeed, throughout the play until to this point—he has the speech prefix "Don Pedro," as if he is letting his hair down and being "one of the boys." However, when he puts the crucial question to Beatrice, "Will you have me? Lady,"[87] the prefix is "Prince," perhaps indicating that the insecure Pedro uses his status to try to make a match. For the rest of the scene (and for the rest of the play[88]), as he issues plans to set up Benedick, he retains the prefix "Prince" but with one exception. "Shee cannot indure to heare tell of a husband"[89] is spoken (with sorrow?) by "Don Pedro." From this point onwards, shunning love as Benedick has done, he retains his formal title of "Prince." Which makes sense of Benedick's penultimate speech in the play: "Prince, thou art sad, get thee a wife, get thee a wife,"[90] almost urging him to become "Don Pedro" again.

Some commentators have written about Shakespeare's use of speech prefixes but approach it from a very different angle. Marjorie Garber correctly spots that Claudius in *Hamlet* is given the speech prefix "King" rather than his own name and asks: "Does this make him more symbolic, one-dimensional, allegorical?"[91] For an actor, Garber poses the wrong question. A director can't suggest to the actor of this great role that it's one-dimensional. Nor is it possible to act a symbol or an allegory. On the other hand, taking the speech prefix as a cue, it might be interesting to examine in rehearsal how far Claudius "plays the King" or is in fact the true king and leader that perhaps Old Hamlet wasn't. Once again the study and the rehearsal room are shown to be very opposing places when considering Shakespeare's plays.

The use of speech prefixes as clues to character is by no means consistent throughout the folio, but clearly it is often more than a coincidence and can be a very useful indicator for the actors playing these roles. The advice to directors and actors should be: check the folio speech prefixes—it could help.

Punctuation

Jaggard's nemesis, the playwright Thomas Heywood, in his book *An Apology for Actors*, printed in 1612, makes the case that watching an actor in a play helps a university student because it:

instructs him to speake well, and with judgment to observe his commas, colons, and full poynts; his parentheses, his breathing spaces, and distinctions.[92]

Heywood is talking about the art of acting and how actors were precise in their observance of punctuation. They could only be precise in their punctuation, of course, if it was written in their scripts. Many people in professional theatre believe that the punctuation in the folio is, for the most part (disregarding printing errors), Shakespeare's punctuation or, put another way, playhouse punctuation. This is a bit of a scholarly minefield, but my personal experience as a director has been that following the folio punctuation rarely lets actors down in helping them to perform the dialogue. It indicates the correct phrasing, the sense, the flow, and the places to take breath. There is commonly much less use of the period than is found in modern texts and more colons, commas, and semicolons, so that the dialogue moves swiftly. In fact, productions that use the folio rather than a script prepared by editor/adaptors are considerably shorter in playing time—the "Two hours traffic of our stage." Over-reliance on folio punctuation, however, could make actors appear to be like Mr. Curdle in Charles Dickens's *Nicholas Nickleby*. Curdle found new Shakespearean meanings by adjusting the punctuation and, in David Edgar's stage adaptation of the book, proposes readings such as: "To be or not? To be that, is the question" and "Oh what? A rogue and peasant slave, am I?"[93]

Considering punctuation in early texts is often dismissed by commentators with an ill-considered thought such as "the Elizabethans and Jacobeans didn't care about punctuation." It's fairly obvious from Shakespeare's plays that they did, and Shakespeare uses punctuation to comic effect in *A Midsummer Night's Dream*. Here's Peter Quince, Curdle-like, introducing the Mechanicals' play (Act 5, scene 1, line 108):

Quince. Prologue.
If we offend, it is with our good will.
That you should thinke, we come not to offend,
But with good will. To show our simple skill,
That is the true beginning of our end.
Consider then, we come but in despight.
We do not come, as minding to content you,
Our true intent is. All for your delight,
We are not heere. That you should here repent you,
The Actors are at hand; and by their show
You shall know all, that you are like to know.

Patrick Tucker writes about this passage, noting that editor/adaptors leave the verse more or less as it was punctuated in the First Folio but alter the punctuation of the dialogue that comes before and after it. Tucker asks whether it is likely, when presented with a copy of this speech from Heminge and Condell, that Jaggard's printers would get the wrongly punctuated text right, and the rightly punctuated text wrong?[94]

Shakespeare himself was a "victim" of the subtle use of punctuation changing sense when he applied for a family coat of arms. The motto he'd chosen was the bullish "Not Without Right"—the Shakespeares deserved it—but the scrivener at first wrote this as "Not, Without Right." The comma conveys completely the opposite meaning; the family should "not" be granted their request as they were "Without Right."[95] Shakespeare knew what a comma was for and has Hamlet describe Claudius's plans for peace with England as an effort to "stand a comma 'tween their amities."[96] The sense is that the two countries are separate but joined by a mutual desire for peace. In language, the comma links phrases that are distinctly defined but connected. Shakespeare also draws the character of a poet in *Timon of Athens* who determines, "No levell'd malice/Infects one comma in the course I hold."[97] The meaning here is that the poet has no malice; even a small comma could not break his course of action. Not just commas are mentioned in the plays but periods too. Immediately before the Quince speech quoted earlier, Theseus sets up the joke (line 96) by talking of nervous clerks who "Make periods in the midst of sentences." A similar reference can be found in Act 3, scene 1, line 15 of *The Merchant of Venice* when Salerio interrupts a rambling speech by Solanio with "Come, the full stop."[98] Clearly Shakespeare knew what punctuation was for and it makes sense that he would apply it practically when writing his scripts.

Three handwritten pages survive of a play called *The Book of Sir Thomas More*, which are believed to be additions to the text in Shakespeare's own hand. There is no direct evidence to prove their authenticity, but the style and sentiment of the language is certainly Shakespearean. If they *are* his words, it underlines the point that Shakespeare was used to working with collaborators. It also supports the view that he first wrote his plays in the messy heat of creativity but delivered a fairly clean script to a professional scrivener that, although it might have needed adjusting according to circumstances, basically worked on the stage. The *Thomas More* pages contain crossing-outs and rethinks—but not as many as might be thought.[99] What can be clearly noticed is the lack of punctuation, italics, and capital letters, and contradictions in the way words are spelled. *Thomas More* is flimsy evidence on which to claim this is how Shakespeare offered all of his plays to his colleagues—the so-called foul papers. The pages probably date from the early 1590s when Shakespeare was at the beginning of his career and not attached to any particular company. It's even possible he might not have written any plays of his own at this point. His working methods would surely have changed over the years, particularly when he became a sharer in his own company, and his later copy to the actors would be as different as the plays he first penned are from his final, deeply complex, "romances."

It's naïve to think that scripts such as the *Thomas More* pages were presented to the actors—there's no way they could have acted from them. We know that Ralph Crane the scrivener, who mainly transposed legal documents and had to have been exact in his work, provided a legible copy of some of Shakespeare's plays for the King's Men.[100] What remains unknown is whether Crane punctuated the script at Shakespeare's request or on his own initiative, or if punctuation was absent in the playhouse texts and was added by the printers. Perhaps a combination of both? Printing-house punctuation without guidance from others seems unlikely. Why would a printer, under pressure to print the copy he is paid for by the page, waste time making grammatical and punctuation adjustments of his own? Joseph Moxon's *Mechanick Exercises on the Whole Art of Printing*, although published in 1683, lays down a (perhaps inherited?) golden rule that a compositor must print only what he finds in his copy and make *no* alterations to it at all:

> By the laws of Printing, a Compositor is strictly to follow his Copy, viz. to observe and do just so much and no more than his Copy will bear him out for; so that his Copy is to be his Rule and Authority.[101]

Doing "just so much and no more than his Copy will bear him out for" is a strong statement, insisting on a complete absence of printing-house "pointing," and there are just too many performance-type punctuations in the folio for it to have been a coincidence. Evidence of the folio version of the plays in performance suggests the punctuation is at least playhouse in origin.

That is not to say that an actor should halt on each punctuation mark—that would create an erratic and stumbling performance. The folio use of punctuation indicates the changes in the pattern of a character's thoughts. Patrick Tucker, who has years of experience directing from the folio, especially with his Original Shakespeare Company, makes a good case for this: "The Folio Punctuation divides the speeches into actor thoughts; these are not necessarily grammatical or even logical, but they are actable."[102]

King Lear's famous first speech in the storm has a curious punctuation in the folio, quite different from modern editions, or indeed performances of it. As printed it interrupts the flow, but read it out loud a few times imagining the actor reacting to the elements and it will be seen to be "actable":

Lear.
Blow winds, & crack your cheeks; Rage, blow
You Cataracts, and Hyrricano's spout,
Till you have drench'd our Steeples, drown the Cockes.
You Sulph'rous and Thought-executing Fires,
Vaunt-curriors of Oake-cleaving Thunder-bolts,
Sindge my white head. And thou all-shaking Thunder,
Strike flat the thicke Rotundity o'th' world,
Cracke Natures moulds, all germaines spill at once
That makes ingratefull Man.[103]

Most productions will have sound cues marked during this speech, responded to by Lear, and they will more or less follow the folio punctuation without being aware of it.

There are many folio punctuation printing errors, and to attempt to act every single dot and comma would be foolish. Often the folio will leave out a period, which folio followers insist is a cue for another actor to interrupt. It would be difficult for an actor to notice a missing period in their script and easy for a period to drop out of a printing frame, so it's sensible to be skeptical (although, perhaps coincidentally, it sometimes works). At moments the folio does the opposite and sets a period when clearly there ought to be none because there is an interjection by another character, as in the following example from *Hamlet*. Barnardo is telling the story of seeing the Ghost when it suddenly reappears:

Barnardo.
Marcellus and my selfe,
The Bell then beating one.

Marcellus.
Peace, breake thee of:
Looke where it comes again.[104]

Usually, but not always, the folio will place a dash at the end of a line to establish an interruption, although a speech in *Love's Labour's Lost* has a novel setting. King Ferdinand is reading a letter (hence the italics) and Costard the Clown struggles to comprehend whether the opaque and flowery language is referring to him. Costard's remarks are placed into the body of Ferdinand's dialogue (and are not in italics) so that the actor playing the king doesn't halt his lines but carries on. The folio setting indicates that two characters are speaking simultaneously:

Ferdinand.
There did I see that low spirited
Swaine, that base Minow of thy myrth, (**Clown.** Mee?)
that unletered small knowing soule, (**Clow.** Me?) *that shallow*
vassall (**Clow.** Still mee?) *which as I remember, hight Costard,*
(**Clow.** O me) *sorted and consorted contrary to thy*
established proclaymed Edict and Continent, Cannon: Which
with, o with, but with this I passion to say wherewith:

Clown.
With a Wench.

Ferdinand.
With a childe of our Grandmother Eve, a female.[105]

Editor/adaptors set Costard's interruptions on separate lines, not only slowing down the speed of the scene but reducing the comic potential of the king's growing frustration with the Clown's interjections. As a monarch, Ferdinand is not used to being interrupted.

Although it is wise to keep an open mind about punctuation, there can surely be no doubt that much of it is placed in the script purely to assist the actors. Examples of the folio employment of commas include Mercutio's "letting it stand/Until she had laid it, and conjured it downe."[106] The image is of an erection deflating after sex and the comma after "laid it," puts the focus on the play on words of "laid" (even today we refer to sex as "getting laid.") Mark Anthony shakes the hands of each of Caesar's assassins, concluding with "my valiant Caska, yours."[107] The comma after "Caska" singles him out for special treatment; he's the one who struck first and from behind, according to a later Anthony speech. Editor/adaptors generally put commas before every conspirator's name and diminish this moment. Iago's words to Cassio, "And good Lieutenant, I thinke, you thinke I love you,"[108] as punctuated in the folio mean "I think you're a good Lieutenant (but you might not be)" and "You think that I love you (but I don't)." Remember these were professional actors speaking the dialogue (Shakespeare was not writing for schools, colleges, or amateur groups) and a professional actor will use the commas to deftly suggest the subtext and ambiguity of the language. This is very different from the way editor/adaptors universally repunctuate Iago's phrasing as: "And, good Lieutenant, I think you think I love you." This punctuation provides much less depth and complexity for the actor and might be translated as meaning the very literal "You are a good lieutenant and I believe that you think I love you." Ophelia explains to her father that Hamlet has made advances towards her and uses the words: "My Lord, he hath importun'd me with love,/In honourable fashion."[109] The comma after "love" marks a qualification or second thought by Ophelia. She tells Polonius that Hamlet has indeed sought her love but, realizing this might be misinterpreted as sex, reflects and adds that Hamlet's intentions were honorable. A few lines earlier (Act 1, scene 3, line 99), there is also a revealing application of a comma, only found in the folio printing:

Ophelia.
He hath my Lord of late, made many tenders
Of his affection to me.

Again Ophelia chooses her words carefully to explain Hamlet's "affection." The First Folio comma after "of late" provides her with a reflective beat: "Why now? He wasn't like this before—what does it mean?" This is significantly different from the editor/adaptor punctuation that paints a picture of a woman who is much more composed:

Ophelia.
He hath, my lord, of late made many tenders
Of his affection to me.

Commas are sometimes used in the folio to indicate interruptions (much more secure evidence than no punctuation at all) as in the following exchange between Austria and Philip the Bastard in *King John*, Act 3, scene 1, line 126:

Austria.
Well ruffian, I must pocket up these wrongs,
Because,

Bastard.
Your breeches best may carry them.

Although it might seem excessive to believe that such an apparently trivial thing as a comma is important, for an actor performing the text, it is.[110] The comma after "Because" indicates fluency in the shared delivery of the two lines. With something like a dash an actor will often "end stop" a phrase, making the response sound contrived.

Not just commas but question marks can indicate performance pointing. In Act 2, scene 2 of *Macbeth* the title character is offstage killing Duncan, leaving his wife nervously wondering if he has gone through with the deed. The pressure she has applied in order to spur him on is all about Macbeth's manhood—"Are you a man?"—so naturally the first words Macbeth's Wife (she is never called "Lady Macbeth" in the folio) utters when she sees Macbeth return from his regicidal act is "My Husband?" The folio has a question mark; she questions whether he has committed the deed as she has urged and is still her husband and therefore a man. In modern copies, such as Kenneth Muir's Arden edition, the question mark that creates tension and doubt is replaced by the editor/adaptor's favorite directorial punctuation, an exclamation point.[111] In fact they make the change but have no notes to tell the reader or performer of the alteration, so the important little question mark is lost to history. It's true to say that question marks were sometimes used as exclamation points in the typography of the time, but to remove them removes from the actor a choice in playing the line. An actor will (quite rightly) feel indignant if a director demonstrates the way to speak the dialogue—a "line reading"—so shouldn't accept the editor/adaptor version of the same thing when they change punctuation.

This is just a small sampling of First Folio punctuation supporting the performances of the actors. Rather than attempt a long catalog of examples similar to the few cited above, I will concentrate instead on the moments when Shakespeare/the folio/the Playhouse either uses little or no punctuation or overpunctuates a passage to create a dramatic effect. A short illustration to begin with, from *Henry V*, Act 5, scene 1, line 48. Fluellen has been insulted by Pistol and in retribution he forces Pistol to eat a leek. Pistol shows both apparent bravado in defending himself and overt cowardice. The following line, in performance, needs no punctuation and isn't punctuated in the folio, since the actor will convey the sense in many different and subtle ways:

Pistol.
By this Leeke, I will most horribly revenge I
eate and eate I sweare.

To print the line in the form the latest Arden edition of *Henry V* does is reductive:

Pistol.
By this Leek, I will most horribly revenge—
I eat and eat—I swear—[112]

Notice the (over) use of the dash—another punctuation favorite among editor/adaptors when they become amateur directors. Consider how clumsy they[113] make Falstaff's speech in Act 3, scene 3, line 13 of Henry IV, Part 1 by employing the dreaded dash. All that is needed is a drum roll after each comic phrase:

Falstaff.
Why, there is it. Come, sing me a bawdy song; make me merry. I was as
virtuously given, as a gentleman need to be. Virtuous enough; swore little;
diced not above seven times—a week; went to a bawdy-house not
above once in a quarter—of an hour; paid money that I borrowed—three or
four times; lived well and in good compass. And now I live out of all order,
out of all compass.

An actor doesn't need such instructions, and it's condescending for the reader too. This is the First Folio punctuation of the same speech:

Falstaff.
Why there is it: Come, sing me a bawdy Song,
make me merry: I was as vertuously given, as a Gentleman
need to be; vertuous enough, swore little, dic'd not
above seven times a weeke, went to a Bawdy-house not
above once in a quarter of an houre, payd Money that I
borrowed, three or four times; lived well, and in good
compasse: and now I live out of all order, out of compasse.

The folio punctuation is lighter and acknowledges an actor will be able to glean many nuances and comic touches beyond what has been written in the script. It also allows for the alternative choice that, from the character's point of view, Falstaff may well believe what he says is true and is not trying to be funny. The audience, of course, will find it humorous whether it's played that way or not, but it's for the actor and director to experiment freely and discover what they feel will be most effective. Editor/adaptor punctuation has already made the choice for them.

Here's another example of punctuation being used sparingly in the First Folio from *Much Ado About Nothing*, Act 3, scene 4, line 74. Margaret is teasing Beatrice for falling in love with Benedick. Again the light punctuation gives the character a bubbling energy— and the actor the freedom to be creative—that the modern editions deny her. Notice that after the first word, "Morall?," the entire speech is one sentence. In fact, although this may well be coincidental and possibly attributed to printing practices, this prose passage as laid out in the folio has the quality of verse; a free verse structure, with each line containing 12–15 syllables. Margaret has a lot to say and won't be interrupted.

Margaret.
Morall? no[114] by my troth, I have no morall meaning,
I meant plaine holy thissell, you may thinke perchance
that I thinke you are in love, nay birlady I am not
such a foole to think what I list, nor I list not to thinke
what I can, nor indeed, I cannot thinke, if I would thinke
my hart out of thinking, that you are in love, or that you
will be in love, or that you can be in love: yet *Benedicke*
was such another, and now is he become a man, he swore
hee would never marry, and yet now in despight of his
heart[115] he eates his meat without grudging, and how you
may be converted I know not, but me thinkes you looke
with your eies as other women doe.

Sometimes the *over*use of punctuation can both establish a character and heighten a response. Take this passage from *Julius Caesar* (Act 3, scene 2, line 13), heavily punctuated in the folio, when Brutus addresses the Plebeians after the assassination of Caesar:

Brutus.
Romans, Countrey-men, and Lovers, heare mee for my
cause, and be silent, that you may heare. Beleeve me for
mine Honor, and have respect to mine Honor, that you
may beleeve. Censure me in your Wisedom, and awake
your Senses, that you may the better Judge. If there bee
any in this Assembly, any deere Friend of *Caesars,* to him
I say, that *Brutus* love to *Caesar,* was no lesse then his. If
then, that Friend demand, why *Brutus* rose against *Caesar,*
this is my answer: Not that I lov'd *Caesar* lesse, but
that I lov'd Rome more. Had you rather *Caesar* were living,
and dye all Slaves; then that *Caesar* were dead, to
live all Free-men? As *Caesar* lov'd mee, I weepe for him;
as he was Fortunate, I rejoyce at it; as he was Valiant, I
honour him: But, as he was Ambitious, I slew him. There
is Teares, for his Love: Joy, for his Fortune: Honor, for
his Valour: and Death, for his Ambition. Who is heere
so base, that would be a Bondman? If any, speak, for him
have I offended. Who is heere so rude, that would not
be a Roman? If any, speak, for him have I offended. Who
is heere so vile, that will not love his Countrey? If any,
speake, for him have I offended. I pause for a Reply.

First notice the italics and capital letters. Of the seven uses of the word "love" in different forms, only two have a capital letter. "Caesar" is placed in italics seven times while the one use of "Death" has a capital letter, contrasting with Mark Anthony who later speaks the word "dead," but it is not capitalized and therefore not overstressed by the actor. Brutus's use of language is a huge mistake. He emphasizes Caesar, fails to hit home the important point that he loved him, yet draws attention to the fact that Caesar is dead—and "I slew him." There's a short, abrupt sentence at the end where the word "Reply" has a capital letter.

It comes across as nakedly brutal in its attempt to coerce the populace around to Brutus's way of thinking. But Brutus's way of thinking isn't of the man in the street and is more like that of a detested lawyer.[116] This chimes nicely with Orson Welles's view of Brutus: "He's dead right all the time and dead at the final curtain…. He's the bourgeois intellectual who, under a modern dictatorship, would be the first to be put up against a wall and shot."[117] Brutus as "bourgeois intellectual" is brought out in the folio punctuation. Rather than silently reading this prose passage, speak it out loud and observe the original punctuation. In the mouth it becomes labored, fussy, stiff, cold, priggish, has too many clauses, and is halting in its delivery. Mark Anthony's "Friends, Romans, Countrymen, lend me your ears"[118] speech by comparison flows freely in soaring verse and appeals to the emotion of his listeners—which is why the opening is one of the most quoted lines in Shakespeare. "Romans, Countrey-men, and Lovers, heare mee for my cause, and be silent, that you may heare" doesn't have quite the same ring to it.

There's another example of folio punctuation establishing mood and character in *Macbeth*, Act 1, scene 6, line 14. Macbeth's Wife has just told her husband that when the king comes to their castle that night he must be killed. Duncan duly arrives and is greeted with the words:

Lady.
                    All our service,
In every point twice done, and then done double,
Were poore, and single Businesse, to contend
Against those Honors deepe, and broad,
Wherewith your Majestie loades our House:
For those of old, and the late Dignities,
Heap'd up to them, we rest your Ermites.[119]

The speech, as punctuated in the folio, sounds unnatural—deliberately so. She's trying too hard to convince Duncan of her loyalty. It's an example of "showing" an emotion rather than "being" connected to the text that a modern director would chide an actor for. The words lack truth and clearly she doesn't mean what she says. On stage the speech doesn't stand in isolation as it's a public scene and is heard, by among others, Banquo and the shadowy figure of Lennox. What is their reaction to this obvious sham? And what does it tell us about the character of Duncan, who doesn't pick up on the deception and has recently executed the traitor Cawdor, a "Gentleman," he says, "on whom I built/An absolute Trust"?[120] The first line of Duncan's reply to Macbeth's Wife, "Where's the Thane of Cawdor?" (now meaning Macbeth), ironically establishes his continued lack of judgment. As a leader of his country he is again found wanting. A power vacuum has emerged and the question for the characters onstage is—who will fill it? Lennox bides his time, but this is the possible moment that Banquo forms ambitions of his own to overthrow the failing monarch. After this scene he cannot, like Macbeth, sleep least he entertain "the cursed thoughts/That Nature gives way to in repose."[121] The "cursed thoughts," it might be surmised, are ways to gain the crown of Scotland. Whereas the folio punctuation supports the actors in this scene, literary commentators are decidedly unhelpful. Frank Kermode completely misses the theatrical impact of this speech and dismisses it with the words, "On many occasions Shakespeare, needing a simple expression, cannot avoid complicating it in this way."[122]

4. Creating a Role from the Folio Text

A final example of overpunctuation can be found in *Othello*. Iago is consciously trying to confuse Othello so that he is receptive to the idea that Desdemona is having an affair:

Iago.
I do beseech you,
Though I perchance am vicious in my guesse
(As I confesse it is my Nature's plague
To spy into Abuses, and of(t) my jealousie
Shapes faults that are not) that your wisdome
From one, that so imperfectly conceits,
Would take no notice, nor build your selfe a trouble
Out of his scattering, and unsure observance:
It were not for your quiet, nor your good,
Nor for my Manhood, Honesty, and Wisdome,
To let you know my thoughts.[123]

The speech is one sentence and is difficult to follow (although the key words have capital letters.) No wonder Othello replies, "What dost thou meane?" This gives Iago license to continue and clarify his words. It is the moment the trap is set and is the purpose of Iago's overuse of punctuation.

Beginning with John Dover Wilson, who wrote of "the beauty of Elizabethan punctuation,"[124] many editor/adaptors have advocated the retention of the folio marking of the text. M. R. Ridley, editor/adaptor of the second Arden *Othello*, is enthusiastic in his support for "playhouse punctuation." Shakespeare, he states,

> was writing for dramatic delivery, while his editors re-write him for logical comprehension from the page....[125]

> To secure a particular effect he deliberately *omits* normal punctuation.[126]

> I think therefore that in the punctuation of the early texts we have, pretty certainly, at least "playhouse" punctuation, and very possibly a great deal of Shakespeare's own ... no editor can desert it without very careful consideration, and if he does so, does so at his peril.[127]

Ridley's version of *Othello* doesn't get off to a promising start and begins with the word "Tush"—not found in any of the folios but added from the two quartos that were published in 1622 and 1630. However, he does attempt to stick to his intentions and retains the folio punctuation in a number of places, certainly more than is usual for an editor. But even though in comparison to other editions Ridley is closer to the folio, consider just how much of an adaptation even a "conservative" modern volume can be. As a small example among many, compare the last speech in *Othello*. First, here's the folio setting:

Lodovico.
Oh Sparton Dogge:
More fell then Anguish, Hunger, or the Sea:
Looke on the Tragicke Loading of this bed:
This is thy worke:
The Object poysons Sight,
Let it be hid. *Gratiano*, keepe the house,
And seize upon the Fortunes of the Moore,
For they succeede on you. To you, Lord Governor,
Remaines th eCensure[128] of this hellish villaine:

>   The Time, the Place, the Torture, oh inforce it:
>   My selfe will straight aboord, and to the State,
>   This he.avie Act, with heavie heart relate. *Exeunt.*

And this is Ridley's version of the same speech:

> **Lodovico.**
>   O Spartan dog,
> More fell than anguish, hunger, or the sea,
> Look on the tragic lodging of this bed:
> This is thy work, the object poisons sight,
> Let it be hid: Gratiano, keep the house,
> And seize upon the fortunes of the Moor,
> For they succeed on you: to you, lord governor,
> Remains the censure of this hellish villain,
> The time, the place, the torture: O, enforce it!
> Myself will straight aboard, and to the state,
> This heavy act with heavy heart relate. *Exeunt.*

In ten and a half lines Ridley makes 10 punctuation changes, realigns one section of verse, alters the folio "Loading" to the quarto "lodging,"[129] removes 17 capital letters and one use of italics. In total that makes 30 alterations to just 85 words.

Read out loud the folio version of the speech and then the editor's adaptation and the difference can be clearly heard. The folio uses more punctuation and breaks up the verse, supporting the actor playing Lodovico, who is overcome with shock and grief. There is a momentary halt in the verse when Iago is forced to look at the victims of his crimes after "This is thy work." Editor/adaptors reset the verse to make it more regular and thus eradicate the drama. How will Iago respond? The capital letters stress the energy and frustration Lodovico feels; it's almost as if he's taking his anger out on the words by hitting them in a way that he's unable to strike the prisoner, Iago. There are two periods after "Let it be hid" and "Succeed on you" as Lodovico struggles to collect his thoughts and feelings, and notice how the comma in the final couplet of the folio splits the line into four to bring the story to a somber conclusion. The Arden version creates a calm and assured Lodovico, although Ridley (and most other editor/adaptors of "Othello") adds a clumsy directorial note by inserting an emotional exclamation point after "enforce it!" (The folio also has the much more powerful word "inforce.") This is a good example of how the First Folio markings support a character's complex emotional journey, whereas the editor/adaptor printings, if used in performance, create a generalized wash of received interpretation. The former is exciting and unpredictable; the latter leads to an obvious and tiresome "cloning."

The statements from Ridley on punctuation in the Arden *Othello* are a repeat of what he'd written in the preface to an earlier Arden Shakespeare he had edited, *Anthony and Cleopatra*, but in that volume he added, "I have in the text which follows retained an unusually high proportion of the F punctuation."[130] It's almost asking for trouble to write such things, and Patrick Tucker duly obliges:

> In the edition that follows these high aims, the Editor in 3,014 lines of text makes 1,466 changes in punctuation (including the addition of 217 exclamation marks and with the removal of just one).[131]

It seems unfair to single out M. R. Ridley when his intentions were honest and admirable, but clearly something like OCD appears to infect editor/adaptors when they sit down at their desks. Ridley's defense of folio punctuation is followed by his colleague E. A. J. Honigmann, the editor/adaptor of the third Arden *Othello*. He warns, "Readers should remember that the editor's choice of punctuation often rests on grounds that could not be defended in a court of law."[132] Honigmann's editing of Iago's first soliloquy, Act 1, scene 3, line 382, would provide strong evidence in any prosecution. Here's the speech as it is found in the folio:

Iago.
Thus do I ever make my Foole, my purse:
For I mine owne gain'd knowledge should prophane
If I would time expend with such Snipe,
But for my Sport, and Profit: I hate the Moore,
And it is thought abroad, that 'twixt my sheets
She ha's done my Office. I know not if't be true,
But I, for meere suspition in that kinde,
Will do, as if for Surety. He holds me well,
The better shall my purpose worke on him:
Cassio's a proper man: Let me see now,
To get his Place, and to plume up my will
In double Knavery. How? How? Let's see.
After some time, to abuse *Othello's* eares,
That he is too familiar with his wife:
He hath a person, and a smooth dispose
To be suspected: fram'd to make women false.
The Moore is of a free, and open Nature,
That thinkes men honest, that but seeme to be so,
And will as tenderly be lead by'th' Nose
As Asses are:
I hav't: it is engendred: Hell, and Night,
Must bring this monstrous Birth, to the worlds light.

There are just six sentences in this passage, the lack of periods suiting the quickness of Iago's mind. When periods are used, they mark a change in tone and thought, before "I know not if't be true," and "He holds me well," for example. The commas help phrase the speech correctly for an actor. Capital letters draw out the important words: Fool, Sport, Office, Knavery, Asses, Nature, Hell, and Birth are just a few. "Hate" doesn't have a capital letter, instructing the actor not to stress words like this, which could lead them to adopt a generalized bitterness and "evil," but rather to discover each thought moment by moment: the colons support this. In the folio speech Iago doesn't reflect but moves swiftly, his adrenalin pumping. One might even say he is shown to be reckless. Here is the case for Honigmann's defense:

Iago.
Thus do I ever make my fool my purse:
For I mine own gained knowledge should profane
If I would time expend with such a snipe
But for my sport and profit. I hate the Moor
And it is thought abroad that 'twixt my sheets
He's done my office. I know not if't be true,

> But I for mere suspicion in that kind
> Will do as if for surety. He holds me well,
> The better shall my purpose work on him.
> Cassio's a proper man: let me see now,
> To get his place, and to plume up my will
> In double knavery. How? How? let's see:
> After some time to abuse Othello's ear
> That he is too familiar with his wife.
> He hath a person and a smooth dispose
> To be suspected, framed to make women false.
> The Moor is of a free and open nature
> That thinks men honest that but seem to be so,
> And will as tenderly be lead by th' nose
> As asses are.
> I have't, it is engendered! Hell and night
> Must bring this monstrous birth to the world's light.

In mitigation Honigmann corrects four possible folio printing errors, changing "She ha's done my office" to "He's done" (although turning two words into one); adds an "a" before "snipe," which the folio printers probably missed out[133]; puts back an "e" in "engendered"; and turns "eares" into the singular "ear." All this is consistent with the two quartos. Nor does Honigmann alter the verse structure or replace the folio's words with any others. Nonetheless in these twenty-one and a half lines, he makes 25 changes of punctuation and removes 14 capital letters and 2 uses of italics. His alterations number 41 in 184 words, which is consistent with the usual editor ratio of changing 20–30 percent of the text. Or, put another way, an actor using a modern edition of a play only receives three-quarters of the original script.

"The editor's choice of punctuation often rests on grounds that could not be defended in a court of law," wrote Honigmann, hoisting himself on his own petard. Why replace the folio's colon after "To be suspected" with a comma, for example? Or change the folio's "Let's see." period and capital letter to a colon and no capital? Surely this denotes one of the few moments when Iago stops to think? Rhythmically the Arden version of the speech works against Iago's desire for speed, setting more periods and removing the elision on words such as "fam'd" and "gain'd." And there's the almost obligatory directorial imposition editor/adaptors favor with the addition, not even found in the quartos, of an exclamation point after "it is engendered!" Within the pages of his *Othello* adaptation, Honigmann informs his readers "F's punctuation is not likely to be Shakespeare's."[134] This may or may not be true, but we can be certain that Shakespeare's punctuation is not likely to be the editor's. The First Folio printing guides the actors; modern editions will almost certainly trip them up. Editor/adaptors generally punctuate for readers, but try to *act* their punctuation in a theatre and the text becomes "unwieldy, slow, heavy, and pale as lead."[135] It doesn't fly off the page as it should. In the folio, after major punctuation such as a question mark, there is often a lowercase letter.[136] Shakespeare wants the actors to drive the text on, push the energy through to the end of the verse line, but also to the end of the character's very long thoughts. In this way, like Hamlet, he is encouraging his actors to "speak the speech *trippingly* on the tongue."[137] Editor/adaptors, on the other hand, have, as Don Weingust puts it, "rendered our Shakespeare more grammatical than dramatic."[138] They fail to realize that the folio/Shakespeare punctuates not only for actors but for *characters*. People don't all talk in the same way but have different speech patterns. The punctuation will change depending on the character—and the situation the characters find themselves in. Punctuating the text along grammatical rather than theatrical lines can remove the drama, the character, and the sense.

Lineation/Meter

By far the biggest alteration editor/adaptors make to the plays of Shakespeare is to the lineation of the verse. Thinking of Shakespeare as primarily a poet, they see it as their duty to make the verse as regular as possible, and for them this means iambic pentameter. What they generally disregard is that while in his early plays Shakespeare's verse was usually (although by no means always) fairly regular, this changed. As he grew in confidence and experience, writing around 40 plays as well as volumes of poetry over 25 years, he began to use a variety of meters to help the actor convey emotion and information.[139] That is *not* to say that short, irregular, lines require an actor to pause at the end of them to complete an iambic verse line. They don't. Shakespeare sometimes writes a different form of verse, for a number of theatrical reasons. As John Jones rightly observes, "As a play lives on the stage, so its language lives in the mouth and upon the ear. The editorial desk is where syllables are counted."[140]

Here's an example from *Othello*, Act 4, scene 2, line 138, of the editor/adaptors attempting to regularize the folio's verse. Emilia believes Othello has been infected by a "cozening Slave" who has "devis'd this Slander," and Desdemona replies, "If any such there be, Heaven pardon him." Emilia's reaction is set in the folio as:

> **Emilia.**
> A halter pardon him:
> And hell gnaw his bones.
> Why should he call her Whore?
> Who keeps her companie?
> What Place? What Time?
> What Forme? What liklyhood?
> The Moore's abus'd by some most villanous Knave,
> Some base notorious Knave, some scurvy Fellow.

Each short phrase is carefully chosen by Emilia[141] (note the capital letters) and each is like a stab in the heart to the listening Iago as he sees his plots begin to unravel. Editor/adaptors construct the speech differently and attempt to fashion it into more regular verse. Even so they are still unable to turn all of the verse into iambic pentameter—the beats are marked next to each line:

> **Emilia.**
> A halter pardon him, and hell gnaw his bones! (11)
> Why should he call her whore? who keeps her company? (12)
> What place, what time, what form, what likelihood? (10)
> The Moor's abus'd by some most villainous knave, (11)
> Some base notorious knave, some scurvy Fellow.[142] (11/12)

One has to question—why bother to change the verse if it still isn't regular? And why would the folio compositor take time to set 8 separate lines rather than the editor/adaptor's 5?

The verse is important to an actor and director not because it may be "correct" or "incorrect" in terms of meter but rather because it can help to establish the mood. There's a truly creepy exchange between Othello and Desdemona (Act 4, scene 2, line 24), which in the folio sets up a slow tempo to the start of the scene and space around the short lines for actions/thoughts/exchanges of looks that are indicated in the text:

Desdemona.
My Lord, what is your will?
Othello.
Pray you Chucke come hither.
Desdemona.
What is your pleasure?
Othello.
Let me see your eyes: looke in my face.
Desdemona.
What horrible Fancie's this?

This is very different from the editor/adaptor version in which the two characters share verse lines, as if they share common thoughts, although only one line is regular pentameter:

Desdemona.
My lord, what is your will?
Othello.
                Pray,[143] chuck, come hither. (11)
Desdemona.
What is your pleasure?
Othello.
                Let me see your eyes. (10)
Look in my face.
Desdemona.
                What horrible fancy's this? (11)

In this version a quick, almost frantic, pace is necessary if the actors pick up the cues as suggested. Any actor will want to begin the scene carefully, as the journey of the emotional arc is long. Continuing with *Othello*, the folio irregular verse supports the actor playing Iago in conveying a guarded disbelief, and a possible struggle for breath, when he is forced to confess (Act 5, scene 2, line 172):

Iago.
I told him what I thought,
And told no more
Than what he found himselfe was apt, and true.

It's a key moment in the play and requires focus; Iago is finally admitting a degree of responsibility, but with a twist—how far did Othello bring this on himself? The editor/adaptor setting, although in iambic pentameter, is much less helpful for the actor and depicts an Iago who is totally composed:

Iago.
I told him what I thought, and told no more
Than what he found himself was apt and true.[144]

That's just three examples from a single play. There are very many more, of course, both in *Othello* and the rest of the canon.

Two highly respected British directors have commented on Shakespeare's use of verse. Peter Hall believes that Shakespeare used irregular verse in much the same way as a film director uses different shots: "It keeps the attention and avoids predictability."[145] Peter Brook warns that if the verse is entirely regular, and the actor tries to deliver it that way, it can lead to "empty music" in the theatre:

> If actors are taught that Shakespeare wrote in pentameters, and the pentameters have a certain beat, and the actors try to use this in their speech, you get a dry, empty music, which is not in the living music that there is in the words.[146]

In other words the verse is there—iambic or not—to convey meaning. Patrick Tucker is astute in observing that Winston Churchill's famous speeches during World War II used a similar approach.[147] It was vital that Churchill communicate with the British nation at a time of crisis, and to do this he rejected prose in favor of a free verse form he called "psalm style." When finished, the speeches were referred to as "hymn sheets." Here's an example from the layout of Churchill's "Give Us the Tools" speech, aimed at soliciting American support for the war in Europe in 1941:

> Put your confidence in us;
>   Give us your faith and your blessing,
>   And under providence all will be well.
> We shall not fail or falter.
> We shall not weaken or tire.
> Neither the sudden shock of battle nor the long-drawn
>   trials of vigilance and exertion will wear us down.
> Give us the tools, and we will finish the job.[148]

The format of Churchill's speeches inspired a piece of sculpture by the Canadian artist Paul De Monchaux in 2004. He was struck by: "Churchill's awareness of the way in which the spaces around words can amplify their meaning."[149] Churchill, like Shakespeare, used meter as a communication tool. Sometimes there is a fortuitous regular iambic line such as "And under providence all will be well," but generally his verse form is varied and matches the message.

It's not only the verse that editor/adaptors restructure; they also change prose into verse. Academics justify their actions by inventing what they call "verse-fossils"; that is, passages of verse that have somehow become buried in the prose. Of course this is sheer speculation, not backed up by any documentary evidence. Most people will not realize that in the First Folio—compiled by his friends and fellow actors, remember—Mercutio's famous story of Queen Mab in Act 1, scene 4, line 53 of *Romeo and Juliet* is actually in prose, not in the verse form you'll see printed in every modern edition of the play. There were six quarto versions of this speech issued between 1597 and 1637 (one a variant of the fourth) as well as the four folios, two published later. Ten printings. In *only* the universally acknowledged corrupt First quarto (which begins "Queen Mab what's she?") is the passage printed in verse—but the lines are assigned to Benvolio rather than Mercutio. For consistency's sake, if editor/adaptors publish the Queen Mab speech in verse they must surely also print "Queen Mab what's she?" and give it to Benvolio. Of course they don't, as the weak phrase and unsuitable character don't suit their adaptations.[150] Here's an editor/adaptor version of the speech, the New Penguin volume edited by T. J. B. Spencer,[151] but all contemporary published texts have more or less the same setting:

Mercutio.
O, then I see Queen Mab hath been with you.
She is the fairies' midwife, and she comes
In shape no bigger than an agate stone
On the forefinger of an alderman,
Drawn with a team of little atomies
Over men's noses as they lie asleep.
Her chariot is an empty hazelnut,
Made by the joiner squirrel or old grub,
Time out o' mind the fairies' coachmakers.
Her wagon spokes made of long spinners' legs;
The cover, of the wings of grasshoppers;
Her traces, of the smallest spider web;
Her collars, of the moonshine's watery beams;
Her whip, of cricket's bone; the lash, of film;
Her wagoner, a small grey-coated gnat,
Not half so big as a round little worm
Pricked from the lazy finger of a maid.
And in this state she gallops night by night
Through lovers' brains, and then they dream of love;
O'er courtiers' knees, that dream on curtsies straight;
O'er lawyers' fingers, who straight dream on fees;
O'er ladies' lips, who straight on kisses dream,
Which oft the angry Mab with blisters plagues,
Because their breaths with sweetmeats tainted are.
Sometimes she gallops o'er a courtier's nose,
And then dreams he of smelling out a suit;
And sometimes comes she with a tithe-pig's tail
Tickling a parson's nose as 'a lies asleep;
Then dreams he of another benefice.
Sometime she driveth o'er a soldier's neck;
And then dreams he of cutting foreign throats,
Of breaches, ambuscadoes, Spanish blades,
Of healths five fathom deep; and then anon
Drums in his ear, at which he starts and wakes,
And being thus frighted, swears a prayer or two
And sleeps again. This is that very Mab
That plaits the manes of horses in the night
And bakes the elflocks in foul sluttish hairs,
Which once untangled much misfortune bodes.
This is the hag, when maids lie on their backs,
That presses them and learns them first to bear,
Making them women of good carriage.
This is she—

The character is in full control of what he is saying and speaks, what is obviously a (prepared?) speech, in a highly structured way. But throughout the play Mercutio is rarely reflective; he's quick-witted, quick-tempered, drunk, bawdy, cynical, and so on, but you wouldn't call him calm. Here's the same speech from the folio, mostly in prose:

Mercutio.
O then I see Queene Mab hath beene with you:
She is the Fairies Midwife, & she comes in shape no bigger
then Agat-stone, on the fore-finger of an Alderman,
drawne with a teeme of little Atomies, over mens noses as
they lie asleepe: her Waggon Spokes made of long Spinners
legs: the Cover of the wings of Grashoppers, her
Traces of the smallest Spiders web, her coullers of the
Moonshines watry Beames, her Whip of Crickets bone,
the Lash of Philome, her Waggoner, a small gray-coated
Gnat, not halfe so bigge as a round little Worme, prickt
from the Lazie-finger of a man. Her Chariot is an emptie
Haselnut, made by the Joyner Squirrel or old Grub, time
out a mind, the Faries Coach-makers: & in this state she
gallops night by night, through Lovers braines: and then
they dreame of Love. On Courtiers knees, that dreame on
Cursies strait: ore Lawyers fingers, who strait dreampt on
Fees, ore Ladies lips, who strait on kisses dreame, which
oft the angry Mab with blisters plagues, because their
breath with Sweet meats tainted are. Sometime she gallops
ore a Courtiers nose, & then dreames he of smelling
out a sute: & somtime comes she with Tith pigs tale, tickling
a Parsons nose as a lies asleepe, then he dreames of
another Benefice. Sometime she driveth ore a Souldiers
necke, & then dreames he of cutting Forraine throats, of
Breaches, Ambuscados, Spanish Blades: Of Healths five
Fadome deepe, and then anon drums in his eares, at which
he startes and wakes; and being thus frighted, sweares a
prayer or two & sleepes againe: this is that very Mab that
plats the manes of Horses in the night: & bakes the Elklocks
in foule sluttish haires, which once untangled, much
misfortune bodes,
This is the hag, when Maides lie on their backs,
That presses them, and learnes them first to beare,
Making them women of good carriage:
This is she.[152]

The moment it goes into verse is very clear. When spoken you can hear the gear change on "This is the Hag, when Maides lie on their backs" as Mercutio's speech gathers momentum and becomes darker and more obscene and has to be interrupted by Romeo. The prose has a distinct rhythm, and the key words have capital letters, but it is appropriate for this tour de force that the actor has more freedom than verse might give him. Not content with setting the description of Queen Mab in verse, the editor/adaptors reorder it so that:

> Her chariot is an empty hazelnut,
> Made by the joiner squirrel or old grub,
> Time out o' mind the fairies' coachmakers.

comes after "Over men's noses as they lie asleep" and before "Her wagon spokes made of long spinners' legs." In this way Mercutio starts with his subject—Mab's chariot—and then describes it in more detail. This may well be good storytelling and logical, each thought proceeding from the previous one, but it kills character. Mercutio hasn't prepared his words; he discovers the lines in the moment, starts a thought and later goes back to it. It might even be said that he doesn't fully know what he is saying or why he is saying it. In fact, that's the first question any actor playing Mercutio asks a director: "Why am I saying this and why now?" The character probably has vague feelings of misogyny, jealousy, and possible homosexual yearnings towards Romeo (brought out in Baz Luhrmann's film), but he hasn't come on stage to recite a piece of poetry. Where is the evidence on which editor/adaptors base their line reordering? There isn't any. The folio helps the actor playing Mercutio—the modern editions hinder the possible development of character.[153] Editor/adaptors seem to believe that verse is always the stronger option in conveying Shakespeare's high emotion, but veteran RSC director John Barton refutes this:

> His prose has very strong rhythms and if an actor does not get in touch with them there will be a loss of definition and energy and clarity.[154]
>
> Many of his heightened passages are in prose and much of his blank verse is naturalistic.[155]

Not content with altering the folio prose to verse, the editor/adaptors also turn verse passages into prose. There's an example of this found at Act 4, scene 2, line 100 of *Measure for Measure*. The Duke (as Friar) and the audience believe that Claudio will be saved from execution since Mariana, pretending to be Isabella, has slept with Angelo. A messenger arrives with the apparent pardon. Editor/adaptors set his speech in prose:

> **Messenger.**
> My Lord hath sent you this note, and by me this further charge: that you swerve not from the smallest article of it, neither in time, matter, or other circumstance. Good-morrow; for, as I take it, it is almost day.

The folio version, however, is in a kind of free verse, certainly not iambic, that assists the actor (who would have been no Burbage) in making each point clear. The important information he has to get across is laid out before him in the text:

> **Messenger.**
> My Lord hath sent you this note,
> And by mee this further charge;
> That you swerve not from the smallest Article of it,
> Neither in time, matter, or other circumstance.
> Good morrow: for as I take it, it is almost day.[156]

It is a list of four distinct instructions as the swift reversal in the plot is emphasized to both the audience and the Duke, neither of whom are expecting this turn of events. The folio setting helps the actor in his phrasing—the editor/adaptor version does not.

A further example of this is Iago's folio reaction (Act 3, scene 3, line 230) when he is told by Othello that he believes Desdemona is "honest":

> **Iago.**
> Long live she so;
> And long live you to think so.

The folio sets this in verse and the meaning is pointed and has its effect. Possibly Iago makes to leave after "Long live she so" and throws the next line casually over his shoulder as he goes. With the editor/adaptor prose version this important moment could easily be lost:

Iago.
Long live she so; and long live you to think so.

There are numerous instances—too many for them to be considered printer error or coincidence—of the First Folio lineation guiding actors in their character responses, but here are two examples from *King Lear* at the end of Act 4, scene 7, line 71. The first removes an action and the second some poignant phrasing. Lear, buffeted by the storm, his mind confused, and approaching death, awakes from a deep sleep and sees his banished daughter Cordelia. He reaches for her in disbelief with the words, set in the folio:

Lear.
Be your teares wet?
Yes faith: I pray weepe not.

It's a heartbreaking scene that requires time in the playing of it. The folio lineation indicates that the old king touches his daughter's face after "wet" and feels her genuine tears. Lear's second short verse line allows the actor to find the emotion of the moment when the previously selfish king begins to think of others, in this case Cordelia. Modern editions set this as one quick, regular iambic line:

Lear.
Be your tears wet? Yes, faith; I pray weep not.

The scene ends at line 83 with Lear's realization of the wrongs he has done. In the folio the phrasing is clearly marked in irregular verse as again the actor will need time to discover these achingly sad reflections (but also not to wallow in them—the verse form prevents this):

Lear.
You must beare with me:
Pray you now forget, and forgive,
I am old and foolish.[157]

Modern editions follow the quartos and set this wonderful speech in prose, also removing the important comma before "forgive":

Lear.
You must bear with me. Pray you now, forget and forgive.[158] I am old and foolish.

Interestingly, although they print the quarto lineation, most include the "you" in "Pray you now," which is only found in the folio, thus creating a clear adaptation of the text.

Two final examples are from *Macbeth* (a play that has admittedly caused a great deal of debate on the security of its meter), and demonstrate how the verse can help actors in connecting to the emotion of the moment in which they find themselves. In Act 2, scene 3, line 53, Lenox reveals that he has spent a sleepless night due to an unnatural storm. He is scared—"freaked out" would be the modern term—of what this supernatural happening might forebode. The folio gives him a number of irregular lines as if in telling his story he is still deeply affected by what he has experienced. Some things, such as "Strange Schreemes of Death," he can barely recount; he is short of breath, halting in his delivery, and as he speaks he seems to see each image again in all of its horror:

Lenox.
The Night ha's been unruly:

> Where we lay, our Chimneys were blowne downe,
> And (as they say) lamentings heard i'th' Ayre;
> Strange Schreemes of Death,
> And Prophecying, with Accents terrible,
> Of dyre Combustion, and confus'd Events,
> New hatch'd toth' wofull time.
> The obscure Bird clamor'd the live-long Night.
> Some say, the Earth was fevorous,
> And did shake.

Editor/adaptors (who have no quarto to refer to) universally set the speech in (fairly regular) iambic pentameter and deny the actor an opportunity to fully convey Lenox's nightmarish vision:

> **Lenox.**
> The night has been unruly: where we lay,
> Our chimneys were blown down; and, as they say,
> Lamentings heard i'th' air; strange screams of death,
> And, prophesying with accents terrible
> Of dire combustion, and confus'd events,
> New hatch'd to th' woeful time, the obscure bird
> Clamour'd the live-long night: some say, the earth
> Was fevorous, and did shake.

As set above, the speech is little different from the exchange between Banquo and Duncan in Act 1, scene 6, line 1, when they calmly describe Macbeth's home—"This Castle hath a pleasant seat"—little knowing what lies within.

Perhaps the most famous incident of editor/adaptors tinkering with the folio verse lineation is "The Bleeding Sergeant" in Act 1, scene 2, line 33, of *Macbeth*. From Flatter onwards it is quoted by all proponents of the First Folio, but is worth repeating here. The Sergeant (the folio speech prefix calls him "Captain," thus raising his status to match Macbeth and Banquo) is recounting to King Duncan the story of the battle, but he is badly wounded and by the end of his speech he is near to fainting. In the First Folio a number of irregular lines help the actor to convey the sense of being initially weak, rallying in pride of the army's victory, and then life draining from the character after this burst of energy and a struggle to finish his tale. Here's the passage as it appears in the First Folio with the number of beats marked next to each line:

> **King.**[159]
> Dismay'd not this our Captaines, Macbeth and
> Banquoh? (prose)
> **Captain.**
> Yes, as Sparrowes, Eagles; (6)
> Or the Hare, the Lyon: (6)
> If I say sooth, I must report they were (10)
> As Cannons over-charg'd with double Cracks, (10)
> So they doubly redoubled stroakes upon the Foe: (12)
> Except they meant to bathe in reeking Wounds, (10)
> Or memorize another Golgotha, (10)
> I cannot tell: but I am faint, (8)
> My Gashes cry for helpe. (6)

It can be clearly seen that at the beginning of the speech the exhausted soldier has difficulty expressing himself and has to stop twice for breath. He makes a final effort to complete the story with five fairly regular lines, but this takes its toll and as he begins to fade away the final three lines have 10, 8, and 6 beats and presumably would descend progressively into nothing and death if Duncan didn't call for a surgeon. Here's what modern editions generally publish, again with the beats marked next to each line:

King.
Dismay'd not this (10—from previous line)
our captains, Macbeth and Banquo?
Captain.[160]
                              Yes—(9)
As sparrows, eagles, or the hare, the lion. (11)
If I say sooth I must report they were (10)
As cannons over-charged with double cracks; (10)
So they (2)
Doubly redoubled strokes upon the Foe: (10)
Except they meant to bathe in reeking wounds, (10)
Or memorize another Golgotha (10)
I cannot tell. (4)
—But I am faint; my gashes cry for help. (10)

Why set the start of the passage with two irregular lines of 9 and 11 beats? What's wrong with the folio setting? There are two breaks in this version of the speech. The first is after "So they" and the editor/adaptors explain that the rest of the line is missing.[161] Quite how they know this is a puzzle, especially as the line as printed in the folio makes perfect sense. In their role as amateur directors, they make an attempt to repeat exactly what the folio has done before them and try to set some of the verse so that it matches the delivery of a dying man. Hence the short four-beat line "I cannot tell" before the Captain/Sergeant reveals he is about to faint. This is pretty ridiculous: why would a dying man speak in coherent iambic pentameter, falter as he gathers his strength, and then revive and continue in regular verse despite the fact that he's about to pass out and is possibly uttering his final breath?

Richard Flatter comments on this speech that Shakespeare's characters "speak each in his own way—and an exhausted man speaks in an exhausted manner."[162] In 1948 Flatter wrote a groundbreaking book, *Shakespeare's Producing Hand*, proposing that in the First Folio Shakespeare demonstrated that "it is for the actor he writes, not for the reader."[163] Flatter had experience of the theatrical profession, having trained under the renowned director Max Reinhardt. Unfortunately his work was published just after World War II and the response to it was sadly colored by an often sickening xenophobia. In Britain Flatter's research was regarded as impertinence by the academic elite. What could a *German* know about Shakespeare? (Actually he was Austrian.) Richard Flatter has consequently become unregarded, although if there's one country outside the English-speaking world that appreciates Shakespeare it's Germany. Actors and directors—and editor/adaptors—should pay close attention to Flatter's words:

> Why not stick to what the Folio says? Why not trust the compositors with the ability to translate into print what they found in the manuscript? And why not believe that he who wrote the script knew his job?[164]

What is frustrating is that in their adaptations editors do sometimes follow the folio's nonpentameter verse. Hotspur in *Henry IV, Part 1* has a speech (Act 4, scene 1, line 31) in which he is reading a letter from his father. He is anxiously scanning the message rather than examining it in detail, and the verse is irregular in order to convey this:

> He writes me here, that inward sicknesse,
> And that his friends by deputation
> Could not so soone be drawne:

There's a clear break after "sicknesse" where modern editors acknowledge a dramatic moment by adding a dash. Few now follow Capell in suggesting that there is a missing word but accept the break as a performance clue, where Hotspur reads the letter quickly and pauses to consider the implications of its contents. Similarly, the final lines of *The Comedy of Errors* are a rhyming couplet and all modern versions agree with the folio in printing them as:

> We came into the world like brother and brother:
> And now let's go hand in hand, not one before another.

Of course they still can't resist a tinker and generally replace the colon after "brother" with a comma, but other than that they bow to the authority of the folio. And yet neither of the lines are set in regular iambic pentameter; the first has 12 beats (known as an Alexandrine) and the second 14 (a "fourteener.") If an unconventional meter is acknowledged as being correct in these plays, why shouldn't it be the right choice in other places too? One of Shakespeare's shamans, R. A. Foakes, thinks he has the answer. Writing in the Arden edition of *The Comedy of Errors* of a passage in the folio that mixes verse and prose (Act 4, scene 3, line 69), Foakes forgives Shakespeare for his apparent carelessness in maintaining meter:

> I suspect that Shakespeare sometimes found it difficult as he was writing to adjust from one rhythm to another, and that a certain amount of overlapping, as here, is the result.[165]

Although in the study this may seem like a problem, on stage it is not and actually helps the performers. A confusion between verse and prose is highly appropriate for *The Comedy of Errors* of all plays, with its mistaken identities, character frustrations, and incredible events. Regular iambic pentameter, suggesting order, is not what the highly charged situations require, and often the verse "breaks down" as the character's emotions run high. A skilled actor will effortlessly be able to convey the switches between verse and prose. Rhythmically the play is pretty much perfect. Dramatically—it works. Equally frustrating is that some editor/adaptors recognize this but then fail to put it into practice. David Bevington, in his New Cambridge Shakespeare version of *Anthony and Cleopatra*, writes, "Shakespeare's verse, especially in his late plays, constantly warns us not to impose preconceived notions of metrical conventionality."[166] He then ignores his own warnings and alters whole passages of folio prose into verse. This lack of consistency, if followed by the actor, can lead only to an inconsistent performance.

Can it really be true that Shakespeare took the time and trouble to include all these actor indicators into the body of his texts? It is well to remember Coleridge's phrase that Shakespeare was "myriad-minded." In his plays Shakespeare says a lot about theatre, actors, and acting, but nothing about authors—to him the words only lived when spoken by the actor. Ben Jonson called him "the wonder of our Stage!"—not of the study. In fact, Jonson probably included the word AUTHOR in capitals in his introductory poem to the First Folio in order to raise Shakespeare's status as a writer. The folio wasn't called Shakespeare's "Works" like Jonson's own collection, but "Mr. William Shakespeares Comedies, Histories, and Tragedies." The very things editor/adaptors attempt to tag on to Shakespeare to assert his poetic credibility are those that attracted criticism from his contemporaries: "small Latin and less Greek," for example.[167] It may stick in the throat of the editor/adaptors but is difficult to argue with William Gaskill:

> Our greatest poet chose to write *plays*. That is, if he is our greatest poet. Would he still be thought so if he had only written the Sonnets, *Venus and Adonis,* and *The Rape of Lucrece?* Probably not.[168]

The fact of the matter is that in basic terms Shakespeare wrote in order to make money. Nearly every historical document related to him is financial, and in the bust over his grave he looks more like a member of the merchant class than a "theatrical."[169] He could only accumulate the cash he needed to return to Stratford as the owner of his grand house "New Place" if his actors did their jobs well. It was in his interest to ensure that they did.

As a conclusion to this chapter, it must once again be made very clear that it is wrong to claim that the First Folio is always right in *everything* it printed. That's obviously not the case. If low on periods, for example, the compositor used a question mark, and some passages are adjusted so that they fit the page to be printed. This included ditching verse and setting it as prose. Contrary to what has been written in this chapter, there are some moments in the setting of the First Folio that if an actor were to attempt to employ the speech prefixes and line assignments the play would become very confusing. *Some* moments—but nowhere near as many as editor/adaptors suggest. If the folio contains indications for an actor, they are not a set of rigid rules that when followed will create the perfect Shakespearean performance. The folio is not to be thought of like the score of a piece of music; if it is like music then it's more like jazz. However, the folio text will undoubtedly support and guide an actor and director in creating productions of vitality and meaning. Modern literary versions of the plays will not.

The next section concerns an area that editor/adaptors have little experience of (although it might be imagined that they share the same enthusiasm for amateur theatricals that Polonius enjoyed) and make little or no comment on—acting.

5

Shakespeare's Rogues and Vagabonds

"Unperfect actors"?

One of the few facts about the life of William Shakespeare (not even disputed by "anti-Stratfordians") is that he was an actor. His name appears on the cast lists of various plays throughout his career and he is even placed in the First Folio of 1623 as one of the "Principal Actors" of his own work. The general public has little idea of the amount of intensive training it takes to become a professional performer; at least four years in most cases, plus a lengthy period appearing in plays in the regions or on the fringe. Actors don't just turn up for an audition and get cast immediately as the lead in a Broadway show. Multiple imaginative solutions to the "problem" of what Shakespeare was doing in his so-called Lost Years between 1585 and 1592 have been proposed, but it seems fair to suggest that, rather than what has been termed "the leap to eminence," he was learning his trade as an actor.[1] As John Dover Wilson put it, "When we find a man of thirty near the top of his particular tree, we must assume some previous climbing."[2]

Seven years, the same period of time when he was apparently "lost," was the term served by an apprentice, and although Shakespeare would have been between 21 and 23, if he was apprenticed as an actor this shouldn't be thought of as unusual. The playwright Anthony Munday was 22 when he signed up for 8 years as an apprentice with the Stationer's Company. Actor/apprentices were normally attached to a trade rather than a theatre company; John Heminge was a member of the Grocer's Company and apprenticed his young actors as grocers. Bottom and his fellows with their various crafts were not so far removed from professional players.

It's true to say that apprentices were not allowed to marry or have a household, and Shakespeare was married with children, of course, but who would check on a man from distant Stratford? Even if Shakespeare wasn't formally indentured as an apprentice, there is evidence that the Queen's Men acting company visited Stratford in 1587 and were in nearby Oxford, Coventry, and Leicester in 1585. It's known that immediately before the Stratford visit the company was short of a performer, William Knell having been killed in a fight with a fellow actor in Oxford. What is interesting, although it cannot be offered as evidence, is that in under a year Knell's widow married another actor in the Queen's Men—John Heminge. The tragic death of William Knell may have been a lucky day for Heminge, providing him with a wife and a working partnership with a man whose plays he would help to print 36 years later.[3]

5. Shakespeare's Rogues and Vagabonds

When Shakespeare reemerges in the records in 1592, he is with the Earl of Pembroke's Men at the Rose Theatre, where the actors included people he was to collaborate with for the rest of his life, such as Augustine Phillips, Richard Burbage, John Sinclair, Thomas Pope, George Bryan, and William Sly. Pembroke's Men and the Rose Theatre premiered the plays of the foremost dramatist of the time, Christopher Marlowe. In his excellent biography of Shakespeare, Peter Levi proposes, "It is extremely likely that he acted in Marlowe's plays, and developed much of his own power by learning Marlowe by heart."[4] Marlowe's *Edward II* probably premiered at the Rose around 1592 and the title character in Act 4, scene 3, line 46, has a speech that contains the words:

> Gallop apace, bright Phoebus, through the sky;
> And, dusky Night, in rusty iron car,
> Between you both shorten the time, I pray,
> That I may see that most desired day,
> When we may meet these traitors in the field![5]

Of course, this speech is remarkably similar to Juliet's at the beginning of Act 3, scene 2, line 1, of Shakespeare's *Romeo and Juliet* thought to have been written in 1595 but possibly earlier:

> Gallop apace, you fiery footed steedes,
> Towards *Phaebus* lodging, such a Wagoner
> As *Phaeton* would whip you to the West
> And bring in Cloudie night immediately.

Did Shakespeare act the part of Edward in Marlowe's *Edward II* and recall his lines when writing Juliet's words? If he did portray Edward, then immediately after his "Gallop apace" speech, he would have been standing in the wings waiting for his cue and heard Queen Isabella say in the very short scene before his entrance:

> In civil broils make kin and countryman
> Slaughter themselves in others...[6]

This is not too far away from the phrase used in the opening chorus (cut in the folio) of *Romeo and Juliet*: "Where civil blood makes civil hands unclean."

There is no actual *proof* to support these speculations—no documents relating to Shakespeare being indentured as an apprentice, for example[7]—but common sense would point to Shakespeare spending a considerable amount of time acting before the public in a wide range of plays that both provided him with an understanding of plot, style, and language, and also help to explain why he appears to have developed such a prodigious memory.[8]

Shakespeare's plays are soaked in theatrical references. It is hard to think of one that doesn't mention the theatre or acting—it's even there in the sonnets (see number 23.) Three of his scripts include a play within a play, and references to actors are put in the mouths of characters you'd least expect—Coriolanus, Othello, Ulysses, Henry IV, Macbeth, the Earl of Warwick in *Henry VI, Part 3*—and Cassius is someone of whom Julius Caesar negatively notes, "He loves no Playes."[9] Shakespeare knew about acting and actors. He made a very good living out of the theatre and it was in his interest that the performers delivered his words in the best possible way. As an actor himself, he was very aware of their needs and he accommodates them in the folio/playhouse setting of his scripts. It would be a mistake to imagine that because Shakespeare's company performed in large arenas, in the open air, before vast numbers of people, their approach to acting differed greatly from that of modern actors. If you visit a production at the present-day Globe on London's Bankside, you will see that, although if it's filmed the acting appears larger than life, in the actual theatre a considerable amount of subtlety can be achieved. Hamlet's advice to the players (Act 3, scene 2, line 2) is exactly *opposite* to the image of the uncultured and declamatory Elizabethan actor:

> If you mouth it, as many of your Players do, I had as live the Town-Cryer had spoke my lines ... use all gently; for in the verie Torrent, Tempest, and, (as I may say), the Whirle-wind of Passion, you must acquire and beget a Temperance that may give it Smoothnesse.... Sute the Action to the Word, the Word to the Action, with this speciall observance: That you o'erstep not the modestie of Nature.

"Gently," "Temperance," "Smoothness," and "modesty" are hardly the words of someone urging the actor to crudely belt out of the lines. Hamlet speculates, after seeing the 1st Player shed real tears when delivering a speech in Act 2, scene 2, line 554:

> What would he doe,
> Had he the Motive and the Cue for passion
> That I have?

Having the *motivation* for an action is the crux of an actor's art, and the practical matter of picking up a cue is essential. A few moments earlier Hamlet had been in wonder at how an actor can produce seemingly authentic emotion:

> But in a Fixion, in a dreame of Passion,
> Could force his soule so to his whole conceit,
> That from her working, all his visage warm'd[10];
> Teares in his eyes, distraction in's Aspect,
> A broken voyce, and his whole Function suiting
> With Formes, to his Conceit? And all for nothing?

For Shakespeare's players, the phrase to "passionate" meant to depict emotion[11] and the reference to "a dream of passion" seems to suggest the actor recalling a previous emotional experience in order to truthfully convey what he found in the script. This would be recognizable to the modern performer as "emotion memory," a technique pioneered by the great teacher of acting in the early 20th century, Constantin Stanislavski. It is a "method" that requires performers to draw from an analogous occurrence in their own lives in order to believe, at that moment, in the reality of the text. In simple terms, the actor playing Hubert in *King John* might think of his own son when attempting to blind Arthur. An actress as Lady Anne, weeping over the coffin that contains her father-in-law, might remember, or imagine, the passing of one of her own family. It doesn't always have to be so direct; the memory of the loss of a beloved pet would not be unusual in enabling a performer to produce real tears. Interestingly, the foremost promoter of Stanislavski's work in America was Lee Strasberg, and he entitled one of his books *A Dream of Passion*, after Hamlet's phrase above.

There are a number of contemporary descriptions of Richard Burbage that survive. He was Shakespeare's leading actor and the creator of many of his most famous characters, including Hamlet. What is astonishing is just how close he appears to be to a modern actor:

So wholly transforming himself into his part, and putting off himself with his clothes, as he never (not so much as in the tiring-house) assumed himself again until the play was ended.[12]

Today we would (sometimes sneeringly) call this "method acting" and associate it with the type of actor who "lives" his roles; Daniel Day-Lewis for example. When Burbage died in 1619, a funeral elegy recorded the audience reaction to his art:

> whilst he but seemed to bleed,
> amaz'd, thought even then he died indeed.[13]

He achieved what every actor strives for; to be utterly convincing, truthful, and believable. This is exactly what the Lord in the Induction to *The Taming of the Shrew* praises a player for—his role was "naturally performed" (line 85). What Shakespeare's company sought to avoid, in the writing as well as the acting, was the situation Fabian describes in *Twelfth Night* (Act 3, scene 4, line 128): "If this were plaid upon a stage now, I could condemn it as an improbable fiction."

A current trend in modern theatre is called "actioning" the text, and this has been championed and effectively employed by the distinguished British director Max Stafford-Clark. In essence it requires the actor to choose a transitive or active verb and apply it to each line, thought, or phrase to give them an action. As an example, take Juliet's mother in Act 3, scene 5, saying to her daughter, "I have done with thee." Juliet has refused to follow her advice and marry Paris, and the actor will connect an action to this line. It could be "disgust," "distress," "discredit," "disown," "dismiss," "discomfort," "disillusion." ... to use just a few words that begin with the letter *D* followed by an "is." There are hundreds of possibilities and the action will be different, and the line sound different, depending on the choice. Speaking the line with an attached action makes it specific, tonally distinct, and avoids generalization. There are volumes of "action" words printed in actor's thesaurus to help the performers choose the unique word they require. In his groundbreaking book *Soul of the Age*, Jonathan Bate quotes Montaigne, whose work Shakespeare was very familiar with, on how to express oneself using the hands. The list of options he gives sound remarkably like those found in an actors' thesaurus for actioning the text:

> threaten, pray, beseech, deny, refuse, demand, admire, confess, repent, fear, doubt, instruct, command, incite, encourage, swear, accuse, condemn, absolve, injure, despise, defy, despite, flatter, applaud, bless, humble, mock, reconcile, recommend, exalt, rejoice, complain, wail, sorrow, discomfort, despair, forbid.[14]

To use a further example, this time taking words from Montaigne's list as a kind of thesaurus, here are some actions that could be attached to probably the most famous line in the English language: "To be, or not to be, that is the question." If the word "fear" is chosen, then Hamlet becomes frightened at the thought of possible death or suicide. Choose the word "mock" and Hamlet becomes a cynic. "Incite" shows us a Hamlet ready to take on the world while "admire" leads him back to an earlier discovery, "What a piece of work is a man!"[15] (The exclamation point at the end of this line is, for once, folio punctuation.)

With Shakespeare's language there's often no need to consult an Actor's Thesaurus as the action words are provided within the script. Here are a few lines from the folio version of Hamlet's "To be or not to be" speech (Act 3, scene 1, line 56.) The possible words that might action it are inserted in brackets before the text. This is only a *possible* reading in order to demonstrate how an actor using this method *could* approach the speech and is not necessarily how the text should be delivered. The three different words/phrases indicate the different approaches to actioning that are used in professional theatre.

Hamlet.
(**Tentatively, doubt, I query**) To be, or not to be, that is the Question:
(**Reverently, dignify, I wonder**) Whether 'tis Nobler in the minde to suffer
(**Wildly, abandon, I release**) The Slings and Arrowes of (**Frustratingly, rebuff, I reject**) outragious Fortune,
(**Defiantly, confront, I oppose**) Or to take Armes against a Sea of troubles,
And by opposing end them: (**Desperately, surrender, I accept**) to dye, to sleepe
(**Aggressively, challenge, I contest**) No more; (**Sadly, despair, I reflect**) and by a sleepe, to say we end
The Heart-ake, and the thousand Naturall shockes
(**Bitterly, disgust, I shun**) That Flesh is heyre too?

Notice the comma in the folio after the first "To be," and how it can help create a Hamlet at the beginning who is unsure of himself and trying to work things out. The 11-beat opening line, with its feminine ending, does this as well. Is the spelling "too" in the line "That Flesh is heir too?" significant? It is often the setting of "to" in the folio but is perhaps worth considering as a pun.[16] Hamlet is heir to a throne but also, as a man, heir to the natural sufferings of the flesh that affect all humans; sickness as well as sex. Notice as well the folio question mark after "heir too?," which editor/adaptors erase. When Hamlet says "Suit the action to the word, the word to the action," it is usually taken as a plea for the actor physicality to match the words and the delivery of the words to be consistent with the physical action. However, it might also be, in a modern context, a call that each phrase/thought should be accompanied by a specific action so that the delivery of it is varied, precise, and distinct. What is really interesting is that most of the "action" words in this speech stand out as they have capital letters. It should be pointed out that modern actors would only "action" complete lines, thoughts, or phrases, not individual words, and would not break up the text quite as much as has been here done for demonstration purposes. The actions would also be used in conjunction with a scene and speech objective.

There is an example of "actioning" in Act 2, scene 1, line 16, of *Romeo and Juliet* when Romeo is hiding from Mercutio in the orchard before he meets Juliet. Mercutio says (in the folio):

> The Ape is dead, I must conjure him,
> I conjure thee by *Roselines* bright eyes,
> By her High forehead, and her Scarlet lip,
> By her Fine foote, Straight leg, and Quivering thigh,
> And the Demeanes, that there Adjacent lie,
> That in thy likenesse thou appeare to us.

In simple terms Mercutio's action is to conjure[17]; a blasphemous act suitable to his obscene objective "I conjure only but to raise up him"—to give Romeo an erection. Editor/adaptors take a scene break after his exit, but the events are continuous and flow naturally on from each other. Romeo later repeats Mercutio's action of conjuring, although now in an appropriately divine sense that invokes Juliet to appear:

> But soft, what light through yonder window breaks?
> It is the East, and *Juliet* is the Sunne,

> Arise fair Sun and kill the envious Moone,
> Who is already sicke and pale with griefe,
> That thou her Maid art far more faire then she:
> Be not her Maid since she is envious,
> Her Vestal livery is but sicke and greene,
> And none but fooles do weare it, cast it off:
> It is my Lady, O it is my Love, O that she knew she were,
> She speakes, yet she sayes nothing, what of that?[18]

There are number of things to note about this passage. Firstly, that no entrance is given for Juliet in the folio. The Arden text, edited by Brian Gibbons (and almost any other modern edition) follows a stage direction in a single corrupt quarto version of the play and puts it after "Window breaks," but Romeo can scarcely be referring to his beloved as an "it." Juliet clearly appears after Romeo has conjured her; that is, at the end of the verse line "cast it off." He is so amazed to see her that his words spill out in one long 16-beat line—"It is my Lady, O it is my Love, O that she knew she were." Notice, too, how the folio punctuation flows. There are no periods, and Romeo, astonished that he has managed to conjure Juliet's appearance, goes straight to "It is my lady" with the shock of seeing her and rushes on in excitement when he hears her speak. He also clearly states she is at a "Window," probably with a light framing her from behind,[19] to reinforce that she is a celestial being whom Romeo, with the help of God, has conjured. His speech goes on to describe her in those terms just as he had earlier referred to her as a saint. There is no mention of a balcony.[20]

Not everyone approves of "actioning" as a secure methodology in achieving truthful performance. Almost the first words Hamlet utters concern themselves with "actions" although, in the theatrical sense of "actioning," he doesn't appear to support their use. In Act 1, scene 2, line 75, Gertrude asks her son why he seems so particularly affected by the death of his father, and Hamlet replies:

Hamlet.
Seemes Madam? Nay, it is: I know not Seemes:
'Tis not alone my Inky Cloake (good Mother)
Nor Customary suites of solemne Blacke,
Nor windy suspiration of forc'd breath,
No, nor the fruitfull River in the Eye,
Nor the dejected haviour of the Visage,
Together with all Formes, Moods, shewes of Griefe,
That can denote me truly. These indeed Seeme,
For they are actions that a man might play:
But I have that Within, which passeth show;
These, but the Trappings, and the Suites of woe.

This is interesting because Hamlet appears to be saying that "actions" are false—a "show"—and he lists the type of things an actor could employ but still not "denote me truly." These include costume ("my Inky Cloake"), sighing with grief ("forc'd breath"), crying ("the fruitfull River in the Eye"), facial expressions ("the dejected haviour of the Visage"), and general outward appearance ("Formes, Moods"). To Hamlet this is all technique and actor tricks—"Trappings"—actions a player might use and "seem" to portray him accurately but not reach the depth of emotion the inner man feels:

> For they are actions that a man might play:
> But I have that Within, which passeth show;

Hamlet doesn't "seem" to be affected by grief—he feels it truly to the core of his being. The same idea is expressed by Helena in the opening scene of *All's Well That Ends Well* (line 47). The Countess, who is seeing her son Bertram leave home for the first time and depart for Paris, chastises Helena for showing excessive emotion at the memory of the death of her father:

> **Mother.**[21]
> No more of this *Helena,* go too, no
> more least it be rather thought you affect a sorrow, then
> to have—

Helena interjects:

> **Helena.**
> I doe affect a sorrow indeed, but I have it too.

She is saying that the tears she is shedding are indeed "affected" and false if related, as the Countess thinks, to the death of Helena's father, but within her she has a heartfelt and true sorrow at Bertram's departure.

Actions are useful when tied to a simple objective such as the Mercutio/Romeo/Juliet scene in the orchard. They will also undoubtedly shape the tonal quality of lines and phrases and make them specific. Using single words to describe a particular moment might be the spark that is needed to unlock a scene and can be enormously helpful. The criticism of "actioning" as an overall rehearsal process is that it can create a lack of spontaneity in performance. It relies on the other actor playing the "correct" action that matches a reaction, and if this is not delivered the response is lost.[22] In early rehearsals the method might prove a solid "comfort blanket" for performers, but in a long run—unless the actions are adjusted through constant negotiation—it could become binding. As with any technique it can be overtechnical, and the danger is that the actors might end up being what is referred to as "in their head" and lacking true emotional connection.

"Actioning" is almost exclusively used on modern plays, perhaps because it can sometimes be difficult to "action" a line and still observe the meter of the verse, as can be seen in the earlier "To be, or not to be" example. There are a number of schools of thought on how the verse should be spoken. Sometimes, especially in education, sadly, you come across people who say, "Just ignore the verse." This isn't particularly good advice. If the verse wasn't important, one wonders why Shakespeare took such trouble with it when he could easily have written the whole play in prose. In fact, while five plays (if you count *Edward III* as Shakespearean) are entirely in verse, none were written in prose alone. At the other end of the scale sit people such as the director Sir Peter Hall who insist that every line of verse takes precedence over the punctuation (and the sense, some would say). Hall requires his actors to speak verse lines rather than grammatical sentences. To be fair to Peter Hall, he isn't asking for each verse line to be "end stopped" to create a rhythmically contrived delivery. He says there should be a "tiny sense break (*not* a stop)"[23] that marks the meter. Hall explains that Shakespeare "didn't want to be poetic, he wanted to be understood"[24] and calculates that 70 percent of Shakespeare's meaning comes at the end of the verse line—although he doesn't say how he arrived at that figure. Take a speech like "To be, or not to be" and cover it with a sheet of paper so that only the end words can be seen. It gives a pretty accurate description of the complete thrust of speech—"question," "suffer," "fortune," "troubles," "sleep," "end," "shocks," and so on.

A good illustration of Peter Hall's view that the meter provides the meaning can be found in Act 3, scene 2, line 1, of *Romeo and Juliet*. The newly married Juliet is looking forward to consummating her match with Romeo and impatiently waiting for the nurse to return with the rope ladder that will allow her elopement:

Juliet.
Gallop apace, you fiery footed steedes,
Towards *Phaebus* lodging, such a Wagoner
As *Phaeton* would whip you to the west,
And bring in Cloudie night immediately.
Spred thy close Curtaine Love-performing night,
That run-awayes eyes may wincke, and *Romeo*
Leape to these armes, untalkt of and unseene,
Lovers can see to doe their Amorous rights,
And by their owne Beauties: or if Love be blind,
It best agrees with night: come civill night,
Thou sober suted Matron all in blacke,
And learne me how to loose a winning match,
Plaid for a paire of stainlesse Maidenhoods,
Hood my unman'd blood bayting in my Cheekes,
With thy Blacke mantle, till strange Love grow bold,
Thinke true Love acted simple modestie:
Come night, come *Romeo*, come thou day in night,
For thou wilt lie upon the wings of night
Whiter then new Snow upon a Ravens backe:
Come gentle night, come loving blackebrow'd night.
Give me my *Romeo*, and when I shall die,[25]
Take him and cut him out in little starres,
And he will make the Face of heaven so fine,
That all the world will be in Love with night,
And pay no worship to the Garish Sun.
O I have bought the Mansion of a Love,
But not possest it, and though I am sold,
Not yet enjoy'd, so tedious is this day,
As is the night before some Festivall,
To an impatient child that hath new robes
And may not weare them, O here comes my Nurse: *Enter Nurse with cords.*

The folio setting has just three sentences, whereas editor/adaptors break it up into around 13. If the actor takes Peter Hall's advice and observes a sense break—in practical terms a short breath after each verse line—Juliet works herself up so that she almost reaches orgasm. The content of the speech with its 5 mentions of "come," phrases such as "Love-performing night," "Amorous rights," "Whiter than new Snow upon a Ravens backe," "when I shall die," and "Not yet enjoy'd, " the descriptions of stars bursting, and Juliet's "unman'd blood" reddening cheeks, all reinforce her sexual ecstasy. Try it yourself and recite the speech out loud. Take a very short breath after each verse line but, rather than halting, use the folio punctuation to give you momentum so that the speech is delivered with speed. By the end you'll find yourself dizzy!

Romeo and Juliet is one of Shakespeare's earlier plays and, as mentioned before, the verse in the early plays is often fairly regular—the verse line and the sense tending to be consistent. This is not the case with the later plays when there is much more use of enjambment—phrases/thoughts that run on past the verse line and stop at a caesura (punctuation mark) in the next line or further. Peter Hall thinks this a "rarity," but consider this speech from Leontes in Act 1, scene 2, line 185, of a late play, *The Winter's Tale*. Leontes has observed his best friend talking with his wife and this has caused him to suffer an agonized jealousy. The thoughts and the verse are appropriately disjointed to reflect the turmoil of his mind:

Leontes.
Gone already,
Ynch-thick, knee-deepe; ore head and eares a fork'd one.
Goe play (Boy) play: thy Mother playes, and I
Play too; but so disgrac'd a part, whose issue
Will hisse me to my Grave: Contempt and Clamor
Will be my Knell. Goe play (Boy) play, there have been
(Or I am much deceiv'd) Cuckolds ere now,
And many a man there is (even at this present,
Now, while I speake this) holds his Wife by th' Arme,
That little thinkes she ha's been sluyc'd in's absence,
And his Pond fish'd by his next Neighbor (by
Sir *Smile,* his Neighbor:) nay, there's comfort in't,
Whiles other men have Gates, and those Gates open'd
(As mine) against their will. Should all despaire
That have revolted Wives, the tenth of Mankind
Would hang themselves. Physick for't, there's none:
It is a bawdy Planet, that will strike
Where 'tis predominant; and 'tis powrefull: thinke it:
From East, West, North, and South, be it concluded,
No Barricado for a Belly. Know't,
It will let in and out the Enemy,
With bag and baggage: many thousand on's
Have the Disease, and feele't not. How now Boy?

Again the subject is sex—"she ha's been sluyc'd in's absence," "his Pond fish'd by his next Neighbor," and "It will let in and out the Enemy,"—but Leontes's diseased condition stands in stark contrast to Juliet's natural attitudes. The verse is far from being regular; in fact there's a predominance of 11-beat lines or "feminine endings" that emphasize Leontes's weak state. "And many a man there is (even at this present," and "Where 'tis predominant; and 'tis powrefull: thinke it": both have 12/13 beats. But what is a performer to make of lines such as "thy Mother playes, and I/Play too"? Should the actor take Hall's advice so that it is spoken "thy Mother playes, and I—Play too" or to use enjambment so that it sounds something like "thy Mother playes and I Play too"? The director William Gaskill is very clear about this speech: "No actor would pause after 'I' in line three, or 'issue' in line four and certainly not after 'by' in line eleven. The actor must go with the sentences."[26] This is not necessarily true. An actor might choose to take a sense break/short breath at the end of each verse line and work himself into a disordered, breathless state in the same way Juliet did in her "Gallop apace" speech. Peter Hall believes that dislocation in verse, as with Leontes, is the result of *containing* the emotion rather than *expressing* it. So perhaps the meter shows Leontes attempting to stop himself from spilling over into a full-blown consideration of the horror that, in his own mind, he has just witnessed? A descent that might lead to madness.

There's no perfect answer. In this passage the actor and director have a choice and will discover what works best for them in rehearsal. The verse is there to help the actor not as a rigid set of rules, but if it is completely ignored it can lead to confused phrasing and a lack of control. Speaking the language in performance, the actor will need to remember that each new phrase/thought requires a new tone/energy and sometimes this can only be conveyed by using enjambment. On the other hand the verse shouldn't be broken up so that it loses its rhythm and becomes slow and emotionally self-indulgent. Most people will have witnessed performances like this where the actor strives to "sound modern." George Bernard Shaw gave some excellent advice to Ellen Terry that still holds true for contemporary actors:

> In playing Shakespear, play *to* the lines, *through* the lines, *on* the lines, but never between the lines. There simply isn't time for it. You would not stick five bars rest into a Beethoven symphony to pick up your drumsticks; and similarly you must not stop the Shakespear orchestra for business.[27]

Hamlet cannot bear to see this acting "between the lines": "Pox, leave thy damnable Faces, and begin," he impatiently snaps at a an actor.[28]

How did Shakespeare's players approach their scripts? Did they agonize for days and weeks on the verse, their motivations, emotional memories, and actions embedded in the dialogue, as modern actors might do? Polonius praises a player for delivering a speech that was "well spoken, with good accent, and good discretion"[29] so the approach to the language, at least as an objective, appears to be pretty similar. In recent years a lot of excellent research from Patrick Tucker, Tiffany Stern, Don Weingust and others has investigated how Shakespeare incorporated into his texts the methods used by Elizabethan actors in preparing their roles. Principally this has focused on the use of "cue scripts." Shakespeare's actors weren't given the full text of a play but just their part of the script—which is where we get the word "part" from in referring to an actor's role. The word "role" comes from the roll of paper the part was written on. There were a number of reasons for this; paper was expensive and to give someone the whole copy of the play left the company open to the theft of the text that Heminge and Condell wrote of. Handing the actors only the parts they speak in a play—plus the three cue words that prompt their dialogue—is actually a very clever technique for bringing a play alive. We know that Shakespeare's company had very little time for rehearsals—if they rehearsed the plays at all, in the modern sense. However, this in itself can be an advantage. One of the major skills a director must learn is not to give an actor too much information. Ignorance can often be a virtue.[30] If Othello and Emilia, for example, have little idea about the rest of the *Othello* narrative, it can help the actors playing those roles towards a more gradual arc of discovery.[31] The contradiction of contemporary rehearsal is that an enormous amount of time, repetition, and detailed study is spent in order for the actor to become spontaneous in performance. And yet the first thing modern actors do when they receive the text is to turn it into a cue script, highlighting their lines and cues with a marker pen and often leaving the rest of the play untouched.

Using a cue script required from the players the very basics of acting—to listen and react. They had to listen so they could hear their cue line, which was embedded among passages that were not in their scripts. They had no choice but to react because they were probably hearing the words from the other characters for the first time or at least one of the few times they had been spoken. Physically it released their bodies and made them active. They were unfamiliar with who would say their cue line so they had to be physically alive to the other actors onstage with them.[32] How different their performances must have been to the often static modern Shakespearean productions that can seem as if a tariff has been set on the actors' movements. Each player must have instinctively developed his own rhythm for his part, avoiding present-day pitfalls Peter Brook describes as "what often happens in Shakespeare ... everyone shares a generalized rhythm that passes impersonally from one to the other."[33] Shakespeare used this cue script method to his advantage when he wrote his plays. In fact he mentions it in one of them and has Buckingham in *Richard III* say (Act 3, scene 4, line 27):

> Had you not come upon your Q my Lord,
> *William,* Lord *Hastings,* had pronounc'd your part;

Acting from cue scripts has been written about extensively elsewhere, so here are just two examples identified by Patrick Tucker in his work as the director of the Original Shakespeare Company.[34] (However, there are countless others.) The first is the Nurse in *Romeo and Juliet*. She has a long speech in Act 1, scene 3, line 16, that describes Juliet as a child, and both Juliet and her mother want to stop the Nurse and get back to the point, which is Juliet's imminent marriage to Paris. A director might say to the actors in this scene "Try to interrupt the Nurse at certain moments." *Shakespeare writes that acting note into the text.* He gives both Juliet and her mother the same cue lines within the Nurse's speech. The actors hear their cue lines and attempt to interrupt too early—the Nurse carries on over them. It will immediately be noticed that whereas editor/adaptors place the Nurse's speech in verse, the folio uses the much more free-flowing prose. This is a passage with the cue line, which is **"and said I"** (**"Aye,"**) highlighted in bold:

Nurse.
...and since that time it is
a eleven yeares, for then she could stand alone, nay bi'th'
roode she could have runne, & wadled all about: for even
the day before she broke her brow, & then my Husband
God be with his soule, a was a merrie man, tooke up the
Child, yea quoth hee, doest thou fall upon thy face? thou
wilt fall backeward when thou hast more wit, wilt thou
not *Jule?* And by my holy-dam, the pretty wretch lefte
crying, **& said I**: to see now how a jest shall come about.
I warrant, & I shall live a thousand yeares, I never should
forget it: wilt thou not *Julet* quoth he? and pretty foole it
stinted, **and said I.**

Old Lady.
Inough of this, I pray thee hold thy peace.

Nurse.
Yes Madam, yet I cannot chuse but laugh, to
thinke it should leave crying, **& say I**: and yet I warrant
it had upon it brow, a bumpe as big as a young Cockrels

stone? A perilous knock, and it cryed bitterly. Yea quoth
my husband, fall'st upon thy face, thou wilt fall back-ward
when thou commest to age: wilt thou not *Jule?* It
stinted: **and said I.**

Juliet.
And stint thou too, I pray thee *Nurse,* say I.

Here's a second cue script example, again using the folio text and identified by Tucker, of an actor being given his cue line early so that he will attempt to interrupt. This is Bottom as Piramus in Act 3, scene 1, line 84, of *A Midsummer Night's Dream*. Bottom is rehearsing a play and both the *character's* cue line and the actor's cue line are the same. The cue words highlighted are **"Never tyre"** ("tire"):

Thysbe.
Must I speake now?

Peter.
I marry must you. For you must understand he
goes but to see a noyse that he heard, and is to come
againe.

Thysbe.
Most radiant *Piramus,* most Lilly white of hue,
Of color like the red rose on triumphant bryer,
Most brisky Juvenall, and eke most lovely Jew,
As true as truest horse, that yet would **never tyre,**
Ile meete thee *Piramus,* at *Ninnies* toombe.

Peter.
Ninus toombe man: why, you must not speak
that yet; that you answer to *Piramus:* you speak all
your part at once, cues and all. *Piramus* enter, your cue is
past; it is **never tyre.**

Thysbe.
O, as true as truest horse, that yet would **never**
tyre:

Piramus.
If I were faire, *Thisby* I were onely thine.

The third time Bottom appears in the scene he is wearing an ass's head, and it's a neat theatrical trick to have him enter twice before without it.

Cue scripts are not the perfect answer when performing the works of Shakespeare. In fact, Original Shakespeare productions were dropped by London's Globe Theatre in 1999 because artistic director Mark Rylance found them "extremely amateur."[35] There are arguments against Shakespeare's company having little rehearsal time and using cue scripts. The Mechanicals in *A Midsummer Night's Dream*, although not professional, have at least two rehearsals; Burbage appears as a character in the anonymous contemporary play *The Return from Parnassus*, auditioning students whom he tells "A little teaching will mend these faults" (Act 4, scene 3)[36]; and a player in *The Knight of the Burning Pestle* (a King's Men production) answers a request to perform a different play with "Oh, you should have told us your mind a month since" (Induction: line 31).[37] So perhaps Shakespeare's players didn't differ too greatly from those of today? Nonetheless, cue script adherents make some valuable insights that an actor should have the option of ignoring or embracing. You won't find such notes appearing in the texts prepared by editor/adaptors.

The next section, expanding points raised in this chapter, examines how Shakespeare's experience of performing helped him to create a character that is the perfect example of a modern actor—Iago.

6

Character as Actor

"I can counterfeit the deep tragedian"

One area where academics regularly stray into the territory usually occupied by actors is seeking motivations for Iago's behavior in *Othello*. It is an easy, but not altogether productive, game to play. One could say, for example, that the starting point of the play, and therefore Iago's actions, is the fact that he was overlooked for promotion. There's a modern precedent for this. Pierre Chanal, a homosexual soldier in the French army, went on a killing spree of young men in the 1980s. It was thought that Chanal's position of authority (like Iago, a sergeant) deluded him into thinking he could do anything he wanted. The FBI Behavioral Science Unit categorized him as "obsessive and sadistic" with "aberrant sexual conduct that leads him to seek pleasure by inflicting humiliation and suffering on others."[1] Could this also be a description of Iago? Of course not. He's much more complicated than that.

Unlike the two dukes of Gloucester, Richard and Edmund, Iago does not have one singular motivation. Edmund is very clear in his objective from the very beginning of *King Lear*—"Legitimate Edgar, I must have your land"[2]—and despite the machinations of both Goneril and Regan to elevate him higher, he shows little ambition to join them in this endeavor. Richard III's motivations actually begin in an earlier play, *Henry VI, Part 3* (Act 3, scene 2, line 168):

> Ile make my Heaven, to dreame upon the Crowne,
> And whiles I live, t'account this World but Hell,
> Untill my mis-shaped Trunke, that beares this Head,
> Be round impaled with a glorious Crowne.

He tells the audience what he wants and then sets out to achieve it. Once he gains the "glorious crown," he lacks further motivation beyond remaining as king and, shorn of an objective, his decline begins. In comparison Iago seems to have a whole book of motivations, some of which are listed below in the order they appear in the narrative:

1. He hates Othello for failing to promote him as lieutenant (Act 1, scene 1); "I hate the Moore" (Act 1, scene 3, line 385). To gain an idea of the scale of the snub, it should be remembered that the cowardly Pistol, like Iago, is an "Ancient."
2. He hates Cassio for taking the position of lieutenant in his place (Act 1, scene 1) and wants him removed from that position—"If such tricks as these strip you out of your lieutenantrie" (Act 2, scene 1, line 171).

3. He does it for fun—"If thou canst Cuckold him, thou does thy selfe a pleasure, me a sport" (Act 1, scene 3, line 369).
4. He does it for money—"Thus do I ever make my Foole, my purse" (Act 1, scene 3, line 382).
5. He feels humiliated and belittled that people believe him to be a cuckold—"And it is thought abroad, that 'twixt my sheets/He ha's done my Office. I know not if't be true,/But I, for meere suspition in that kinde,/Will do, as if for Surety" (Act 1, scene 3, line 386).
6. He's jealous of Cassio's good looks and success with women—"the knave is handsome, young: and have all those requisites in him, that folly and greene mindes looke after" (Act 2, scene 1, line 243); "He hath a dayly beauty in his life,/That makes me ugly" (Act 5, scene 1, line 19).
7. He loves Desdemona—"Now I do love her too,/Not out of absolute Lust, (though peradventure/I stand accomptant for as great a sin)" (Act 2, scene 1, line 289).
8. He believes Othello is sleeping with his wife—"For that I do suspect the lustie Moore/Hath leap'd into my Seate. The thought whereof,/Doth (like a poysonous minerall) gnaw my Inwardes:/And nothing can, or shall content my Soule/Till I am eevened with him, wife, for wift" (Act 2, scene 1, line 293).
9. He believes Cassio is sleeping with his wife—"(For I feare *Cassio* with my Night-cape too)" (Act 2, scene 1, line 305).
10. He is sexually impotent (his only truly sexual thoughts are in a dream) and believes his wife has given birth to a bastard child. This latter idea is entirely a matter of interpretation, especially of Act 2, scene 1, line 135. Emilia says, "How if Faire, and Foolish?," and if Iago's reply is directed back at her, he bitterly exclaims, "She never yet was foolish that was faire" (Desdemona is fair and has not been unfaithful, Emilia dark and unfaithful); "For even her folly helpt her to an heire." Emilia's folly in having sexual relationships outside of marriage led to the birth of a child. If Iago knows he is impotent, then the child couldn't be his. Perhaps tellingly, Emilia is silent for the rest of the scene. At the end of the exchange, line 161, Desdemona's reaction to Iago's behavior is, "Oh most lame and impotent conclusion."
11. He has a general hatred of women, evidenced by his behavior throughout the play but particularly in his attitude towards Emilia and the "trash" Bianca. It might also be thought that he has a distaste for the sexual act: "This is the fruits of whoring" (Act 5, scene 1, line 116), and the fact that his marriage to Emilia appears to be childless. This interpretation depends in part on whether Iago is to be believed when he tells the audience "Not out of absolute Lust, (though peradventure/I stand accomptant for as great a sin)." Having lustful thoughts, however, is different from carrying them out.
12. He loves Othello—"Make the Moore thanke me, love me, and reward me" (Act 2, scene 1, line 306). This becomes more apparent in the "Marriage Ceremony" in Act 3, scene 3, beginning line 466, "Witnesse that heere *Iago* doth give up/The execution of his wit, hands, heart,/To wrong'd *Othello*'s service," and ending at line 482 with Iago's "I am your owne forever."
13. He loves Cassio—"I lay with *Cassio* lately.... And then (Sir) would he gripe, and wring my hand:/Cry, oh sweet Creature: and then kisse me hard,/As if he pluckt up

kisses by the rootes,/That grew upon my lippes, laid his Leg ore my Thigh,/And sigh, and kisse, ..." (Act 3, scene 3, line 416). Iago says this was Cassio's dream, but it could equally be interpreted, especially in performance, as Iago's dream, or fantasy. And there's no evidence to contradict that it actually happened.

14. He is simply, as the folio "Names of the Actors" describes him, "A Villaine." The text partially contradicts this. When Othello, now fully aware of the events that have led him to kill Desdemona, confronts Iago in Act 5, scene 2, he says at line 283: "I look downe towards his feet; but that's a Fable." So Iago isn't a devil with hoofed feet. However, he continues: "If that thou bee'st a Divell, I cannot kill thee." Despite the attack from Othello's sword of Spain, Iago isn't killed: are we to assume he is then the Devil? Later in the scene, at line 298, Othello calls him a "demy-Divell," which might be more correct.

It's interesting that the one motivation Iago doesn't appear to have is racial hatred. In fact Emilia is far more racist towards Othello.[3] At the very least, the actor playing Iago has 14 motivations to inspire his conduct—which might be a surprise to literary-minded commentators such as Levin L. Schucking, who confidently states, "In no department of Shakespeare's art do we find such irregularity as in his dealing with the motives for action."[4]

Which of these motivations should the actor choose? Even if some can be discounted, most are clearly there in the text. And many contradict themselves—does Iago love or hate Othello, love or hate Cassio, is his objective promotion, money, or fun? Shakespeare seems to have deliberately embraced this ambiguity. When Iago is asked directly to explain his actions, he gives an opaque reply (Act 5, scene 2, line 300): "What you know, you know," and never speaks again. Emilia's conclusion (Act 3, scene 4, line 159) is that people like Iago have *no* motivation:

> But Jealous soules will not be answer'd so;
> They are noter jealious for the cause,
> But jealious, for they're jealious. It is a Monster
> Begot upon it selfe, borne on it selfe.

This chimes with what Coleridge termed Iago's "motiveless malignity." All very well, but how is the actor to play this? In order to portray a role truthfully, actors need to be clear on a character's motivations and objectives. Even if jealousy inspired Iago's conduct, an actor cannot play a generalized "envy" but needs to be specific in his responses to each and every event. "Identity" is the key that can help unlock this puzzle.

In many of Shakespeare's plays, characters and situations become confused because the protagonists lack an identity or feel their identity has been usurped by someone else. Nowhere is this more evident than in Act 1, scene 2, line 33 of *The Comedy of Errors*. Here we have two sets of twins who cannot exist until they find their brother:

Antipholus of Syracuse.
He that commends me to mine owne content,
Commends me to the thing I cannot get:
I to the world am like a drop of water,
That in the Ocean seekes another drop,
Who falling there to finde his fellow forth,
(Unseene, inquisitive) confounds himselfe.

So I, to finde a Mother and a Brother,
In quest of them (unhappie a[5)] loose my selfe.

It's not just the twins who lose themselves. Egeon seeks to be a father but has failed to find the sons that would identify him as that, Adriana cannot be a wife without a husband, and Emilia is forced to take on the role of Mother Superior rather than mother because she is a woman bereft of her children. *The Comedy of Errors* is an early play, but the theme persists in the later *Anthony and Cleopatra*. When Mark Anthony pursues the retreating Cleopatra's ship at the height of battle, he realizes, "I have fled my selfe."[6] Cleopatra literally has to rebuild him by strapping on his armor before he can resume the character of a warrior and live up to his earlier proclamation that "I am *Anthony* yet."[7] Of course it's just a fiction, a role he plays, and ultimately he loses the war against Octavius. When this happens, he once again is deprived of a sense of himself: "Heere I am *Anthony,*/Yet cannot hold this visible shape."[8] Cleopatra tries to keep his image alive by remembering him with a eulogy:

Cleopatra.
His legges bestrid the Ocean, his rear'd arme
Crested the world: His voyce was propertied
As all the tuned Spheres, and that to Friends:
But when he meant to quaile, and shake the Orbe,
He was as ratling Thunder. For his Bounty,
There was no winter in't. An *Anthony* it was,
That grew the more by reaping.[9]

She asks Dolabella, "Thinke you there was, or might be such a man/As this I dreampt of?" to which he simply answers: "Gentle Madam, no." The character Anthony has created for himself never existed; it was as ephemeral a dream.

There are numerous examples of Shakespearean characters who assume an alternate persona in order to survive: Kent, Edgar, Duke Vincentio, Viola, Innogen, Rosalind, Helena, Julia—even the lady Macbeth "unsexes" herself. The characters become actors and this causes them problems. Despite professing "(by the verie phangs of malice, I sweare) I am not that I play,"[10] Viola has to learn to cope with the fact that "I am the man."[11] This is the danger of acting, which is a kind of madness in that the individual becomes possessed. As William Hazlitt wrote of actors in his 1817 essay "On Actors and Acting," "Their life is a voluntary dream; a studied madness."[12]

The idea of acting as a type of "madness" is perhaps most evident in Richard of Gloster. Like Antipholus of Syracuse, he feels he is "scarse half made up" and compensates for this by taking on various roles. Richard ambles through two plays (quoted below, *Henry VI, Part 3*, Act 3, scene 2, line 184) gleefully boasting of his skill as an actor who can:

wet my Cheekes with artificiall Teares,
And frame my Face to all occasions.

But this does for him in the end. The role of king he conspired to be cast as is not one that naturally fits, and in gaining it he loses his familiar identity. Richard becomes schizophrenic, as can be seen in this brilliant speech from Act 5, scene 3, line 182, of *Richard III*, which is beautifully punctuated in the First Folio. He is now two people, conversing in a split personality and obsessing about "self," which he repeats 13 times in 23 lines ("I" is mentioned 14 times and "My" or "Me" 16):

Richard.[13]
Cold fearefull drops stand on my trembling flesh.
What? do I feare my Selfe? There's none else by,
Richard loves *Richard,* that is, I am I.
Is there a Murtherer heere? No; Yes, I am:
Then flye; What from my Selfe? Great reason: why?
Lest I Revenge. What? my Selfe upon my Selfe?
Alacke, I love my Selfe. Wherefore? For any good
That I my Selfe, have done unto my Selfe?
O no. Alas, I rather hate my Selfe,
For hatefull Deeds committed by my Selfe.
I am a Villaine: yet I Lye, I am not.
Foole, of thy Selfe speake well: Foole, do not flatter.
My Conscience hath a thousand severall Tongues,
And every Tongue brings in a severall Tale,
And everie Tale condemnes me for a Villaine;
Perjurie, in the high'st Degree,
Murther, sterne murther, in the dyr'st degree,
All severall sinnes, all us'd in each degree,
Throng all to th' Barre, crying all, Guilty, Guilty.
I shall dispaire, there is no Creature loves me;
And if I die, no soule shall pittie me.
Nay, wherefore should they? Since that I my Selfe,
Finde in my Selfe, no pittie to my Selfe.

Richard has achieved, tragically, the goal of any actor, which is to create the conditions whereby, as Constantin Stanislavski wrote, "You will be incapable of distinguishing between yourself and the person you are portraying."[14] Stanislavski's work with the Moscow Art Theatre at the turn of the 20th century and his books *An Actor Prepares, Building a Character, Creating a Role,* and *My Life in Art,* are probably the single biggest influence on modern acting and led to the rise of the present day "Method" actor.

Iago, like Richard, has a number of soliloquies, but they are enigmatic and the audience is never entirely sure whether to believe him or, indeed, if he believes what he says himself. There are 3 soliloquies in the first half, but in the second, apart from 9 lines explaining the handkerchief plot, there are none. Take away the boasting and bravado and he actually tells us very little. And what he reveals at one point is negated by a later conflicting statement. That is, apart from one short line—"I am not what I am." It comes at the end of a speech in the very first scene of the play (line 63) and is almost a *non sequitur:*

> But I will weare my heart upon my sleeve
> For Dawes to pecke at; I am not what I am.

This is interesting because it is exactly the same description the disguised Viola makes of herself in Act 3, scene 1, line 138, of *Twelfth Night*: "I am not what I am." In other words, the character that is seen by other people is not who Iago and Viola truly are. Sartre, in his book *Being and Nothingness,* categorized three states of being—the body for me (who I think I am), the body for the other (the image I project), and the body seen by the other (how people perceive me).[15] Generally, the first two categories have an element of free will, but how people perceive us is outside our control. Iago's desire is the ultimate power, Sartre's third state of being: the ability to influence how people perceive him. To do this he must bury his own personality—who he thinks he is, the image he projects—and become another. Or a number of others. Iago lacks a coherent motivation because he lacks a consistent character. He is the ultimate actor; out of nothingness he is able to conjure multifaceted beings. This is something a character in one of Shakespeare's other plays had recognized. Richard II contemplates, "Thus play I in one Prison, many people."[16]

One of the great essays on acting is "The Paradox of the Actor" written by Denis Diderot in 1769. It has become unfashionable in modern times because it seems to be a slight on actors, although this was never his intention. Diderot proposes that in order to truthfully portray a character, actors must subvert any character of their own:

> Perhaps it is just because he is nothing that he is before all everything. His own special shape never interferes with the shapes he assumes.... It has been said that actors have no character, because in playing all characters they lose that which nature gave them ... they are fit to play all characters because they have none.[17]

Hazlitt supports Diderot's view: "It is only when they are themselves, that they are nothing."[18]

Both Richard II and Edgar are conscious of the fact that to successfully play the role they desire, they must give up whatever "special shape" they have and become nothing. Edgar, before transforming into the "studied madness" of Poor Tom, declares, "Edgar I nothing am,"[19] while the play-acting King Richard II gives a typically ambiguous response when he is asked if he will give up the Crown: "I, no; no, I: for I must nothing bee."[20] The pun on "I/Aye" meaning "yes" and "myself" shows us a character who both wants and doesn't want something. In a more complex sense, he is also suggesting that up until that point he has played the role of king badly. Once he is "nothing," he can truly inhabit the character. From this point in the play, Richard never behaves more like a king than when he is "nothing" and no longer the monarch. The man who usurps him, Henry Bullingbrooke, knows that he has never been able to perform his stolen part with any degree of truth: "For all my Reigne, hath beene but as a Scene/Acting that argument."[21]

This idea of "nothingness" is a recurrent Shakespearean theme and is sometimes linked to the fear of a loss of masculinity. In basic terms a man has a "thing"—a penis—while a woman has a vagina—"no-thing."[22] The horror of impotency and the attendant "no-thing" that comes with it haunts Leontes, Anthony, and Macbeth, among others, and is present in the sonnets. Coriolanus seems to reject not just Rome but his masculine self when he enters into a complex (pseudo sexual?) relationship with Aufidius: "Wife, Mother, Child, I know not. My affaires/Are Servanted to others."[23] Cominius observes of Coriolanus that he is now "a kinde of Nothing"[24] ("Nothing" is capitalized in the First Folio). Rosalind, on the other hand, has the opposite desire, a return to womanhood, and says "I will weepe for nothing."[25] However, in spite of Emilia's comments about jealous people, Iago actually displays little sign of the passionate jealousy and fear of "nothing" that consumes Othello: "Othello's Occupation's gone."[26] He is fairly cool in relating to the audience his suspicion of Emilia's extramarital relations with Othello (Emilia confirms his imaginings), and although he claims the thought "Doth ... gnaw my Inwardes,"[27] we never see any physical evidence of this and as a possible motive for action it is quickly dropped. This supposed infidelity has no impact on the plot. Iago kills Emilia to stop her from revealing his scheming not because of her suspected unfaithfulness. He embraces nothingness because it allows him to be all things. To be all things he becomes an actor.

But which of the 14 incidents for action listed above does Iago believe? Probably all of them *at the moment he thinks them.* When he is prompted to explain his behavior, it might be said that he genuinely believes what he says:

Iago.[28]
I told him what I thought,
And told no more
Than what he found himselfe was apt, and true.[29]

What he has told Othello is true, but it is a stage truth, prompted by circumstances. "Stage truth is that in which the actor sincerely believes,"[30] wrote Stanislavski. Something similar may be seen today when criminals, faced with overwhelming evidence of their guilt, still deny any wrongdoing and ardently profess their innocence. Often they will have broken down in tears at a press conference held to remember the victim(s) while simultaneously being responsible for committing the crime. Tabloid newspapers will label them something like "callous monsters," but although they may be monsters there's no conscious attempt to be callous. Like the actor Iago they have set their minds in a place where they can sincerely believe in a fiction.

The job of the actor is to live in an imagined present. There will be moments when their characters carry out an *action*—placing the handkerchief in Cassio's chamber is a good example—and others when there is a *reaction* to an event—the unforeseen arrival of Bianca with the same handkerchief prompting Iago to incorporate her into his deception.[31] What Iago is brilliant at is committing to each moment. If we examine his behavior moment by moment, it will be seen what a truly great actor he is. The first thing to notice is that it is not Iago who begins the chain of events with an action but rather he reacts to somebody else's needs. Rodorigo has the opening lines of the play, and it is Rodorigo's reaction to Desdemona's marriage to Othello that Iago has to respond to. Although it is also revealed that Cassio has been promoted over his head, Iago has no plan to deal with that: "Why, there's no remedie./'Tis the cursse of Service." The marriage and the promotion are circumstances outside of his control, and Iago's simple objective at this stage is to rouse Brabantio in order to "poison" Othello's "delight." However, he also says "I follow him, to serve my turne upon him." When events change, his reactions will change too. At this present moment, Iago plays the dual roles of friend to Rodorigo and enemy of Othello. In the next scene the roles have been reversed so that he is now friend to Othello and enemy of Rodorigo. The description of how he dealt with Rodorigo's words about Othello is a lie, but his dialogue is in character for "Honest Iago," the loyal subordinate, and much else of what he says is true. He warns Othello that Brabantio "will divorce you" and there is indeed an attempt to do this, which might on another occasion have succeeded had it not been for the crisis in Cyprus. Iago's actions in the play support the self-revelation "I hold it very stuffe o'th' conscience/To do no contriv'd Murder: I lacke Iniquitie/Sometime to do me service." He will not commit a murder (although he will contrive to get others to murder for him). The two deaths he personally carries out were not planned. Rodorigo is disposed of after his botched attack on Cassio leaves him vulnerable to exposing Iago's part in the assault and Emilia is killed as an instinctive reaction to her unmasking her husband. Neither are done out of a "contrived" or premeditated malice but rather the need to survive.

What actors must always do is listen and watch carefully so they can react with conviction, although some will, frustratingly, act in isolation. In the first scene with Othello, Iago begins to form his narrative and store away things he has heard for a later part of his play. He is not responsible for Brabantio's racism and dream/nightmare of Desdemona's betrayal or that her father will cut off all ties with her when she marries Othello. However, Iago will make use of these events. He has the magpie instinct of an actor and steals the "wronged" parent's lines. Brabantio claims that Desdemona was:

> So opposite to Marriage, that she shun'd
> The wealthy curled Deareling of our Nation,[32]

Iago remembers this and in a later scene reminds Othello of her behavior:

> Not to affect many proposed Matches
> Of her owne Clime, Complexion, and Degree,
> Whereto we see in all things, Nature tends.[33]

When we see Iago again, it is in the long Act 1, scene 3, where he says little and is absent for part of it. He is invisible to the major players—he has made himself "nothing"—but is actively listening and picks up useful knowledge such as an apparent difference of opinion in the Othello/Desdemona union. Whereas she clearly has a need for sex, "the Rites for why I love him, are bereft me": Othello wishes to be "bounteous to her minde." If their relationship is not sexual (Iago takes the opportunity to interrupt any possible coupling with the riot in Cyprus) it's easy to imagine that she is having sex elsewhere, away from the marital bed. Another snippet of information is gleaned from Brabantio, who tells Othello:

> Look to her (Moore) if thou hast eies to see:
> She ha's deceiv'd her Father, and may thee.

Iago repeats this back to Othello in Act 3, scene 3, line 209: "She did deceive her Father, marrying you." What Iago is engaging in is the actor task of research. An actor will often go through a play and make three lists: What I say about myself, what I say about others, what others say about me. However, Iago is doing this not to analyze his own character but the characters of others. Once he has a fully developed idea of who a character is, then he can use his research to exert pressure on their weakest points. Rodorigo, for example, thinks money will solve everything, Cassio has a problem with drink, and Emilia will do anything to make Iago her husband again. It is the characters he has been unable to study in depth, such as Lodovico and Bianca, who cause his plots to unravel.

Having been quiet, or "nothing," throughout Act 1, scene 3, Iago springs to life in a new guise at its close, demonstrating how adept he is at handling the tricky actor problem of status. In the scenes with Othello he had adopted a suitably low status, but now, with Rodorigo, he creates what in theatre is called a parent/child relationship. It is Iago, of course, who is the parent, and he treats Rodorigo to advice worthy of Capulet to Juliet, Polonius to Ophelia, or Brabantio to Desdemona:

> Vertue? A figge, 'tis in our selves that we are
> thus, or thus.

And "Love":

> It is meerly a Lust of the blood, and a permission
> of the will.

At the very end of Act 1, scene 3, after about 20 percent of the action in the play has passed, Iago finally has a soliloquy, but it is a list of stated facts rather than a character revelation. He tells us Rodorigo is his "fool" whom he will use to get money, he hates Othello and suspects him of sleeping with Emilia, he will keep in character as the friend of Othello, he wants the job for which he was passed over, Cassio is "fram'd to make women false," and Othello is gullible. These are more the rough notes for a script than a fully-worked-out plan. The major plot point of his play will be to persuade Othello that Desdemona is having an affair with Cassio. The detail has not yet been thought through, but it will happen "after some time." As with any good playwright, the idea is "engendered" and he will now let it rest and see how it develops.

The journey to Cyprus provides Iago with what any actor craves—an audience. His gender immediately gives him a higher status among the women on the quayside and he takes advantage of this to perform a series of epigrams in his new role as sparkling wit; a "ladies' man." However, the text is not his own, he is quoting, playing the parts of both lover and clown. It's interesting that despite Desdemona's put-down of him ("Oh most lame and impotent conclusion"), he seems to bear her no malice and certainly has no plans for her death. Ambiguity is the subject of the next chapter, but it should be pointed out that it is possible for an actor to convey Iago's sense of affection for Desdemona while simultaneously involving her in his schemes. He later reveals, "I do love her too,/Not out of absolute Lust"[34] ("absolute" meaning "as simple a thing as"). Cassio, on the other hand, who has usurped Iago's position of alpha male, he now decides to bring down alongside Othello. This might also be the moment, having seen Cassio's over-friendly welcoming of Emilia, that the seeds are sown for Iago's suspicion, "I feare *Cassio* with my Night-Cape too."[35] (The use of italics is how the First Folio prints names rather than a word that needs to be stressed.) With the arrival of Othello safe from the storm, Iago once again retreats into "nothing"; a loyal servant who is neither greeted nor acknowledged but given the offhand instruction to deal with the luggage. What he observes in his silence is significant. Othello's greeting to Desdemona is "O, my faire Warriour." This is a gender reversal that Iago can later use to stir Othello's fear of "no-thing" and impotency and to point out to Cassio—who has also witnessed the exchange—"Our General's Wife, is now the Generall."[36]

There follows a mirror scene with Rodorigo, but this time the status is that of teacher/pupil as Iago now issues instructions for a specific action; Rodorigo is to engage Cassio in a fight that will cause Cyprus to mutiny and Cassio to lose his place. First though, Iago must convince (an actioning word) Rodorigo that Cassio is in love with Desdemona and she with him. In the soliloquy after the scene Iago says: "That *Cassio* loves her, I do well beleev't." His hunch is right, and he later teases from Cassio the information that he thinks her "perfection." Desdemona is a different matter: "That she loves him, 'tis apt, and of great Credite." "Credit" means it is credible and "apt" appropriate or likely. The foremost teacher of acting in the 20th century, Constantin Stanislavski, writes of the "given circumstances" in a situation that will lead to truthful playing, and Iago is efficient when listing these: Desdemona has fallen for Othello's wild stories about himself rather than the man he truly is, he is older than her, the heat of sexual love will soon die, and they are from different races and classes, which (in Iago's view) is against nature. An actor will translate these circumstances into the "Creative If" (also known as the "Magic If") and behave as if they were true. Stanislavski explains:

In precisely the same way as a child believes in the existence of its doll and the life in and around it—when the "if" appears, the actor is transported from real life into another life that he has built in his imagination. Once he believes in it, he can begin to be creative.[37]

In Iago's actor imagination, the Cassio/Desdemona relationship has a stage truth that he can absolutely believe in.

There is an evaluation of Cassio that Iago makes in the scene which has no veracity given events in the play. In this, like Richard III, he demonstrates that the state of "nothingness" can lead to a split personality. He projects his own "character" onto Cassio because Iago is now a different being. This description of Cassio, an audience might say, is actually an accurate summary of Iago but rather it is an outline of one of Iago's many selves:

> A slipper, and subtle knave, a finder of occasion:
> that ha's[38] an eye can stampe, and counterfeit Advantages,
> though true Advantage never present it selfe.[39]

At the moment he says it, this is not him. He is now playing a different role and has a different identity. The scene is brought to its conclusion by Iago's second soliloquy. In order to address the audience he must drop any previous characters and speak as "himself." This proves difficult and is a good example of what Hazlitt meant when he offered his opinion about actors, "It is only when they are themselves, that they are nothing." Lacking a character, Iago becomes "confus'd" and does not know "which thing to do." His lines are conflicting, beginning with an extraordinary opinion that seems to completely oppose his previous actions:

> The Moore (how beit that I endure him not)
> Is of a constant, loving, Noble Nature,
> And I dare thinke, he'll prove to *Desdemona*
> A most deere husband.

Each thought he has in the soliloquy is qualified by a counterthought: he cannot endure Othello, but Othello has a "loving Noble nature"; he loves Desdemona, not out of lust (although he is lustful) but only so he can "dyet my Revenge"; he will be "eeven'd" with Othello for sleeping with Emilia, but "fayling so" will make him jealous; Rodorigo will help him bring down Cassio because Iago suspects Cassio is also having an affair with Emilia, yet he will also slander Cassio and this will make the Moor love Iago, whom Iago will then turn mad. There is no clear line or logic to Iago's rambling thoughts because he has no distinctive role to play. Is he the wronged husband, the revenger on Cassio or lover of Othello? The only way out of this conundrum is to create another character for himself and like Richard III he seems "determined to prove a Villaine."[40] ("Prove" in this context means "become.") The closing lines of Iago's speech are worthy of the "baddie" in a Victorian melodrama:

> 'Tis heere: but yet confus'd,
> Knaveries plaine face, is never seene, till us'd.

This is not a role he keeps up for long, and in the very next scene he introduces another new character. On the Cyprus quayside he was a "ladies' man," but Iago is now a "man's man" drinking heavily, leading the singing of songs, and engaging in sexual banter about the boss's wife. He is secure enough in his acting skills to be able to switch parts for a moment and become the "subtle knave" who tells the audience of his plotting. His plan works like his dream (helped by some well placed lies [?] to Montano about Cassio's excessive alcohol consumption), a fight duly occurs, which in turn results in rioting among the Cypriot populace. Othello arrives and immediately Iago mirrors him. The governor/general stops the fight with the words, "Hold for your lives," which Iago translates into "Hold Hoa ... Hold ... hold for shame." In a demonstration of how apparently unified they are in their desires, Othello now mirrors Iago: "Why how now hoa?" Othello wants to know the cause of "this barbarous Brawl." In a telling response, Iago says he will "perswade my selfe,[41] to speake the truth"—like an actor he persuades himself into the role (or "self") of "honest Iago"—and the story he relates is more or less accurate. By way of a defense he once again projects onto Cassio one of his own characters; "Men are Men." This might actually have backfired on Iago and worked, had not Desdemona suddenly turned up—something Iago has no control over—and it is immediately after she appears that Othello decides to make an example of Cassio.

In past scenes Iago has played the parts of friend to Othello and teacher to Rodorigo. He now merges and moderates these two roles into the sympathetic supporter of Cassio. As with Iago's previous admiration for Othello and love of Desdemona, there seems to be a genuine concern for Cassio's welfare. He is totally in character—if he wasn't, then Cassio would see through him. What Iago tells Cassio is not villainous; in fact it's sound practical advice. He is quick to point out to the audience:

> And what's he then,
> That saies I play the Villaine?
> When this advise is free I give, and honest,
> Proball to thinking, and indeed the course
> To win the Moor againe.
>
> How am I then a Villaine,
> To Counsell *Cassio* to this paralell course,
> Directly to his good?

His final major soliloquy is as elusive as its predecessors in uncovering what really makes Iago tick as a person—the word "person," etymologically, is appropriate in that it means "mask." Iago takes great pains to defend himself against any charges of villainy, but as the speech develops he becomes most like Richard III; no doubt with a twinkle in his eye as he challenges the audience to disagree with him. He is not an undefined "nothing" at this moment, floundering around without a role; the choice he has made is to "play the Villaine"—a title in keeping with his description in the cast list of the First Folio. How else is the audience to interpret lines such as:

> Divinitie of hell,
> When divels will the blackest sinnes put on,
> They do suggest at first with heavenly shewes,
> As I do now.

Because he has a fully formed character when making this speech, his argument is consistent, his plan precise, and there are none of the equivocations found in the previous soliloquies. The narrative for the rest of his play is laid out by the "Villaine" in very simple terms: Desdemona is someone who will go out of her way to help others, Othello will do anything for her but has a "weak function" (the fear of impotency and "no-thing" again), so when Desdemona pleads to her husband on Cassio's behalf Iago will:

> powre this pestilence into his eare:
> That she repeales him, for her bodies Lust,

As Peter Quince might say: "Here is a play fitted."[42] Except that there is a character in the script that Iago thought had been cut but who suddenly returns, and he has to deal with the now extraneous Rodorigo. The only thing Iago can do is get rid of him as quickly as possible, and he repeats his desire four times "Retire thee, go…. Away … get thee gone." Rodorigo duly disappears for a third of the play.

A little time passes, but enough for Emilia to notice that Iago has been playing the role of "friend to Cassio" with complete conviction, particularly when it comes to Cassio being stripped of his rank:

> I warrant it greeves my Husband,
> As if the cause were his.

The phrase "As if" takes us back to Stanislavski's words on the power of the "Creative/Magic If" in creating a credible performance, but there is another Stanislavski technique called "Emotion Memory" that Iago is also now using. This allows actors to empathize with their character by recalling similar emotional situations in their own lives that can be applied to events in a play. For Iago to empathize with Cassio's feelings when being demoted, he has only to emotionally recall how he felt when he was passed over for the position of lieutenant. In his own mind, this was as sharp a sleight as being cashiered out of the army. Of course, "Emotion Memory" cannot work in isolation. Stanislavski gives instruction to actors that Iago follows closely:

> You must play yourself. But it will be in an infinite variety of combinations of objectives and given circumstances which you have prepared for your part and which have been smelted in the furnace of your emotion memory.[43]

The next two scenes are crucial to Iago if his play is not to close before the intermission. This is the moment when he will raise the subject of Desdemona's affair, but "Which thing to do?" Should he "play the Villaine" or be "super-subtle"? He chooses the latter and begins with a short exchange that confirms his role as "nothing" or silent servant:

Iago.
Hah? I like not that.
Othello.
What dost thou say.
Iago.
Nothing my Lord;

He behaves exactly "as if" he genuinely suspects there is something going on between Cassio and Desdemona and, as we have seen, the given circumstances make it "probal." If it were true, then the character of "loyal subordinate," rather than seeking to reveal the affair, would want to remain impartial. He would not wish to tell the husband about his suspicions but would do everything he could to relieve Othello's mind. Iago's character therefore doesn't attempt to spill the beans but on the contrary makes a great effort not to reveal his thoughts, as he later explains to Othello:

> It were not for your quiet, nor your good,
> Nor for my Manhood, Honesty, and Wisedome,
> To let you know my thoughts.[44]

Back in silent mode, Iago is watching and listening as Desdemona tests the waters in trying to persuade Othello to reinstate Cassio into the army. She appears to be successful and this causes a potential crisis for Iago, but he stays cool and in character. He has heard her plead:

> What? *Michael Cassio,*
> That came a woing with you? and so many a time
> (When I have spoke of you dispraisingly)
> Hath tane your part,[45]

This provides Iago with the first line of his scene, which is simply to ask Othello to confirm that this is correct. The great acting teacher Lee Strasberg, who developed Stanislavski's work, told his students that if they prepared for the first moment the scene would then play itself. Iago does exactly that, and from this innocuous first question Othello's descent begins. There are three recognizable acting techniques that Iago uses to obtain his objective: truth, emotion memory, and research.

Truth is important if Othello is to believe Iago's words and behavior (and the audience not think Othello a fool). Roma, in David Mamet's play *Glengarry Glen Ross*, advises another character to "always tell the truth. It's the easiest thing to remember,"[46] and this phrase is often used to support Mamet's opinion that actors should simply play the text. Iago seems to be taking Mamet's advice on board and there are a number of examples in this scene when he is consistent in relating the true facts:

> For *Michael Cassio,*
> I dare be sworne, I thinke that he is honest.
>
> Utter my Thoughts? Why say, they are vild, and falce?
>
> Though I perchance am vicious in my guesse
> (As I confesse it is my Natures plague
> To spy into Abuses, and of my jealousie
> Shapes faults that are not) that your wisdome
> From one, that so imperfectly conceits,
> Would take no notice, nor build your selfe a trouble
> Out of his scattering, and unsure observance:
>
> Good Heaven, the Soules of all my Tribe defend
> From Jealousie.
>
> I speake not yet of proofe:
> I am to pray you, not to straine my speech
> To grosser issues, nor to larger reach,
> Then to Suspicion.
>
> Should you do so (my Lord)
> My speech should fall into such vilde successe,
> Which my Thoughts aym'd not.
> *Cassio's* my worthy friend.
>
> My Lord, I would I might intreat your Honor
> To scan this thing no farther: Leave it to time,
> Let me be thought too busie in my feares,
> And hold her free, I do beseech your Honor.

Notice how the folio use of meter and punctuation works on Othello by giving him a hint that what Iago says is the opposite to what he means—a brilliant double-bluff. It might be said that lines such as the instruction not to take his words "to larger reach,/Then to Suspicion" and to "Leave it to time," as well as the claim that he is concerned "My speech should fall into such vild successe,/Which my Thoughts aym'd not" are all falsehoods, but they are not. Iago wants to poison Othello's mind, and leaving him in the limbo of suspicion over a period of time will surely achieve the stated objective of driving him to madness.

To support this objective, emotion memory is very easy for Iago to call on and he is able to genuinely convey the horror of jealousy to Othello because he has suffered from it himself. For once he is in agreement with his wife and speaks from experience in describing jealousy as "the greene-ey'd Monster, which doth mocke/The meate it feeds on." What, and who, he is jealous of is a matter for debate. In building the dialogue for his part in this scene, Iago employs research[47] to draw on things he has heard and seen thus far.

> Good name in Man, & woman (deere my Lord)
> Is the immediate Jewell of their Soules;

is a neat summing-up of Cassio's views on reputation, and Iago reminds Othello of how Desdemona had reacted to his stories[48]:

> And when she seem'd to shake, and feare your lookes,
> She lov'd them most.

"Seem'd" marks her out as a dissembler, and there is further evidence of this by the act of her elopement to get married:

> Shee that so young could give out such a Seeming
> To seele her Fathers eyes up, close as Oake,

Desdemona has been forward in expressing her sexual needs and Iago uses this to propose that her behavior is typical of all Venetians:

> In Venice, they do let Heaven see the prankes
> They dare not shew their Husbands.

It might be said that there's an emotional truth to these lines if Iago believes his wife is one of those Venetians he describes. He now becomes fully integrated into the role of "Othello's trusty adviser" and—like Nick Bottom—he has the skill and confidence to take on other roles too. It is Emilia who feels herself "nothing," lacking an identity, and without a part in Iago's play: "I nothing, but to please his Fantasie." The word "fantasy" (imagination) is revealing in a modern context (and it will only ever be perceived in a modern context since it is performed to a modern audience) as it suggests an unconventional sexuality—something that will be examined shortly.

Buoyed with the success of his script as it reaches exactly the halfway point, Iago becomes more ambitious and introduces a key prop—Desdemona's handkerchief. It is a beautifully simple visual image of feminine fragility, but to obtain it Iago must give Emilia a more significant part. It is an error in casting since it is Emilia (in her new role as "Desdemona's trusty advisor") who will eventually bring Iago down. The attainment of the handkerchief leads to a short domestic scene between husband and wife in which Iago wants Emilia to be fully aware of the character he is playing—"dissatisfied partner." For once he is "showing" or "demonstrating" the character rather than "being" it, but his behavior is recognizable in life as "truth." A parallel example might be that anyone in a relationship would have suffered at some point from their partner's demonstration of "the silent treatment." From this point on, "nothingness" takes a back seat for Iago. He is secure in the parts he will play, and it is the last time he speaks directly to the audience.

It's perhaps significant that this husband/wife exchange is followed by a similar domestic squabble between Othello and Iago. This is the most curious and ambiguous encounter in the play and is (and has been) open to numerous interpretations. Iago's "pestilence" has taken hold of Othello, and after a sleepless night thinking of the events of their earlier scene he has now bought into the possibility that Desdemona has cuckolded him. Rather than confronting her directly, he turns on the person closest to him, a part Iago has established for himself. The reaction from Iago is hysterical. The word "hysteria" comes from the Latin *hystericus*, meaning "of the womb," and in the 19th century female neurosis was thought to be caused by a disease of the uterus—hence a woman with heightened emotion was "hysterical."

Iago.
O Grace!⁴⁹ O Heaven forgive me!
Are you a Man? Have you a Soule? or Sense?
God buy you: take mine Office. Oh wretched Foole,
That lov'st to make thine Honesty, a Vice!
Oh monstrous world! Take note, take note (O World)
To be direct and honest, is not safe.
I thanke you for this profit, and from hence
Ile love no Friend, sith Love breeds such offence.

Iago seems to be equally at home when playing male or female roles, and he slips easily into the character of "wronged wife." His question to Othello, "Are you a man?," is exactly the same phrase Macbeth's Wife chooses in Act 3, scene 4, line 68, of *Macbeth* to taunt her husband about his masculinity. The word "office" is one Iago used earlier to describe his suspicion that Othello has taken the part of husband from Iago. Here it suggests the office of wife with Iago seemingly overreacting and demanding a divorce—"take mine Office." Although Iago might claim to be affected, like Othello, by a fear of cuckoldry, his words and actions show how seamlessly he can incorporate the feminine "no-thing" into his characters. Iago's response is similar to Emilia's confrontation with Othello:

Emilia.
                Oh Gull, oh dolt,
As ignorant as durt: thou hast done a deed
(I care not for thy Sword) Ile make thee known,
Though I lost twenty lives. Helpe, helpe, hoa, helpe:
The Moore hath kill'd my Mistris. Murther, murther.⁵⁰

and also when she discovers Iago has caused the death of Desdemona:

Emilia.
Villany, villany, villany:
I thinke upon't, I thinke: I smel't: O Villany:
I thought so then: Ile kill my selfe for greefe.
O villany! villany!⁵¹

The last two lines of Iago's speech to Othello are a rhyming couplet and sound very like the conclusion to a sonnet, the poet speaking to his lover:

> I thanke you for this profit, and from hence
> Ile love no Friend, sith Love breeds such offence.

The following extract from Sonnet 82 would not sound out of place if said by Iago in this scene:

> Thou, truly fair, wert truly sympathized
> In true plain words, by thy true-telling friend;

"Friend," of course, has the meaning of sexual partner as well as buddy,[52] and Bianca uses it in this way when she suspects the handkerchief belongs to an imagined new lover of Cassio: "This is some Token from a newer Friend."[53] Much of the vocabulary Iago chooses is sexual: sense, honesty, vice, love, breeds. It's not stretching things too far, given the context of this argument, to suggest that Iago is now playing the role of "Othello's Wife." In other words, he mimics Desdemona. If we look closer at his earlier words, they could indicate that because Othello stole Iago's Wife, leaving him a "no-thing," Iago will become wife to Othello, "wife, for wife":

> And nothing can, or shall content my Soule
> Till I am eeven'd with him, wife, for wift.[54]

The folio comma after the first "wife" seems to support this idea.[55] Perhaps this is what Emilia meant by "I nothing, but to please his Fantasie." She is "no-thing"—just a vagina to fuel his sexual imagination. Setting on both Rodorigo and Cassio to steal Desdemona will leave a position open that Iago can take up. He has also said to Rodorigo, "If thou canst Cuckold him, thou dost thy selfe a pleasure, me a sport."[56] To "sport" with someone can have the meaning of a sexual dalliance. Rather than fearing cuckoldry, it could be said that Iago demands it.[57] He has the twin desires of seeing his wife sleep with another man, which would result in a subsequent loss of masculinity, allowing him to embrace the female in himself and become the "wife."

Iago describes what appears to be a sexual fantasy when he "lay" (which also has an obvious double meaning) with Cassio. He is awake because he has a toothache. This in itself is significant, as the toothache was associated with people suffering the anguish of sexual passion. Benedick, for example, has a toothache after falling in love with Beatrice. The Arden editor of *Much Ado About Nothing*, A. R. Humphreys, cites Beaumont and Fletcher's *The False One*: "You had best be troubled with the *Tooth-ach* too,/ For *Lovers* ever are."[58] In Cassio's dream (or Iago's fantasy), Iago literally plays the role of Desdemona:

> In sleepe I heard him say, sweet *Desdemona*,
> Let us be wary, let us hide our Loves,
> And then (Sir) would he gripe, and wring my hand:
> Cry, oh sweet Creature: then kisse me hard,
> As if he pluckt up kisses by the rootes,
> That grew upon my lippes, laid his Leg ore my Thigh,
> And sigh, and kisse, and then cry cursed Fate,
> That gave thee to the Moore.

Cassio is jealous and curses Fate because Iago, as pseudo Desdemona, belongs to Othello. Casting himself as Desdemona allows Iago to perform her dual function in his play as lover to Cassio and wife to Othello. It should be recalled that Iago describes Cassio as "handsome" and Othello as having a "loving, Noble Nature." The transformation into Desdemona is completed through the act of kneeling next to Othello, holding his hands, and reciting lines that have very strong echoes of the marriage ceremony:

> Witnesse that heere *Iago* doth give up
> The execution of his wit, hands, heart,
> To wrong'd *Othello*'s Service. Let him command,
> And to obey shall be in me remorse,
> What bloody businesse ever.

As in a marriage where partners give up their individual identity and two become one flesh, Iago is no longer "nothing," like Emilia, but has merged with Othello in the character of Desdemona. His final words to Othello before leaving are the highly resonant: "I am your owne for ever." Iago has embraced "no-thing" so far that he now displays the feminine trait of mercy and asks that Desdemona be spared from death—"But let her live."[59] (It might be said that, since Iago is playing Desdemona, this is a plea for his own life or at least that she should live on through him.) The next time we see Iago he is in the company of Desdemona, who reveals "My Lord, is not my Lord." Stealing her function, her husband, and her form of words—"Is my Lord angry?"—Iago rushes off in concern to find his new "spouse."

The problem with this argument is that it can be contradicted by other words and events in the play. Remember, though, that Iago defines himself not by a single role but by a series of "other selves" and when he is "in the moment" what he says and does is consistent with the character he has created. He only seems to be inconsistent when he switches character. And switch characters is exactly what he does in his next scene. It isn't Iago as Desdemona/loyal wife who returns, but rather the Devil/Villain and tormentor of Othello. In just 34 lines he achieves his new objective of driving Othello into a fit of madness. Iago then makes a curtain speech over Othello's prostrate body that is the conclusion to his play:

> Thus credulous Fooles are caught,
> And many worthy, and chast Dames even thus,
> (All guiltlesse) meete reproach.

Othello has (literally) fallen, Iago has gained the lieutenancy, Cassio will not be allowed to rejoin the army and save his reputation, and Desdemona will be divorced—presumably to marry Rodorigo, if he pays Iago enough money. But as for Richard III and Macbeth, it is this pinnacle of attainment that marks the beginning of Iago's descent. As an actor Iago has been performing in isolation and has forgotten the maxim of Sanford Meisner (another noted 20th century acting teacher): "What you do doesn't depend on you; it depends on the other fellow."[60] The "other fellow" in this case is Cassio, who has been acting in a subplot of his own and, unknown to Iago, has passed the incriminating evidence/prop of the handkerchief on to Bianca. He now makes an inconvenient entrance to interrupt Iago in mid-scene, the first of seven such interruptions from various characters in which Iago is called upon to demonstrate his skill at improvisation. Initially, the response from the surprised Iago is fairly weak. He (probably) lies about Othello being subject to epilepsy and the added detail that "he had one yesterday" would surely raise Cassio's suspicion or concern. The only thing Iago can do, as in the earlier scene with Rodorigo, is get Cassio off stage as quickly as possible and buy some time to think of some additional material and rewrites. This he swiftly does and manages to join the subplot with the major narrative by incorporating Cassio and Bianca into his cast.

Iago's actor instinct returns and he convinces Othello to hide himself and watch the upcoming scene by once again stating the truth:

> Whil'st you were heere, o're-whelmed with your griefe
> (A passion most resulting such a man)
> *Cassio* came hither: I shifted him away,
> And layd good scuses upon your Extasie,
> Bad him anon returne: and heere speake with me,
> The which he promis'd.

By "encaving" himself in readiness for Cassio's return, Othello effectively becomes the audience and Iago gives him a quick acting lesson so that he is able to critically comprehend the players' actions:

> marke the Fleeres, the Gybes, and notable Scornes
> That dwell in every Region of his face ...
> I say, but marke his gesture:

The scene, to Othello, is in dumb show so he is unable to hear the words and has to rely on the performer's body language in order to understand the meaning. "Mark his gesture" is a telling phrase in terms of actor technique and is reminiscent of the "psychological gesture" taught by Michael Chekhov.[61] In essence this is the view that every character's psychology can be revealed through physical gesture. Iago has been employing this throughout the play in order to give the characters he has created a physical and psychological truth, although his real objective has often been counter to the role he plays. For example, when Othello sees Iago after the Cyprus riot he observes, "Honest *Iago* that lookes dead with greeving."[62] Iago only *looks* like he's grieving, and we later learn that the events have been a "pleasure" to him. However, gestures that convey Iago's pleasure would not match his objective of wanting to be perceived as upset and concerned. He has used an acting technique both to play truthfully and to turn the truth on its head and he will now work the same trick on the watching Othello. Iago will engage Cassio in a conversation about Bianca but Othello, who is unaware of the real "Given Circumstances," will interpret them in accordance with the circumstances Iago has given him:

> For I will make him tell the Tale anew;
> Where, how, how oft, how long ago, and when
> He hath, and is againe to cope your wife.

Othello is instructed to carefully watch the gestures made by Cassio and match them to a scenario he believes is Cassio retelling the story of how Cassio seduced Desdemona. Iago's plan is:

> As he shall smile, *Othello* shall go mad:
> And his unbookish Jelousie must conserve[63]
> Poore *Cassio*'s smiles, gestures, and light behaviors
> Quite in the wrong.

It is the use of gesture that gives the scene authenticity, and Othello misconstrues both Cassio's body language and his mimicking of Bianca's gestures through the context that Iago has provided:

Cassio.
She was heere even now: she haunts me in every place. I was the other day talking on the Seabanke with certaine Venetians, and thither comes the Bauble,[64] and falls me thus about my neck.
Othello.
Crying oh deere *Cassio,* as it were: his jesture imports it.
Cassio.
So hangs, and lolls, and weepes upon me:
So shakes, and pulls me. Ha, ha, ha.
Othello.
Now he tells how she pluckt him to my Chamber:

The improvisation between Iago and Cassio plays out in exactly the way Iago had predicted, and the scene should have cut straight to the discussion on how to punish the unfaithful couple had there not been a second interruption that is not in Iago's script. Not only does Bianca now enter, but she has Desdemona's handkerchief in her hand. This represents another potential crisis just at the point of success, and Iago's reaction is to fall back into silence and "nothing." Fortune is on his side, and rather than contradict the plot Iago has constructed, Bianca unwittingly confirms it.

In the exchange with Cassio, the parts of "man's man" and "friend to Cassio" had helped to secure Iago's objective. Now, no doubt with his adrenaline pumping from the success of the scene he has just played, Iago returns to another familiar character; the Devil/Villain and tormentor of Othello. He had earlier asked for Desdemona to be saved from death, but at that point he was playing a different role. In his present guise, perhaps becoming too immersed in the character he has created, Iago commits his first truly appalling act, instructing Othello that not only should Desdemona be killed but:

> Do it not with poyson, strangle her in her bed,
> Even the bed she hath contaminated.

Iago will dispatch Cassio personally along the way; he extracts the information of where Cassio dines that evening. Events are moving quickly (the folio's extensive use of elided words helping to drive the plot on) and there ought to have been a jump forward to Othello and Desdemona in their bedchamber were it not for a third unplanned entrance, this time of Lodovico and others on a mission from the Senate in Venice. This is something Iago cannot have known about or been responsible for and there is a very real danger that the story will now turn in another direction.

In effort to stave off potential disaster, Iago takes the initiative and greets the senators immediately and directly. The recently bestowed role of lieutenant allows Iago the status to do this, but events turn away from him. He can only stand silently as he hears the news that Cassio has been promoted over his head again, this time to governor of Cyprus, and they are to return to Venice. To make matters worse, Othello strikes Desdemona in public. The latter action is precisely the type of thing Iago had advised Othello NOT to do:

> I am to pray you, not to straine my speech
> To grosser issues, nor to larger reach,
> Then to Suspition.[65]

Like a (bad) director giving notes to one of his actors, Iago's assessment is: "'Faith that was not so well." Iago's plans are now in tatters, his play cancelled due to unforeseen circumstances. When Lodovico questions him about Othello's behavior, he seems oddly disconnected, unwilling to talk (unsure what to say), and can only come up with a cryptic answer, "He's that he is." This is a foreshadowing of almost the last statement Iago makes, which is "what you know, you know" and stands in contrast to his assessment of himself, "I am not what I am." He seems to be telling Lodovico not to judge Othello on any previous evaluation of his character—"the Noble Moore, whom our full Senate/Call all in all sufficient"—but on the evidence of his eyes. What Othello has become is what Lodovico has seen; and that's a madman. Othello lacks Iago's actor imagination to become "nothing" and is therefore unable to switch personas as events unfold. He's always simply "that he is." Sending the party from Venice off to confirm the former "Noble Moore's" insanity will at least have the effect of securing Othello's downfall, but any hope of destroying Cassio, let alone causing the demise of Desdemona, has now gone. The ending seems to be on course for a mirroring of *King Lear* with the now insane protagonist realizing he had foolishly misjudged an innocent young woman, and slipping away in a tragic death. All that remains is a postscript, but not one added by Iago. Othello has called Desdemona a whore three times and, overcome with shock and grief, she seeks comfort from the only man she can trust, and that's her "Good Friend" Iago. Cassio cannot be summoned, of course, without attracting the ire of Othello still further and, although she doesn't know it, her father is dead. It is in the role of "father" that Iago returns, drawing on his experience of the parent/child relationship he had used in an earlier scene with Rodorigo. Desdemona encourages this: "I am a Child to chiding." It is well to remember that, like Macbeth, "He has no children," and Iago plays a kind of reverse to Capulet's response to his weeping daughter Juliet.

At this point literary critics like to comment on Iago's hypocrisy and devilish behavior. After all, it's only been a short while since Iago not only passed a death sentence on Desdemona but also suggested the method of execution. The conflicting motivations of trying to ease Desdemona's mind—"Do not weepe, do not weepe: alas the day"—while simultaneously wishing her dead can cause problems for actors. The one thing they can't do is act in a generalized "devilish" manner. They need to be specific in their objectives; but how can they do that when on the one hand Iago says "all things shall be well" while on the other he knows things certainly won't be well for Desdemona since he's set Othello on the path to killing her? Actors (and critics) will often tie themselves in knots, twisting the lines to fit some manufactured theory that reduces the ambiguity and attempts to impose consistency. At moments like this it's useful to remember David Mamet's "KISS" rule: "*K*eep *I*t *S*imple, *S*tupid."

The simplest solution is to the play the truth. Iago has taken on a different identity from when he goaded Othello into murdering Desdemona; if he has a different identity he is a different person. The Devil/Tormentor is left in the wings as he assumes the personality of "father." For an actor, this is usual behavior. Gratiano, as an example, is nearly always played by the actor who has portrayed Brabantio in earlier scenes, and this doesn't present him (or the audience) with any difficulties. Iago is not a hypocrite or, indeed, a devil/tormentor. He cannot be, since he is not Iago in this scene but "Iago"—one of his "many selves"—and he behaves "as if" he will protect the distraught and helpless "daughter" Desdemona.

An alternative possibility to consider is that perhaps this is where we see another side of Iago, one where he is *not* performing. Despite what he has said and done, this *could* be the moment when, conscious of his actions thus far, he decides to pull back and throw his script in the flames. It should be acknowledged that any actor—even if they keep in character in the Tiring House as Burbage did—is always aware that they are in a play. If they weren't, then they wouldn't be acting—they'd be insane. Stanislavski quotes the Italian actor Salvini on this phenomenon: "Salvini said: 'An actor lives, weeps and laughs on the stage, and all the time he is watching his own tears and smiles. It is this double function, this balance between life and acting that makes his art.'"[66] Although fully immersed in his roles, Iago would still retain a sense of his previous actions and the events surrounding them. He has observed of Othello, "He is much chang'd," and it's possible for Iago to change, too, moved by Desdemona's words.

What most people fail to realize in life is that our character personas are fluid and shift depending on circumstances. For example, a crisis at work may be greeted with good humor if our sports team has won, our partner has revealed their deep love for us, and we've bought a winning lottery ticket. Change the circumstances to a sleepless night, an argument with our partner, and the car breaking down on the way to work and the reaction to the crisis will be somewhat different. This is why we mistakenly comment that someone's actions are "out of character." The character of the person hasn't changed, but the circumstances have. No one behaves in completely the same way at all times, nor can we know how they will respond in the future. This change in Iago, prompted by the situation, would be in keeping with other characters in Shakespeare's plays who are transformed from "bad" to "good" such as Duke Frederick in *As You Like It*, Proteus in *The Two Gentlemen of Verona*, and Leontes in *The Winter's Tale*. It would provide an active reason for his sharp responses to Emilia, who has taken on the unconscious role of tormentor to Iago by reminding him of one of his former parts:

> I will be hang'd, if some eternall Villaine,
> Some busie and i nsinuating Rogue,
> Some cogging, cozening Slave, to get some Office,
> Have not devis'd this Slander:

Iago's reply is "Fie, there is no such man," and he's correct—there no longer is such a man since Iago has discarded that character. The "eternal Villain" doesn't exist, although Iago is conscious that he has existed in the past, and that he played him. Rather than trying to remain unexposed, Iago might be regretful of what, in character as "insinuating Rogue," he has done. Significantly, there is no soliloquy at the end of this scene in which Iago attempts to defend himself or boast of his power to gull the innocent. Actioning his dialogue, one might conclude he is "ashamed."

Rousseau should be credited with the belief that deep down all men are good, although circumstances can make them evil, and it's these "given circumstances," to use their theatrical term, that actors seek too. "When you act an evil man look to see where he is good" is the advice Stanislavski gave his students.[67] If an actor simply plays what is on the page—the "given circumstances"—the scene will often work without any problem or need for discussion, even if it appears on reading the whole script to be contradictory. (Shakespeare's actors, remember, were not provided with the complete script.) However, any decision must be supported by the text in conjunction with the use of the actor's imagination. In this instance we know Iago has revealed his feelings for Desdemona—"I do love her too"—and he acknowledges her "virtue" and "goodness." The circumstances are that he has no child of his own but is "father" to his surrogate "daughter" Desdemona, who is in distress. Combining the role-playing of "father" with an awareness of things he has said and done in the past, it's credible to suggest that when Iago says, "Go in, and weepe not: all things shall be well," he really means it. Academics might think this is straining the text, but theatre-makers would recognize the potency of such imaginative engagement. Iago is reformed, about to bring the curtain down on his play and his acting career ... when there is a fourth unexpected entrance, this time from Rodorigo, and again Iago cannot have anticipated it. Richard III, Edmund, and Macbeth plan their actions carefully, step by step, but much of what Iago does is governed by chance. One can only speculate how events might have turned out if Rodorigo had not appeared at this point, but it is a shock to Iago and a surprise to the audience, both of whom had all but forgotten him. It's a master stroke from Shakespeare.

Iago's epic narrative has come to an abrupt halt, but it is events outside of Iago's control—"What the other fellow does"—that revive it once more. Just as it was Rodorigo who began the tragedy, so it is he who gets it back on track. Iago has provoked Othello into action and Rodorigo now does the same to Iago. The "improvisation" that follows is initially more of a monologue from Rodorigo, and apart from a few short lines such as "Well, go too: very well," "Very well," and "You have said now," Iago contributes little. Perhaps he is still coming to terms with the feelings he experienced in the previous scene? One of the things Rodorigo accuses him of is being a bad actor, displaying a lack of consistency:

> ...your words and
> Performances are no kin together.

From his own point of view he is correct in that Iago has said Rodorigo will "enjoy" Desdemona and "thou shalt know more hereafter," but he has not delivered on either of these things. Iago might also reflect that his words in the last scene with Desdemona were not "kin" to his performances in the scenes before. Rodorigo threatens, "I will make my selfe knowne to *Desdemona*," and with these words he unconsciously seals both her death and his own. Having his "daughter" find out about his past is not something Iago can risk. He slides into a status relationship once again, but this time it is Rodorigo who is teacher/parent and Iago the pupil/child. The roles are thrust upon Rodorigo through flattery:

> Why, now I see there's mettle in thee: and
> even from this instant do build on thee a better opinion
> then ever before:

Iago praises Rodorigo's "purpose, Courage, and Valour" and begins to persuade him to kill Cassio that night. Urgency is needed because Othello and Desdemona are leaving for Mauritania—one of Iago's few outright lies. The folio has typecast Iago as "Villaine" and almost without realizing it he has reverted to type. Even Richard of Gloster realizes:

> I cannot flatter, and looke faire,
> Smile in mens faces, smooth, deceive, and cogge,
> Ducke with French nods, and Apish curtesie,[68]

Iago can. Like an old-stager he cannot give up this role. The "smell of the greasepaint" leads him to wish for one last play, one last scene, one last part—and his next act will stretch him to the limit.

Before setting events in motion, Iago ponders the wisdom of what he is about to do. If Cassio, Rodorigo, or both die in this action, "Every way makes my gaine," but after further consideration he decides that Cassio is the one he needs to dispose of most because:

> ...the Moore
> May unfold me to him: there stand I in much perill:

It's important to note that Iago *doesn't* want Cassio dead as part of his earlier stated bargain with Othello, who will in turn kill Desdemona. He is never aware that Othello watches the assault on Cassio or that Othello believes Iago "teachest me." Iago doesn't place him as an audience to view the scene as he had previously, and he is only partially responsible for Othello's actions afterwards. In fact, Iago's focus is on saving himself, he seems to have almost forgotten Othello's murderous intentions, and it suits his purposes that no one is witness to the planned dual murders. Rodorigo and Cassio fight and both cry out in pain; the former with "Oh, I am slaine" and the latter "I am maym'd for ever." From their words it sounds very like the plan has worked and Iago leaves, taking his character of "Villain" with him. (There is no exit point printed in the folio, but since Iago reenters in his nightshirt 20 lines later, enough time is needed for his costume change. Either he has confidence in the scenario he has created and leaves as soon as Cassio enters or he waits until he can be sure both Rodorigo and Cassio are dead.)

Readers of the play will immediately spot that an important detail appears to have been left out. All editions of *Othello* since Theobald in 1733 insert his imagined stage direction "*Fight. Iago cuts Cassio behind in the leg, and Exit*" or something like it. This makes sense since Iago has decided that Cassio "must die," Cassio says he is protected from sword thrusts to his upper body by his coat, and he later provides the information, "My legge is cut in two." As a professional soldier, he certainly hasn't done that to himself. Someone must have cut him in the leg and the obvious candidate is Iago. However, there is no such stage direction in either the quarto or folio versions of the play when you would expect there ought to be since the events are not wholly evident from the dialogue. What ought to be considered is that it's possible Rodorigo cut Cassio in the leg during their fight. An alternative interpretation to the editor/adaptor imposition is that Iago told the absolute truth when he revealed of himself:

> I hold it very stuffe o'th' conscience
> To do no contriv'd Murder: I lacke Iniquitie
> Sometime to do me service.[69]

This is supported by his actions in this scene. Iago only kills Rodorigo after he calls out his name, "O damn'd Iago!," which might expose him. It isn't a "contriv'd Murder" but one done out of necessity.[70] The editor/adaptor insertion of a stage direction where Iago cuts Cassio in the leg has validity and can be powerful in performance, but it changes the character of Iago. Any modern actor who has played the role will tell you that the practicalities of cutting the leg of Cassio, exiting, changing costume, and returning in a very short space of time are extremely difficult to achieve. The stage direction from the editor/adaptors is a complete fabrication, and directors and actors should have the choice[71] of whether or not to include it in their productions.

Let's suppose for a moment that the only concrete evidence contained in the copies printed by Shakespeare's contemporaries is correct and that Iago doesn't strike Cassio and leaves before or just after the fight. In either instance he wouldn't be aware that Rodorigo and Cassio are only injured; this was not an option he had considered. Iago returns with a new character and costume and is not only surprised to find them both living but that there has been a fifth unplanned entrance, this time from Lodovico and Gratiano. Thinking quickly, Iago turns this to his advantage by, in his role of "Lieutenant," demonstrating he is a hero, a decisive man with a clear head in a crisis—"a very valiant Fellow" as Lodovico calls him—and one who cares enough for his "Brother" to bind Cassio's wounds with his own shirt. No doubt the plan was to blame the deaths on some unnamed "bloody Theeves," but a sixth interruption comes quickly when Bianca rushes on to help her lover. Iago doesn't make the same mistake as he had previously with Bianca, underestimating the effect the "other fellow" can have on a scene, and he immediately improvises a solution that will remove her as a possible source for revealing what he has done. To do this he relies on male prejudice against women of a certain class—"O notable Strumpet"—and takes on the parts of both Investigator and Judge, concluding:

> Gentlemen all, I do suspect this Trash
> To be a party in this Injurie.
> Patience awhile, good *Cassio*.

Notice how he refers to the all-male assembly with the class-conscious "Gentlemen" and in his final line doesn't allow Cassio to protest Bianca's innocence. The speed of events is key to preventing Lodovico and Gratiano from having time to think rationally. Iago deliberately switches focus from Cassio to the slain Rodorigo. He asks Gratiano if he knows Rodorigo, aware that as brother to Brabantio and uncle to Desdemona he would certainly know Rodorigo, and in an unfavorable light. In the very first scene of the play, Iago has heard Brabantio describe Rodorigo's behavior as "madnesse" and "malitious knaverie." Iago gambles that Brabantio had relayed this to his brother, and that Gratiano would share his view.

If it were not for Gratiano's prejudices, he might have stopped for a moment and asked why Bianca would be involved in the killing of Rodorigo. There's cause enough for Rodorigo to attempt to kill Cassio—failure to marry Desdemona and Cassio becoming the lover of his beloved—although this is never said. Or for Bianca to attack Cassio in a fit of jealousy. But what is Bianca's connection with Rodorigo? Lacking any evidence, Iago calls on his acting experience, proposing again that gesture reveals thought. Interestingly, he shows how the same gesture or expression can mean completely different things. To Cassio, fast losing blood from his wounds, he says, "What? looke you pale? Oh beare him out o'th' Ayr," and this enables Cassio to be taken away before he can tell the truth. Bianca also looks pale, but this indicates her guilt:

> Looke you pale, Mistris?
> Do you perceive the gastnesse[72] of her eye?
> Nay, if you stare, we shall heare more anon.
> Behold her well: I pray you looke upon her:

> Do you see Gentlemen? Nay, guiltinesse will speake
> Though tongues were out of use.

Iago looks set to escape responsibility once again were it not for the seventh and final unplanned entrance, this time from Iago's own wife. She supports her husband's view of Bianca—"Oh fie upon thee Strumpet"—and her suspicions are confirmed when Iago asks Emilia to find out where Cassio dined that evening. Iago knows from an earlier scene, of course, that Cassio had dinner with Bianca, which Bianca confirms. Seemingly now in tune with each other—the first and only time we truly see them act in partnership—Iago sends Emilia off to tell Othello what has occurred. This is in keeping with his character as someone in authority, but he has once again forgotten "the other fellow." Although a part of him might guess that Emilia will find Desdemona dead, he doesn't bargain that she will confront Othello on his reasons for killing her.

Othello claims it was Iago who told him of Desdemona's affair with Cassio, but Emilia cannot believe it and questions if he means "My Husband?" three times. Iago has been wholly credible in playing the role of "Husband"—Emilia has seen his tenderness towards the wronged Desdemona—so that that she is unable to comprehend that the person she knows so well could do such a thing. Of course, it wasn't the character of "Husband" who did this but "Villaine." Even when Iago returns, she still finds it impossible to conceive that he may have spurred Othello on to murder:

> He sayes, thou told'st him that his wife was false:
> I know thou did'st not: thou'rt not such a Villain.

Iago's reply demonstrates that he is slipping into madness and he now thinks the fictional events he scripted were "true." He has become so far immersed into his characters and plot that he totally believes in them. The great 19th century actor Coquelin warned about this—losing the "inner self" and control of your part so that there is no longer an awareness of the duality of actor and role:

> The actor ought never to let his part run away with him ... if you have no more consciousness where you are and what you are doing—you have ceased to be an actor: you are a madman.[73]

When Emilia asks Iago if he ever said Desdemona was false, he is almost nonchalant in his simple, short response, "I did." The modern equivalent would be "Of course," and is a stark contrast to his earlier long soliloquies. Iago, in his own mind, is speaking truly, but he cannot recognize it is only a stage truth. Unable to distinguish between reality and fiction, he accuses Emilia of madness. She must be mad if she thinks what is "apt, and true" is a lie. His last words to his wife before killing her are "Filth, thou lyest," so it might be said that he does this as a reaction to her apparently lying rather than to stop her from speaking the truth. Iago flees the scene because he has finally managed to find the courage to commit a "contriv'd murder." He doesn't run from the accusation that his "reports have set the Murder on" since he still believes he acted in accordance with the truth—although to everyone else it is "a strange Truth," as Gratiano puts it.

Academics write that Iago has been making a justification of his actions in the sense that he manufactures excuses for his behavior. In the theatre world, Iago's "justification" means something different, as Stanislavski explains:

> Put life into imagined circumstances and actions until you have satisfied your sense of truth and ... you have awakened your sense of faith in the reality of your sensation. This is what we call justification.[74]

At the end of any play, particularly if the work is complex and multilayered, actors are often approached by members of the audience who eagerly demand answers from them—"What did that mean?" "What happened to your character when ... ?" "Why did you do that?" They can come up with numerous ingenious "solutions" that surprise the author and had not been thought of in rehearsal. The temptation is to reply, "Well, you saw the play—it is what it is." Iago's final lines have a flavor of this:

> Demand me nothing: what you know, you know:
> From this time forth, I never will speake word.

Iago began as "nothing" and now, through a series of carefully chosen roles played with absolute conviction, he has disappeared into the vortex of his own imagination.

"Character as actor" is seldom paid much attention either in the rehearsal room or the study. We examine the text closely to identify when a character is lying, but that's quite a different thing from recognizing when a character is *performing*. Cleopatra, it might be said, plays the role of lover because that is how history has cast her. There is a sense that her behavior displays little genuine affection for Mark Anthony. Her self-obsession gives her an artifice, and although she may be passionate she is rarely sincere. Other Shakespearean character/performers include Romeo as lover of Rosaline, Edmund as devoted son, Hal as a reprobate, Holofernes as a scholar, the "friends" of Timon of Athens, and arguably both Claudius and Richard II as king.

To the Elizabethan/Jacobean actor, "studying a part" meant learning it—Hamlet asks a player if he can "study a speech of some dosen or sixteene lines,"[75] and Viola cannot reply to Olivia as "I can say little more then I have studied, & that question's out of my part."[76] One of the most frustrating things people who "study" Shakespeare, in the modern use of the word, constantly bang their heads against is his ambiguity. They sit down to write an essay and have to decide whether *The Taming of the Shrew* is sexism or satire, *All's Well That Ends Well* is genuinely a comedy, if Hamlet is mad or sane, Brutus a hero or a fool, or Coriolanus a tyrant or a patriot. Actors, on the other hand, love contradiction as it gives their characters depth. They will not want their portrayals to be neutral, so decisions have to be made, but they will also desire their work to display complexity. This is what Alan Howard, a leading actor with the Royal Shakespeare Company, called the search for "positive ambiguity." Only a close reading of their character's words and actions, free from preconceptions, will allow actors to discover this—as we shall see in the following chapter.

7

Ambiguity

"Faire is foule, and foule is faire"

The Merchant of Venice is one of Shakespeare's most controversial plays and the way it is produced tends to reflect the social mores of the time it is performed in. Some scholars argue that it was originally a full-blown comedy (the folio groups it among the comedies[1]) with Shylock the funny Jew dressed in a red wig (Judas is traditionally thought to have had red hair). In other periods Shylock was portrayed as a sinister "bogeyman" figure and a warning to the audience about the evils of Judaism. Nowadays Shylock is most often a sad and oppressed man "more sinned against than sinning," and directors will sometimes set the play in fascist Germany or Italy in order to focus on its supposed anti–Semitism. *Merchant* is a complex piece that divides opinion. Making Shylock convert to Christianity, taking his soul as well as his worldly goods, is hardly a laudable act, but then neither is plunging a knife into a living man's chest to cut away a pound of flesh to settle a financial debt. Actors and directors in the modern age will "study" *The Merchant of Venice* in order to find the moments of contradiction and ambiguity. Shakespeare's players, of course, didn't have to do this as the author was on hand to answer their questions. With a lack of rehearsal time, where they needed guidance was in the minutiae of how to deliver the lines and, as we have seen, the folio/playhouse setting helped them with this. In considering a Shakespeare play, it is important that modern actors and directors read *out* of the text, basing their work only on what they find in Shakespeare's script, and not read *in* to the text, pasting their own values, politics, or preoccupations onto the play, where they might sit in an uneasy alliance.[2]

Michael Bogdanov is a director who found the Christians in *The Merchant of Venice* to be less than Christian, and his reading has validity. Describing the match between Portia and Bassanio with the truly wonderful phrase "a marriage made in lead,"[3] he points out that one of Antonio's last acts in the play is another oath: "My soule upon the forfeit."[4] Clearly, he has learned little from his near-death experience. Bogdanov makes the important discovery in the text that almost the final words from Portia reveal she has received a sealed letter from Bellario, whom she had sent to for advice and legal garments before Shylock's trial began. She seems to know the contents and says to Antonio:

> There you shall finde three of your Argosies
> Are richly come to harbour sodainlie.[5]

If she knew from the outset that Antonio's ships had literally come in and he could easily pay back the money he owed to Shylock, then the proceedings of the court were a sham—a "show trial" against a token Jew. The text bears this out, and Portia's speech once Antonio is saved is worth quoting in full[6]:

Portia.
                    Tarry Jew,
The Law hath yet another hold on you.
It is enacted in the Lawes of Venice,
If it be proved against an Alien,
That by direct, or indirect attempts
He seeke the life of any Citizen,
The party gainst the which he doth contrive,
Shall seaze one halfe his goods, the other halfe
Comes to the privie coffer of the State,
And the offenders life lies in the mercy
Of the Duke onely, gainst all other voice.
In which predicament I say thou standst:
For it appeares by manifest proceeding,
That indirectly, and directly to,
Thou hast contriv'd against the very life
Of the defendant: and thou hast incur'd
The danger formerly by me rehearst.[7]
Downe therefore, and beg mercy of the Duke.

Why didn't she say this at the beginning? The words Portia chooses, such as "Jew" and "Alien" (both with capital letters), along with the action of making Shylock fall to the ground and beg for his life, seem to have the simple objective of humiliating a non–Christian. Apparently the law demands "the offenders life lies in the mercy/Of the Duke onely," rather than a jury. The Duke, of course, is the man who allowed Shylock's claim in the first place. If it was illegal in Venice to ask for a pound of flesh in settlement of a debt, why wasn't the case thrown out of court? Rather than a display of justice, the trial might be considered a set-up.

Running alongside this is what might be called "Shylock's Revenge." Ask any National Socialist and they will tell you that Jewishness descends through the maternal line. When Jessica and Lorenzo have children, then Shylock's grandchildren will be considered Jews. The less than satisfactory coupling of Jessica and Lorenzo is supported by Shakespeare's play. In Act 5, scene 1, line 1, they share a passage of verse that you can sometimes find included in volumes of poetry[8]:

Lorenzo.
The moone shines bright. In such a night as this,
When the sweet winde did gently kisse the trees,
And they did make no noyse, in such a night
Troylus me thinkes mounted the Trojan walls,
And sigh'd his soule toward the Grecian tents
Where *Cressed* lay that night.

Jessica.
In such a night
Did *Thisbie* fearefully ore-trip the dewe,
And saw the Lyons shadow ere himselfe,
And ranne dismayed away.

7. Ambiguity

Lorenzo.
In such a night
Stood *Dido* with a Willow in her hand
Upon the wilde sea bankes, and waft her Love
To come againe to Carthage.

Jessica.
In such a night
Medea gathered the inchanted hearbs
That did renew old *Eson*.

Lorenzo.
In such a night
Did *Jessica* steale from the wealthy Jewe,
And with an Unthrift Love did runne from Venice,
As farre as Belmont.

Jessica.
In such a night
Did young *Lorenzo* sweare he lov'd her well,
Stealing her soule with many vowes of faith,
And nere a true one.

Lorenzo.
In such a night
Did pretty *Jessica* (like a little shrow)
Slander her Love, and he forgave it her.

Jessica.
I would out-night you did no body come:
But harke, I heare the footing of a man. *Enter Messenger.*

There's no doubting the beauty of the language, but it requires closer examination. All of the examples they give—Troilus and Cressida, Pyramus and Thisbe, Dido and Aeneas, Medea and Jason—are doomed love affairs. Lorenzo's words to his supposed beloved are financial rather than romantic with the play on words of "steale"—theft and running away—and Jessica's "Unthrift Love"; she has not provided a significant dowry:

Lorenzo.
In such a night
Did *Jessica* steale from the wealthy Jewe,
And with an Unthrift Love did runne from Venice,

Jessica's response also focuses on theft—"Stealing her soule"—and question Lorenzo's fidelity:

Jessica.
In such a night
Did young *Lorenzo* sweare he lov'd her well
Stealing her soule with many vowes of faith,
And nere a true one.

Her use of vocabulary—sweare, soule, vowes, faith—seems to suggest Lorenzo has stolen her religion too. It's a choice for the actress playing Jessica whether she is happy or regretful about this, but it's possible to consider that "nere a true one" could refer to religious belief (that is, Christianity is not the true faith). Certainly there are double meanings in both Lorenzo's and Jessica's lines. There's also a contradiction in the character of Jessica because she has hardly been true to her father, taking a ring that was probably given to him by his wife before they married and committing the very unthrifty act of swapping it for a monkey. The ring had no monetary value for Shylock, but it's priceless to him and he "would not have given it for a wildernesse of Monkies."[9]

The role of Jessica as a commodity is reinforced at the conclusion when she and her husband learn they will receive Shylock's wealth after he dies; an event, we can assume, that will not be long in coming. Lorenzo's reaction to this news is perhaps ill chosen, perhaps a tasteless joke, perhaps deliberately ironic from Shakespeare:

> Faire ladies, you drop Manna in the way
> Of starved people.[10]

"Manna from Heaven" is, of course, an Old Testament story from the Book of Exodus, when God sent manna to save the Jews. The marriage of Jessica to Lorenzo is far from secure, and perhaps this is why Portia's arrival at Belmont is delayed because, Stephano explains:

> ...she doth stray about
> By holy crosses where she kneeles and prayes
> For happy wedlocke houres.[11]

It might be said that Portia is praying not just for her own happy marriage but also the match between a young Jewess and a Christian. After all, she would be acutely aware of the lesson provided by the casket test: "All that glisters is not gold."[12]

Unlike Lorenzo but like Orsino, whose love is misdirected, Jessica confesses that she is "never merry when I heare sweet musique."[13] Lorenzo launches into a 19-line defense of the values of music before, seeing Jessica is unconvinced, he concludes with the somewhat brutal command: "Marke the musicke." According to Lorenzo:

> The man that hath no musicke in himselfe,
> Nor is not moved with concord of sweet sounds,
> Is fit for treasons, stratagems, and spoyles,[14]

which is a pretty accurate description of Jessica's behavior in the play. Clearly, despite Portia's prayers, this is far from being a marriage made in heaven. All of this has to be balanced with other occurrences in the play: Portia's speech on mercy, for example. She practices what she preaches and encourages Antonio to show mercy to Shylock, a man who moments before had been prepared to kill him. Shylock finally only loses half his goods, which is a kind of justice. After all, he would have preferred to kill Antonio rather than accept any amount of money, and he'd brought the knife and scales to court in what was obviously a premeditated act. The contradictions and ambiguities in the play, as discovered moment to moment by the actors, are what make it so compelling.

Perhaps the most ambiguous play in Shakespeare's canon is *Henry V*. Again, productions tend to reflect the times in which they are performed. Olivier's film, made in Britain in 1944, took a decidedly heroic stance on the warrior king, and was intended as a morale booster during World War II. Kenneth Branagh filmed the play in 1989, a period of political and social unrest in the UK, and the realism of the battle scenes in particular was much admired. Nowadays *Henry V* is commonly presented from an antiwar point of view—it would be a brave, perhaps foolish, director who sought to produce it as "the national anthem in five acts."[15] The opinion of *Henry V* as a piece that criticizes armed conflict has validity and may be read in the first few lines of the play when the Chorus says the actors will tell the story of Henry "On this unworthy Scaffold."[16] A "scaffold" in this context can mean simply the stage, but it also has an obvious secondary meaning as a place of execution. Thomas More, in his biography of Richard III, combines both meanings when writing about the Wars of the Roses: "These matters be King's games, as it were stage plays, and for the most part played upon scaffolds."[17] And yet *Henry V* was one of only 4 books thought worthy to be issued free to U.S. armed services throughout the world in 2002. The introduction (adapted from Sidney Lee who was writing in the early 20th century) believes the play "lacks plot" but nonetheless recommends it for the "joyous sense of satisfaction in the high potentialities of human character" in "this inspiring combat."[18] So who is right? Is *Henry V* a critique or a celebration?

As long ago as 1817, William Hazlitt wrote a startling essay on the character of Henry, calling him a "very amiable monster" and his wars in France a "Royal Gadshill." Hazlitt's view was that

> Henry, because he did not know how to govern his own Kingdom, determined to make war upon his neighbours. Because his own title to the crown was doubtful, he laid claim to that of France.[19]

This is partially true—but for the politics of the time the play was written, this was not necessarily a bad thing. In Act 4, scene 5, line 213, of *Henry IV, Part 2* Henry Senior had given his son the specific advice:

> Be it thy course to busie giddy Mindes
> With forraigne Quarrels.

The Elizabethan audience would have recognized that the Henrys were practicing the Machiavellian princely ideal of *virtu;* that is, any action is justified that protects and supports the state. The rule of Henry V brought a kind of stability to England after the turmoil of the reigns of Richard II and Henry IV and would be followed by the bloody War of the Roses. The Chorus makes this clear in the epilogue to the play:

> *Henry* the Sixt, in Infant Bands crown'd King
> Of France and England, did this King succeed:
> Whose State so many had the managing,
> That they lost France, and made his England bleed.

Henry V was written and performed in 1599, a time of insecurity in England as the old Queen Elizabeth approached death. The hot topic of the day was who would succeed her and, more importantly, how they would deal with Catholic foes at home and abroad. In a passage (line 44) that precedes Act 5, scene 1, the Chorus claims that in the description of history s/he is "remembering you 'tis past," but this only draws attention to the present.[20] This speech contains a direct comparison between the "usurper" warrior-king, Henry V, and the Earl of Essex, shortly to rebel against Elizabeth I. Shakespeare seems to be following Ben Jonson's advice that theatre should be "near, and familiarly allied to the time."[21]

Although this is relevant history for an edited version of the play, a student, a critical commentator, a modern actor or director will find it of little practical use. After all, their audience will not be comprised of a group of 450-year-olds who understand the intricacies of Elizabethan politics. Shakespeare is always in the present, and for any of his plays to work they must have relevance to the people who are watching, or why bother to perform them? This is exactly what Hamlet (Shakespeare?) tells us the "purpose of Playing" is; in other words why all professionals involved in staging a play do what they do. The "end":

> both at the first and now, was and is, to hold as 'twer
> the Mirrour up to Nature; to shew Vertue her owne
> Feature, Scorne her owne Image, and the verie Age and
> Bodie of the Time, his forme and pressure.[22]

The use of "at the first and now" is interesting retrospectively because it tells us that Shakespeare's purpose in first writing a play and producing it "now" in our own age have a twin objective. And the objective is to accurately portray contemporary situations. Hamlet called Players "the abstract[23] and brief chronicles of the time."[24] In a literal sense this means they give a summary account of contemporary events (that is, both of the period the play is set in and the period in which it is performed). The word "abstract" can mean, (although Shakespeare never used it in this way) "apart" and "impersonal," and in this respect actors might, in a Brechtian sense, tell a story "impartially" and let the audience conclude its meaning.

For a modern spectator, *Henry V* is a chronicle that takes place in 3 time periods; medieval, Elizabethan, and contemporary. This is possibly what Shakespeare had in mind when he wrote Cassius's words that come immediately after the assassination of Julius Caesar:

Cassius.
How many Ages hence
Shall this our lofty Scene be acted over,
In States unborne, and Accents yet unknowne?[25]

Shakespeare's Cassius originally delivered this speech in Elizabethan England, depicting an event from ancient Rome, but he also looks forward to the future. The word "acted" suggests both others carrying out a similar act of political violence but also generations of players acting out the same story. "States unborne" recognizes the flux and fragility of nationhood and how this may alter at a later date. Although Shakespeare wouldn't have known it, we could say this might include the Commonwealth State of England and the regicide of Charles I, the birth of the United States of America, the emergence of former Soviet countries, or nations still struggling for independence such as Palestine. A group of murderers washing their hands in the blood of the head of state after he has just died from multiple stab wounds is hardly a "lofty scene," and that immediately sets up an audience debate—in any time period—about "regime change."[26]

Shakespeare's history plays, especially *Henry V*, seem to have the purpose Thomas Fuller wrote of in his 1639 book *The History of the Holy War*:

> [History] not only maketh things past present but enableth one to make a rational conjecture of things to come. For this world affordeth no new accidents ... old actions return again, furnished over with some new and different circumstances.[27]

So we watch the old story of *Henry V* and the words, characters, and incidences remind us of contemporary events. "What's past is prologue" is how Shakespeare phrased it in *The Tempest*.[28] The Bishop's biased reasoning that opens *Henry V* would surely be regarded unfavorably in the late 20th century and recognized as similar to the arguments made about weapons of mass destruction before the second Iraq war. A mid–20th century audience may well support the Bishop's objective, recollecting the failure to respond to the aggression of Nazi Germany. The purpose of the play is that it "enableth one to make a rational conjecture of things to come." An audience watches *Henry V*, spots the same problems encountered in their own time, and this enables them to address the crisis in their present by taking the best qualities in the narrative—courage, leadership, inspiration, resolve—and balancing them against the worst—political opportunism, lying to the people, slaughter of the innocent, and military folly.[29]

This is easy to write—but much more difficult to act. When faced with a text full of moral and political contradictions, what is an actor to do? It is the "circumstances" in the play and a character's "actions," to use Fuller's words in a theatrical context, that are the only things actors should concern themselves with. Yeats thought *Henry V* was meant to be ironic, and irony is something specific an actor can convey, although it is difficult to read in the study. For example, when the King insists that "God fought for us," the actor playing Fluellen might consider the circumstance of the remaining fragment of an army full of sick and exhausted soldiers surrounded by at least ten thousand dead bodies, including children, before he says, "Yes, my conscience, he did us great good."[30] Fluellen's "conscience" after such a bloodbath is all-important. Similarly, a director and actor will wish to focus on a character's actions, such as Henry's famous appeal to his troops (set here in the folio's irregular verse):

King.
Once more unto the Breach,
Deare friends, once more;
Or close the Wall up with our English dead.[31]

Like a general in World War I sending waves of troops over the top, Henry's action is a military catastrophe and he has to resort to threats such as the horrific image of "naked Infants spitted upon pykes"[32] before the town surrenders and he can enter Harfleur. The circumstances are that the breach is never entered, and one assumes his stirring rhetoric resulted precisely in the wall being closed up with English dead. To take Fuller's warning that "old actions return again," the same situation reoccurred in the 19th century when the British attempted to capture a breach at Gate Pa in New Zealand, with disastrous results. Perhaps Pistol, Nym, Bardolph, and the Boy show, not cowardice in refusing to charge the breach, but common sense?

The English playwright John Arden proposed that in *Henry V*, Shakespeare had written "a secret play within the official one."[33] In other words, it's deliberately ambiguous. He may be right, but this gives the actors a difficult challenge. They have to present the "official" play, as John Arden terms it, of the overall narrative of events but also the "secret" play that might be critical of them. This can only be achieved through the arduous work of closely studying what characters actually say and do in order to tease out the subtext. And sometimes what a character says and does is contradictory. To demonstrate this, let's look at just the first 50 lines of Act 4, scene 7, of *Henry V* (as it is set in the folio) and chart some possible actor choices.[34] It's important to remember these are only *choices*, not certainties, but the approach used can be applied to any Shakespeare play. The scene comes at a crucial point during the Battle of Agincourt and the Welsh Captain Fluellen and his English friend Captain Gower come across a group of boys in the rear of the conflict who have been killed by the enemy:

Enter Fluellen and Gower.

Fluellen.
Kill the poyes and the luggage, 'Tis expressly
against the Law of Armes, tis as arrant a peece of knavery
marke you now, as can bee offert in your Conscience
now, is it not?

Gower.
Tis certaine, there's not a boy left alive, and the
Cowardly Rascalls that ranne from the battaile ha' done
this slaughter: besides they have burned and carried away
all that was in the Kings Tent, wherefore the King
most worthily hath caus'd every soldiour to cut his prisoners
throat. O 'tis a gallant King.

Fluellen.
I, hee was porne at *Monmouth* Captaine *Gower:*
What call you the Townes name where *Alexander* the
pig was borne?

Gower.
Alexander the Great.

Fluellen.
Why I pray you, is not pig, great? The pig, or
the great, or the mighty, or the huge, or the magnanimous,
are all one reckonings, save the phrase is a litle variations.

Gower.
I thinke *Alexander* the Great was borne in
Macedon, his Father was called *Phillip* of *Macedon,* as I
take it.

Fluellen.
I thinke it is in *Macedon* where *Alexander* is
porne: I tell you Captaine, if you looke in the Maps of
the Orld, I warrant you sall finde in the comparisons betweene
Macedon & Monmouth, that the situations looke
you, is both alike. There is a River in *Macedon,* & there
is also moreover a River at *Monmouth,* it is call'd Wye at
Monmouth: but it is out of my praines, what is the name
of the other River: but 'tis all one, tis alike as my fingers
is to my fingers, and there is Salmons in both. If you
marke *Alexanders* life well, *Harry of Monmouthes* life is
come after it indifferent well, for there is figures in all
things. *Alexander* God knowes, and you know, in his
rages, and his furies, and his wraths, and his chollers, and
his moodes, and his displeasures, and his indignations,
and also being a little intoxicates in his praines, did in
his Ales and his angers (looke you) kill his best friend
Clytus.

Gower.
Our King is not like him in that, he never kill'd
any of his friends.

Fluellen.
It is not well done (marke you now) to take the
tales out of my mouth, ere it is made and finished. I speak
but in the figures, and comparisons of it: as *Alexander*
kild his friend *Clytus,* being in his Ales and his Cuppes; so
also *Harry Monmouth* being in his right wittes, and his
good judgments, turn'd away the fat Knight with the
great belly doublet: he was full of jests, and gypes, and
knaveries, and mockes, I have forgot his name.

Gower.
Sir John Falstaffe.

Fluellen.
That is he: Ile tell you, there is good men porne
at *Monmouth.*

Gower.
Heere comes his Majesty. *Alarum. Enter King Harry and Burbon with prisoners. Flourish.*

This is a scene that doesn't appear in the quarto versions of the play—neither does Henry's "Once more unto the Breach" speech and the Epilogue—but the quartos claim their text was "as it hath been sundry times played." The lines either have been added by Shakespeare or were never played before an audience. The scene has been split up into short passages that will indicate the possible contradictions in the character's responses. There are numerous possibilities of how the lines can be delivered, but for demonstration purposes only a few of the most contradictory are noted. As with previous examples, this is not to state that this is how the text *should* be played but rather illustrates the type of choices that *could* be made. A number of Fluellen's words might seem odd in their spelling. This is an excellent example of the folio printing Shakespeare's phonetic setting of words to convey the flavor of a Welsh accent.[35] Fluellen's name is in itself phonetic; his true name is likely to be Llewellyn.

For a reader the scene starts with "*Enter Fluellen and Gower*," but for the actors it begins way before this. Firstly they will want to consider the immediate circumstances that both characters have been fighting a bloody battle where they are considerably outnumbered—a conflict that might result not only in their own demise but in possible shame and conquest of their country by a foreign power and the complete collapse of the Lancaster monarchy.[36] Henry's "Crispin's Day" speech (it's a production choice whether to have Gower and/or Fluellen present when it is delivered) emphasizes the courage of the men who fight on his side, but their names are also places in England that could be lost to the French—Bedford, Exeter, Warwick, Salisbury, and Gloucester. It's extremely frustrating to see productions of the play in which Gower and Fluellen stroll on from the side of the stage as if they've just enjoyed a picnic in the Lorraine sunshine.

The second circumstance is the events in the play itself; the long trek to Agincourt in which much of the army has been lost to sickness, the massacre at Harfleur and the threats to its populace (which both Gower and Fluellen witness), the hanging of Bardolph (again, both are there when it is carried out), and the summary executions of Cambridge, Scroop, and Grey. Both Gower and Fluellen would undoubtedly know that Mortimer, brother-in-law to Cambridge, had a far more legitimate right to the crown than Henry.[37] Mortimer's claim to the throne of England was through the female line—exactly the same reasoning that provokes Henry's adventures in France. It's a mistake to believe that because a character is not a lord or a king he won't have an attitude to world events. Although they might buy into the Bishops' insecure arguments for invading France as an opportunity for colonial expansion and national pride, it would not have escaped them that Edward III had renounced the English claim to the French throne 55 years earlier.

The third circumstance is the history prior to Henry's invasion of France—in this case the actors have three previous Shakespeare plays to refer to. Under Richard II, to use the words of John of Gaunt:

> That England, that was wont to conquer others,
> Hath made a shamefull conquest of it selfe.[38]

However, the reign of Henry IV had hardly brought stability to the country and was marked by numerous insurrections. The methods employed by the House of Lancaster ushered in a new age of brutality from the chivalrous Middle Ages. After all, they were prepared to risk the wrath of God in overthrowing an anointed monarch.[39] Act 4, scene 2, of *Henry IV, Part 2* demonstrates just how far they would go in their pursuit of power. Prince John, Henry V's brother, meets a rebel army and agrees to their demands if they will disband their forces. This done, he promptly has them arrested and executed as traitors. The rebels protest that such an action is dishonorable, but John counters this with the quibble that he promised to address their concerns but he didn't promise that he wouldn't kill them. He echoes Falstaff, whose view of honor is:

> ...What is Honour
> A word. What is that word Honour? Ayre: A
> trim reckoning. Who hath it? He that dy'de a Wednesday.[40]

Prince John, the Duke of Gloucester, is the man who is directly in command of Captain Gower in the English effort to mine Harfleur and blow it up. Henry was just 16 months into his reign when he set sail for France, and although he had shown courage and some success in battle, what had distinguished him most was his debauched lifestyle—he was a playboy prince. Taking on the French in their own backyard was a whole new tennis-ball game. The fourth circumstance for the actors in this scene is what would come after the reign of Henry V. Again, Shakespeare is helpful in providing 4 further plays that need to be looked at. Each is distinguished by the depiction of a bloody and protracted civil war culminating in the reign of the tyrant Richard III. Fluellen and Gower have no way of knowing this, of course, but they might fear it.

Finally are the circumstances of the characters' words and behavior in the play before the scene begins. Gower is an enigmatic character and until this point appears emotionally contained; he is a depiction of the typical English "stiff upper lip." Fluellen, on the other hand, has constantly urged "the disciplines of War," and "discipline" is a word he repeats many times. Actors will wish to examine their character's biography up to this moment. Captain Fluellen enjoys an easy relationship with the King, who later plays a practical joke on him, and seems to have been with Henry for a long time since Henry often addresses him directly as if he were a friend. Gower is perhaps an English patriot, loyal to whoever is in power. He might come across as a bit of a "cold fish" and he's certainly prepared to obey controversial orders such as mining Harfleur. Fluellen is Welsh and Henry had cut his teeth in battle fighting the Welsh. Much of *Henry IV, Part 1* concerns itself with the activities of Owen Glendower and his struggle to free Wales from English occupation. This isn't necessarily a contradiction for Fluellen—although it could be played that way. Another Welshman, Davy Gam, is one of the few named by Henry who lost their life on his behalf at Agincourt. Historically, in one of Henry's early actions as king, the Welsh rebels were pardoned and Henry sought peace with Wales.[41] Perhaps Fluellen wishes an end to suffering in the country he loves so much by throwing in his lot with the English? He won't do this easily and would know that his namesake Llywelyn the Last, who died 133 years before Agincourt, had been the final king of Wales. Or maybe Fluellen is a career soldier, prepared to go where the work takes him, who nonetheless objects when the "Lawes of the Warres is not kept." What attracts Fluellen to a life in the army is "the Ceremonies of the Warres, and the Cares of it, and the Formes of it, and the Sobrietie of it, and the Modestie of it."[42] Unlike Gower, he disapproves of using mines, which would inevitably inflict civilian casualties.

After all this preamble, the actors can now begin the scene, but it's crucial for them to remember that at this point both characters don't know the battle has been won:

Enter Fluellen and Gower.

STOP!

A reader will scan the entry and rush through to the dialogue, but the two actors need to pause and take in the enormity of what they see in front of them before they utter a word. On Shakespeare's bare open stage, they would have to use their imaginations: in their minds perhaps some of the children are still alive but gasping for their final breath or screaming out in dying agony; toys are scattered around, a last letter remains unfinished, a pot of food is boiling over; perhaps there's mocking French graffiti scrawled on the tents, evidence of sexual molestation and torture, the children's throats are cut. Certainly the Boy who accompanied Bardolph, Pistol, and Nym, would be among the dead as Shakespeare makes clear in an earlier speech[43]:

Boy.
  ...I must stay with the
Lackies with the luggage of our camp, the French might
have a good pray of us, if he knew of it, for there is none
to guard it but boyes.[44]

He will never again see the London Alehouse he yearned for. Gower and Fluellen, over a long campaign, would have got to know the boys in the luggage/supply camp very well. Perhaps they have children of their own? The silence and the unspoken thoughts that fill it are important because they inform the rest of the scene. This initial emotional response has to be carried through by the actors and not dropped. The circumstance of the slaughtered boys remains all around them as they speak. What they feel at this moment will stay with them for the rest of their lives. A common problem with less accomplished actors is that they react to the situation initially but discard their emotional connection as soon as the dialogue switches away from the children. It's vital that what should be evident in their minds, faces,[45] bodies, and voices at the start—anger, despair, grief, confusion, guilt, and so on—is still there when Henry enters and remains when they discover they have won a famous victory.

Appropriately, the English Gower displays outward reserve as he struggles to keep his emotions under control and says nothing, but he will still be viewing the carnage and thinking and feeling. Fluellen speaks first, although it might be a character choice that he can barely speak:

Fluellen.
Kill the poyes and the luggage,[46] 'Tis expressely
against the Law of Armes, tis as arrant a peece of knavery
marke you now, as can bee offert in your Conscience
now, is it not?

FLUELLEN: The easiest approach to this speech is for Fluellen to show anger, and many editor/adaptors direct the actor towards this by adding an exclamation point after "luggage," even though it's not found in any of the folios or quartos that were published. The folio text is lightly punctuated and leaves room for the actor's dexterity. Nonetheless, anger is a legitimate choice—who wouldn't be angry when witnessing such an event? The massacre of undefended children might stiffen Fluellen's resolve to win the battle and strengthen his support for Henry's claim to rule these barbarous French. It could also do exactly the opposite. Fluellen may now believe they have no chance of victory in a conflict against people who are prepared to go to lengths that are "against the Law of Armes." A further choice might be disbelief but also a gradual dawning of what the killing of the boys represents. Fluellen is looking at dead children, but what he also sees is the end of an era; the age of chivalry is over. The realization probably began when Gower, the other person in this scene, remember, instructed Fluellen to help with the mines under Harfleur. "The mines is not according to the disciplines of the wars," is Fluellen's reply.[47] Does he recall this when looking at his friend? There's probably a moment when Fluellen begins to feel very old. There is no "Sobrietie" or "Modestie" in what is laid out before him; this is very unlike the "Pristine wars of the Romans."[48] The problem with beginning the lines in anger is that it leaves little room for the development of the speech and scene. A quick-witted actor will be able to convey a number of conflicting emotions. As an example, taking each phrase as marked by the commas, it *might* be a journey of: disbelief—fear—accusation—guilt. You'll notice that using single words like this is "actioning" the text. Fluellen ends with a question—not necessarily a rhetorical one—that confronts Gower's "Conscience" (set with a capital C in the folio.)[49]

GOWER: While Fluellen has been speaking, Gower has been listening; perhaps only half listening, but certainly thinking and reacting. He may also be gradually comprehending the significance of this event. Henry had prayed to the "God of Battles" not to remember the usurpation of Richard II when the English are fighting. In *Edward III* (now generally thought to be at least partly written by Shakespeare) Edward had proclaimed that "Heaven aids the right,"[50] so perhaps they are not in the right? There's no evidence of God aiding their cause here. For Henry and the Lancasters it looks like the party is over. Who will succeed? What does the future hold for England? On the other hand, Gower had previously witnessed Henry offer peace to the French:

King Henry.
And tell thy King, I doe not seeke him now,

But could be willing to march on to Callice,
Without impeachment
We would not seeke a Battaile as we are,
Nor as we are, we say we will not shun it.[51]

So it's the enemy's fault for rejecting peace in favor of "a peece of knavery." A contradictory thought, recalled from that earlier scene, might be that this was almost asking for trouble, and the King's arrogance in revealing they are weak and few in number, along with the equivocal "could," has caused this mess.

Rather than just standing and waiting for his turn to speak (which seems to be a technique often employed when producing Shakespeare), the actor playing Gower will wish to have an action. The first line of his reply, "'Tis certaine, there's not a boy left alive," suggests he has been searching for survivors and desperately trying to save them.

Gower.
'Tis certaine, there's not a boy left alive, and the
Cowardly Rascalls that ranne from the battaile ha' done
this slaughter: besides they have burned and carried away
all that was in the Kings Tent, wherefore the King
most worthily hath caus'd every soldiour to cut his prisoners
throat. O 'tis a gallant King.

GOWER: There's a clear choice for the actor in delivering this speech, which, simply put, is whether it should be heroic or ironic. The heroic has substance for a man like Gower who is apparently loyal to the King. He was prepared to kill civilians when attempting to blow up Harfleur, so executing captives shouldn't cause him a problem. There's not a single child living, the act was committed by "Cowardly Rascalls" (both words set in capitals in the folio) who have got behind the English lines, burnt the King's headquarters and now seem bent on a crazed rampage. Earlier in the battle, Gower was possibly present to hear the King report, "The French have re-enforc'd their scatter'd men,"[52] and the danger is that this could happen again. Henry has to kill the French prisoners in order to prevent them escaping and committing further outrages. This is a tough decision to make, but their military leader hasn't shirked from his responsibilities, as he is a "gallant King." Moreover, he did this "worthily," as he could have made ransom money on the prisoners, but the lives of his men are worth more to him than lining his own pockets. Bates had claimed that the rich will be ransomed and the poor footsoldiers dispatched, but Henry will kill all prisoners, regardless of their station in life—a socialistic but unchivalristic act.

An opposing choice helps to reveal John Arden's "secret play." Gower has been asked a direct question from Fluellen, which could be paraphrased as, "Search your conscience; can you think of a worse war crime than this?" The answer is deflected—Gower simply confirms that all the boys are dead—but his conscience would probably focus on the killing of prisoners, which is why he mentions it in his speech. Shakespeare clearly establishes the link between Henry cutting the throats of those who are now technically noncombatants and the French cutting short young lives. The flow of action is continuous on stage, not divided into scenes as in the editor/adaptor publications, and Henry's lines that immediately precede the entry of Gower and Fluellen are carefully placed in the narrative:

>Then every souldiour kill his Prisoners,
>Give the word through.[53]

We are never told the number of boys who died, but according to Exeter's later speech, at least 1,503 French officers were captured and an undisclosed, presumably larger, amount of common soldiers. It would require nerves of steel to take out each of these bound men, who would no doubt be pleading for their lives, and individually cut their throats. Holinshed's *Chronicles*, on which Shakespeare based his play, records that Henry did indeed kill prisoners, but we never actually see this happen in the play, only Henry demanding it is done. However, after the King's order, the quartos retain an interesting interjection from Pistol—"Couple gorge"—which might mean that Pistol cuts the throat of the "funny Frenchman" he is holding captive, Monsieur Le Fer. The quartos, as mentioned previously, claimed they were setting the script "as it hath been sundry times played," so it's possible that the Lord Chamberlain's men acted the cutting of prisoner's throats[54] but Heminge and Condell didn't dare print it, or it was censored by the authorities, or Shakespeare changed his mind about including this action. The Olivier and Branagh films both omit any lines or references that refer to the incident, still toeing the "official play" line against the "secret" one even in the 20th century. A. R. Humphreys, editor/adaptor of the New Penguin *Henry V*, makes just 3 notes on the hilariously obscene misunderstandings of Katherine's English lesson,[55] as if he wished it wasn't there, while perversely he finds Pistol's "Cut the throats" and the death of Monsieur Le Fer a moment of comedy. It's a production choice whether or not to stage the executions, but the passion of Gower's responses in the scene will be different if he has heard the order (possibly secondhand) or actually witnessed the event.

What Gower actually says deserves closer scrutiny. He *doesn't* say the throats of the prisoners were cut in retaliation for the murder of the boys or to stop "Cowardly Rascalls" evading capture and committing further atrocities. He records that the King's tent had been burned and looted and *this* is why (the "wherefore" in his words means "why") Henry gave the order: "Wherefore the King most worthily hath caus'd every soldiour to cut his prisoners throat." Depending on the actor interpretation, "most worthily" can be delivered as praise or sarcasm. The verb tense of "hath caus'd" suggests the executions have already been performed. Whether Gower saw this massacre, heard about it, took part in it, or was present when the order was given, there might be one thing on his conscience—he didn't voice any objection or step in to prevent it. A twist in the tale, one that an actor can convey but is impossible to read, is that Gower's words might firmly support the King but his thoughts are critical of him. Fluellen would pick up on this, and perhaps it is pointed in his direction? Why would Gower do this? His conscience screams at him that what has been happening is wrong, but he's an officer commanding part of an army in a battle that will decide not just the fate of his country but whether he will live or die. He's also in the presence of another officer, one who has always stressed the need for discipline in fighting. The events they have witnessed may be despicable, but it's vital at this stage of the conflict that the men who are actively engaged in the combat show solidarity or they will sink. Praising Henry is the most practical option.

An example of a possible journey for Gower—and this is only *one* example of multiple choices an actor might make—is that initially he feels responsible in some way for the death of the boys, and this turns to anger towards the people who have carried out the crime and frustration that they weren't stopped. His bitterness is then directed against the King in the same kind of class-conscious statements Williams made earlier in the play. (Williams presumably represents the views of the rank and file.) Burning a tent and losing some valuables is hardly comparable to children losing their lives. He would no doubt be sickened by the killing of prisoners and may fear that the same thing will happen to ordinary English soldiers if they are captured. Williams makes exactly that point about Henry: "When our throats are cut, hee may be ransom'd, and wee ne're the wiser."[56] Gower concludes that Henry's actions are not those of God's deputy on earth; he is not a truly anointed king. A simple way for the actor to convey this vocally is to put quotation marks around a word, as in "O 'tis a gallant 'King.'" The same thing will happen if the choice is made to treat "gallant" and "most worthily" in a similar way or employ a combination of an earlier "King" and the later "gallant." The actor must watch out for overdoing this or the sarcasm will cause the speech to lose its subtlety.[57]

FLUELLEN: Fluellen's reaction will very much depend on how the actor playing Gower delivers his dialogue and this will vary for both of them from performance to performance. The original Fluellen, if the cue script method is to be believed, would have the benefit of being helped in his responses as he would hear about Henry ordering French prisoners' throats to be cut for the first time. There was nothing about this in his roll. The King is a man Fluellen has idolized, especially as Henry is from Wales and historically was actually fighting under the banner of the Welsh dragon. Gower's description of the incident sounds like a desperate and undisciplined act. Has the King lost control? Fluellen would need to convince himself otherwise; that although it doesn't fit in with his personal philosophy, these things happen in war. It's been a common theme throughout the play with cutting throats mentioned 13 times, although significantly never by the French. This was a period of plague (medieval and Elizabethan) and life was cheap, Henry had offered peace and was rejected, the French were reinforcing and the English were heavily outnumbered—what choice did the King have? No doubt Fluellen's confidence is shaken—he may be shocked and disappointed—but his overriding objective, as with any soldier, is to win the war and survive.

Fluellen.
Aye, hee was porne at *Monmouth* Captaine *Gower:*
What call you the Townes name where *Alexander* the
pig was borne?[58]
Gower.
Alexander the Great.

FLUELLEN: The first thing Fluellen stresses is that Henry was born in Wales. Replying to Gower's comment of "a gallant King" this could be said with pride, the use of "Captain Gower" giving the statement a greater formality while simultaneously excluding Gower, reminding him he is, unlike them, English. Or he could say the line expressing regret; puzzlement that someone Welsh would do such things, and chastisement towards Henry—a man born in Wales shouldn't behave in this way. They appear to share a friendly relationship, and as someone Fluellen regards as a friend, Henry's actions cut deeper. If the actor stresses the word "porne," the meaning becomes that the King was born in Monmouth, but that has no bearing on his later actions. It's a bit like the Duke of Wellington, who is commonly thought to have said of his birth in Ireland: "If a gentleman happens to be born in a stable, it does not follow that he should be called a horse."⁵⁹ With the next line, *now* comes the comedy—a brilliant way for Shakespeare to break the tension that has built up. It would be a mistake for the actor to play it for comedy; Fluellen doesn't know he's being funny. What he's seeking to do is make a comparison between Alexander the Great and Henry to justify the King's behavior. Or to admire it. Or criticize it. Perhaps above all, in order to understand it. The latter choice prevents the actor from suddenly launching into a speech and allows him to discover each phrase and image in the words that follow. Fluellen's accent substitutes a *P* for a *B*, as with "porne" for "born," and there are numerous other examples of this in his language throughout the play, such as "bridge" pronounced "pridge," as well as "prains," "prave," "pashful," "prawls," and "plows." Of course, Fluellen is saying "Alexander the Big," but the effect of his Welsh pronunciation is that he calls Henry a pig three times—surely a deliberate choice by Shakespeare in writing his "secret" play?

GOWER: A common reaction for actors playing Gower is to laugh at Fluellen's mistake. It could be an affectionate chuckle at his friend's odd speech patterns, relief that a moment of humor can take him away from the dead children, or a wry exclamation that suggests Fluellen's mistake is nearer the truth—Henry is a pig. Correcting the English of Captain Fluellen is a typically superior English thing to do. Even today you will find British people pontificating on the pronunciation of the English language, particularly that of Americans, and it is seen at its worst in the insistence of a "correct" way to speak Shakespeare. It could be that Gower meant no harm in pointing out the error to his friend and it was just an instinctive reaction. Or that Gower's mind is elsewhere, performing another action with the dead boys such as closing their eyes, and he doesn't fully realize what he's said.

> **Fluellen.**
> Why I pray you, is not pig, great? The pig, or
> the great, or the mighty, or the huge, or the magnanimous,
> are all one reckonings, save the phrase is a litle variations.
>
> **Gower.**
> I thinke *Alexander* the Great was borne in
> *Macedon,* his Father was called *Phillip of Macedon,* as I
> take it.

FLUELLEN: This might be a moment of anger and frustration from Fluellen as he is sick and tired of being mocked for his Welsh heritage. He later teaches the taunting Pistol a lesson by making him eat a national symbol of Wales, a leek. It would be appropriate, given what Fluellen has heard of his compatriot Henry killing captives and seen the aftermath of the slaughter of innocent children, that he would take out the anger he feels on his "dear friend" Gower. This reaction is recognizable from everyday life when at moments of high emotion we turn on those closest to us. Or the actor could simply take the lines at face value and genuinely question whether he has chosen the right words in naming "Alexander the pig." It would be an interesting production choice for Fluellen to speak English as a second language, his thesaurus of alternative words identifying him as someone who has learned English in the classroom (from Gower?). The same thing can be experienced today when overseas students amaze native English speakers with their complex knowledge of English grammar; details most native speakers are completely unaware of. Fluellen later beats Pistol, who has mocked him, Gower says, "because he could not speake English in the native garb."⁶⁰

GOWER: If there is an outburst from Fluellen at a supposed slight to Wales, Gower doesn't respond to it. Perhaps he's used to his friend being touchy on the subject? At any event he doesn't react—maybe he's learned not to—and instead he answers the earlier question put to him about Alexander the Great's birthplace, with the extra detail of Alexander's father. It's possible their shared knowledge of the ancient world is what draws Fluellen and Gower towards each other. Fluellen later remarks, "Gower is a good Captaine, and is good knowledge and literatured in the Warres."[61] The actor might imaginatively suppose Gower to be, rather than a career soldier, a classics teacher in a private school who volunteered or was conscripted and now faces the full horror of war. Certainly, some of Gower's corrections and sharpness throughout the play have an air of the pedagogue about them. Do the dead boys remind him of faces in the choir at his school back in comfortable England? Visit any private school in the Commonwealth of Nations and it will have a desperately sad plaque on the wall of its chapel recording the names of long-forgotten ex-pupils who lost their lives in "the Great War" for the benefit of the British Empire.

An alternative is that Gower answers the question in a perfunctory manner, a banal response, and wishes to end any conversation about Alexander the Great. Given the circumstances it's hardly an appropriate subject. Rather than prompting Fluellen into speaking further, he wishes to stop him in order to more fully comprehend the present moment. The military man in him might be thinking that this action was something the French had to do in order to win the battle. The boys were "runners," supplying the arrows to the troops in the front line that had resulted in the English archers causing such utter devastation. But could they or should they have been defended? Were there enough men to do that? As an officer, could he have done more to stop this from happening?

Fluellen.
I thinke it is in *Macedon* where *Alexander* is
porne: I tell you Captaine, if you looke in the Maps of
the Orld,[62] I warrant you sall finde in the comparisons betweene
Macedon & Monmouth, that the situations looke
you, is both alike. There is a River in *Macedon,* & there
is also moreover a River at *Monmouth,* it is call'd Wye at
Monmouth: but it is out of my praines, what is the name
of the other River: but 'tis all one, tis alike as my fingers
is to my fingers, and there is Salmons in both. If you
marke *Alexanders* life well, *Harry of Monmouthes* life is
come after it indifferent well, for there is figures in all
things. *Alexander* God knowes, and you know, in his
rages, and his furies, and his wraths, and his chollers, and
his moodes, and his displeasures, and his indignations,
and also being a little intoxicates in his praines, did in
his Ales and his angers (looke you) kill his best friend
Clytus.

FLUELLEN: What is an actor to make of this strange speech? Why did Shakespeare include it at all? Probably to delay the rest of the battle and the entry of Henry so that full focus can be given to the children who have lost their lives. But that's no help to the actor who is playing Fluellen, who will want to know what his character is saying and why he is saying it. As a simple action, the Welsh captain is "comparing" Harry of Monmouth and Alexander the Great, but the arguments—"there is Salmons in both"—are odd and pretty weak. The speech lacks a clear structure and the ending, which concerns Alexander killing a friend when drunk, contradicts Fluellen's earlier words about "Sobrietie" and veers off the point. Whatever approach to the lines an actor takes, it seems apparent that they haven't been prepared. The character is extemporizing and, although a scholar of antiquity, forgets the name of the river in Macedon. This is either because he is attempting to convince himself of the justice of Henry's conduct or to persuade Gower, who he might perceive is critical of the King. To deliver the speech in a "heroic" vein has legitimacy as a choice. Alexander was one of the world's greatest soldiers and conquered other countries to the glory of his nation. Henry is attempting to do the same. The key sentence is: "If you marke Alexanders life well, Harry of Monmouthes life is come after it indifferent well, for there is figures in all things." Henry life follows Alexander's life "indifferent well"; in other words they are fairly similar, "indifferent" meaning "fairly." "Figures in all things" carries on this idea of comparison, and "figures" can be glossed as "to portray or represent or a symbol of." To paraphrase the sentence, Fluellen is claiming that Alexander and Henry share similar glorious lives, and we know that because we can see symbols of such comparisons everywhere, as if they were meant to be. The King is a kind of reincarnation of Alexander, sent by God to lead his people to victory and honor.

Of course, this is an argument that doesn't really hold water, certainly not in the circumstances, and Fluellen's twisted logic is surely deliberate. The words are opaque. "Indifferent" can also mean "unconcerned or neutral" and "figure" is often used by Shakespeare elsewhere in the sense of something imaginary or made up. If the actor adopts the choice of these readings, then Fluellen is saying that the lives of Henry and Alexander are insignificantly similar but might be imagined to be similar because anything can be made up. It's not necessarily what the character is attempting to say, even though he could be thinking it, but this is a meaning that will no doubt be conveyed to parts of the audience and possibly Gower. The audience, like Fluellen, will be divided on its attitudes to the imagery. But what's the purpose of using the flimsy argument of there being rivers in both Monmouth and Macedon? Neither Henry nor Alexander is responsible for that and it has no bearing on their characters. Fluellen is correct that there is a River Wye in Monmouth, but the larger and more famous river in Wales is the Severn. In fact the Severn is Britain's longest river and is used as a land marker in Act 3, scene 1, of *Henry IV, Part 1* when Hotspur, Glendower, and Mortimer divide England and Wales between them. It is true that the river at Monmouth is called the Wye, but it also presents the actor with a marvelous opportunity for a pun of Wye/why.[63] In his incoherent and rambling speech, Fluellen is struggling to make sense of his words and sense of what has happened. Both he and Gower will have a single thought uppermost on their minds: *Why???* So, while babbling on about rivers in Greece and Wales, the actor might also convey the subtext of a bitter disbelief at the pointless action of killing the boys. If this choice is made, the line would be said something like: "It is call'd—*Why?*—at Monmouth." Wales, like France, is occupied by the English, and Fluellen might also be wondering if such ruthless actions are likely to be repeated in his own country. He only makes one direct comparison between the *behavior* of the two kings and his description of Alexander could be said to be an apt summary of Henry's state of mind when giving the order to kill prisoners. He did this "in his rages, and his furies, and his wraths, and his chollers, and his moodes, and his displeasures, and his indignations, and also being a little intoxicates in his praines." "Intoxicated" can be used to describe someone who is drunk ("pissed out of their brains" would be the current British slang) but it also has the sense of thoughts and judgments being out of control.

The speech is in prose, and this allows the actor more freedom to convey Fluellen's conflicting thoughts and emotions. One path through the speech *might* be that he at first defends Henry—"the situations looke you, is both alike." Not just the geographical locations but the political situations both leaders found themselves in. Alexander had ascended to the throne after the assassination of his father, Phillip, and Alexander's own death was followed by civil war and the break-up of his empire. Clytus was not only Alexander's "best friend" but someone who had saved his life on the battlefield. To win a war and achieve conquest, it is often necessary and acceptable to take extreme measures. Pistol had appealed directly to Fluellen to save Bardolph's life only to receive the reply: "If, looke you, he were my Brother, I would desire the Duke to use his good pleasure, and put him to execution; for discipline ought to be used."[64] The same view stays with him so that later in the play he urges that Williams be hanged under "martial law." However, Fluellen has also said that the death of Bardolph "is not a thing to rejoyce at,"[65] so he obviously has a conscience. He can see the logic of needing to be ruthless and maintain discipline, but that thought breaks down under the reality of dead children and prisoners with severed necks. He has to ask himself—why? The feeling is so strong it causes him to keep talking to drive the images from his mind. He is grasping for words and finds them in fingers and salmons but even then can't remember the name of a river in the classical world that he has studied so closely. Fluellen recovers and is about to remark, before Gower interrupts him, that Henry would never kill his friends. Fluellen would regard the King, despite their differences in social status, as a Welshman and therefore a friend. Henry wouldn't lead them all to their deaths and possible everlasting damnation. Would he? Numerous approaches can be taken to this speech (including comedic), but the overall impression from Fluellen will be confusion. The actor can't play "confusion" but will instead seek to be active and give himself a note such as "I'm trying to understand."

GOWER: Gower has been listening closely to Fluellen's words. The time for stage business like searching the bodies is over and would be distracting. He finds himself in the awful situation of being among the dead but with little to do now but wait for others. Gower might be struggling to comprehend exactly what Fluellen is trying to say: there's nothing "great" about what has been done, and Harry of Monmouth is not Henry the Great. He may also show concern for his friend who, emotionally affected by events, has lost his usual clear-headedness and certainty. The comparisons Fluellen is making conclude that the King is subject to drunken rages that could result in him killing those closest to him, perhaps even the two of them for not guarding the boys and the luggage.

Gower.
Our King is not like him in that, he never kill'd
any of his friends.

GOWER: There is a comma after "in that" (editor/adaptors set a less subtle colon), which divides Gower's reply into two phrases. Either he is saying Henry is not like Alexander in the detail of killing a friend but like him in other respects or that the King is not at all like Alexander; for example he didn't kill a friend. The meaning behind Gower's words depends on where the actor chooses to employ a stress. If "that" or "not" is stressed, then it conveys the former meaning. Stressing "he" will mean Gower is correcting Fluellen again; Alexander killed a friend, Henry has not. A stress on "killed" delivers the thought that he didn't physically kill anyone but he as good as did. At the end of *Henry IV, Part 2*, Hal has cut off Falstaff with the cold words, "I know thee not, old man: Fall to thy Prayers."[66] Gower later reveals that he knows Falstaff by name. Although the "fat Knight" doesn't appear in *Henry V*, his death is directly attributed to Henry. As Nym puts it: "The King hath run bad humors on the Knight, that's the even of it."[67] If the actor playing Gower stresses the word "friends," then yet another meaning is conveyed. Henry didn't kill friends, only enemies. These would include the French who have carried out a genocide, the traitor and apparent close friend Scroop, and Bardolph. (The Boy tells us Nym was hanged too, presumably with the King's knowledge.) Or the whole sentence can be delivered with sarcasm, and this is difficult to convey in writing. A paraphrase of the sentiment might read something like "Kill his friends? Oh no, our 'King' would *never* do something like that, now would he? He wouldn't kill anyone who was a friend. Well, only Falstaff, Cambridge, Scroop, Grey, Bardolph, Nym and, at a conservative estimate, two-thirds of the army that landed with him in France."

FLUELLEN: There could be indignation from Fluellen at yet again being admonished by an Englishman, but that comes with his later lines. His reaction will depend on how the actor playing Gower delivers his words. If he chooses sarcasm, for example, then it might pull up Fluellen for a moment and make him think. After all, it was Fluellen who did Henry's dirty work and beat the soldiers towards the breach and certain death at Harfleur. He might also remember how ruthless the King had been in executing so-called traitors, one of whom, Scroop, the King describes as knowing "the very bottome of my soule,"[68] and yet he still goes to the axe. In this action alone, Henry has behaved very much like Alexander in murdering Clytus. The speeches the conspirators make when sentenced to death sound similar to the forced confessions in the Soviet show trials of the 1930s. If Fluellen wasn't actually present to hear their recantations, he would certainly have known about them, as it was in Henry's interest to publicize the threat to national security from the "enemy within." On the other hand, Fluellen might see the clear necessity of leaving a stable and united country behind when fighting a war abroad. It's bad enough having to deal with a possible invasion from the "weasel Scot" without internal threats from fifth columnists in positions of high power who are passing themselves off as the King's friends.

> **Fluellen.**
> It is not well done (marke you now) to take the
> tales out of my mouth, ere it is made and finished. I speak
> but in the figures, and comparisons of it: as *Alexander*
> kild his friend *Clytus,* being in his Ales and his Cuppes; so
> also *Harry Monmouth* being in his right wittes, and his
> good judgments, turn'd away the fat Knight with the
> great belly doublet: he was full of jests, and gypes, and
> knaveries, and mockes, I have forgot his name.
>
> **Gower.**
> *Sir John Falstaffe.*

FLUELLEN: Fluellen is floundering. He doesn't want to stand accused of suggesting the King would commit cold-blooded murder (even if he might think it), so he has to rephrase his words. Henry hasn't killed anybody, just "turn'd away" Falstaff, although he again can't remember the detail of a name. This was "good judgment" on the part of Harry Monmouth, and Fluellen qualifies his earlier statement to emphasize Henry was not "a little intoxicates in his praines" when he did this but in his "right wittes." However, Fluellen's description of Falstaff seems affectionate rather than critical: "He was full of jests, and gypes, and knaveries, and mockes." Of course the opposite might also be said to be true; someone who is full of "knaveries" is not the right company for a future King.

GOWER: There is a simple three-word response from Gower—"Sir John Falstaffe"—but the delivery can convey conflicting meanings. Picking up on Fluellen's description of Falstaff, he could be thinking wistfully of the "jests" and fun that now seem to come from another, happier, age. On the other hand, he could be considering how Falstaff's relationship with Hal might well have brought down the whole monarchy. He remembers Falstaff's name and would know he was an associate of Pistol, and in an earlier scene Gower describes Pistol as "an arrant counterfeit Rascall"[69] and "a Gull, a Foole, a Rogue."[70] A stern reaction, then—unless the actor takes the view that if Hal had stayed carousing with Falstaff in a London alehouse they wouldn't find themselves in the present situation.

> **Fluellen.**
> That is he: Ile tell you, there is good men porne
> at *Monmouth*.

FLUELLEN: This is another example of how the choice the performer makes in stressing certain words can give completely opposite meanings. If the actor leans on the word "is"— "there *is* good men porne at Monmouth"—Fluellen might be conveying the idea that despite Henry's dishonorable acts, there are others born in Monmouth who are not like this. Davy Gam, for example (listed as one of the few "English" dead), reputedly had a home in Monmouthshire and is commemorated in a stained-glass window that can be seen to this day in Llantilio Crosseny church.[71] Another interpretation of this stress on "is" might be that Fluellen is trying to convince himself that Henry *is* still a good man, in spite of everything that has occurred. If the stress is taken on "good men"—"there is *good men* porne at Monmouth," then Fluellen is saying that there is a history of good men being born at Monmouth and the King is one of them. Put the stress on "good" alone, though, and we're back to a criticism of Henry. He is bad but there are others who are good.

GOWER: Again, Gower's unspoken reaction will be governed by the choices the actor playing Fluellen makes. He could be sympathetic and recognize the difficult situation his friend is in and the serious dent to Fluellen's Welsh pride. He might, weighing up the pros and cons, decide in favor of the King and that, to use Hamlet's words, "He was a man, take him for all in all:/I shall not look upon his like againe."[72] On the other hand, he is perhaps sick and tired of all this baloney about Wales—there are good men born everywhere, including England, and the arbitrary circumstance of someone's geographical birth has nothing to do with their morality.

> **Gower.**
> Heere comes his Majesty. *Alarum. Enter King Harry and Burbon with prisoners. Flourish.*

GOWER: Henry's appearance, if not a shock, is certainly a surprise. He should be in the vanguard of the battle and not here. Not only that, but they have just been speaking about him, perhaps in unflattering terms. How will the King respond when he sees the dead boys? Gower also spies the unexpected presence of the Duke of Burbon and a number of French prisoners. (Burbon is only found in the folio stage directions of this entry and might represent a deliberate addition from Shakespeare.) The slaughter of the children suggests the English are losing the conflict—and the stage direction "Alarum" a moment of crisis—but this is something new. Are they, against all the odds, actually winning? If Burbon is a prisoner, will they be required to cut his throat? Or, as Williams suggested, will the Duke's high profile save him for ransom while poor French recruits of a lesser status are put to the sword? It won't be Henry personally who does the killing but people like Gower and Fluellen. There's a clear alternative in delivering this line as supportive of Henry or sarcastic. If the latter choice is taken, then Gower will quote "His Majesty" as if Henry is neither by right or action a true King.

FLUELLEN: When Henry enters Fluellen will see him with new eyes and be anxiously waiting for—needing?—the correct response from the King. If the folio stage directions are taken literally and Fluellen is not onstage for the "Crispin's Day" speech, then this is the first time the two men have met since the fight at the bridge on the march to Calais. In that scene (Act 3, scene 6) Henry addresses Fluellen by his first name twice, without his military title, as if he were a friend. Bardolph is hanged and the King issues the direct order (which Fluellen and Gower both witness) that he wishes:

> none of the French
> upbrayded or abused in disdainefull Language; for when
> Levitie and Crueltie play for a Kingdome, the gentler
> Gamester is the soonest winner.[73]

Will Henry still hold to this noble ideal? Fluellen may be mentally urging restraint or vengeance. He might be proud of the young monarch; the presence of Burbon suggests he has managed to pull off an unlikely victory. Or he may now see him as a hypocrite. Harry of Monmouth has let "Levitie and Crueltie play for a Kingdome" in cutting captive throats and this is the result. On the other hand, being "the gentler Gamester" at this moment will result in capitulation to the cruel French who have carried out the atrocity seen all around them. Fluellen's head will be buzzing with conflicting thoughts, and he may well feel relief that he can hand over responsibility to the King in the hope that he will know what to do. Both Fluellen and Gower wait with bated breath. Henry's reaction to these events is certainly one of the most important decisions of his reign:

King.
I was not angry since I came to France,
Untill this instant. Take a Trumpet Herald,
Ride thou unto the Horsemen on yond hill:
If they will fight with us, bid them come downe,
Or voyde the field: they do offend our sight.
If they'l do neither, we will come to them,
And make them sker away, as swift as stones
Enforced from the old Assyrian slings:
Besides, wee'l cut the throats of those we have,

And not a man of them that we shall take,
Shall taste our mercy. Go and tell them so.⁷⁴

Gower: Gower might think that the King doesn't get off to a very good start by saying "I was not angry since I came to France." What were the appalling threats to the citizens of Harfleur if not anger? If these words were said without anger, then that's even worse and Gower is in the presence of a cold-blooded psychopath. This is the second time Henry has ordered the throats of prisoners to be cut—no doubt there's a flinch from Burbon at the phrase "of those we have," because it includes him. If we ignore the quarto "couple gorge" (and the Oxford Shakespeare) and follow the folio, then there is no indication that either of these specific orders are obeyed. Gower could be seeing the King lose the support of his army. What good will executing prisoners do? Surely it can only lead to further French retribution and certain death for them all?

An alternative interpretation from Gower might be that Henry is quick and decisive in his assessment of what the fallen children represent. This is now a fight to the death and all-out war. In such circumstances, it is necessary to kill any Frenchman that stands in their way. As an Englishman, the challenge of overcoming impossible odds would appeal to Gower's national psyche. The English are still proud of the "Spirit of Dunkirk and the Blitz" in World War II. The soldier in Gower may acknowledge that their only hope is to take on the enemy in the way Henry describes and throw his support fully behind the King.

Fluellen: Henry's opening line, "I was not angry since I came to France," is possibly a phrase that Fluellen agrees with. Anger is the correct human response—Fluellen was no doubt angry himself when he first encountered the bloody scene. He had witnessed the King make threats at Harfleur, but they were only threats of what *could* happen *if* they didn't surrender and the army was let loose on the town. He offered peace:

> Whiles yet the coole and temperate Wind of Grace
> O're-blowes the filthy and contagious Clouds
> Of heady Murther, Spoyle, and Villany.⁷⁵

They are now in a very similar situation in which Henry makes a *threat* to kill prisoners *if* the French in the strong military position above them on the hill don't retreat. He is honorable in giving them fair warning. At Harfleur when the English were in the ascendancy, Henry showed himself to be "coole and temperate." Times have changed and, according to Exeter, their army is outnumbered at odds of five to one and the French have raised the stakes by committing a war crime. Fluellen might conclude that the more of these Gallic monsters are disposed of the better. What would certainly play well with him is the reference to classical combat:

> we will come to them,
> And make them sker away, as swift as stones
> Enforced from the old Assyrian slings:

However, it's not as simple as that. The thoughts and feelings Fluellen has experienced throughout the scene will still be with him. Although he may be partially satisfied with Henry's words, he is unable to probe him further and receive a more balanced response as the sudden entry of the French Herald interrupts them. At this point Fluellen will have very mixed emotions. A helpful Shakespearean passage from Act 4, scene 3, line 68, of *All's Well That Ends Well* is a good note not just for the actors playing Fluellen and Gower but for any actor:

Cap.G.[76]
The webbe of our life, is of a mingled yarne,
good and ill together: our vertues would bee proud, if
our faults whipt them not, and our crimes would dispaire
if they were not cherish'd by our virtues.

In other words, most situations and characters are not 100 percent right or wrong, good or bad. Fluellen bides his time and listens to the exchange with Montjoy that initially tells him the King will still not surrender himself to ransom, but then later that the day is won. When he does speak it is not to praise Henry or to rejoice at the victory but a tentative series of statements considering the past history of England "as I have read in the Chronicles." The first person he makes reference to is another young hero, Edward the Black Prince, whose father, as mentioned earlier, had given up England's claims in France. Is he hinting that the Battle of Agincourt might be over but the legitimacy question still persists? Edward III had, like Henry, won a famous battle but still didn't capture the French throne. Fluellen's next action is to remind Henry that Welsh soldiers fought valiantly that day, too, and that Henry is himself Welsh, which the King in his reply confirms. Then comes a curious speech:

Fluellen.
All the water in Wye, cannot wash your Majesties
Welsh plood out of your pody, I can tell you that:
God plesse it, and preserve it, as long as it pleases his
Grace, and his Majesty too.

This is ambiguous. The first two lines can obviously be played as a statement of national pride: the victor of Agincourt is, and always will be, a Welshman. But what is the actor to make of the abrupt "I can tell you that," which is hardly a suitable phrase to be used before a king? An alternative option is that Fluellen chides the King for what he has done this day. With this interpretation, "All the water in Wye" (he does not say *the* Wye, as is usual) might be glossed as "All the incidences (water, as in the phrase 'That's water under the bridge') cannot take away the fact that a Welshman has committed some of these terrible acts today and has left me wondering Wye/Why they had to happen." "I can tell you that" would then become "and you'd better prepare to meet your maker and explain yourself."

The second part of Fluellen's speech is also generally taken as praise of Henry, and editor/adaptors universally add an (unacknowledged) exclamation point after "and his Majesty too." The exclamation point leaves no room for interpretation other than that Fluellen blesses Henry's Welsh blood. The ending of the phrase, however, suggests that the King will only continue to be Welsh as long as it pleases God and Henry himself, which doesn't make sense. T. W. Craik, editor/adaptor of the third Arden Series of *Henry V*, sidesteps the issue with the unlikely "Fluellen's patriotism pushes him to the verge of incoherence."[77] In the New Penguin volume the editor/adaptor A. R. Humphreys provides no comment at all on these lines but makes the obvious note that "Welsh plood" refers to Henry being born in Monmouth. This is another example of an editor/adaptor telling the actors what they already know but completely ignoring a major textual crux. The key question in this passage is what "it" means in "God plesse it, and preserve it, as long as it pleases his Grace." If Fluellen when saying "it" is talking of Welsh blood—the people of Wales—then he is asking God to bless and preserve the Welsh nation but suggesting that Henry has the power to wipe it out in the same way he has removed much of the French bloodline by slaughtering a whole generation on the field of Agincourt. The Welsh blood will continue "as long as it pleases his Grace, and his Majesty too." Grace, in this interpretation, would mean "God's grace," as in the phrase "there but for the Grace of God go I." Wales will survive not only if it is God's will but Henry's too. Fluellen connects God and majesty, which is a reminder that a king is merely God's deputy on Earth. The Bishop of Carlisle in *Richard II*, Act 4, scene 1, line 125, describes a monarch as "the figure of God's Majesty."

Another option is that the "it" refers to Henry himself; Henry's blood. Fluellen wishes the King a long life "God plesse it, and preserve it," but adds the qualification that he will only do this if Henry acts honorably: "As long as it pleases his Grace, and his Majesty too." If Henry's life shows itself pleasing by acts of grace—that is, mercy, fitness, goodwill, things sanctified by God—then Fluellen will bless him. To "fall from grace" is to relapse into sin. In Act 1, scene 2, line 16, of *Henry IV, Part 1*, Falstaff accuses Hal of lacking grace:

> ...And I
> prythee sweet Wagge, when thou art King, as God save
> thy Grace, Maiesty I should say, for Grace thou wilte
> have none.

Majesty is not just another name for king but can also mean dignity. Fluellen urges Henry to retain kingly qualities while Falstaff is suggesting that Hal might gain the title of a monarch but will never have the grace that fits the position. None of these glosses are entirely satisfactory, but the actor should remember that Fluellen's words, whichever way they are interpreted, are not fully supportive of Henry and he hedges his bets with the statement "as long as," something he more or less repeats in his next speech:

Fluellen.
By Jeshu, I am your Majesties Countreyman, I
care not who know it: I will confesse it to all the Orld, I
need not to be ashamed of your Majesty, praised be God
so long as your Majesty is an honest man.

This seems to be the end of Fluellen's journey. After a long struggle with his conscience, he finally decides that he "need not to be ashamed of your Majesty," a phrase that suggests he had previously believed Henry's actions to be shameful. With the praise comes another qualification: "So long as your Majesty is an honest man." There is no folio punctuation after "praised be God," as if this is an unconsidered and emotional blurting out of his thoughts. If the King does not behave in an honest way, then Fluellen will not support him. So it might be said to be a warning. There's no question mark at the end of this speech, either in the folio or elsewhere, but it might be an interesting actor choice that Fluellen does a final check before acknowledging his conclusion is the right one. Whatever option is taken, there has to be a form of resolution or the later comedic part of the scene between Fluellen and Williams will prove difficult to play.

What has Gower been thinking all of this time? According to the folio, he's not there, or rather he has no stage direction to exit so it's unclear whether he is in the scene or not. Gower has to be offstage at some point, as Henry asks both Williams and Fluellen to fetch him, so when did he leave? Editor/adaptors generally give him an exit when the King orders the fallen to be counted:

> Our Heralds go with him,
> Bring me just notice of the numbers dead.[78]

Gower, however, is not a Herald, so why would he leave at this request when he hasn't been directly asked? A positive alternative is that the English captain exits in disgust after his line "Heere comes his Majesty," as if he didn't wish to meet Henry or look him in the eye. The problem this raises, detractors will point out, is that Gower is later part of the duping of Williams, so he can't be disapproving of the King. In actual fact Gower is not privy to the plot and is completely unaware of Henry's intentions. This moment with Williams is the only time in the printed script that he actually meets Henry—he never exchanges a single word with him either here or anywhere else in the play—and his action in the later part of the scene is to defend Fluellen rather than the King. He may well disapprove of what has happened at Agincourt, but he is a soldier and he obeys orders.

Whatever choices the actors in this short passage make—even if they highlight the comedy—they might reflect on the words of the Duke of Wellington, who had experienced the reality of death on the battlefield firsthand: "Believe me, nothing except a battle lost can be half so melancholy as a battle won."[79] Literature students may have found this chapter frustrating and confusing and will have been screaming at the pages as they read, "Make your mind up and stop equivocating!" For an actor and director, the range of conflicting choices—this chapter has only scratched the surface—will be familiar territory, and they should be free to contradict the options and conclusions that have been outlined. The beauty of theatre is that, unlike film, it's possible to play scenes differently every night. Not completely differently, of course, as this will create a lack of consistency that would bewilder an audience, but subtly distinct in hundreds of ways. Robert Louis Stevenson recognized this when he wrote that the great Italian actor Salvini "night after night does the same thing differently, but always well."[80] In simple terms, such detailed work gives the performers a road map for their role that includes not just the main routes but the back streets as well. This ensures they will never get lost.

The different approaches an actor might take in order to create a character are many and varied. The British director Katie Mitchell is correct when she says that actors arrive for the first rehearsal all speaking contrasting languages.[81] There is no right or wrong way, but the work should always begin with the script. If the responsibility for the text is given to editor/adaptors, then this crucial part of the process is handed to people who have no experience of professional acting. The next chapter, based on personal experiences from my working life, examines some of the possible ways directors might help their actors to lift Shakespeare's words from the page and place them on the stage.

8

A Director's Approach

"The rich advantage of good exercise"

I'm often asked about my "method" for directing a Shakespeare play. Apart from the close scrutiny of Shakespeare's script and an agnostic attitude to editor/adaptors, I'm sure it will be no surprise to learn that I don't pay too much attention to the A. D. Nuttalls, Frank Kermodes, or Marjorie Garbers of this world. Directors and actors who base their work on academic theories might reflect on Berowne's words in Act 1, scene 1, line 86, of *Love's Labour's Lost*:

> Small have continuall plodders ever wonne,
> Save base authoritie from others Bookes.

Resisting the accusation of being a "plodder," I, and most other directors, will strive (within time limits) to look at the text with fresh eyes and without preconceptions. Rather than repeating the opinions of scholars on words, phrases, scenes, and characters, I attempt to test them in partnership with the actors. That doesn't mean I come to rehearsal with a completely blank page and no ideas or opinions but that I will try to discover the play on the rehearsal room floor. Early in my career I worked for the Royal Shakespeare Company, and rehearsals in those days (I'm sure it doesn't happen now) began with a long speech from the director about the script we were about to produce. I found it very interesting but couldn't help wondering how he[1] knew these things since we hadn't started work yet.[2] In my opinion, the three simple words "I don't know" really ought to be cherished; they stir curiosity and creativity.

Nearly all modern professional rehearsals of a Shakespeare play will start with what is called "table work," where the actors and director sit down around a table and collectively work through each and every moment of the script. If "actioning" is included, it can take many days before the performers get on their feet and attempt to act the play.[3] It would be wrong to say that my approach is greatly different and that I don't spend time with the actors "studying" the text. I do. At the very least, actors need to be sure of the meaning of the lines and why they are speaking them. However, I try to do no more than a few days of this type of work and get the actors moving as quickly as possible. All script work needs to be seen as a preparation for performance and not an opportunity for individuals—especially the director—to demonstrate their intellectual prowess. I have a simple rule: "If you can't play it, don't say it." Any remark or observation must be able to be translated into persuasive performance or it is at best a distraction and at worst self-indulgent. It's all too easy to waste time and for the rehearsal to drift towards a university seminar and not a *practical* engagement with the text. Many actors, it must be remembered, come from an acting school rather than a university background, and it's often their instinct rather than the application of their intellect which produces such sparkling performances. Too much academic chit-chat will make them feel inhibited and quell their natural desire to take risks and trust their imaginations. The actor Brian Cox found this at the National Theatre of Great Britain when he played King Lear, and wrote of early rehearsals: "There's a certain atmosphere that makes me lose my bottle."[4]

The focus of rehearsal is in building a solid foundation so that *in performance* the actors can engage imaginatively with the words and with each other. Much of the preparation is concerned with practical considerations such as where an actor stands on the stage, but even this, unless the script calls for it, can be fluid. In a production I directed of *Much Ado About Nothing* in New York City, performed outside in-the-round, I instructed the actors playing Don John and Conrad to come on from different places each time they played their scene together without telling the other, and this had the effect of keeping the scene alive and spontaneous. For the same reason I rarely give general notes to a company of actors as this can lead to generalized playing. I prefer to speak to each performer individually. The results of this conversation will be discovered by the rest of the cast in the only place that really matters—the onstage event—and allows them to react spontaneously. The Holy Grail for any actor and director is to create the conditions whereby the performers can instinctively respond in character to events happening around them. For actors this is the joy of "playing."

As an example of onstage spontaneity, I directed *Othello* for the Fairbanks Shakespeare Theatre, Alaska, and set it in 1950s America. We had placed Act 3, scene 3, where Iago first plants the idea of Desdemona's infidelity in Othello's mind, at a military office with Iago typing documents and seemingly making offhand remarks as he worked. We'd rehearsed that after line 132—"Why then I thinke *Cassio*'s an honest man"—Iago would pull a document from the typewriter and make to exit. At one performance the document ripped, leaving a small piece of it on the desk. Rather than panic that a rehearsed action had gone wrong, the superb actor playing Iago, Tom Robenolt, simply picked up the remains of the document on the word "complexion" during the later passage:

> Not to affect many proposed Matches
> Of her owne Clime, Complexion, and Degree,
> Whereto we see in all things, Nature tends.[5]

The white piece of paper became a visual image for the dark-skinned Othello of the cultural differences between him and his wife. This was an excellent piece of spontaneous engagement by the actor ... which he never repeated again. The objective of rehearsals then, as British director Mike Alfreds puts it in his appropriately entitled book *Different Every Night*, is to "activate the instinct."[6]

When directing Shakespeare, it's all too easy to resort to "cloning" the characters (Luciana wearing spectacles), to repeat a piece of "traditional" stage business (Hotspur having a stutter), or to rely on cliché (battle scenes using flags, smoke, and kettledrums). Production ideas become fashionable and are taken up by directors with relish.[7] For example, in his 1978 *The Taming of the Shrew* for the Royal Shakespeare Company, Michael Bogdanov put an actor on a motorbike and other directors quickly began to do the same thing in other plays, downgrading to a bicycle if the production had a tight budget. It sometimes seems when watching modern Shakespeare play as if an edict has gone out that when a coin is passed onstage it must then be bitten by the receiver, all Shakespearean actors (whether in a comedy or a tragedy) must wear work boots and suspenders, and there must be at least one scene where a character drinks from a hip flask or eats an apple (a banana if it's a comedy).

In defense of directors, the received interpretation of some scenes and characters would disappoint (possibly offend) an audience if they weren't played, even though they don't appear in Shakespeare's script. I have already commented that Shakespeare didn't write of a balcony in *Romeo and Juliet* and yet it's an iconic image worldwide. Similarly, Othello isn't black or African American but closer to Arabic in appearance; hence the "Moor" of the title. Details such as these are inherited rather than what is actually in the play. So how can a director hope to avoid cliché? The important thing to accept is that any Shakespeare production will include some kind of repetition from other productions, even if it wasn't planned that way. It can be very frustrating when, after you have discovered in rehearsal a seemingly brilliant and original way of playing a scene, an audience member cheerfully points out that another director did exactly the same thing in a previous production, something you were completely unaware of.[8] Over 400 years of accumulated production history makes it inevitable that there will always be some kind of crossover of ideas. The danger of attempting to be original is that it can lead to perverse production choices simply in order to be different. A smart director will realize that it's not the choice of setting that makes a Shakespeare play original but the choices an actor makes in performance. As the RSC's veteran voice coach, Cicely Berry, has written: "It is the detail in the dialogue which creates the world."[9]

To help obtain a basic overview of a Shakespeare play I'm working on, I always begin with single, individual words, found in the word frequency lists. The number of times Shakespeare uses certain words can be very revealing. One of the most frequent words found in *Macbeth*, for example, is "all" (employed 82 times), while "temperate" is used just once. The latter is easy to understand, but what about "all"? It helps put a different slant on the play. Rather than an audience witnessing the downfall of a tyrant and going home to sleep easy in their beds, Shakespeare seems to be saying that we are *all* responsible for breeding these political dictators. I have no idea if Declan Donnellan examined the word counts when he directed the play, but he concluded:

> Macbeth stirs terrifying feelings in us. It's as if we are part of Macbeth. We put a Jung quote in the programme: "None of us stands outside mankind's infernal shadow." The more you pretend you're not part of that evil, the more you become an instrument to that evil.[10]

When I directed *Macbeth* in Dublin, the single word "all" and its meaning led me towards Goya's haunting images in his series of sketches "Los Caprichos," particularly "The sleep of reason produces monsters."[11] It also helped when deciding the age-old question of whether Banquo's Ghost is seen or not seen. The folio has a very clear stage direction: "*Enter the Ghost of Banquo, and sits in Macbeths place.*" Only Macbeth and the audience are able to see the Ghost; Shakespeare places us *all* in the same position as Macbeth.

Some word frequencies are hardly surprising; "love" is one of the most used words in *Romeo and Juliet* (137 appearances) and "will" can be found 186 times in *Henry V* but "guilt" only twice. The word "will" also predictably occurs 198 times in *Much Ado About Nothing* while "punishment(s)" appears on only three occasions. In *The Merchant of Venice* the word "Jew" is spoken at 57 moments with similar words such "Jew's" adding another 14 to that, 71 in total, whereas "Shylock" is named in just 17 places. Looking at the word count can help to dispel received ideas about a particular play. There are no prizes for guessing "Caesar" is a frequently used word in *Julius Caesar* (198 uses), but who would have thought "good" would crop up 71 times, "love" at 34 moments, but that "justice" is rarely spoken of and can only be found twice? Or that "Cassio" is the name on everyone's lips in *Othello*, spoken on 112 occasions, almost as much as Othello (24), Desdemona (41), and Iago (60) put together.

Word frequency can either confirm an impression of a play or challenge it. One of the most frequently reoccurring words in *The Winter's Tale* is "good" (103), which supports the goodness of Hermione. "Tyranny" is included just 3 times and "madness" on only two occasions, which seems to tell us that Leontes is neither a tyrant nor mad. The ending of the play is ambiguous and it is often pointed out that Hermione doesn't say anything directly to Leontes when they are reconciled. Perhaps it is then significant that "forgiveness" is only spoken twice in the play? As the title suggests, *Anthony and Cleopatra* is a play about pairings, arguably opposite pairings, and the words reflect this. Notice that the following words occur almost the exact amount of times: shall (127), will (125), would (65), should (64), give (51), take (48). The most-used words are not Anthony and Cleopatra but rather Anthony (133 times) and Caesar (132). "Octavius" is only mentioned twice. From this it would appear that the real battle within Mark Anthony is the memory of the assassination of Julius Caesar rather than concern over Caesar's nephew ("concern" is another word that only comes up twice). More interestingly, "Cleopatra" occurs at just 28 points, almost the same as Octavia (23). "Queen," however, does appear 45 times. If the word count suggests the play is actually about Mark Anthony and Julius Caesar, it also underlines the high stakes; "Egypt" is used on 41 occasions and "world" 43. Whoever controls Egypt controls the world.

Moving on from single isolated words, I next look at the first and last lines in the play. The first phrase of *Hamlet*—"Who's there?"—is a neat encapsulation of what the play is about (which is why Peter Brook directed a version of it in French which he called "Qui Est La?"). The last words in *Hamlet*, from Fortinbras, "Go, bid the Souldiers shoote," hardly paint a picture of a new harmony in the rotten state. *Richard III* opens with the word "now" and, like *Macbeth*, reminds the audience that the events they are about to witness are happening in their own time rather than in the distant past.[12] With this in mind, Richmond's plea for peace that concludes the bloody story asks for the intervention of God to help fallen Man: "God say, Amen."

A number of the endings to Shakespeare plays are ambiguous or provisional. The Bastard closes *King John*, for example, with: "Naught shall make us rue,/*If* England to it selfe, do rest but true" (my italics). Similarly, the last line of *The Taming of the Shrew* throws into doubt everything the audience has seen: "Tis a wonder, by your leave, she will be tam'd so." *Henry V* is supposedly a play about England's glorious victories in battle, but almost the final phrase focuses on defeat: "They lost France, and made his England bleed." Octavius Caesar is the victor of the Battle of Philippi, but with Brutus, Cassius, and many thousands lying dead and the beginning of the end for the Roman republic, his closing epitaph in *Julius Caesar* can't help but sound ironic:

> So call the Field to rest, and let's away,
> To part the glories of this happy day.

The idea of the ending being the beginning of a much longer story of repeated events can be found in *Romeo and Juliet*, a play, incidentally, in which the words "pair" and "parents" only appear twice:

Prince.
A glooming peace this morning with it brings,
The Sunne for sorrow will not shew his head;
Go hence, to have more talke of these sad things,
Some shall be pardon'd, and some punished.
For never was a Storie of more Wo,
Then this of *Juliet,* and her *Romeo. Exeunt omnes*

The conclusion is of a "glooming peace" on which the sun will not shine; only "some" will be punished, and in the meantime they will all talk about it. It's reminiscent of a modern-day press conference after some particularly horrific child murder where it's always said that lessons have been learned from this "story of Woe" … until the next time.

There's a similar unsettling conclusion to *Macbeth*. In an earlier scene, Malcolm has related to Macduff a long list of the excesses he will resort to when he is King: "Had I powre, I should/Poure the sweet Milke of Concord, into Hell,/Uprore the universall peace, confound/All unity on earth."[13] He later retracts this, explaining he was simply testing Macduff's loyalty, an excuse Macduff doesn't completely believe because he finds it "hard to reconcile."[14] The new king's address to his assembled thanes carries a barely disguised threat that he will be "even with you," and he already begins to rewrite history with his talk of the "Fiend-like Queene" whose strange death he spins as suicide (the Gentlewoman was explicitly told to "Remove from her the meanes of all annoyance,/And still keepe eyes upon her"[15]). The invitation to see Malcolm crowned recalls Macduff's failure to observe Macbeth's coronation, which led to dire consequences for his family:

Malcolm.
We shall not spend a large expence of time,
Before we reckon with your severall loves,
And make us even with you. My Thanes and Kinsmen
Henceforth be Earles, the first that ever Scotland
In such an Honor nam'd: What's more to do,
Which would be planted newly with the time,
As calling home our exil'd Friends abroad,
That fled the Snares of watchfull Tyranny,
Producing forth the cruell Ministers
Of this dead Butcher, and his Fiend-like Queene;
Who (as 'tis thought) by selfe and violent hands,
Tooke off her life. This, and what needfull else
That call's upon us, by the Grace of Grace,
We will performe in measure, time, and place:
So thankes to all at once, and to each one,
Whom we invite, to see us Crown'd at Scone. *Flourish. Exeunt Omnes.*

In 1995 Saddam Hussein's two daughters and their husbands defected to Jordan but returned home after being pardoned by the Iraqi dictator. The husbands were, of course, immediately executed on arrival. I think there's a flavor of this in Malcolm's "calling home our exil'd Friends abroad." These exiled friends would include his brother Donalbain, who "for certain" chose not to fight alongside his brother to free Scotland, and Banquo's son Fleance. Picking up on my earlier point of the extensive use of the word "all" suggesting collective accountability, part of Malcolm's speech might be read as a belief that by fleeing the country these exiles were responsible for "producing forth" Macbeth:

> As calling home our exil'd Friends abroad,
> That fled the Snares of watchfull Tyranny,
> Producing forth the cruell Ministers
> Of this dead Butcher, and his Fiend-like Queene;

Both Malcolm and the audience know that Malcolm's crown is insecure since it was predicted that Banquo would be "Father of many Kings" and there is no sign of young Fleance—yet (a word that appears 56 times.)

Examining individual words alongside endings and beginnings can be a liberating experience in releasing a play from the shackles of hundreds of years of preconception. However, it's important to physicalize the language and get it in the actor's bodies. Too much sitting around discussing the play and the actors can find themselves bound in the pages of the script. After all, the basic objective of any theatre performance is simply to tell a story, and it's crucial that the narrative doesn't get lost through too narrow a focus on the minutiae of the words. To help avoid this, and as a storytelling exercise, I ask the actors to perform some of Shakespeare's sonnets in rehearsal. This is done in character, with a defined imagined setting and situation given, and addressed to other characters to whom the words and sentiment might seem appropriate. The sonnets, small stories in themselves (or, directly translated, "Little Song"), often seem to predict what Shakespeare included in his plays. Benedick attempts to write a poem in *Much Ado About Nothing* and Sonnet 130, "My Mistress' eyes are nothing like the sun," could be an apt description of his view of Beatrice. Berowne in *Love's Labours Lost* is also a failed sonneteer, but Sonnet 127, "In the old age black was not counted fair," sums up his feelings for the dark-skinned Rosaline. *The Comedy of Errors* depicts the relationship between Adriana and her husband Antipholus of Ephesus as one built on lies so they might both speak Sonnet 138, "When my love swears that she is made of truth." Taking this latter sonnet as an example of how the exercise works, it could be set it in a bar at the *Porpentine* with a drunken Antipholus spilling his heart out to the Courtizan and/or Balthasar after being excluded from his home. Changing the gender in the verse, it might equally be set in the Priory and see Adriana confessing to the Abbess who has blamed her for the apparent failure of her marriage or at home in the *Phoenix* debunking Luciana's idealized view of men.

I've used the sonnets on mature love when working with actors playing Anthony and Cleopatra. They write to each other a lot—what do they say? Perhaps Anthony, keenly aware of Cleopatra's preoccupation with her "Sallad dayes,/When I was greene in judgment, cold in blood,"[16] would pen something like Sonnet 104:

> To me, fair friend, you never can be old,
> For as you were when first your eye I eyed,

> Such seems your beauty still. Three winters cold
> Have from the forests shook three summers' pride,
> Three beauteous springs to yellow autumn turn'd
> In process of the seasons have I seen,
> Three April perfumes in three hot Junes burn'd,
> Since first I saw you fresh, which yet are green.
> Ah, yet doth beauty, like a dial-hand,
> Steal from his figure and no pace perceived;
> So your sweet hue, which methinks still doth stand,
> Hath motion and mine eye may be deceived:
> For fear of which, hear this, thou age unbred;
> Ere you were born was beauty's summer dead.

Notice the verse mentions "yet are green" and that "mine eye may be deceived," which chimes nicely with Anthony's later suspicion that Cleopatra is unfaithful. Cleopatra could reply by using the words of Sonnet 123:

> No, Time, thou shalt not boast that I do change:
> Thy pyramids built up with newer might
> To me are nothing novel, nothing strange;
> They are but dressings of a former sight.
> Our dates are brief, and therefore we admire
> What thou dost foist upon us that is old,
> And rather make them born to our desire
> Than think that we before have heard them told.
> Thy registers and thee I both defy,
> Not wondering at the present nor the past,
> For thy records and what we see doth lie,
> Made more or less by thy continual haste.
> This I do vow and this shall ever be;
> I will be true, despite thy scythe and thee.

There's the obvious mention of pyramids and Anthony's scythe/sword/penis, but more importantly, if Cleopatra has written "I will be true, despite thy scythe and thee," imagine her shock when the next message she receives tells her that Anthony has married Octavia.

The Winter's Tale is a complex play, one of Shakespeare's greatest achievements, and in it Hermione is wrongly accused of cuckolding her husband Leontes. In order to help him see the error of his ways and be fully contrite for his actions, she pretends to be dead for 16 years. When Hermione "comes back to life," she says nothing to Leontes. If she had spoken, she might well have used the words of Sonnet 112:

> Your love and pity doth the impression fill
> Which vulgar scandal stamp'd upon my brow;
> For what care I who calls me well or ill,
> So you o'er-green my bad, my good allow?
> You are my all the world, and I must strive
> To know my shames and praises from your tongue:
> None else to me, nor I to none alive,
> That my steel'd sense or changes right or wrong.
> In so profound abysm I throw all care
> Of others' voices, that my adder's sense
> To critic and to flatterer stopped are.
> Mark how with my neglect I do dispense:

> You are so strongly in my purpose bred
> That all the world besides methinks are dead.

Leontes's problem is that he hasn't been able to reconcile his intense male friendship with Polixenes and his marriage to Hermione. Sonnet 144 might indicate to the actor playing Leontes his dilemma:

> Two loves I have of comfort and despair,
> Which like two spirits do suggest me still:
> The better angel is a man right fair,
> The worser spirit a woman color'd ill.
> To win me soon to hell, my female evil
> Tempteth my better angel from my side,
> And would corrupt my saint to be a devil,
> Wooing his purity with her foul pride.
> And whether that my angel be turn'd fiend
> Suspect I may, but not directly tell;
> But being both from me, both to each friend,
> I guess one angel in another's hell:
> Yet this shall I ne'er know, but live in doubt,
> Till my bad angel fire my good one out.

Sometimes a sonnet can describe a character's feelings and situation fairly accurately. In *All's Well That Ends Well*, Helena uses her father's medicine to cure the King of a life-threatening disease. Her reward is to choose a husband, but Bertram, the man she longs for, will have none of it and runs away from the match. What Helena might feel at the moment she learns of this is expressed in Sonnet 147:

> My love is as a fever longing still,
> For that which longer nurseth the disease;
> Feeding on that which doth preserve the ill,
> The uncertain sickly appetite to please.
> My reason, the physician to my love,
> Angry that his prescriptions are not kept,
> Hath left me, and I desperate now approve
> Desire is death, which physic did except.
> Past cure I am, now Reason is past care,
> And frantic-mad with evermore unrest;
> My thoughts and my discourse as madmen's are,
> At random from the truth vainly expressed;
> For I have sworn thee fair, and thought thee bright,
> Who art as black as hell, as dark as night.

Similarly, Sonnet 140 with its mention of madness, slanders, patience, cruelty, ill-advised words, the world growing bad, and "Bear thine eyes straight" could be addressed by King Lear to his daughters, particularly Cordelia, and is perfectly in tune with the themes of the play:

> Be wise as thou art cruel; do not press
> My tongue-tied patience with too much disdain;
> Lest sorrow lend me words, and words express
> The manner of my pity-wanting pain.
> If I might teach thee wit, better it were,

> Though not to love, yet, love to tell me so;
> As testy sick men, when their deaths be near,
> No news but health from their physicians know;
> For, if I should despair, I should grow mad,
> And in my madness might speak ill of thee;
> Now this ill-wresting world is grown so bad,
> Mad slanderers by mad ears believed be.
> That I may not be so, nor thou belied,
> Bear thine eyes straight, though thy proud heart go wide.

Shakespeare's poems can also sometimes contain an apt scene or character description that is relevant to one of his plays. The following example, from *The Rape of Lucrece*, line 1513, fits Iago although it is actually a depiction of Sinon:

> Like a constant and confirmed devil,
> He entertain'd a show so seeming-just,
> And therein so enscounc'd his secret evil,
> That jealousy itself could not mistrust
> False-creeping craft and perjury should thrust
> Into so bright a day such black-fac'd storms,
> Or blot with hell-born sin such saint-like forms.

And this extract, found in *Venus and Adonis*, line 1123, could be said to be a description of Juliet when she wakes up in the tomb and finds Romeo dead:

> She looks upon his lips, and they are pale;
> She takes him by the hand, and that is cold;
> She whispers in his ears a heavy tale,
> As if they heard the woeful words she told;
> She lifts the coffer-lids that close his eyes,
> Where, lo, two lamps, burnt out, in darkness lies;
>
> Two glasses, where herself herself beheld
> A thousand times, and now no more reflect;
> Their virtue lost, wherein they late excell'd,
> And every beauty robb'd of his effect:
> 'Wonder of time,' quoth she, 'this is my spite,
> That, thou being dead, the day should yet be light.

The sonnets and narrative poems are a rich source of information and inspiration for actors tackling a Shakespearean text and shouldn't be ignored. Nor, indeed, should his other plays. When Heminge and Condell wrote, "Reade him, therefore; and againe, and againe," it wasn't so much a sales pitch as a directorial note. Whatever play is worked on or character created, there will always be supplementary material found in the poems and sonnets. Their effectiveness will depend on the degree of imagination with which they are used in rehearsal. It's not enough just to look at a passage of verse and exclaim, "Oh, yeah, isn't that interesting?" Any discoveries must be able to be applied to performance.

Some highly successful directors, such as Katie Mitchell, make extensive use of improvisation exercises as part of their rehearsal process. The benefits of this are without question and can be particularly enlightening when filling in the back story by improvising scenes that Shakespeare didn't include in his plays; Hamlet and Horatio at university in Wittenburg, for instance, or Romeo's courtship of Rosaline. The danger is that improvisation can become an end in itself and cause the actors to lose sight of the text they are working on. Rather than complementing a script, it can create a parallel play, and too much attention be paid to this "back story" at the expense of what the author has actually written on the page. As with "actioning," I have the utmost respect for directors who use improvisation in their work and their achievements cannot be denied. Instead of improvisations, which can sometimes be undefined and unfocused, I prefer to keep a firm anchor on Shakespeare by roughly staging scenes in rehearsal from some of his other works that seem to have relevance to the play being produced. When directing *King Lear*, for example, we looked at Hubert's attempted blinding of Arthur in *King John*,[17] Launcelot Gobo meeting his "sand blind" father Old Gobo in *The Merchant of Venice*,[18] and Desdemona's speech to her father, Brabantio, about a woman's split loyalty to both a husband and father, in *Othello*.[19] The effect of the first scene was that it helped Cornwall to become more hesitant and much less sadistic when blinding Gloster (and therefore more believable), the second made the actors aware of the large number of comic moments in *King Lear*, and the third gave Cordelia some thoughts to run through her head when her father asks about her love for him, which she chose to suppress and say nothing. The value of working on extracts from other Shakespeare plays is threefold: it can support the work by examining how Shakespeare approached the same situation in similar scenes, it can help to explain textual cruxes, and it can act as a bridge in providing "missing" events.

Shakespeare liked to recycle; if an idea worked, he wasn't afraid to visit it again in a different form. Like women disguising themselves as men or, more generally, characters adopting an alternative persona, *As You Like It* and *The Tempest* both tell the story of a wicked brother who banishes a father and his daughter to an enchanted place, where the daughter finds love and helps restore a ruler to his rightful throne. *Measure for Measure* and *All's Well That Ends Well* both employ the "bed trick" to resolve their plots, and *Much Ado About Nothing* and *The Winter's Tale* have a wronged woman pretending to be dead and then "coming back to life" when her husband displays forgiveness. Similar "mirroring" can be found in numerous individual scenes. Falstaff and Hal role-playing the King chastising his wayward son in *Henry IV, Part 1* is more or less repeated in *King Lear* in the hovel when Lear puts his daughters on trial. Perhaps this is one reason why it was cut in the folio/performance? What "mirror scenes" do is take the actors away from the text they are working on and refresh it by seeing (approximately) the same scene from a different angle. This helps both the actors and director consider alternative approaches and can assist them in avoiding clichéd interpretations. If Shakespeare did the same thing differently, why shouldn't they apply their imaginations to follow him? There are numerous examples of mirror scenes throughout the canon. Working-class men in both *Love's Labour's Lost* and *A Midsummer Night's Dream* put on a play that is duly ridiculed by the gentry. *Richard III*, Act 4, scene 2, has the King suggest to Buckingham that he might kill Prince Edward in a very similar way to King John asking Hubert to dispose of Arthur in Act 3, scene 2, of *King John*. Lady Percy in Act 2, scene 3, of *Henry IV, Part 1* makes almost the exact same speech to her husband as she does to her father in Act 2, scene 3, in the second part of *Henry IV*.[20] And both her scenes are reminiscent of Calphurnia pleading with Caesar not to go to the Senate and Portia pleading with Brutus to share the cause of his unrest in Act 2 of *Julius Caesar*. The argument between Brutus and Cassius in Act 4, scene 3, of *Julius Caesar* has a mirror in the argument between Anthony and Octavius in Act 2, scene 2, of *Anthony and Cleopatra*. There are scenes before the battlements of a besieged town in *Henry V* and *King John*, shipwrecks in *The Tempest*, *Twelfth Night*, and *The Comedy of Errors*, Britain is divided up in *King Lear* and *Henry IV, Part 1*, scenes with murderers appear in *Richard III* and *Macbeth*, and what is the attack on Parolles by "Russians" in Act 4, scene 1, of *All's Well That Ends Well* but another Gadshill?

Sometimes passages of thought from one character are apt for another. The following words from Macbeth might have been said by Richard III:

> I am in blood
> Stept in so farre, that should I wade no more,
> Returning were as tedious as go ore.[21]

Richard, after all, expresses a very similar sentiment:

> But I am in
> So farre in blood, that sinne will pluck on sinne,
> Teare-falling pittie dwells not in this eye.[22]

The stubborn and sleep-deprived Leontes could use these lines of Macbeth's:

> But let the frame of things dis-joynt,
> Both the Worlds suffer,
> Ere we will eate our Meale in feare, and sleepe
> In the affliction of these terrible Dreames,
> That shake us Nightly.[23]

Or Hamlet have spoken Macbeth's:

> Light thickens,
> And the Crow makes Wing toth' Rookie Wood:
> Good things of Day begin to droope, and drowse,
> Whiles Nights black Agents to their Prey's doe rowse.
> Thou marvell'st at my words: but hold thee still,
> Things bad begun, make strong themselves by ill[24]:

This speech is not a million miles away from Hamlet's:

> 'Tis now the verie witching time of night,
> When Churchyards yawne, and Hell it selfe breaths out
> Contagion to this world. Now could I drink hot blood,
> And do such bitter businesse as the day
> Would quake to looke on.[25]

And that's just three examples from one character in a single script.

An action in one play can often be repeated in another; Othello and Romeo both die with a kiss (to some extent so does Mark Anthony), Juliet and Innogen take sleeping potions that make them appear to be dead, and there's an astonished reaction when twins are revealed in *Twelfth Night* as well as *The Comedy of Errors*. Antipholus of Syracuse in *The Comedy of Errors* (Act 2, scene 2, line 212) is claimed by a lady he does not know (Adriana) in exactly the same way as Sebastian in *Twelfth Night* (Act 4, scene 1, line 59) is enticed into a strange woman's house (Olivia.) Notice how the words each uses at the end of these scenes echo each other:

Antipholus of Syracuse.
Am I in earth, in heaven, or in hell?
Sleeping or waking, mad or well advisde:
Knowne unto these, and to my selfe disguisde:
Ile say as they say, and persever so:
And in this mist at all adventures go.

Sebastian.
What rellish is in this? How runs the streame?
Or I am mad, or else this is a dreame:
Let fancie still my sense in Lethe steepe,
If it be thus to dreame, still let me sleepe.

Comparing speeches from other parts of the canon can throw light on character problems. For example, is "The quality of mercy" speech from Portia in *The Merchant of Venice* (Act 4, scene 1, line 180) really her genuine, extempore words or merely repeated by rote from some pious volume she has read? You can make up your own mind, but contrast it with the following passage from Thomas More in *The Book of Sir Thomas More*[26]—apparently the only section of one of Shakespeare's plays that has come down to us in his own handwriting. The Attorney More, with equal logic as Portia, asks of a crowd that seeks to remove "strangers" from England how they would feel if they were likewise banished. In other words, it's a plea for mercy. How far it's a heartfelt plea for mercy or legal-speak is the purpose of comparing the following speech with Portia's famous lines:

> would you be pleased
> To find a nation of such barbarous temper,
> That, breaking out in hideous violence,
> Would not afford you an abode on earth,
> Whet their detested knives against your throats,
> Spurn you like dogs, and like as if that God
> Owed not nor made not you, nor that the claimants
> Were not all appropriate to your comforts,
> But chartered unto them, what would you think
> To be thus used? this is the strangers case;
> And this your mountainish inhumanity.[27]

Kate's declaration on marriage at the end of *The Taming of the Shrew* (Act 5, scene 2, line 137) with its talk of "Thy husband is thy Lord, thy life, they keeper" has an obvious parallel with Luciana's words in Act 2, scene 1, line 15, of *The Comedy of Errors*, in which she expresses the point of view that men "are masters to their females, and their Lords." The $64,000 question is: does either of them really mean it? Emilia's views on the same subject (Act 4, scene 3, line 92, of *Othello*) have a touch more realism about them: "Let Husbands know,/Their wives have sense like them: They see, and smell,/And have their Palats both for sweet, and sowre,/As Husbands have." That doesn't mean that any of the opinions expressed by the characters are wrong or a lie, especially taking into account the context, or that these are Shakespeare's own beliefs. For the actors playing Kate and Luciana, it simply presents another way of looking at things; an option.

It's possible to imagine from mirror speeches how a character's future might develop. The last we hear of the cowardly braggart Pistol in Act 5, scene 1, line 81, of *Henry V* is when he tells us:

Pistol.
Doeth fortune play the huswife with me now?
Newes have I that my *Doll* is dead i'th Spittle of a malady
of France, and there my rendevous is quite cut off:
Old I do waxe, and from my wearie limbes honour is
Cudgeld. Well, Bawd Ile turne, and something leane to
Cut-purse of quicke hand: To England will I steale, and
there Ile steale:
And patches will I get unto these cudgeld scarres,
And swore I got them in the Gallia warres.

The cowardly braggart Parolles in Act 4, scene 3, line 320, of *All's Well That Ends Well* holds a very similar ambition:

Parolles.
     Captaine Ile be no more,
But I will eate, and drinke, and sleepe as soft
As Captaine shall. Simply the thing I am
Shall make me live: who knowes himselfe a braggart
Let him feare this; for it will come to passe,
That every braggart shall be found an Asse.
Rust sword, coole blushes, and *Parrolles* live
Safest in shame: being fool'd, by fool'rie thrive;
There's place and meanes for every man alive.
Ile after them. *Exit.*

Parolles survives to return later in the play, and although down on his luck he has lost none of his wit. "Simply the thing I am/Shall make me live" is a highly appropriate phrase to describe Pistol's thoughts as he makes his way back to London.

 Perhaps the most useful application of using other scenes from Shakespeare is providing "missing" information. One of the problems with *Anthony and Cleopatra* is that we meet the protagonists when their relationship is at a crisis point but don't see them in the early, passionate days of their blossoming love. I've used sections of *Romeo and Juliet* to fill in this gap. After all, what is Act 4, scene 15, of *Anthony and Cleopatra*—where the dying Anthony is lifted above to be reunited with Cleopatra—but a triumphant version of the scene in the orchard in *Romeo and Juliet* when Romeo strives to reach Juliet at her window. Similarly, I've staged in a rehearsal of *The Comedy of Errors* the last scene of *Shrew* as the "Gossip's feast" where the characters go off to celebrate at the conclusion of the play. There are many correspondences between these two early works. We never learn how the marriage between Antipholus of Ephesus and Adriana has deteriorated in *The Comedy of Errors*—perhaps there has been a touch of Kate in *The Taming of the Shrew* about Adriana? Both plays were written at about the same time and there's sibling rivalry between sisters in each of them.

 The story of *Othello* reveals that Cassio wooed Desdemona on Othello's behalf, but these are scenes that aren't in the play. Is there a suggestion that Desdemona enjoyed the meetings? Somewhat controversially, I've taken the exchanges between Cesario/Viola with Olivia in *Twelfth Night*, when she is a substitute suitor for Orsino, and had Cassio speak Viola's lines and Desdemona, Olivia's. As with all exercises, this was done not to confirm a predetermined idea but in the spirit of genuine inquiry. It may well be that the actors discover no impropriety in the Cassio/Desdemona relationship, perhaps just a simple flirtation between a young woman and a glamorous man. Or they may find something more unsettling. If the latter choice is made, it must be remembered that Desdemona ultimately chooses Othello just as Olivia finds true love with Sebastian. Staying with *Othello*, how far are the scenes between Iago and Rodorigo supposed to be light relief? My own view is that they are comic, and this was confirmed (to me at least) by working on scenes in *Twelfth Night* when Sir Toby gulls Sir Andrew, replacing Iago and Rodorigo for the two knights. Whatever scene you rehearse in Shakespeare, it nearly always has a "friend" in one of his other plays. If this is the case, the need for improvisation to help create the back story[28] becomes less important. Why use spurious words of your own when you can engage with what Shakespeare has written? Or, sometimes, what others have written. Working on scenes from Norton and Sackville's 1561 play *Gorboduc* (the first play in English to employ blank verse) was particularly enlightening when rehearsing *King Lear*. Not only is it a source for Shakespeare's play but it contains scenes and characters that Shakespeare chose to leave out, notably Gorboduc/Lear's wife. It's important to stress again that these are *exercises*; if they are taken too far, a production can veer dangerously towards adaptation.

John Dryden wrote a version of *Anthony and Cleopatra* in 1678 and titled it *All for Love*—which in itself is a pretty good note for the two leading actors. Unlike Shakespeare's play, in which they never meet, Dryden has Anthony's wife Octavia confront his mistress Cleopatra. Their exchange in Act 3, line 417, begins with:

Octavia.
I need not ask if you are Cleopatra;
Your haughty carriage—
Cleopatra.
Shows I am a queen.[29]

This scene helped the actors playing these roles to have a fixed memory and image of her rival when speaking Shakespeare's lines. Sometimes in rehearsal things can become intense, and there is always a point when the actors are so saturated with information that they become frustrated that their knowledge of the text isn't translating into persuasive performance. In this situation, all that is often needed is some relief from the everyday grind of grappling with a role. For example, the exchange between Romeo and Juliet in the orchard—which in places is light and fun—can develop into a sickly seriousness, certainly for those of cynical tastes. Ben Jonson's *Poetaster* (1601) parodies the scene and has the recently banished Ovid meet Julia under her chamber window (Act 4, scene 9).[30] There's little in Jonson's reimagining of significance to assist the actors beyond a few good phrases, such as Julia's "O, Father, since thou gav'st me not my Mind,/Strive not to rule it."[31] The benefit is simply in coming at a similar scene from a different angle without the pressure of having to deliver a performance.

An alternative approach to engaging with the text is used by the British director Deborah Warner, who starts with (among other exercises) lots of read-throughs of the play she is working on but with the actors speaking roles that aren't their own. This has the effect of ensuring the actors have a very full understanding of the script and allows them to recite lines that, in performance, they should be listening to. Warner's productions are rightly lauded for their imaginative detail, but an overuse of this method can be counterproductive. Actors hear others inadvertently giving them "line reading"; they can lose confidence as they imagine the actor reading their part is "better" than them; a sense of ownership of the role is leased out to the whole cast; and it can waste vital rehearsal time. When Warner directed *King Lear* at the National Theatre in London in 1991, it was only at the 7th rehearsal, after 6 read-throughs, that the leading actor, Brian Cox, got to speak the words of his character, King Lear. Cox wrote about the production in a published diary: "Deborah should have started earlier; I think her pace of work is far too slow."[32] Often, using rehearsal exercises can be an excuse to delay the inevitable of getting on and working through the nuts and bolts of a play. As with improvisation, they can become an end in themselves and quickly be forgotten as opening night approaches and the actors begin to panic about simple necessities such as remembering the words and standing in the right place. Nonetheless, I have used something similar to Deborah Warner and asked actors, after the read-through, to swap roles with a scene partner and treat the dialogue as if said by their own character. Leontes and Polixenes, for example, Mark Anthony and Brutus, Romeo and Juliet, each pair of twins in *The Comedy of Errors*, and Henry IV and Hal. The effects of this are often productive and surprising, particularly if it is an event that the character doesn't appear in. These scenes are invariably ignored by the actors after the first read-through. An academic approach to character will list the ways in which characters differ, but actors need to know what connects them to the other characters as well, since this is how relationships are formed and broken. For instance Fortinbras, like Hamlet, has recently lost a father and is ruled by an uncle he despises. Reading another's role can help to identify the extremely important connections that lie hidden in the text.

The idea present in *The Comedy of Errors* is that human beings can only be whole when joined to another; a married couple are literally, in church teaching, one flesh. Antipholus and Dromio have no identity without their "other half," Emilia (Abbess) can only be "Mother Superior" rather than mother as she has lost her sons, and Adriana cannot be "wife" without a husband. If the characters have "another half," then it's important for the actors to look at the words and behavior of these "mirror" characters when creating their own. They will find Antipholus of Syracusa will be like Luciana, Adriana similar to Antipholus of Ephesus, and Emilia like Egeon, and vice versa. That is not to say that charting character differences is not without value. I use it sparingly, however, since it comes close to essay writing rather than performing and can remind actors of horrifying experiences answering seemingly irrelevant examination questions about the plays when at school. Sometimes, though, it can achieve clarity and serve a distinct purpose. When I directed *The Comedy of Errors*, just two actors (because of budget constraints) played both Antipholuses and Dromios, and the following chart of differences helped them to make each character singular and defined:

ANTIPHOLUS OF SYRACUSE	**ANTIPHOLUS OF EPHESUS**
No mother	No father (Duke = surrogate)
Rescued by father but leaves him. Perhaps desperate for a female "mother figure" in his life?	Rescued by mother but "rejected" by her. Perhaps an indication of why he finds it difficult to to be close to Adriana?
Similar to Luciana—she is his "other half."	Similar to Adriana—she is his "other half."
Searches for (needs) brother—and is also searching for his mother; an important point to remember	No effort made to find his brother—possibly because he has the "stability" of Adriana, possibly because he is living the image of his own creation
The son who would take a gap year to travel before studying	The son who would skip university for a job; possibly in the City where it's big money and wild entertainment

No job—dependent on Dad	"Self-made man" (with Duke's help)
Unmarried (unhappily)	Married (unhappily)
Poor	Rich
Gold attracts to him	Rope attracts to him
Anonymous	Well known
A wanderer but wants stability	Stable at home—but wanders
Open spaces—no home	Keys and locks—Secure home
From the North (think England, where people from the North are often considered to be less sophisticated than those from the South)	From the South (think England, where people from the South are often considered to be more sophisticated than those from the North)
From the sea	From land
Naïve	"Man of the world"
Religious—spiritual—superstitious	Exists in the present
Romantic—would marry Luciana on first meeting	
	Businessman—buys wife gifts for her love/obedience
Melancholic (witches take advantage of this)	
	Bon viveur
Soliloquies—introspective	No soliloquies—less reflective
Impulsive	Calculating (Buying chain, etc.)
Calmer (like Luciana)	Hot-headed (like Adriana)
Thinks he's mad	Thinks everyone else is mad
Soft	Hard
Jokes with Dromio	Colder towards Dromio
Beats Dromio (an apparent contradiction?)	Unusual to beat Dromio (an apparent contradiction?)
Classless	Sense of social position
Less confident, especially with women	Confident, especially with women
Is never arrested although he takes sanctuary in the Priory	Is arrested and often falsely accused
Larger, more sympathetic role	Smaller, less sympathetic role
Seems physically more bound in contrast to Antipholus of Ephesus	Seems physically looser in contrast to Antipholus of Syracuse

DROMIO OF SYRACUSE

DROMIO OF EPHESUS

No mother or father—except Egeon and Antipholus	No mother or father—except Antipholus—Luciana and Adriana seem especially spiteful towards him, taking out on the slave what they can't on the master
Sold by his own mother at birth—no mention as to whom his father is	Sold by his own mother at birth—No mention as to whom his father is
Rescued by Egeon	Rescued by Emilia
Not searching for his brother and makes no mention of him	Not searching for his brother and makes no mention of him
Superstitious—knows about the Bible and witches and Latin	Practical
Beaten by Antipholus	Rarely beaten by Antipholus although beaten by the women
Tells Antipholus jokes and has a "buddy" relationship	More distant from Antipholus
Doesn't ask audience for sympathy	Asks audience for sympathy
Hates Nell (unattached)	Loves Nell (attached)
The only person in the play who doesn't find a partner	Finds a partner in Nell and has a good relationship with Luce
Fetches gold	Fetches rope
From the North (think England, where people from the North are often considered to be less sophisticated than those from the South)	From the South (think England, where people from the South are often considered to be more sophisticated than those from the North)
From the sea	From land

Anonymous	Known
His master is poor	His master is rich
Is never arrested but takes sanctuary in the Priory	Is arrested and often falsely accused
No home	Secure home
Used to traveling and seeing different places and people	Probably never traveled or seen different places and people
Often transcends his class position	Sense of social position
The clown	The "doormat"

There are many places in this book where I have shown how referring to Shakespeare's other plays can help to settle textual problems, so I shall use just one example here. In 1933 L. C. Knights wrote a satirical essay called "How Many Children Had Lady Macbeth?"[33] in response to what he regarded as irrelevant commentary on Shakespeare's plays. For actors though, such questions are often pertinent. Macbeth's Wife says:

> I have given Sucke, and know
> How tender 'tis to love the Babe that milkes me.[34]

so it's clear she has given birth. Either this was from another relationship or the Macbeths had a child and it died, perhaps in infancy. There is no talk of a successor and Macbeth seems to envy the fact that Banquo's son Fleance will be heir to a line of kings. If Macbeth is impotent—and his wife seems to harp on his supposed lack of manhood—this might be used by the actor to explain Macbeth's preoccupation with killing (even before the murder of Duncan, he has cold-bloodedly sliced Macdonwald "from the Nave to th'Chops"). If he can't deliver life, then he will deliver death. The textual crux comes in Act 4, scene 3, line 213, just after Macduff has been told that his wife and children have been murdered by Macbeth:

Malcolm.
Be comforted.
Let's make us Med'cines of our great Revenge,
To cure this deadly greefe.
Macduff.
He ha's no Children. All my pretty ones?
Did you say All? Oh Hell-Kite! All?[35]

The question is—*who* has no children? Malcolm or Macbeth? In the play neither is shown to have any offspring, so is it a slight against Malcolm or an explanation of Macbeth's actions? A. C. Bradley, the target of L. C. Knights's essay, believed the "he" referred to was Malcolm, and that Macduff is saying that because Malcolm hasn't experienced fathering children he has no authority to suggest that Macduff should stop grieving and use the death of his family to spur him on to depose Macbeth. The current Arden editor, Kenneth Muir, takes the opposite view—it's Macbeth who has no children—but with a twist. Rather than the view that Macbeth can coldly slaughter children because he has no offspring of his own, Muir comes up with something different. He defers to the editor/adaptor of the first Arden edition, Henry Cunningham, and argues that what Macduff means is that because Macbeth has no children, Macduff cannot take his revenge by killing them too, like for like. This, of course, makes Macduff as bad as Macbeth, and although it fits with the theory that Macbeth is not an isolated case but, given the circumstances, we might all behave in the same way, it's a huge character leap for the actor. Macduff has shown no sign of brutality thus far and doesn't in the rest of the play. In fact he warns Malcolm's army not to engage in revenge attacks but rather "Let our just Censures/Attend the true event,"[36] and he makes it very clear that the fight is between him and Macbeth and he has no interest in killing anyone else:

> Tyrant shew thy face,
> If thou beest slaine, and with no stroake of mine,
> My Wife and Childrens Ghosts will haunt me still:
> I cannot strike at wretched Kernes, whose armes
> Are hyr'd to beare their Staves; either thou *Macbeth,*
> Or else my Sword with an unbattered edge
> I sheath againe undeeded. There thou should'st be,
> By this great clatter, one of greatest note
> Seemes bruited. Let me finde him Fortune,
> And more I begge not.[37]

The point is surely that Macduff strives to stay honest when the world around him is turning mad. He has fled Scotland and left his wife and children behind because he cannot conceive that Macbeth would kill them. The most he can imagine is the tyrant might have "batter'd at their peace." Like the nuclear bomb and the Holocaust in modern times, Macbeth's infanticides have ushered in a new age in conflict, one Macduff struggles to understand. In this he displays the same reaction as Fluellen to the killing of the boys at Agincourt. The only answer Macduff can think of is that because Macbeth has no children he is capable of killing children; anyone who has known the joys of parenthood couldn't commit such an appalling act. Another of Shakespeare's plays can be called on to support this interpretation. In Act 5, scene 5, line 63, of *Henry VI, Part 3* Queen Margaret, who has just seen her son Prince Edward stabbed to death, says:

> You have no children (Butchers) if you had,
> The thought of them would have stirr'd up remorse,

To sum up: because Macbeth has no children with his wife or anyone else or, indeed, stepchildren or children who died in infancy or were stillborn, he can, without remorse, order the slaughter of the young Macduff's. Since Macbeth's Wife has been able to bear a child with another man, a "real" man in the Macbeths minds, the inference must be that Macbeth is sexually impotent and this has major repercussions for the portrayal of the role. We can reach this conclusion by referring to one of Shakespeare's other plays.

Thus far in this chapter you might be forgiven for spying an apparent contradiction in my approach to Shakespeare. If I warn of over-intellectualizing the scripts and the dangers of "faculty thinking," as it has become known, doesn't such close examination of the texts encourage exactly that? It's a fine line, and one constantly to beware of. Unless the study of the text is matched with a character physicality, it's pretty much useless and a complete waste of the actor's time. We've all seen productions where the actors stand with perfect balance, speak the text with commendable clarity, and have a uni-focus on the person they are talking to, as if everyone else around them doesn't exist. No living human being is perfectly balanced, but some Shakespearean performances display the physical fluidity of characters from *South Park*. And yet the human body is about 60 percent fluid; our movements literally flow. Sit in a café and observe people for an afternoon and you will quickly notice that *no* part of them ever stops moving. If you've ever had the misfortune to see a corpse, you will know why the phrase "dead weight" is so evocative. In performance an actor's whole body must be alive; they need to spot thoughts in the other actor/characters' faces and body language and respond to them. As Declan Donnellan has written, "Actors see with their entire bodies."[38] Unfortunately this is rare. A locked stance and closed physicality seem to be the accepted hallmark for acting Shakespeare.[39] This is not a mere preference for a performance style. Consider these statistics on human communication from Dr. Albert Mehrabian of the University of Southern California.[40] Seven percent of communication is verbal. In other words, Shakespeare's language is the best the world has ever seen, or is likely to see, and yet only around 7 percent of what he writes actually hits home. Thirty-eight percent of communication comes from the tone of voice/inflection—the actor's job. Take three simple words such as "I love you" and the meaning will be different depending on where the actor places the stress. "**I** love you" tells the listener that I'm the one who loves you and not anyone else. "I **love** you" conveys that I don't hate you, I have strong feelings for you. "I love **you**" indicates that there is no one else in the equation. Said with sarcasm, the words are completely different again; the speaker doesn't really love you but parodies the line. Overwhelmingly, at 55 percent it is body language that communicates the most, which is why it is vital that a character's thoughts have a physical manifestation in performance. Any discoveries in the text are only fully effective if they can be expressed through movement.

Performing *Richard III* in the 21st century it is rightly unacceptable to link Richard's physical disability to his moral irresponsibility, so a different approach is required.[41] If you examine the text of *Richard III alone* there is arguably only one reference to his hump— "bunch backed toad"—although there are many in *Henry VI, Part 3*. Poisonous toads do indeed puff up their backs before striking, but this is one curse among many; Richard is called a spider, hog and so on—most often a boar or a dog. When Catesby and Ratcliffe support Richard, it is interesting to note that the Cat and the Rat join the Dog. That's an intellectual point, but how to translate this so it's evident in the actor's bodies? Most acting schools have a block of work they call "animal study" where the students visit a zoo, choose an animal, and recreate its movements in the rehearsal room. This helps them with attaining the practice of concentrated and detailed observation but also with developing their performances away from a too-cerebral approach to the text. Sometimes animal study can work for a character. Bullingbrooke might be portrayed as a fox, for example, or Edmund as a lizard. In *Richard III* Catesby as a cat could be a sly, devious person, with slow, subtle movements. For Ratcliffe, a rat is small, mean, quick, and spiteful. A dog, of course, is apparently very loyal but can also be fierce, ruthless—and make a lot of noise!

Anthony Sher famously portrayed Richard III at the Royal Shakespeare Company in 1984 and used shortened crutches for his arms so that he resembled an animal—a "bottled spider," most reviews remarked, although that creature wasn't foremost on Sher's mind. This wasn't an imposition; the stimulus for it came from the text. Sher had seen a television program on bullfighting and wrote in his notes when preparing the role:

> Watching the fighting bulls today, I realize they have many of the qualities that I've been thinking about for Richard…. When they burst into the ring there is a great agility, they spring, change direction, like they're dancing. The massive hump … is full and hard, a pack of muscle.[42]

In rehearsal, Sher says, director Bill Alexander talked to the cast "about finding more tribal/animal behavior. Getting away from the stiff formality of history-play acting."[43] Sher observes "You can find any character by watching animals."[44] His was an outstanding Richard III that has arguably yet to be surpassed in the modern age.[45]

A popular approach to developing an actor's physical awareness is to play theatre games. In essence these are children's street and party games adapted to suit situations in the script. Competitive games, for example, could be used to help establish the rivalry between the Montagues and Capulets in *Romeo and Juliet*. Game playing can help to break down barriers and bond a new company of actors, release a performer's energy, and are a fun way of warming up the body prior to going onstage. In 1977 Clive Barker wrote *Theatre Games*, probably the definitive book on using games as a rehearsal technique. His work is extremely valuable to the actor, particularly the objective of "getting the direction of activities switched from the conscious front brain to the subconscious back brain."[46] When rehearsal becomes overcerebral, a simple game can relax a group and is a timely reminder that theatre is a performance where the actors are "players" and the text is not, as Barker points out, "inadequately spoken literature."[47] The word "drama," after all, comes from the Greek for "action."

The problem with games is that they can become unconnected to the script unless they are really specific, and rather than break down barriers they can be exposing and a source of deep embarrassment to actors. Many of the most accomplished performers are actually pretty shy offstage. Brian Cox wrote about director Deborah Warner's extensive use of game playing in their *King Lear* rehearsals: "For me these games reflect a bourgeois English childhood which means nothing to me and I'm not sure of their value here."[48] Playing too many games can eat up important rehearsal time, take the work off at a tangent, and have little impact on the final performance. That is why I tend to use theatre games selectively, depending on the play, actors, and progression of rehearsal. Games are most beneficial when applied to a specific area of the script, particularly if the participants are in character. I used pillow fights, the card game Snap, and darts when attempting to cultivate the combative natures of Beatrice and Benedick. A game of Twister was productive when working through the tangled relationship of Hermia, Helena, Demetrius, and Lysander, playing "killer" helped to establish the suspicious atmosphere of Duncan's court, and a rehearsal snowball fight between Leontes and Polixenes eventually found its way into a production of *The Winter's Tale*.

As with improvisation, theatre games can take place in isolation from the text, so I try to connect the physical actions of a game to the language. Act 1, scene 2, of *Richard III* is one of the most famous and most difficult scenes in Shakespeare. Lady Anne has to be persuaded to marry Richard in the presence of the corpse of her father-in-law, Henry VI. She knows it is Richard who has killed him, as well as her husband Prince Edward, and her exchanges are full of anger and bitterness. At least they ought to be. An actor's natural respect for a fellow performer can lead to the lines sounding considered rather than emotional and instinctive. To counter this, and to fill the scene with physical energy, as an exercise I had each actor move around the space and fling a ball to the other on the last syllable of their line, and only to begin their retort when they received the ball. The high energy of the exercise exhausted the actors and left them no room to think other than to pick up their cues. The next time the scene was played (without the ball, of course), it was less intellectual and more visceral, and was rhythmically diverse. There are many other ways that ball games can be imaginatively adapted to tease out the actor physicality when performing the text.

The trick is to identify the problem and choose a game that might help to solve it rather than playing a game for its own sake with no real purpose.

Perhaps the most common trap actors can fall into when performing Shakespeare is not conveying an understanding of the language and speaking it in a perceived "Shakespeare voice" that is fully articulated but lacks variation in pace, pitch, and tone. This is what Peter Brook described as everyone sharing "a generalized rhythm that passes impersonally from one to the other."[49] These two problems are linked; if you don't understand the words then it's not possible to make them vocally distinct. When this situation occurs, there are two complimentary exercises I employ. They're pretty standard in modern rehearsals and I certainly make no claim to have created them.

The first exercise is simply to have the actor, with a strong arm, point at him- or herself when the script says "I," to the person being addressed when "you" is spoken, and to whoever else is mentioned in the dialogue. This helps to pick out the detail in a long, complicated speech, such as Egeon's story, which begins *The Comedy of Errors*. If none of the other characters are actually present in the room or in the cast, then chairs can be used. As an example, let's take this complex passage from Jaques De Boys (called "2nd Brother" in the folio) that wraps up *As You Like It* (Act 5, scene 4, line 150). It's the denouement to the play, and unless the audience has a clear sense of what he is saying they won't understand the ending. It's very difficult to describe the exercise in writing, but I have placed in bold the moments when the actor would point:

2nd Brother.
Let **me** have audience for a word or two:
I am the second sonne of old **Sir Rowland**,
That bring these tidings to this **faire assembly**.
Duke Frederick hearing how that everie day
Men of great worth resorted to this forrest,
Addrest a **mightie power**, which were on foote
In **his** owne conduct, purposely to take
His brother **heere**, and put **him** to the sword:
And to the skirts of this wilde Wood **he** came;
Where, meeting with an old **Religious man**,
After some question with **him**, was converted
Both from **his** enterprize, and from the world:
His crowne bequeathing to **his** banish'd **Brother**,
And all **their** Lands restor'd to **him** againe
That were with **him** exil'd. This to be true,
I do engage **my** life.

The problem is to whom "his," "him" and "he" refer, and the exercise makes this evident. To paraphrase the pointed words: Jaques begs to be listened to as his information is important, tells everyone that he (Jaques) is the middle son of the deceased Sir Rowland De Boys (Oliver is the eldest son and Orlando the youngest), and relates the story of how Duke Frederick, usurper of the throne, heard that "men of great worth" were making their way to the Forest of Arden on a daily basis to be with Duke Senior, Duke Frederick's brother. Alarmed at this news, Duke Frederick had raised and led an army to find and kill Duke Senior. On approaching the forest, Duke Frederick met a man of religion who, after some discussion, persuaded Duke Frederick from his murderous enterprise. This religious man had such a profound effect on Duke Frederick that Duke Frederick immediately converted to the spiritual life and retreated to a monastery. As he did so, Duke Frederick gave back the crown to Duke Senior and restored the lands to all of Duke Senior's followers who had been exiled with Duke Senior. Jaques swears on his life that his story is true. This paraphrase sounds even more convoluted than Shakespeare's speech, but the exercise of pointing gives the actor a specific image in his mind when saying the lines. If the actors can see the various people they are talking about, then the tone of their voice naturally changes when they mention each one and the narrative becomes clear.

I have used the "pointing exercise" on Henry's speech that contains a long list of the fallen at Agincourt in *Henry V* (Act 4, scene 8, line 81). In the wrong hands, this can sound about as interesting as reading from the yellow pages (it is often cut), but Shakespeare's purpose is to honor each of the victims of the war against France. This has a resonance in modern times when each September 11, the names of those who died in the attack on the Twin Towers in New York City are recited at Ground Zero. When employing the exercise, Henry can point to empty chairs, random photographs, or people in the room who then have to leave. It's a powerful moment as the actor playing Henry realizes the consequences of his actions. In performance I had the King read the names from the military "dog tags" of men that had been slain. Not only single speeches but duologues, too, can benefit from the "pointing exercise," such as Act 4, scene 3, of *Julius Caesar*. There is an exchange between Brutus and Cassius at line 41 in which each accuses the other of impropriety in their conduct of the war against Mark Anthony and Octavius. It's a long scene, so here is just a short extract with the moments when the actors point marked in bold.[50] Give the exercise a try and you'll notice just how violent they are towards each other. It's a verbal fight as both call on the gods to support their point of view and Brutus compares Cassius to a lowly slave:

Cassius.
O ye **Gods**, ye **Gods**, Must **I** endure all this?
Brutus.
All this? Ay more: Fret till **your** proud hart break.
Go shew **your Slaves** how Chollericke **you** are,
And make **your Bondmen** tremble. Must **I** bouge?
Must **I** observe **you**? Must **I** stand and crouch
Under **your** Testie Humour? By the **Gods**,
You shall digest the Venom of **your** Spleene
Though it do Split **you**. For, from this day forth,
Ile use **you** for **my** Mirth, yea for **my** Laughter
When **you** are Waspish.

The second exercise I often use helps a speech become tonally interesting. It's simply to move when the character has a thought change; normally this would be done by switching chairs. The rule when speaking text is "New thought = New tone" and this exercise not only physicalizes the words but is a reminder that there must be a key change in the notes of the voice with each movement/thought. The First Folio doesn't punctuate the words as editor/adaptors do so that it's much freer. If a modern edition is used in this exercise the actors will generally simply move on the major punctuation, but a speech is much richer and more complex when spoken rather than read. The exercise is of most benefit when applied

8. A Director's Approach

to the later plays. In Shakespeare's early works, the characters tend to more or less switch thoughts on the ends of verse lines. Helena's speech that concludes Act 1, scene 1, of *A Midsummer Night's Dream*—"How happy some, ore others, some can be?"[51]—is a good example of this. The following passage from *Timon of Athens* was probably written in Shakespeare's mature period (1607?), although an exact date of composition is unknown.[52] It begins Act 4, scene 1, and the misanthropic Timon is leaving Athens and cursing the city as he goes. The lines need to be heartfelt and specific or the speech will become one long boring rant. I have marked with a forward slash the places where the character *might* be changing thought and the actor moves to a different chair:

Timon.
Let me looke backe upon thee./O thou Wall
That girdles in those Wolves, dive in the earth,
And fence not Athens./Matrons, turne incontinent,/
Obedience fayle in Children:/Slaves and Fooles
Plucke the grave wrinkled Senate from the Bench,
And minister in their steeds,[53]/to generall Filthes.
Convert o'th' Instant greene Virginity,/
Doo't in your Parents eyes./Bankrupts, hold fast/
Rather then render backe; out with your Knives,
And cut your Trusters throates./Bound Servants, steale,/
Large-handed Robbers your grave Masters are,
And pill by Law./Maide, to thy Masters bed,
Thy Mistris is o'th' Brothell./Some[54] of sixteen,
Plucke the lyn'd Crutch from thy old limping Sire,
With it, beate out his Braines./Piety, and Feare,
Religion to the Gods,/Peace,/Justice,/Truth,/
Domesticke awe,/Night-rest, and Neighbourhood,/
Instruction,/Manners,/Mysteries, and Trades,/
Degrees,/Observances,/Customes, and Lawes,/
Decline to your confounding contraries./
And yet Confusion live:/Plagues incident to men,
Your potent and infectious Feavors, heape
On Athens ripe for stroke./Thou cold Sciatica,
Cripple our Senators, that their limbes may halt
As lamely as their Manners./Lust, and Libertie
Creepe in the Mindes and Marrowes of our youth,
That 'gainst the streame of Vertue they may strive,
And drowne themselves in Riot./Itches,/Blaines,/
So we[55] all th' Athenian bosomes, and their crop
Be generall Leprosie:/Breath, infect breath,
That their Society/(as their Friendship)/may
Be meerely poyson./Nothing Ile beare from thee
But nakednesse,/thou detestable Towne,/
Take thou that too, with multiplying Bannes[56]:/
Timon will to the Woods,/where he shall finde
Th' unkindest Beast, more kinder then Mankinde./
The Gods confound/(heare me you good Gods all)/
Th' Athenians both within and out that Wall:/
And graunt as *Timon* growes, his hate may grow
To the whole race of Mankinde,/high and low./
Amen. *Exit.*

It's an astonishing speech and one that belies the play's reputation as being an inferior *King Lear*. The language suddenly comes alive when using this exercise and each of Timon's curses will display a different weight and tone. Notice that there are no exclamation points in the folio printing, indicating that the outpouring of vitriol should be performed with a degree of subtlety. The Arden editor, H. J. Oliver, adds 19 exclamation points in just 40 lines.[57] If this were followed in performance, the speech would quickly become very tedious to the ear and consequently hard to follow.

An alternative way to employ the "thought change" exercise is to ask the actors to stand when speaking and to take a step when they discover a new thought. Try this with Emilia's speech that begins Act 4, scene 2, of *The Two Noble Kinsmen* (a section probably written by Shakespeare)[58] when she enters with pictures of Arcite and Palamon and attempts to decide who she loves most. If the two actors playing her objects of affection are placed at the opposite sides of the rehearsal room, Emilia can move towards either when she expresses a positive thought about them and away from them when she doesn't. You'll discover that after the speech Emilia is back in the middle, where she started from, and "Cannot distinguish, but must cry for both."

To someone reading this chapter who has no experience of performing or rehearsing a Shakespeare play, my descriptions may appear all too simplistic. I can only refer them to Declan Donnellan's words that "exercises are to be used rather than understood."[59] This is excellent advice from a director since it insists on discovery rather than dogma. In conclusion, let me give my own practical advice to anyone considering directing a Shakespeare play. In no particular order of importance:

- Don't sprinkle your discussion with words such as "trochee," "dactyl," "spondee," "anapest," and "amphibrach."[60] Some actors can become fixated on such terms, which can lead to a performance that is stale and "intellectualized" rather than spontaneous and free. If the director insists on repeatedly using these words, the play will bounce back to the study and away from the stage.
- Only read what is relevant to performance—this generally won't include literary commentators. Shakespeare's plays illustrate human behavior. Books from the modern age such as Erving Goffman's *The Presentation of Self in Everyday Life*,[61] which examines how people act to survive, and Deborah Tannen's *You Just Don't Understand*,[62] which investigates gender differences when using language, support Shakespeare's ideas. Tannen, for example, points out that, contrary to the production style of many modern Shakespeare companies, in conversation men will rarely lock eyes. Her analysis of how the two genders misinterpret language proved vital to me in directing *The Comedy of Errors* and took me away from preconceived ideas about the characters. Whereas Adriana's speech "Ay, ay, Antipholus, look strange and frown"[63] is often cloned as a "masculine" scolding, her language is in fact, by Tannen's definition, the feminine "rapport-talk" and an appeal to her husband's emotions. Luciana, on the other hand, is often presented on stage as a "girly-girl" although her views clearly display a masculine "report-talk" and seek to find solutions rather than offer support. It would be an interesting exercise to have the assistance of sociologists, behavioral psychologists, and sociolinguists in rehearsal rather than dramaturges, voice coaches, and historians.

- Make sure your historical, social, and character research is applied to performing the play in the 21st century. As Mike Alfreds has written, "We cannot (and shouldn't bother trying to) recreate the theatrical conditions we believe operated, say, four hundred years ago; there's no way we can respond to the play in the same way as its original audience."[64]
- Referring only to books is not a particularly productive way of working with actors, who tend to think in images rather than intellectual concepts. Listening to music and looking at selected paintings and photographs are far more likely to fire their imaginations.
- Edit the text yourself, based on the First Folio. If you're unable to do this because of time constraints, at the very least remove editor/adaptor impositions such as exclamation points.
- Be bold with cutting the text and do it before rehearsal begins, although the places where passages have been extracted should be clearly indicated to the actors so that they are aware of the need for a possible bridge. Much valuable rehearsal time can be lost with a seemingly endless group debate about whether a single word or phrase should be left in or taken out. Waiting until later to introduce cuts can be disastrous. When Sir Trevor Nunn directed *King Lear* for the Royal Shakespeare Company, it wasn't until the 12th week of rehearsals (they were also producing *The Seagull* in tandem with *Lear*) that additional cuts were made. These were rehearsed in an afternoon, causing actors at that evening's performance to stumble on passages they had become familiar with over three months. Sir Trevor wished to be fair, so spread the edits across each company member. The reward for these efforts was just 3 minutes removed from the overall playing time—a minute of which was put back on at the next performance.[65]
- All of the published quartos are available online on the British Library website, as well as many other places that display a facsimile of the folios, such as the Folger Shakespeare Library. If there is a textual crux—use them!
- Get to know the play inside out before rehearsal. This will allow you to watch the actors and listen to the rhythms of the language rather than placing your nose in the script and ignoring the action. Listening and observing will nearly always present you with a surprising discovery that hadn't occurred when reading the play alone.
- Place the actors on their feet early with their lines learned as quickly as possible. Actors need to get on with their job—acting. It will also change the atmosphere in rehearsal away from a university tutorial and more towards performance. Mike Alfreds is again spot on when he writes, "I've come up against glosses of Shakespeare texts in which the editor agonises about the possible meaning of a phrase and offers convoluted, totally unplayable options, whereas an actor, in the process of playing, makes instant sense of it."[66]
- Don't begin with exercises, begin with acting out the play. Exercises only become useful once the actors know the script in depth.
- There is no single magic "method" to apply when directing a play. Shakespeare usually invented a new color with every script he wrote and this means that each play requires a different—and imaginative—approach.

- Any statement made by the director should be provisional—tomorrow and tomorrow and tomorrow brings a new thought/approach/feeling for a scene.
- It's OK to experiment.
- It's OK to change your mind.
- It's OK not to know.

Throughout this book I've concentrated on words, lines, speeches, scenes, and characters. The final chapter looks at a single Shakespeare play—*Measure for Measure*.

9

Weighing Up the Options

"Measure for Measure"

Academics have labeled *Measure for Measure* a "problem" play. Ostensibly this is because the audience is presented with a number of moral "problems" that exist in society (and still exist) and a debate is set up around them. There's an underlying feeling they also use the word because the text causes them problems when trying to locate a central "meaning"—a pretty fruitless task in such a multifaceted, complex, and deliberately ambiguous play. Despite it being included under the grouping "Comedies" in the First Folio, the modern trend among directors is to find something darker in Shakespeare's script, and it is generally now performed as a pseudo-tragedy. The "problem" for editor/adaptors and director/interpreters alike is how to categorize *Measure for Measure* without getting tangled in a Polonius-like flurry of definitions such as:

> Tragedie, Comedie, Historie, Pastorall: Pastoricall-Comicall-Historicall-Pastorall: Tragicall-Historicall: Tragicall-Comicall-Historicall-Pastorall.[1]

The title suggests balance, so there are a number of juxtaposed situations and contradictory characters.[2] This idea of balance extends to the words Shakespeare uses in the text with their frequency often matching each other: virtue (used 12 times) and vice (11), wife (14) and husband (15), life (48) and death (42) and, interestingly, woman (19) and bawd (19). We might use the Duke's words to describe the language in the play: "Such a dependency of thing, on thing."[3] And so we have, to use just a few examples, lines such as "the goodness that is cheap in beauty, makes beauty brief in goodness,"[4] "Pay with falsehood, false exacting,"[5] "My mirth it much displeas'd, but pleas'd my woe,"[6] and "Who thinks he knows, that he ne'er knew my body,/But knows, he thinks, that he knows Isabel's."[7] (The folio punctuation gives the actor the precise phrasing.) The scenes and characters likewise juggle darkness and delight.

The word frequency also makes a strong case for the play being a comedy,[8] with "good" being one of the most used words (100 instances) and "punishment" (only mentioned twice) the least. *Measure for Measure* has a comic structure, ending with 4 weddings and a whipping, and draws elements found in many of Shakespeare's other comedies: the "Bed Trick" from *All's Well That Ends Well*, the Puritan from *Twelfth Night*, and a mispronouncing constable and a friar with a crazy plan from *Much Ado About Nothing*. In both *Measure* and *Much Ado* there is instruction given to "Kill Claudio"—an instruction that is not carried out—and the "baddie" (Don John, Lucio) is dispatched for future punishment. Both plays end, like *The Winter's Tale*, *Much Ado About Nothing*, and *All's Well That Ends Well*, with the miraculous resurrection of someone thought to be dead. The Duke's line "Believe not that the dribbling dart of Love/Can pierce a complete bosom"[9] is reminiscent of the vows taken against love by Benedick in *Much Ado*[10] and the King in *Love's Labour's Lost*. It might even be said that *Measure* is a comedy of mismatched lovers like *A Midsummer Night's Dream* and *The Two Gentlemen of Verona* as both the Duke and Angelo form "attachments" to someone else before finding their true partners. Angelo, through Isabella, finds Mariana, while the Duke, through Mariana, finds Isabel. It might be stretching things to gloss the Duke's line "Weed my vice, and let his grow"[11] as jealousy and a reference to Mariana's vice (vagina) and Angelo's "growing" erection, although Isabella uses the word "vice" in this sense to Claudio: "Wilt thou be made a man, out of my vice?"[12] Nonetheless it is clear the Duke has been visiting Mariana for a period of time, perhaps the 5 years of her exile to the Moated Grange. So perhaps it is Mariana who Friar Thomas has spoken about offstage that provokes the Duke to claim that love cannot pierce him? "Perhaps"—a word academics would read as speculation; an actor reads "perhaps" as imagination. If the play is a comedy of mismatched lovers, then in order to follow this through in performance some imaginative application to the script is necessary. Actors work from specifics so a plausible back story, based on the text, has to be created for each character. *It does not mean this is the actual true back story*—we simply don't know what that is, or if Shakespeare had one in mind—but one that can work as a catalyst in creating a role.[13]

Let's first look a little more closely at the "given circumstances" that establish the character of Duke Vincentio. He clearly knows what has happened to Mariana in great detail (he is her confessor, after all) and she recognizes him in his friar disguise. He asks Friar Thomas to "Supply me with *the* habit"[14] (my italics), which suggests he has used it before to visit Mariana. This time, however, he will also be traveling throughout Vienna meeting his subjects, so he needs Friar Thomas to "instruct me how I may formally in person bear/like a *true* Friar"[15] (my italics). The Duke has "ever loved the life removed"[16]—a nice ideal but irresponsible for a ruler. In order to achieve political stability, he needs to marry and have children to continue his lineage but, according to Lucio at least, "He's now past it."[17] One wonders if Vincentio is subconsciously describing himself when he says to Claudio, "When thou art old, and rich,/Thou hast neither heat, affection, limb, nor beauty,/To make thy riches pleasant."[18] Clearly he needs to learn a lot about justice and kingship, but he also needs to learn about love—and with it marriage. This is a common Shakespearean comic device (see Bertram and Proteus as examples). Visiting Angelo's jilted betrothed and her secluded world just won't do. The "Duke of dark corners,"[19] absent from public life, leads directly to his slander, since if people don't know their leader they will, like Lucio, fill in the details themselves.[20] Vincentio comes to accept this and his entrance in the last act, in public, is the very "loud applause and Aves vehement"[21] he had previously shunned. (The use of the word "aves" highlights his role as both political and spiritual leader of his subjects.) He demonstrates open government, before the people and outside the walled city or moated grange. The place he chooses to display his justice is, of course, in the very suburbs where the brothels had been pulled down.

Looking at the history of Shakespeare's time is not always useful for actors performing in the 21st century, but sometimes it can help them to more fully comprehend a role. One of the more interesting contemporary documents relating to Shakespeare allows for the purchase of scarlet cloth for him and his fellow actors to be in attendance at King James's coronation in July 1604—the same year *Measure for Measure* was first performed and probably written. So we can be pretty sure he was at that event and would have heard Bishop Bilson declaim:

> Since then Princes can not be Gods by nature, being framed of the same metall, and are in the same moulde, that others are; It foloweth directly, they are Gods by Office; Ruling, Judging, and Punishing in Gods steede, & so deserving Gods name here on earth.[22]

That is the view of Cardinal Pandulph in *King John*, who greets the kings of England and France with "Haile, you anointed deputies of heaven"[23] and, pursuing this idea, *Macbeth* relates the commonly held view that a king could perform miracles.[24] In a way the Duke in *Measure for Measure* does exactly that by resurrecting Claudio from the dead. He behaves "like power divine,"[25] the stage image of removing the bags from the heads of Claudio and Barnadine becoming a reheading or rebirth for these two characters. They are, as Isabella says, "Like man new made."[26] What is often overlooked when reading but clear in production is that Vincentio undergoes *exactly* the same process when Lucio pulls off his friar hood and the head of the Duke is revealed. It is at that moment that he begins to act like a true monarch with his costume—half duke, half friar—reinforcing the idea that a king is appointed by God.

Any directors preparing a production of *Measure for Measure* will tear their hair out pondering the question of Vincentio's marriage to Isabella and consider if there is genuine love between the two partners or if it is simply a more sophisticated version of Angelo's assault on a would-be nun. What mustn't be forgotten is that this is no ordinary betrothal but one ordained by God himself. Marrying Isabella, certainly in Jacobean terms, would be an ideal match. As a young woman she will bear him children and, crucially, as a Catholic, also help mend the schism in the Church. It's interesting that the three places mentioned in the text as possible venues for the Duke's "remove"—Russia, Rome, and Poland, as well as Vienna itself—all had strong Catholic connections at this time. The Duke appears to want his subjects to believe he is negotiating an end to religious conflict for a people tired of the constant fractures in the church. As Lucio puts it, "Grace is Grace, despite of all controversy."[27] In 1604 Shakespeare's audience, like the Duke's subjects, were presented with a choice between a protestant monarch with Catholic connections (James's mother being the Catholic martyr Mary, Queen of Scots) or a Taliban-like Puritanism. Both King James and the Duke have a religious balancing act to perform. History supports this idea. One of James's first acts as king, in August 1604, was to arrange a treaty that ended the Anglo-Spanish war. Preparation for this had begun in 1600 when the Cardinal Archduke of Austria, who was married to Isabel, Infanta of Spain, and ruled the Spanish-occupied Netherlands, sent his secretary Lodovick Vereiken to England on a peace mission. Vereiken attended a performance the Lord Chamberlain's Men gave at court, mostly likely of *Henry IV, Part 1*, so it's possible Shakespeare met him. At the very least he would certainly have known of Lodovick. It can surely be no coincidence that Shakespeare included in his first play under James's rule such details as a *Cardinal*/Duke from Austria, who marries someone called Isabel and uses the alias Lodovick, at a time when there was a push in England towards a resolution of doctrinal strife. None of Shakespeare's sources use these names or location. This is useful detail for an actor. The Vincentio/Isabella marriage will be a balanced partnership—her merciful nature is matched by her husband's strong judgment. Significantly, the Duke's pardon of Barnadine comes *after* Isabella pleads for Angelo's life; he learns from her example. However, unlike some commentators seem to think, he *does not* release Barnadine unconditionally but gives him over to the hands of Friar Peter, who will advise him spiritually so he may "provide for better times to come."[28] Barnadine is "a Bohemian born" and Bohemia is another Catholic country. It's a smart political move on the Duke's part not to execute a Catholic foreign national despite him being a confessed murderer. He has learned that to be a leader sometimes means "Craft against vice, I must apply."[29]

It has become a theatrical cliché for actresses playing Isabella not to accept the Duke's offer of marriage at the end of the play, or at least to equivocate on it. Apart from the age difference, it's difficult to understand why their relationship should not be successful since they are so alike. Both are isolated, flawed people who learn from their mistakes. As to age, Henry VIII was 45 when he married the 28-year-old Jane Seymour and she bore him his only surviving male heir, Edward VI. The love between Isabella and the "Fantastical" Duke is defined not only by such lines as the Duke's insisting he will stay true to her "(Not changing heart with habit)"[30] (picked out by the use of brackets in the folio) but also by the fact that both are accused of madness. And as we know from *A Midsummer Night's Dream*, Act 5, scene 1, line 4:

> Lovers and mad men have such seething braines,
> Such shaping phanasies, that apprehend more
> Then coole reason ever comprehends.
> The Lunaticke, the Lover, and the Poet
> Are of imagination all compact.

The marriage is set up by Isabella's words (surely deliberately chosen by Shakespeare?) in reply to the Duke's "Make it your comfort." She says, "I do my Lord."[31] His proposal is that they should be equal partners in marriage and in ruling the State (my italics):

> I have a motion much imports your good,
> Whereto *if* you'll a *willing* ear incline;
> What's mine is yours, and what is yours is mine.[32]

A final "measure for measure"—balance and harmony. Critics of this view argue that there is no stage direction for them to leave together although, since the play is over, an indication to exit isn't really necessary. However, there is an interesting stage direction at the end of *The Taming of the Shrew* (another play only published in the First Folio) that states "Exit Petruchio" but not Katherina. If this is taken literally and is not a printing error, then she is left on her own. When Shakespeare wanted to signify a fractured relationship he did so, as he appears to have done in *Shrew*.

Since marrying has made the Duke "one flesh" with Isabella, to better understand him we must look more closely at his partner. What is the path she travels that can make a prospective nun accept an older man's offer of marriage and with it the responsibilities of monarchy?

A journey that begins in a convent cell and ends with her jointly ruling an entire city-state. It should be noted immediately that Isabella is *not* a nun. The Provost notes (my italics) that she is "to be *shortly* of a Sister-hood"[33] while Claudio comments, "This day, my sister should the Cloister enter,/And there receive her approbation."[34] In other words, she was entering the nunnery in order to become a nun *on probation*. Lucio's arrival prevents even this, which, of course, is the point of the scene. But what prompted Isabella's decision to enter holy orders? Her relationship with her father seems all-important, and in her exchange with the condemned Claudio she invokes his memory twice. The first is idolization—"there my father's grave/did utter forth a voice"[35]—while the second glances at her mother being guilty of the same crime Claudio is to die for: "Heaven shield my Mother played my Father fair:/For such a warped slip of wilderness/Ne'er issued from his blood."[36] It's a revealing overreaction to the circumstances.[37]

It might be imagined that Claudio and Isabella's father had died fairly recently; Escalus's words, "Alas this gentleman,/Whom I would save, had a most noble father,"[38] seem to suggest that. If he was recently deceased, and idolized by Isabella, it would make sense for her to renounce all men, none of whom could live up to her image of her father, and enter a convent. Perhaps it was also this death that prompted Claudio's decision to marry and have children to continue his father's line? In Isabella's second scene with Angelo there is an interesting and often overlooked passage where she offers the opinion:

> Women? Help heaven; men their creation mar
> In profiting by them: Nay, call us ten times frail,
> For we are soft, as our complexions are,
> And credulous to false prints.[39]

Is it personal experience that makes her speak these words? Has she, at some point in her life, been credulous to the false prints of a man? Was she, like Angelo, betrothed to someone she later believed was untrue? Perhaps it was her father who chose a partner for her, whom she later rejected? This imagined back story more sharply defines for the actress playing Isabella the similarities between her situation and that of both Mariana and Angelo. Even more interesting to speculate is whether, like Brabantio in *Othello* (written around the same time as *Measure for Measure*), it was this failed or inappropriate love match that caused her father's death.

None of these speculations can be backed with hard evidence, but for the actress playing Isabella it makes the guilt at her brother *and* father's death a powerful ingredient that can give vigor and depth to her scenes. It also provides a plausible enough reason for her to desire "a more strict restraint"[40] on the already overly strict Votarists of Saint Clare and a subtext to lines such as "Th'impression of keen whips, I'd wear as rubies."[41] Like Angelo in the last act of the play she feels guilty ("I am no better")[42] and in need of punishment. However, unlike Ophelia, who has also lost a father, brother, and boyfriend, she doesn't go mad from guilt.[43] What is apparent from the text is the father/daughter relationship Isabella and Vincentio enjoy. The first time Isabella calls him "father" is marked in the folio with a capital letter and comes immediately after he tells her, "The cure of it not only saves your brother, but keeps you from dishonour in doing it."[44] She generally continues to afford him this title thereafter. Mariana never addresses the Duke as father but chooses "Frier" instead. The

Duke's first use of the word "daughter" to Isabella occurs much later, at the appropriate point when he is comforting her after delivering the false news of Claudio's death.[45] He does, however, call Mariana "daughter" in his first scene with her but not after—perhaps another indication of his developing affections away from Mariana and towards Isabella? There is a similar use of the word "father" in *Romeo and Juliet*. Surprisingly, there are only two moments in the play when Juliet meets Frier Lawrence; Act 2, scene 6 (her marriage to Romeo) and Act 4, scene 1 (when she receives the sleeping potion). She refers to him as "my ghostly Confessor," "the Frier," "Holy Father" (in front of Paris), "Frier," and finally "Farewell deare father"; the last time Lawrence sees her alive. Since Juliet's real father has just disowned her in very brutal terms, this final phrase is poignant and is perhaps set up by Paris's second line in the scene: "My Father Capulet will have it so." It might be argued that marrying Vincentio helps Isabella regain her lost father in the same way that Frier Lawrence becomes a surrogate parent to Juliet.

These contexts help clarify Isabella's acceptance of the Duke's offer of marriage. Here is a man who, unlike Claudio, could genuinely speak her "father's voice" and fill the void created by his loss. As a prospective nun, Isabella was literally seeking to become "God's bride." What better and more holier match than to marry the Almighty's appointed deputy on earth, the Duke who has "power divine"?

His proposal to her is made in two stages, marked by the meter. The first is immediately after Claudio is revealed as being alive:

> Give me your hand, and say you will be mine,
> He is my brother too: But fitter time for that[46]:

The language Vincentio chooses—"Say you will be mine"—is a request and not a command. In modern parlance he "pops the question," but like any suitor he is unsure of a positive answer. The folio colon in the middle of the second line depicts a shy bachelor quickly qualifying his words, although he does indicate that he will repeat his intentions later. The second proposal is made with almost the last words of the play and comes at the end of a verse line, another of the balanced statements found throughout the play: "What's mine is yours, and what is yours is mine."[47] The short break at the line's end allows Isabella the action of taking the Duke's hand, and the next two lines, which conclude the play, clearly point to a partnership rather than a coercion (my italics):

> *So* bring *us* to *our* palace, where *we'll* show
> What's yet behind, that's meet you all should know.[48]

"So" means "And so" or "So now" and signifies a resolution—Isabella uses the word in this context at Act 2, scene 4, line 84, when she is resigned to Claudio's death.[49] This is the typical form of Shakespearean comedy, one definition of a comedy being that there is a positive resolution, consistent with the plot. The rhyming couplet enforces the sense of closure. More importantly, Isabella and the Duke taking hands in public at this point is a handfasting ceremony. They are married in exactly the same way as Mariana/Angelo and Juliet/Claudio, underlining the legality of these previous matches.

When we weigh up the characters in *Measure for Measure* their follies are generally matched by compensatory finer qualities, as is evident in the pairing of Isabella and the Duke. Modern productions embrace this idea of balance but tend to use it to pitch the "bad"

Angelo against the "good" Vincentio. Rather than comedic harmony, this creates a distortion of Shakespeare's text into something simplistic, confusing, and dissatisfying. What is the impression the audience is to leave with? That the Duke is jilted but Angelo is coerced into a life of married misery with Mariana? Hardly the stuff of comedy. There are positives and negatives in both Angelo and Vincentio, although ultimately they attain equilibrium. If this were not the case, then the actor playing Angelo has to undergo a melodramatic transformation from pervert to penitent without any stages being marked in between. Angelo is a complex character who is depicted as being neither wholly bad nor wholly good. Without doubt he genuinely believes his style of governance will benefit Vienna, and in many ways it's difficult to argue that it won't. However, he's not the only character in the play who walks a see-saw of change, and Angelo's behavior might be placed in perspective by noting what happens to Escalus, who travels in the opposite direction.

The first word in the play is "Escalus," which points to him having a key role in the narrative. He is initially described in praiseworthy terms that indicate he is the ideal candidate to become deputy:

> Of Government, the properties to un-fold,
> Would seeme in me t' affect speech & discourse,
> Since I am put to know, that your owne Science
> Exceedes (in that) the lists of all advice
> My strength can give you: Then no more remaines
> But that, to your sufficiency, as your worth is able,
> And let them worke: The nature of our People,
> Our *Cities Institutions,* and the Termes
> For Common Justice, y'are as pregnant in
> As Art, and practice, hath inriched any
> That we remember.[50]

The Duke's words are carefully chosen: "your owne Science" and "y'are as pregnant in/As Art." "Science" and "Art," both capitalized in the First Folio, suggest a man whose legal knowledge comes from a book and not practical experience. He knows the law but doesn't practice it. The Viennese list of statutes is a long one, but the problem is that these statutes are not being applied. If Escalus were to become deputy, he would continue down the route of legal laxity. At first he lives up to the Duke's expectations. His first act of "justice" is to plead for Claudio's life on, not a point of law, but class—he "had a most noble father."[51] This is quickly followed by releasing Froth on the basis that he was born in Vienna and was "of fourscore pounds a year,"[52] while Pompey is allowed to "continue in his courses"[53] and has to be rearrested. "Pardon is still the nurse of second woe"[54] states the man who has just pardoned two criminals, Pompey and Froth.

Escalus is part of the Vienna the Duke describes as having "Laws, for all faults,/But faults so countenanc'd, that the strong Statutes/Stand like the forfeits in a Barber's shop,/As much in mock, as mark."[55] There is a whiff of corruption in the air where "money talks" and class matters. This not only applies to the release of Froth but Barnadine too, whose "friends still wrought Reprieves for him,"[56] and Pompey expects to escape a prison sentence if Lucio pays his bail. "Reprieves" has a capital letter in the folio, which might suggest that extra emphasis on this word is required from the actor playing the Provost. "Reprieves" thus becomes a euphemistic word for bribery. The Duke has seen "corruption boil and bubble,/Till it o'er-run the Stew"[57] and Escalus has contributed to that world, a world where the murderer Barnadine was "Nursed up and bred." The "precise" Angelo knows precisely what has made Barnadine so flagrantly disregard the law: "Thieves for their robbery have authority,/When Judges steal themselves."[58] Whatever may be said of Angelo, he at least attempts to end this corruption, although it partly continues on his class-conscious watch. The brothels in the suburbs are torn down, but those in the city are bought by a capitalist-minded "wise Burger" who will no doubt make a quick profit when the Duke returns. And, as Pompey points out, lechery might be quashed, but usury continues. However, even Lucio admits, "Lord Angelo Dukes it well."[59]

There can be little doubt that Escalus is fully aware of Angelo's goal in executing Claudio; it is a test case to demonstrate the law which, as Angelo says, "like a Prophet/Looks in a glass that shows what future evils.... Are now to have no successive degress,/But here they live to end."[60] Angelo's objective is to eliminate crime, and he will start with Claudio, who Lucio immediately realizes has been arrested "to make him an example."[61] Escalus understands the wider implications of the death of Claudio: "There are pretty orders beginning I can tell you: It is but heading, and hanging,"[62] but his oft-repeated remedy is, "There is no remedy."[63] As the plot progresses, the person who Mistress Overdone describes as "accounted a merciful man"[64] begins, to use his own words, to "play the tyrant."[65] He is like some Nazi bureaucrat, quickly embracing the new regime with gusto, while persuading himself he is "only following orders." His journey is one from excessive leniency to draconian repression. Escalus's actions become more and more extreme, so that by the end the "old Escalus" whom the Duke knew is replaced by a man who jails Mistress Overdone, leaving a 15-month-old child without a mother, attempts to arrest 4 people, and wants to torture a friar. Coming out of character for a moment, the Duke has to warn him to "be not so hot."[66] The "lack of temper'd judgment"[67] Escalus is quick to see in Angelo could equally be applied to himself. There is not just one "corrupt Deputy" in Vienna but two, and of the pair Angelo is the more honest.

Of course, there's no getting away from the fact that the story could have ended very differently with Claudio dead and his sister deflowered, yet one might say that Angelo's "indecent proposal" to Isabella is how things operate in the corrupt Vienna. It is another "measure for measure," little different from the "reprieves" that have been bargained for Barnadine's life.[68] This may be a provocative view, but it's the type of textural discovery that can help the actor playing Angelo attain a more balanced view of his character. The term most critical commentators use to describe Angelo is the generalized and pejorative "hypocrite," which is something an actor can't play. A performer will want to be specific in identifying Angelo's actions and deliver them with truth. The audience and other characters might judge some of these actions to be hypocritical, but Angelo's objective was not to be a "hypocrite." His singular motivation is to make Vienna a safer place for its citizens to live, and although his justice is strict, it's consistent, and comes from a desire to do good rather than evil. It is Richard III who is "determined to prove a Villaine,"[69] not Angelo. If the actor portraying the "corrupt Deputy" is to create a fully rounded and believable character, then it is necessary to mount a defense of what Angelo says and does.

The first important thing to note is that Angelo never commits any crime, although he certainly had intentions to do so and would have carried out a rape had not Mariana kept the late-night appointment in his garden instead of Isabella. The execution of Claudio, in which he is only guilty of breaking a promise and not having a "special warrant," isn't murder and is within the law. The Duke condemns Angelo's "salt *imagination*"[70] (my italics) and not his actions while Isabella is clear in her view that "his Act did not o'er-take his bad intent/And must be buried but as an intent/That perish'd by the way."[71] Angelo is no Demetrius and Chiron, who rape Lavinia in *Titus Andronicus*, but a man who is all too human, with his prominent characteristics after meeting Isabella being doubt and regret. Angelo's first soliloquy in the play (Act 2, scene 2, line 163) is punctuated with 13 question marks in the folio,[72] which demonstrate that he steps back to search his conscience rather than pushing forward with a plan:

> What's this? what's this? is this her fault, or mine?
> The Tempter, or the Tempted, who sins most? ha?
> Not she: nor doth she tempt: but it is I,
> That, lying by the Violet in the Sunne,
> Doe as the Carrion do's, not as the flowre,
> Corrupt with vertuous season: Can it be,
> That Modesty may more betray our Sence
> Then womans lightnesse? having waste ground enough,
> Shall we desire to raze the Sanctuary
> And pitch our evils there? oh fie, fie, fie:
> What dost thou? or what art thou *Angelo*?
> Dost thou desire her fowly, for those things
> That make her good? oh, let her brother live:
> Theeves for their robbery have authority,
> When Judges steale themselves: what, doe I love her,
> That I desire to heare her speake againe?
> And feast upon her eyes? what is't I dreame on?
> Oh cunning enemy, that to catch a Saint,
> With Saints dost bait thy hooke: most dangerous
> Is that temptation, that doth goad us on
> To sinne, in loving vertue: never could the Strumpet
> With all her double vigor, Art, and Nature
> Once stir my temper: but this vertuous Maid
> Subdues me quite: Ever till now
> When men were fond, I smild, and wondred how. *Exit.*

Unlike Escalus, Angelo reflects on his behavior and recognizes he is the one who "sins most." With refreshing honesty, no excuses are offered to justify his temptations and he lays the blame squarely on himself. There is no hint of an "indecent proposal" to seduce Isaballa and nor does he conclude, like Iago:

> I have't : it is engendred : Hell, and night
> Must bring this monstrous Birth, to the worlds light.[73]

In fact, the solution he reaches is to "let her brother live," the first of three times he admits that executing Claudio is wrong. Later, believing Claudio to be dead, he immediately regrets it: "He should have liv'd ... would yet he had lived."[74] In almost his last words in the play, he speaks of his "Penitent heart."[75] ("Heart" is an apt choice of word connecting his thoughts to Mariana.)

When the "indecent proposal" first enters his mind (although there are seeds of the idea earlier in the scene), he is clumsy and uncertain in delivering it, couching it in terms not of himself but an imagined "supposed," an oblique testing of the waters rather than an assault. Notice how the First Folio punctuation (the speech is one sentence) helps the actor create Angelo's sense of unease[76]:

> Admit no other way to save his life
> (As I subscribe not that, nor any other,
> But in the losse of question) that you, his Sister,
> Finding your selfe desir'd of such a person,
> Whose creadit with the Judge, or owne great place,
> Could fetch your Brother from the Manacles
> Of the all-building-Law: and that there were
> No earthly meane to save him, but that either
> You must lay downe the treasures of your body,
> To this supposed, or else to let him suffer:
> What would you doe?

It could be said that "or else to let him suffer" refers to himself as much as Claudio since he is again wrestling with his conscience, striving to square his newfound sexual feelings with his long-held moral probity. There is no sign of a potential rape or physical attack seen in some modern productions (usually over a desk). The only time he spells out the bargain directly comes later: "Redeem thy brother,/By yielding up thy body to my will."[77] It is said in reaction to Isabella's rejection of him. He tells her (my italics), "*Now* I give my sensual race, the rein,"[78] and later "by the affection that *now* guides me most,"[79] which suggests it is only after a personal internal struggle that he resolves to give in to his desires and complete "what is't I dream on."[80] It's a dream, a sexual fantasy, and not his habitual behavior.

Angelo appears to be a grown man who reaches puberty in the play. He is characterized by Lucio as someone "who never feels/The wanton stings, and motions of the sense,"[81] preferring to "blunt his natural edge."[82] Angelo lives in a world without sex—until he meets Isabella. The moment is marked in their first scene together and occurs immediately after Isabella pleads with him to "ask your heart ... if it confess/a natural guiltiness."[83] These few short words are incredibly evocative for Angelo. "Heart" gives him the idea of love, which, like the Duke, he has previously shunned, especially from Mariana. "Confess" reminds him of God and the confessional, "natural" the "natural edge" Lucio spoke of, while "guiltiness" will be a powerful motivating factor in his future actions, as it is with Isabella. It's a neat summary of his conflicting emotions. Angelo's response is an aside to the audience describing the awakening sexual feelings within him. "She speaks, and 'tis such sense,/That my sense breeds with it"[84] repeats the language previously used by Lucio. The choice of "breeds" seems obvious enough, while "sense" can mean "stimulus" as in "sensual" or "sensation." By the time Isabella has left the scene, Angelo is at full sexual potency and it is arguably his erection he is talking about when he asks, "What's this? What's this?" Following puberty is adolescence and his words are those of a doting lover rather than a ravisher. Isabella's voice and eyes are the images that strike him most—there is no mention of her body.

Angelo's major concern in his first soliloquy is crucial to the development of his character—"What, do I love her." It is *love* he later asks from Isabella in return for Claudio's life. He repeats this twice in their second meeting: "Plainly conceive I love you"[85] being followed by "He shall not Isabell if you give me love"[86]—the first time he uses her name directly when addressing her. To emphasize his sincerity he concludes with a solemn vow, "Believe me on my Honour/My words express my purpose,"[87] his purpose being to receive *love*, not sex, although the two are obviously linked. This schoolboy crush is followed by a schoolboy tantrum when Isabella rejects him. For the rest of the play it is *fear* that motivates him most: fear of love, fear of God and the hereafter, fear Claudio might, Laertes-like, return to kill him if pardoned, but most of all fear of women. This fear of women isn't something experienced by Angelo alone but seems to be universally present in the male psyche. *The Hite Report on Male Sexuality*, published in 1978, has a respondent describe his feelings when a woman rejects him and he writes in words that could be spoken by Angelo: "I feel worthless ... mad that someone has this power over me against my better judgment. Against my will. Mind rape, the kind women do."[88]

My 2010 production of *Measure for Measure* in Alaska, which presented the play in a Jacobean setting, opened with Angelo delivering a sermon that was written in 1615 by Joseph Swetnam[89] and is typical of the misogyny that was rife at this time and still exists today, although it is more hidden. It was included so that the audience could see Angelo performing an action—preaching (a veiled Mariana watching)—rather than just hearing his views described in the text. It also helped place those views in the context of the age—many of Shakespeare's audience would have agreed with Angelo/Swetnam. More importantly, it served to help the actor playing Angelo construct a back story for his character. Consider lines Swetnam wrote, such as "A woman which is fair in show is foul in condition." This is exactly Angelo's problem; Isabella looks fair but may have been sent by the devil to tempt him: "Oh cunning enemy, that to catch a Saint/With Saints dost bait thy hook."[90] Swetnam constantly warns men that to consort with women is a danger to their souls and Angelo, believing Claudio dead and Isabella "deflowered" by him, becomes a kind of Raskolnikov fearing for his soul.[91]

One of the principal accusations leveled at the "cruel" Angelo is that he abandoned Mariana once her dowry had been lost at sea. There's no doubt this was a callous act, especially since her brother was drowned at the same time. Swetnam explains the logic of not marrying unless a dowry is in place (Claudio and Juliet lack a dowry too) and his words provide a clear defense of Angelo's behavior:

> There are many which think when they are married that they may live by love, but if wealth be wanting, hot love will soon be cold, and your hot desires will be soon quenched with the smoke of poverty.

Swetnam, like Angelo, appears to have had some kind of failed love affair which had broken his heart and shaped his extreme views: "A woman is like to a pumice stone, for which way soever you turn a pumice stone, it is full of holes; even so are women's hearts, for if love steal in at one hole, it steps out at another." He concludes with the revealing words that he has spoken out against women "for it may be a warning to make others wise." This suggests he has not been "wise" in the past and wants other men to learn from his experience. The problem for the Jacobeans, and Angelo, was that the Bible told them humanity suffered as a result of Eve's original sin yet one of these "daughters of Eve" was the recently deceased Elizabeth, the "Virgin Queen." Swetnam acknowledges this: "And yet I will not say but amongst dust there is a Pearl found, and in hard rocks, Diamonds of great value. And so amongst many women there are some good, as that gracious and glorious Queen of all womankind, the Virgin Mary, the mother of all bliss. What won her honor but a humble mind and her pains and love unto our Savior, Christ?" In Swetnam's mind women are either saints or whores,[92] and that corresponds to the world of the play where, as noted previously, the words "woman" and "bawd" are used an equal amount of times. And so Isabella is "a thing en-skied, and sainted"[93] while the prostitute Kate Keepdown is a "rotten Medler."[94] The Duke spells out the limits imposed by gender when he tells Mariana: "Why you are nothing then: neither Maid, Widow, nor Wife?"[95] Bearing in mind the comments in an earlier chapter that "nothing" or "no-thing" was a term for woman/vagina, it might be crudely said that Vincentio is telling Marianna, "You're just a cunt." Lucio backs up the Duke by saying, "My lord, she may be a punk"[96]—if she doesn't conform to any of society's definitions of a woman's role in life, then she can only be a hooker.

Angelo is no different to other men. His first assessment of Isabella is that she is a "virtuous maid" but he later changes his view to the only other option available to him by the mores of the time and he calls on her to play the role God chose for women:

> Be that you are,
> That is a woman; if you be more, you're none.
> If you be one (as you are well exprest
> By all external warrents) show it now,
> By putting on the destin'd Livery.[97]

With Mariana he travels in the opposite direction and initially believes that "her reputation was dis-valued/In Levity."[98] What has led Angelo to this opinion? Probably that old Shakespearean favorite, jealousy. The Duke hints at this when he feels the need to reassure Angelo that Mariana has been faithful: "I have confess'd her, and I know her virtue."[99] It's easy to imagine Angelo having had the sudden burst of jealousy that overcame Leontes in *The Winter's Tale* or to be described in the terms used by Iago in *Othello*:

> Trifles light as ayre
> Are to the jealious, confirmations strong
> As proofes of holy Writ.[100]

What "trifles" led Angelo to think Mariana was disreputable we don't know, but Swetnam provides a clue when he writes of women that "lust and uncleanness continually keeps them company." The prepubescent Angelo, holding this to be true, may well have recoiled when Mariana, fervently in love and newly "married," made a sexual advance towards him. It might even be argued that Mariana is "the strumpet" he is speaking of when he says:

> never could the Strumpet
> With all her double vigour, Art, and Nature
> Once stir my temper.[101]

The difficult but crucial transition any actor playing Angelo faces is accepting marriage to Mariana, and along with it manhood and responsibility. Like Isabella he stays silent at the end of the play, but he *must* be affected by Mariana pleading for his life. His final soliloquy is one of despair when he believes God has deserted him. It concludes:

> Alack, when once our grace we have forgot,
> Nothing goes right, we would, and we would not.[102]

Mariana provides that grace, touching the common Shakespearean theme of a woman's love redeeming a man. "Power divine" ensures Angelo receives his God-given partner. The Duke explains Mariana's love for Angelo has "like an impediment in the current made it more violent and unruly."[103] The use of the word "impediment" recalls Sonnet 116: "Let not to the marriage of true minds/Admit impediments" while "unruly" again hints at love and madness being closely allied. Witnessing the actions of Mariana, it is not too difficult to rewrite Swetnam's earlier words so they become a thought of Angelo's when she pleads for his life: "What won her honour but Mariana's humble mind and her pains and love unto myself." Which is why he has a "penitent *heart*" (my italics).

Measure for Measure is a play that teeters on tragedy. Angelo could easily have become another Macbeth, and there are similarities between the two characters. Both lose their sense of identity; "What art thou Angelo?" and "This deed unshapes me quite"[104] being reflected by Macbeth's "To know my deed 'twere best not know myself."[105] Both have thoughts that are interrupted by knocking—the devil knocking at the door—and the imagery that describes them is similarly of ill-fitting clothes. Macbeth immediately regrets killing Duncan as Angelo does Claudio, while Isabella is urged to be a woman by Angelo, "if you be more you're none,"[106] in the same terms Macbeth protests he is a man "who dares do more is none."[107] Once Claudio is dead, Angelo could have embarked on a Macbeth-like bloodbath of "heading and hanging." There is the hint of a possible coup with Angelo suggesting the Duke might be insane: "His actions show much like to madness, pray heaven his wisdom be not tainted."[108] Pompey says much the same thing when he warns Escalus, "If you live to see this come to pass."[109] Will there be some kind of Thermidor that "neutralizes" Escalus in the same way Banquo is removed? Or a revolt of the young that, like Malcolm, overthrows the regime? Happily, neither Isabella nor Mariana are Lady Macbeth and the resolution is not nihilistic. There is humanism in the play that is found in the all-too-human characters. Each might well say, along with Pompey: "Truly sir, I am a poor fellow that would live."[110]

The play is a comedy; a moral comedy, perhaps, but still a comedy. Balance is the strongest theme in the text, and the characters have to be carefully scrutinized so that their actions are consistent but nonetheless complex and convincing. Apply too great a pressure to a single aspect of their behavior and the characters and narrative tip the scales towards melodrama. The "problems" presented to the audience are ones that still concern us today. Which is better—Angelo's "zero tolerance" against the perpetuators of crime or the Duke's liberal forgiveness? Is marriage the sacred foundation of a stable society? Should sexual behavior be kept between consenting adults or be a matter for state control? Do we want a "strong," decisive leader or one who champions the sanctity of individual choice? Considering such problems requires some measure.

Conclusion

"I'll to my book, for yet ere supper-time I must perform"

One of the most popular editions of Shakespeare used in professional theatre is the New Penguin printing of the text. This has nothing to do with the quality of the notes and the commentary, the emendations being precise, correct, and imaginative, or that the meter and punctuation assist the actors in creating their roles. It's not particularly any of those things. The choice is based purely on the size of the script and the layout. The New Penguin fits easily into a pocket or purse and has no notes on the same pages as the dialogue that interrupt the flow. The notes are at the back of the book with no indication on the page that they are there to help clarify a passage. Generally placed after the notes, on the very last pages, is a section called "An Account of the Text," which lists in almost cryptic form the folio/quarto differences. It takes a lot of page-turning back and forth to identify where these occur, and it would be a rare actor or director who took the time to do so. Usually this section is simply ignored by the profession. When choosing a script for rehearsal, the most common practice is described by Anthony Sher when he was directed by Bill Alexander as Richard in *Richard III*:

> Bill says he'd like to use the New Penguin edition to rehearse with, and the Arden for notes—these are much better and wittier, but so profuse there are only about two lines of the play itself per page. Alison [assistant director] will cross-check both versions and when there are discrepancies we'll choose which-ever is more useful for our purposes.[1]

The Arden is used for reference when a passage is unclear but is too unwieldy to be a practical rehearsal script. The New Penguin edition is what the actors actually hold in their hand.[2] This can cause problems. For a play like *Richard III*, there were six quarto versions published up until the folio was released in 1623, and two after, plus a further 3 folios. On top of that is now added another two modern editor/adaptor editions, which the director conflates again to make their own. That makes *fifteen* separate versions of the same play. It's no wonder that Sher, a hugely experienced actor, had trouble learning his lines:

> I can find no logic as to why he sometimes uses "hath" instead of "have," a "thee" instead of "you," or vice versa. These little dents in the road trip me up constantly, making the journey rather nerve-racking.[3]

In the event, the production turned out to be groundbreaking and Sher and Alexander were rightly lauded for their collective efforts in presenting the play anew. It's not always the case.

This is the moment I have to turn on my own profession and admit that, when it comes to altering Shakespeare's text, directors can be the very worst offenders. In 2006 Alan Dessen wrote an essay for *Shakespeare Survey # 59*[4] in which he listed all of the changes directors made to Shakespeare's language in the considerable amount of productions he had seen worldwide the previous year. It makes sobering reading. The alterations, big and small, appear to have been made without reference to any evidence that might suggest them and with little thought beyond the director's whim (and ego.) Time after time Dessen describes plays butchered by directors; the crassness of some choices is truly cringeworthy. The word "niggard," for example, is often removed from modern productions as it apparently could be misinterpreted as a racial slur. Of course this is in itself racist since it supposes that African Americans can't understand the difference between niggard/"miserly" ("niggardly" is still current in the English language) and a highly offensive insult. Shakespeare seems to attract the worst type of director dilettante. I do not, by any means, advocate a stifling conservatism in producing a script—just a little more integrity.

In defense of directors, I would say that some of the changes they make are purely practical. No matter what level of professional theatre you work at, a director will always be encouraged to save money. So two settings become one, characters are edited out or conflated to save on actor salaries, an intermission must be included because of the revenue from bar sales, the choice of modern dress is made simply because it's cheaper, and plays are extensively cut in length to enable an audience to catch the last bus or train home. This is understandable and the reality of modern theatre. If directors lack money, they have even less time. Rarely is a director allowed the opportunity to explore the text with the actors, to prepare in depth, or to experiment. The very idea of "experimentation" is dismissed as self-indulgence. In fact the most common amount of time a director is able to devote to a production (and be paid for) is one week for preparation, three to four weeks rehearsal, half a week technical rehearsal, followed by half a week of dress rehearsals and, if you are very lucky, previews. Six weeks maximum. And don't think the actors are always available throughout this period. There's quite rightly an Equity restriction on the amount of hours an actor can work and, as an actor can also be performing in an evening show, rehearsal time is reduced still further. The larger companies work a little differently, but not much differently. The woefully small fee directors receive will mean that they, as well as the designer, are already planning their next production—and the one after that—as rehearsals progress. They have to do this, simply to make ends meet. With a lack of time and money, the simplest expedient when it comes to the text is for the director to defer to the editors, little realizing how much an editor's role has become that of an adaptor. The director is blindly allowing an editor/adaptor to guide the actors and make some of the most important decisions in the production. These decisions, as we have seen, can often be made with little or no evidence, are literary in nature and, since the editor/adaptor has a conflicting objective, are not only unhelpful to an actor and director but can stifle their creativity. The director Katie Mitchell recognizes this and advises fellow directors, "Literary criticism may encourage generalisation and vagueness in your thinking about the play."[5] Both actor and director need to be specific in their choices and would do well to remember David Mamet's KISS rule: Keep It Simple, Stupid.[6]

The bottom line for an actor rehearsing a Shakespeare script is, "What does this passage mean?" Sources of the line, possible printer error, reference to Latin texts, historical background, and word etymology, are of lesser concern than this one simple need—"What does it mean?" Once they know that they can get on with their job. An actor wouldn't dare enter a rehearsal room with a copy of "No Fear" Shakespeare or "Shakespeare Made Easy" in which the Bard's words are printed alongside modern "translations." They would risk mockery and being thought of as uneducated. Yet sometimes, in working on a speech, a simple illustration in everyday English is exactly what actors need in order for them to make progress with a role. This is why actors read the "No Fear"/"Made Easy" editions in secret in the privacy of their homes, like some sort of Shakespearean pornography.[7] I'm not, of course, suggesting a "dumbing down" in working with the language; precisely the opposite. I'm advocating a practical and physical engagement with the words that releases actors and enables them to become more creative and spontaneous in performance. Rehearsing Shakespeare today has become more like a university seminar with a good chunk of time spent mimicking editor/adaptors and endlessly discussing the text rather than putting it on its feet and attempting to act it. As John Barton warns, "Beware of jargon. It can lead to *talking* about acting taking the place of actually *doing* it."[8] The manifestation of this is that a lot of Shakespearean acting appears to be above the shoulders. So many academic ideas are whizzing around an actor's head that it leads to neutrality and a lack of immediacy. You can almost see the editor/adaptors onstage, whispering in their ears. For an actor it can be fatal. The respected British director Declan Donnellan recognizes this: "If you can explain it, it's dead; that is why we cannot explain acting."[9] I'm not asking for an anti-intellectual approach; actors are highly intelligent people, much more intelligent than the general public give them credit for. What I'm warning against is what in theatre is called "an overeducated response." Strictly speaking, it's not a response at all, since the actors aren't genuinely reacting in the moment to events around them. How can they if they've followed the editor/adaptors and have everything worked out before the performance? A director's work with an actor ought to be a catalyst to creativity rather than a substitute for it.

Directors are acknowledged as interpreters of Shakespeare's plays and are under pressure to reinvent them with each new production. When working for the Royal Shakespeare Company (many years ago), I remember a director asking the tech team, "What hasn't been done before?" He was less anxious about understanding Shakespeare's script and more concerned with scoring a point over his colleagues and being recognized for his originality. Audiences expect and encourage this. The most common question I'm asked by people before one of my Shakespeare productions opens is: "What's your concept?" If the answer sounds fresh and intriguing, it encourages them to attend the performance. This recognition of artist as interpreter may be gleaned from the titles given to certain productions. They often become associated with the director, actor, or the company that produced them: "Brook's Dream," "Olivier's Hamlet," or "The RSC History Cycle." Personally, I prefer to talk about the "context" of my productions rather than the "concept"—the setting chosen to allow a play to have meaning for a particular group of people at a particular time. My choices in directing a play will change according to different circumstances. In 1993 I directed a modern dress *Romeo and Juliet* in England that cast the Capulets as Muslims and the Montagues as white Christian colonists. My point was that there are more similarities between Islam and Christianity than differences, and mistrust between the two groups can be based on "ancient grudge."[10] Thankfully it was well received. Imagine the reception had it been performing in New York City on the night of September 11, 2001? Some directors eagerly jump on events such as this and base a production around them in order to make a play seem contemporary. This tends to have the effect of making the work a news story, and the parallel is made but the play is lost. Peter Brook warns that "modern" is not necessarily "contemporary."[11] We can place cell phones in the hands of characters, which is how a modern person would behave, but to be contemporary a production has to truly resonate with the times. Brook explains that a newspaper is modern but is rarely reflected upon and simply thrown away—"tomorrow's chip paper" is the British phrase used to describe this. I did in fact direct another production of *Romeo and Juliet* in Germany late in 2001. This time my approach was much more abstract and employed a Japanese theatrical style. If there was a comparison to be had with 9/11 or anything else, the audience could make it themselves.[12]

That is not to say I abdicate my responsibility as a director and therefore interpreter of the script. Peter Brook is again surely correct when he writes, "If you just let a play speak, it may not make a sound."[13]

If there's anything worse than an eccentric production of a Shakespeare play, it's one that makes no decisions at all and seems content to present "BBC Shakespeare—Live!" Directors of this type of production are Shakespeare's draymen; slow, ponderous, steady, but completely uninspiring. Often their work (or lack of it) is disguised as "original practices" and masquerades as Shakespeare's "true intention." We don't know what Shakespeare's intentions were, of course, but we can be sure it wasn't to bore the audience. In some ways not setting a play in the contemporary world is exactly what Shakespeare did in his writing, although this was almost certainly because English law meant that he couldn't place the plays in his present. He could have been thrown in jail, or suffered a much worse punishment. In fact, apart from the history plays, only *The Merry Wives of Windsor*, *Cymbeline*, *Macbeth*, and *King Lear* are set in Britain, and the last three take place in a Britain long before the Shakespearean period. And yet Shakespeare's plays always seem to be about the present; simultaneously his own present and the time they are later performed in. What we know of the production style of the King's Men indicates a radical approach was used to convey this. Henry Peachum's drawing of *Titus Andronicus* has actors wearing a kind of toga on top, indicating the surface meaning and setting, while underneath is the contemporary Elizabethan doublet and hose—perhaps a pointer to the subtext?

Shakespeare set all of his plays, nominally perhaps, in periods other than his own. Many sections of his history plays (especially the early ones) are obviously directed against the Spanish rather than the French who are the subject of the story—although England was no lover of the French and they were still an enemy.[14] *Richard II* takes place in medieval times but has obvious associations with Queen Elizabeth I, prompting her supposed comment, "I am Richard, know ye not that?"[15] *Macbeth* and *King Lear* are clearly written with the new King James in mind. (Why wasn't Shakespeare imprisoned?) Even *Twelfth Night*, in the character of Malvolio, depicts the rise of a Puritan class that, less than 25 years after the publication of the First Folio, would establish the Interregnum. Little did Shakespeare know that Malvolio's vow "I'll be revenged on the whole pack of you"[16] would see his puritanical vengeance manifest itself in the complete closure of the theatres after the English Civil War.

Malvolio, according to the setting, is Croatian, but the text points in a different direction. There's nothing Viennese about Mistress Overdone or Danish about Hamlet, the Nurse is far from being Italian in *Romeo and Juliet* and the characters and location of *A Midsummer Night's Dream* are Greek only in name. It could be said that Shakespeare's style was close to Brecht's theories of "historicization." That is, looking at the past to highlight problems in the present. Close, perhaps, but very different. Whereas Brecht urged historical accuracy rather than a contemporary setting (his opinion being that unless a difference in period was indicated the audience would believe social conditions had always been like this and couldn't be changed), Shakespeare was far from historically accurate. A clock in *Julius Caesar* and the game of billiards in *Anthony and Cleopatra*, for example. Which is ironic, given the lengths some productions go to in creating a supposedly authentic depiction of Shakespeare's time or the period the plays are set in. Where Brecht and Shakespeare might agree is Brecht's view that: "The bourgeois theatre's performances always aim at smoothing over contradictions, at creating false harmony, at idealisation."[17]

It's Shakespeare's ambiguity, his ability to question and see several sides of every story, argument, and character, the refusal to package a play and present it as completed, that is the very thing that makes him so contemporary in our present skeptical and cynical age. And this is why his stories can be told over and over again using different styles and from often conflicting angles. Is *Henry V* pro- or antiwar? Does *Hamlet* work better in modern dress or in doublet and hose? Did Peter Brook's production of *A Midsummer Night's Dream* with its circus skills and undefined costumes bring the play closer to Shakespeare's "intentions" than an "original practices" presentation at the present-day Globe in London?

Shakespeare seems to have developed a production style that was at once modern dress, historical, and abstract, and that provides more than enough meat for the director/interpreter. The question is: how much of that meat is it acceptable for a director to take? Declan Donnellan's view is that "the most important thing to remember about Shakespeare is that he's dead and we're alive."[18] In many ways his statement is persuasive; a director and actor should feel free to re-create the plays in whichever way they wish. However, Donnellan is wrong on one point; Shakespeare isn't completely dead. His texts are very much alive. That was the objective when printing the First Folio and why Ben Jonson could write within its pages that Shakespeare "art alive still, while thy Book doth live." Shakespeare is most alive in the First Folio and performance clues are found in almost every line.

On the other hand, too great a reverence for the folio can be reductive. Hardcore First Folio followers come across like born-again Christians who think they have found the answer and bore their friends in attempting to guide them towards enlightenment. An actor needs to have an open and questioning mind in considering the text—the folio text and any other. As with directors, Peter Brook warns actors against "letting the words do the work" as they did in productions he watched early in his career:

> Many a young actor was led to believe that in front of great words he was a sort of newsreader and that his primary function was to let the lines be heard and speak for themselves. From this came the worst of all horrors. The "Shakespeare" voice.[19]

My own opinion is that whatever path actors and directors choose in producing the text, they will find little assistance from editor/adaptors and critical commentators. Consider for a moment that some of the greatest theatrical writers of all time were also actors—Shakespeare, Molière, Pinter—while some of the most stolid, dull, and untheatrical playwrights (in my opinion) were also critical commentators: Bernard Shaw, W. H. Auden, and T. S. Eliot, for example. Eliot believed, "The whole of Shakespeare's work is one poem,"[20] but actors and directors should pay less attention to Shakespeare the poet and more to Shakespeare the theatre-worker. If the words are spoken clearly and the meter is observed, the poetry shines through without needing much extra help from an actor. That is not to say I advocate that an actor and director should ignore the wonderful poetry of Shakespeare's language. My objective is a *closer* attention to that language in performance, to use and pay more respect to the original text as prepared by his close colleagues and not abdicate it to editor/adaptors who, when working on the plays, have a different agenda. The First Folio, although flawed in places, is where Shakespeare guides the performer. It's the obvious and most helpful place to *start*.

Let's give up the pretense that editor/adaptors publish a consistent and reliable script. They don't. Equally, let's frown on the cavalier practices of directors who approach supposed textual problems with a knife and correction pen. Let's publish the text of Shakespeare's First Folio as we do a new play or film script, with 12 point Courier typeface, and put it in a loose-leaf ring binder that is the size of a paperback novel. That way the performers won't have a barrier between them when rehearsing and can take out pages and hold them in their hands. Let's dispense with extensive notes and print only what will genuinely guide actors towards making choices in their unique interpretation of their characters. Actors should treat the texts as they do new writing: roll them up in their pockets and purses, spill coffee on them, write notes all over them. Let's get out of the mindset that the performance script is a piece of world literature.[21]

Above all—disagree with my views. Pick them apart, argue, go back to the script and make your own discoveries, neither repeating the work of previous productions nor allowing editor/adaptors to make decisions for you. As a guide, remember Heminge and Condell's instruction: "Read him, therefore; and again, and again": They warned only to let others lead you if you need to: "If you need them not, you can lead yourselves, and others." In writing this they seem to have followed their friend Shakespeare, who gave actors and directors the single piece of advice that should always be remembered:

"Let your own discretion be your tutor."

Chapter Notes

Introduction

1. Clive Priestley, *Financial Scrutiny of the Royal Shakespeare Company* (London: HMSO, 1984).
2. All Shakespeare quotations, unless otherwise indicated, are from Charlton Hinman, *The First Folio of Shakespeare: The Norton Facsimile*, 2d ed. (New York: W. W. Norton, 1996).
3. *Henry IV, Part 1*, ed. John Dover Wilson, New Cambridge Shakespeare (Cambridge: Cambridge University Press, 1968), 157.
4. *King Henry IV, Part 1*, 3d ed., ed. David Scott Kastan, Arden Shakespeare (London: Thomson Learning, 2002), 279.
5. *The First Part of Henry the Fourth*, ed. Frederic W. Moorman, The Warwick Shakespeare (London and Glasgow: Blackie & Son, 1922?).
6. *Oxford Shakespeare: Complete Works of William Shakespeare*, ed. W. J. Craig (Oxford: Clarendon Press, 1914).
7. *Henry IV, Part 1*, ed. David Bevington, Oxford Shakespeare (Oxford: Oxford University Press, 1987).
8. *The Oxford Shakespeare: The Complete Works*, 2d ed., gen. eds. Stanley Wells and Gary Taylor (Oxford: Oxford University Press, 2005).
9. Ibid., introduction, xxxii.
10. Introduction to *Othello*, ed. M. R. Ridley, Arden Shakespeare (London: Methuen, 1958), xxxii.
11. A. D. Nuttall, *Shakespeare the Thinker* (New Haven: Yale University Press, 2007), 330–331.
12. Richard Levin, *New Readings vs. Old Plays* (Chicago: University of Chicago Press, 1979), 28.
13. Editors alter the folio "hither" to "he there," a gloss that makes sense and has stood since the first editor of Shakespeare, Nicholas Rowe, in 1709. There is no quarto version of *Anthony and Cleopatra* to refer to, so the change is basically guesswork. "Hither" is equally valid and works in the sense of "hither and thither," meaning "here and there" or "a state of confusion." The First Folio description of Anthony depicts a man giving away honors without thought and threatening the unity of the Roman state.
14. Peter Brook, *The Empty Space* (London: Pelican Books, 1972), 17.
15. Jonathan Miller, *Subsequent Performances* (London: Faber & Faber, 1986), 37.
16. Similarly, although nearly always present in productions, there is no "heath" mentioned in *King Lear* or balcony in *Romeo and Juliet* (de Witt's famous drawing of the Swan Theatre shows no acting area that is a balcony). Nor does Petruchio carry a whip—that first appears in print in 1788 and can still be seen in productions over 200 years later. The world's most famous soliloquy, "To be or not to be," isn't, strictly speaking, a soliloquy—"a speech made alone"—as Ophelia, and arguably Claudius and Polonius, are onstage too, albeit not interacting with Hamlet.
17. The second quarto version of *Henry IV, Part 1*, claims it has been "Newly corrected by W. Shakespeare" but whether this is true or hype by the publisher in order to sell the play we don't know.
18. It's perhaps more accurate to say five years after his death as the actual printing process began in 1621. The plan to compile and print the folio was probably conceived soon after Shakespeare died, since in 1619 the Lord Chamberlain sent a letter to the Stationer's Company directing that none of Shakespeare's plays owned by the King's Men should be printed without their consent. See W. W. Greg, *The Shakespeare First Folio* (Oxford: Clarendon Press, 1955), 15–16.
19. *Hamlet*, ed. Philip Edwards, The New Cambridge Shakespeare (Cambridge: Cambridge University Press, 1985), 32.
20. Bernice W. Kliman, Introduction to *The Enfolded Hamlet,* http://triggs.djvu.org/global-language.com/enfolded/enfolded.intro.html.
21. Hinman, *The First Folio*.
22. In 1627 the Red Bull Company, no doubt calculating that a new play cost £5–8 whereas at least 36 of Shakespeare's "proved" plays might be pirated for nothing, attempted to stage some of them, and Heminge paid Henry Herbert, Master of the Revels, £5 to stop this. Herbert records: "From Mr. Hemming, in their company's name, to forbid the playing of Shakespeare's plays to the Red Bull Company ... £5."

The Dramatic Records of Sir Henry Herbert, ed. J. Q. Adams (New Haven: Yale University Press, 1917), 64.

23. Perhaps deliberately and subtly, not wishing to bring a furor upon themselves such as greeted Jonson's use of the word "works" (regarded as pretentious), Heminge and Condell say it was their job to "gather his works" in their introduction.

24. The word "numbers" refers to the structure of the verse.

25. Hinman, *The First Folio.*

26. Ridley, Introduction to *Othello,* xxx.

27. *Hamlet,* ed. Harold Jenkins, Arden Shakespeare (London: Methuen, 1982; rpt., London: Routledge, 1989), 63.

28. This doesn't mean that they weren't prone to mistakes. The presence of a prompter in drawings and documents of the time indicates that a sharp eye was kept on making sure the actors delivered the author's words correctly.

29. Leo Kirschbaum, *The True Text of "King Lear"* (Baltimore: Johns Hopkins Press, 1945), 6. Bottom urges his fellow actors to "Take pains, be perfect" (Act 1, scene 2, line 101). The two quarto versions have him say "be perfit"—asking for perfection while messing up the word—which is possibly an actor's joke that found its way into the script, as sometimes happens in modern theatre. However, "perfect" spelled "perfit" can also be found in the setting of Act 3, scene 7, line 89, of *Richard III* in the First and Second Folios. The Third Folio corrects this to "perfect."

30. The idea of "foul papers" comes from a comment written in the manuscript copy of John Fletcher's *Bouduca.* Edward Knight, book keeper for the King's Men, wrote: "The booke where by it was first Acted from is lost: and this hath beene transcrib'd from the fowle papers of the Authors wch were found." Gabriel Egan, *The Struggle for Shakespeare's Text* (Cambridge: Cambridge University Press, 2010), 25. Although Heminge and Condell refer in their introduction to the folio to "his papers," it doesn't necessarily follow that they printed plays from "foul papers." They are probably writing about how they encountered the work originally. It's difficult to believe they would, running a commercial enterprise, have allowed plays by their top money-spinning writer to be lost. Extensive (and often convoluted) arguments are made that some plays in the folio were set from "foul papers," but as to direct evidence, there is none.

31. Knight had no financial accounting responsibilities and his role should not be confused with that of a present-day bookkeeper.

32. W. W. Greg believed that, because Heminge and Condell were busy running a theatre, it was Knight who acted as editor/proofreader of the First Folio. Greg, *Shakespeare First Folio.*

33. Peter Levi, *The Life and Times of William Shakespeare* (London: Macmillan, 1988), 311. The importance and accuracy of the prompt copy might be gleaned from the Induction to John Marston's *Jack Drum's Entertainment* (1600), where the "author" takes away the prompt copy and the actors can't proceed without it.

34. Egan, *Struggle for Shakespeare's Text,* 17.

35. *Sir Thomas More,* ed. John Jowett, Arden Shakespeare (London: Methuen, 2011), 139.

36. *Julius Caesar* is a text believed to have been set in the First Folio from a prompt copy and this play is one that the editor/adaptors find hard to make any significant changes to. John Jowett acknowledges, "The play was exceptionally well printed." *William Shakespeare: A Textual Companion,* eds. Gary Taylor and Stanley Wells (Oxford: Oxford University Press, 1987; rpt., New York: W. W. Norton, 1997), 386.

37. There is evidence to suggest that *Timon of Athens* is the exception to this and probably wasn't performed until the 18th century. If this is indeed the case, it's tantalizing to wonder why it was never staged and why Heminge and Condell included it in the collected works. We will probably never know.

38. It's a stretch of the imagination to believe that Shakespeare didn't visit London when he learned that his livelihood had disappeared among the ashes of the Globe. It's also unlikely that a playwright would sit at home rather than watch the performance or rehearsal of one of their plays. The whole reason they write is to see a play performed.

39. A copy of Thomas Middleton's *A Game at Chess* (a King's Men production from 1624), survives in his own handwriting as well as the prompt copy from Philip Massinger's 1631 *Believe as You List* (another King's Men play). Neither was used by printers and both were published after the First Folio.

40. Craig, Preface to *Oxford Shakespeare.*

41. John Cocke (probably), in a book called *Description of a Common Player,* published in 1615, calls the players a "Brother-Hood." Reprinted in *English Professional Theatre, 1530–1660,* eds. Glynne Wickham, Herbert Berry, and William Ingram (Cambridge: Cambridge University Press, 2000), 179. Further evidence of this may be found by players giving their children first names such as Burbage and Beaumont.

42. The work of these two astonishing female Victorian scholars, two Americans, it might also be added, has been seriously overlooked by the still predominantly Anglo "men's club" world of the editor/adaptors.

43. Preface to Charlotte Porter and Helen A. Clarke, *Shakespeare's Complete Works* (London: George G. Harrap, 1903), ix.

44. This comment was made by the York Herald, Ralph Brooke, who complained of the number of undeserving people who were receiving coats of arms. Fourth on the list of his examples was "Shakespeare ye Player." See Samuel Schoenbaum, *William Shakespeare: A Compact Documentary Life* (Oxford: Oxford University Press, 1977), 231–232.

45. Alexander Pope, *The Works of Alexander Pope,* Vol. 9 (London: J. F. Dove, 1822), 399, 409.

46. Ibid., 412.

47. Frank Kermode, *Shakespeare's Language* (London: Allen Lane/Penguin, 2000), 17, 18.

48. The retirement myth, and many others, is the work of Shakespeare's acknowledged first editor, Nicholas Rowe.

49. Jonathan Bate, *Soul of the Age* (London: Pen-

guin, 2009), 144. Of course, this quote might also be used as a charge against directors of Shakespeare's plays.

50. *King Richard III,* prepared by Pat Baldwin and Tom Baldwin, Cambridge Student Guide (Cambridge: Cambridge University Press, 2002), 64.

51. Introduction to *1 Henry IV,* ed. G. L. Kittredge (Boston: Ginn, 1940), xi.

52. If an actor studies the play in an academic way, this often leads to what is called a "studied" performance, that is, overtly technical and lacking in spontaneity.

53. Identifying the events in a play is a common modern rehearsal process. The events will always stay the same, but the actor/character's response to them may differ in each performance.

54. Peter Brook's words on this are pertinent: "Once I have finished working on my plays, I can begin to produce my theories." Peter Brook, *The Shifting Point* (London: Methuen, 1988), 97.

55. Levin, *New Readings*.

56. Ibid., 35. See Chapter 8 of this book and the section on Shakespeare's word frequency that refutes this view.

57. Ibid., 80.

58. Ibid., 81.

59. Ibid.

60. Ibid.

61. Ibid., 82.

62. Kastan, Preface to *King Henry IV, Part 1,* xv.

63. Heminge and Condell didn't prepare an edition of the text as modern editor/adaptors do. They printed a version that was a record of performance designed to be read with this in mind. As Stanley Wells notes, "Shakespeare seems to have had no interest in preparing his plays for the reader." Stanley Wells, *Re-Editing Shakespeare for the Modern Reader* (Oxford: Clarendon Press, 1984), 57.

64. Throughout his long career, Frank Kermode was fond of using the telling phrase "ordinary readers" to distinguish those who are not part of this academic elite.

65. Kermode, *Shakespeare's Language,* 245.

66. *In Arden: Editing Shakespeare: Essays in Honour of Richard Proudfoot,* eds. Ann Thompson and Gordon McMullan (London: Arden Shakespeare Library/Thomson Learning, 2003), 136. The actor use of "actions" is considered in Chapter 5 of this book.

67. Ibid., 112.

68. In Act 3, scene 5, line 75, Richard, Duke of Gloster, instructs Buckingham to go out among the people and "Tell them, how Edward put to death a citizen,/Onely for saying, he would make his Sonne,/Heire to the Crowne, meaning indeed his House,/Which, by the Signe thereof, was tearmed so." Even Sir Thomas More, who was no friend of Richard when he wrote his biography, acknowledged this was true and adds the detail that Edward had the man arrested, tried, hanged, drawn, and quartered within 4 hours.

69. *Richard III,* Act 1, scene 4, line 93.

70. The historical Brackenbury was a close associate of Richard, from whom he received many lands and honors, including Lieutenant of the Tower, and as such he is implicated in the disappearance of the princes. But Shakespeare used history for his own dramatic purposes—hence the seemingly endless number of books, articles, and societies that seek to refute that Richard was the monster Shakespeare painted him as. They are missing the point. Shakespeare wrote what worked theatrically and was never one to get sidetracked by historical detail. The real Hotspur, for example, was actually 23 years older than Hal and three years older than Henry IV, but Shakespeare makes Hotspur and Hal about the same age to contrast the actions of two sons.

71. Thompson and McMullan, *In Arden,* 117.

72. *Julius Caesar,* ed. David Daniell. Arden Shakespeare (London: Thomson Learning, 1998), 227.

73. George Bernard Shaw, *Shaw on Shakespeare,* ed. Edwin Wilson (New York: Applause Theatre & Cinema Books, 1989), 259.

Chapter 1

1. The Second Folio, which can be a guide in correcting errors, only picks up and adjusts two Beros back to Hero.

2. *King John,* ed. R. L. Smallwood (Bungay, UK: New Penguin Shakespeare, 1974), 356.

3. Introduction to *King John,* ed. E. A. J. Honigmann, Arden Shakespeare (London: Methuen, 1954), xliii. Even John Jones, defending the authority of the First Folio, can write: "I have corrected F's mislineation of 107—8 and I shall do likewise hereafter without noting the fact." John Jones, *Shakespeare at Work* (Oxford: Clarendon Press, 1995), footnote 8, 80.

4. Honigmann, Introduction to *King John,* xliii.

5. Honigmann, *King John,* 178.

6. Smallwood, *King John,* 352, 356.

7. Ibid., 360.

8. There is no exit marked in the folio, but since there is a lot of stage action it might be assumed the Citizen disappears into the town.

9. Raphael Holinshed, *Holinshed's Chronicle, as Used in Shakespeare's Plays,* ed. Allardyce Nicoll and Josephine Nicoll (London: Everyman's Library, Dent, 1969), 2–3.

10. Ibid., 13.

11. T. J. King, *Casting Shakespeare's Plays* (Cambridge: Cambridge University Press, 1992), 182.

12. In place of character names, the folio prints "Enter Tawyer with a trumpet" in *A Midsummer Night's Dream,* "William Kemp" in *Romeo and Juliet,* "Sinklo" in *The Taming of the Shrew* and *Henry VI, Part 3,* and "Jack Wilson," "Cowley," and "Kemp" are all found in *Much Ado About Nothing*.

13. Honigmann, Introduction to *King John,* xxxvii.

14. There are, however, some instances where a character's *function* is used rather than their name. The folio prints "Andrew" in *Much Ado About Nothing* instead of "Dogberry"; it's a reference to the type of character and the actor who played him. Dogberry is

a clown's role, also known as a "Merry Andrew." Similarly, in *Love's Labour's Lost,* Holofernes often has the speech prefix "Pedant" and Don Armado "Braggart."

15. *The Troublesome Reign of King John* was first acted by the Queen's Men and was published in quarto in 1591, 1611, and 1622. This last edition, coming just before the release of the First Folio, cites Shakespeare as the author. How far this is true or an attempt to take advantage of Shakespeare's popularity we don't know.

16. David Crystal, *"Think on My Words": Exploring Shakespeare's Language* (Cambridge: Cambridge University Press, 2008), 18.

17. Act 4, scene 2, line 249.

18. Act 2, scene 1, line 457.

19. Act 3, scene 2, line 64.

20. Introduction to *King John,* ed. John Dover Wilson (Cambridge: Cambridge University Press, 1936), xlvii.

21. An alternate reading is to follow the First Folio exactly and have the Citizen who refuses to let King John enter Angiers appear first, and then his role is taken over by Hubert where the folio text marks it at Act 1, scene 2, line 337. Which means it is Hubert who suggests the marriage between the Dauphin and Blanche. As Arthur is sent to Angiers after the ensuing battle, it would make sense if Hubert of Angiers became his "protector," especially after giving John such wise counsel. Even though it doesn't fully explain some of the points raised above, this interpretation provides a director with another powerful choice.

22. E. A. J. Honigmann, *The Stability of Shakespeare's Text* (Lincoln: University of Nebraska Press, 1965), 171.

23. If Lewis retains these lines, it makes him very like the hot-headed Dauphin in *Henry V.*

24. *King Henry IV, Part 1,* 3d ed., ed. David Scott Kastan, Arden Shakespeare (London: Thomson Learning, 2002), 131.

25. Demonstrating a lack of consistency, the Oxford *Complete Works* editor/adaptors do not retain the original name of the King—"Bullingbrooke"—but alter it to "Bolingbroke" since Henry was named after his place of birth, Bolingbroke Castle in Lincolnshire. *William Shakespeare: The Complete Works,* eds. Gary Taylor and Stanley Wells, Oxford Shakespeare (Oxford: Clarendon Press, 1988).

26. Act 5, scene 2, line 703. Both the New Penguin and Arden editions alter the folio and Quarto 2's "He wears" to Quarto 1's "a' wears." Neither volume offers any explanation for this change.

27. The Nurse's words to Juliet about Paris—"Romeo's a dishclout to him" (Act 3, scene 5, line 219)—are much more charged than is commonly supposed.

28. *Love's Labour's Lost,* ed. John Kerrigan (St. Ives, UK: New Penguin Shakespeare, 1982), 232.

29. Act 5, scene 3, line 322.

30. Albany is also probably not "young" and in his final words has abdicated his right to the throne in favor of Kent and Edgar.

31. Lewis Theobald, *The Works of Shakespeare,* Vol. 5 (London, 1733). *King Lear,* ed. Nick de Somogyi (London: Nick Hern Books, 2004), 247.

32. *A Midsummer Night's Dream,* ed. Harold F. Brooks, Arden Shakespeare (London: Methuen, 1984).

33. Ibid., 106.

34. Brooks, Introduction to *A Midsummer Night's Dream,* xxvii.

35. The subject of Shakespeare's rewrites is looked at more closely in Chapter 3.

36. Act 5, scene 1, line 35.

37. Notice how the editor/adaptor removes this comma. It's an example of hundreds of subtle changes they make that pass without comment. The comma emphasizes that it is a play Theseus wants to see that night rather than a singer.

38. Two quarto versions of *Othello* were published. The first, in 1622, does not contain this line or indeed other passages in the scene, such as Emilia's famous "But I do thinke it is their Husbands faults/If Wives do fall" speech (Act 4, scene 3, line 85), indicating the folio incorporated a Shakespearean rewrite. The second quarto, published in 1630, follows the folio and assigns the line to Desdemona.

39. *Othello,* ed. E. A. J. Honigmann, Arden Shakespeare (London: Thomas Nelson and Sons, 1997; rpt., London: Thomson Learning, 2006), 291.

40. The previous Arden editor, M. R. Ridley, also appears to have a crush on the "saintly" Desdemona. Her exchange with Iago on the Cyprus quayside he calls "unnatural" and "one of the most unsatisfactory passages in Shakespeare." His reason? "It is distasteful to watch her engaged in a long piece of cheap backchat with Iago.... All we gain from it is some further unneeded light on Iago's vulgarity." Of course he believes it was added as "a sop to the groundlings." *Othello,* ed. M. R. Ridley, Arden Shakespeare (London: Methuen, 1958), 54. People from superior classes, like editor/adaptors, couldn't possibly find such language acceptable and amusing, or the working-class groundlings appreciate anything other than low comedy.

41. Act 1, scene 3, line 160.

42. *Othello,* ed. Kenneth Muir (Bungay, UK: New Penguin Shakespeare, 1968), 188.

43. Ridley, *Othello,* 30.

44. *King Henry IV, Part 1,* 3d ed., ed. David Scott Kastan, Arden Shakespeare (London: Thomson Learning, 2002), 346, 348.

45. John Russell Brown, *Free Shakespeare* (New York: Applause, 1997), 101.

46. *King Lear,* ed. G. K. Hunter (Bungay, UK: New Penguin Shakespeare, 1972), 214.

47. Ibid.

48. Some productions have Goneril heavily pregnant at this moment because of Lear's later curse: "Strike her yong bones/You taking Ayres, with Lamenesse" (Act 2, scene 4, line 160). Children in the womb are referred to in other plays of the period as "young bones." Leaving aside the practicalities of giving the actor playing Goneril a literal burden throughout the play, a stronger choice might be that Goneril and Albany are unable to conceive a child and this might be a reason why Goneril is attracted to the more virile Edmund. The curse of sterility is pretty stupid from King Lear since it leaves Britain without an heir.

49. *Love's Labour's Lost,* ed. John Kerrigan (St. Ives, UK: New Penguin Shakespeare, 1982), 171.
50. Frank Kermode, *Shakespeare's Language* (London: Allen Lane/Penguin, 2000), 106.
51. Peter Brook, *Evoking (and Forgetting!) Shakespeare* (London: Nick Hern Books, 2002), 43.
52. As the plays were mainly performed in daylight, Othello's line also tells the audience it is night and he can only see torches. Even with 20/20 vision, Othello wouldn't fully recognize people in the dark.
53. Honigmann, *Othello,* 129.
54. E. K. Chambers, *William Shakespeare: A Study of Facts and Problems* (Oxford: Clarendon Press, 1930), 483.
55. Introduction to *Macbeth,* ed. Henry Cunningham, Arden Shakespeare (London: Methuen, 1912), xxiii.
56. James Joyce, *Ulysses,* 1922, Episode 1.
57. *King Lear,* Act 3, scene 4, line 21.
58. Selected quickly at random from a few copies of various editions of the plays, here are ten examples of editors explaining the obvious: "good morrow" = "good morning," "fall" = "drop," "beholding" = "beholden," "bring" = "conduct," "burst" = "broken," "arms" = "weapons," "husht" = "be quiet," "curtsy" = "bow," "sweeting" = "darling," "deny" = "refuse."
59. This occurs widely throughout the published texts. Here are just three separate instances from well-regarded scholarly editions: "Unexplained," *The Comedy of Errors,* ed. R. A. Foakes, Arden Shakespeare (London: Methuen, 1962), 70; " not susceptible of satisfactory explanation," *Measure for Measure,* ed. J. M. Nosworthy (St. Ives, UK: New Penguin Shakespeare, 1969), 167; "hitherto unexplained," *The Merry Wives of Windsor,* ed. Sir Arthur Quiller-Couch, The New Shakespeare (Cambridge: Cambridge University Press, 1969), 104.
60. Most editions emend "fight" to "sight."
61. *Measure for Measure,* ed. J. W. Lever, Arden Shakespeare (London: Methuen, 1965), 21.
62. A glance at *Henry V* would find a line from Montjoy to the King in Act 3, scene 6, line 113, "You know me by my habit," or *Henry IV, Part 1,* Act 1, scene 2, line 165, "I, but 'tis like they will know us by our horses, by our habits, and by every other appointment to be our selves."
63. Honigmann, *King John,* 163–164.
64. Ibid., 139.
65. *All's Well That Ends Well,* ed. G. K. Hunter, Arden Shakespeare (London: Methuen, 1959), 104.
66. Ibid., 97.
67. In the First Folio "Esperance" is in italics to distinguish it as a motto and the O has been excluded. Hotspur thus exclaims the single powerful word "hope."
68. *King Henry IV, Part 1,* 2d ed., ed. A. R. Humphreys, Arden Shakespeare (London: Methuen, 1960), 53.
69. Declan Donnellan observed (although not of this passage), "Even the suicide hopes for death." Declan Donnellan, *The Actor and the Target* (London: Nick Hern Books, 2002), 199.
70. Preface to *Troilus and Cressida,* ed. Kenneth Palmer, Arden Shakespeare (London: Methuen, 1982), vii.
71. Preface to *Cymbeline,* ed. J. M. Nosworthy, Arden Shakespeare (London: Thomson Learning, 1995), ix.
72. *The Taming of the Shrew,* ed. Brian Morris, Arden Shakespeare (London: Methuen, 1981), 218.
73. Ibid.
74. Simon Callow, *Being an Actor* (London: Methuen, 1984), 129.
75. Act 3, scene 3, line 113.
76. *The Tragedy of King Richard III,* ed. John Jowett (Oxford: Oxford University Press, 2000).
77. A lack of sophistication in the use of language would be in character for one so young.

Chapter 2

1. *Macbeth,* ed. Kenneth Muir, Arden Shakespeare (London: Methuen, 1951), 37.
2. Interestingly, a First Folio stage direction after line 17 in Act 3, scene 3, of *The Tempest* reads: "Enter several strange shapes, bringing in a banke." In this instance "banke" means a "banquet"—almost identical in spelling (but not meaning) to "banquette."
3. Act 4, scene 1, line 80.
4. Act 4, scene 2, line 3. Since Sutton Coldfield is a place fairly close to Stratford-upon-Avon, it might be thought that Shakespeare is poking fun at a "rival" town.
5. The quarto text prints "Four days."
6. Notice the folio comma after "revok'd," which suggests Lear's rant will carry on, but he is disrespectfully interrupted by Kent. A closer look at the folio performance punctuation is covered in Chapter 4 of this book.
7. *King Lear,* ed. R. A. Foakes, Arden Shakespeare (London: Thomas Nelson and Sons, 1997; rpt., London: Thomson Learning, 2001), 170.
8. Ibid., 178.
9. Act 2, scene 2, line 117.
10. *Measure for Measure,* ed. J. M. Nosworthy (St. Ives, UK: New Penguin Shakespeare, 1969), 166.
11. *King Lear,* Act 2, scene 2, line 63.
12. *Measure for Measure,* ed. J. W. Lever. Arden Shakespeare (London: Methuen, 1965), 72.
13. Patrick Tucker, *Secrets of Acting Shakespeare: The Original Approach* (New York: Routledge, 2002), 250.
14. The apparent clumsiness of "are become" and "achieves" has comic potential for the actor playing Malvolio, rather like Polonius's response to Hamlet's letter to Ophelia "That's an ill phrase, a vile phrase" (Act 2, scene 2, line 110). The letter, after all, has been written not by Olivia but in her style by Maria. The less than sophisticated opening line allows for a moment when Malvolio could smell a rat and the three people watching might curse Maria for an apparent mistake. She knows what she is doing; giving Malvolio such obvious clues increases their enjoyment at his vanity when he ignores them. Further evidence that the folio phrase "are become" is correct may be pro-

vided by the fact that it is also used by Shakespeare in *Richard III* when Lady Anne tells Gloster: "and much it joyes me too,/To see you are become so penitent" (Act 1, scene 2, line 223).

15. Here we find another instance of the editorial habit of writing "unexplained." The Arden editors comment on "The Lady of the *Strachy*": "No satisfactory, historical or literary allusion has been traced ..." while a fellow editor's theory is dismissed as "no more probable than the rest." *Twelfth Night,* eds. J. M. Lothian and T. W. Craik, Arden Shakespeare (London: Methuen, 1975), 65.

16. Act 2, scene 5, lines 23 and 39.

17. Notice how Malvolio also changes "em" to "them," using more sophisticated language before Olivia.

18. There could also be a play on words of "throwne"/"throne" as in *Coriolanus,* Act 5, scene 4, line 24: "He wants nothing of a God but Eternity, and a Heaven to Throne in."

19. *Twelfth Night,* ed. M. M. Mahood (Bungay, UK: New Penguin Shakespeare, 1968), 162.

20. Maynard Mack, *King Lear in Our Time* (London: Methuen, 1966), 5.

21. *Othello,* Act 1, scene 3, line 341.

22. Act 3, scene 1, line 28.

23. Act 4, scene 1, line 153.

24. Act 3, scene 2, line 65.

25. Act 3, scene 2, line 131.

26. The Fourth Folio, printed in 1685, changes "Holy" to "Hobby."

27. Some editors print Desdemona's words in the Second Folio—"My mother had a maid called Barbara"—rather than First Folio's "My mother had a maid called *Barbarie*" (Act 4, scene 3, line 24). Sometimes, in making corrections, the Second Folio got it wrong and further confused things. Clearly the Barbary maid was, like Othello, a Berber or Moor from North Africa and had been rejected by her love—perhaps, we might imagine, by a white European, as often happened when traders visited this coast. A neat reversal of Desdemona's situation and one underlining that failed relationships have nothing to do with the actions and attitudes of a particular race.

28. George Bernard Shaw, *Shaw on Shakespeare,* ed. Edwin Wilson (New York: Applause Theatre & Cinema Books, 1989), 262.

29. E. A. J. Honigmann, *The Stability of Shakespeare's Text* (Lincoln: University of Nebraska Press, 1965), 171.

30. Nosworthy, *Measure for Measure,* 154.

31. Lever, *Measure for Measure,* 15.

32. Nosworthy, *Measure for Measure,* 159.

33. Ibid.

34. Lever, *Measure for Measure,* 99.

35. Nosworthy, *Measure for Measure,* 179.

36. There are many words such as this that the editor/adaptors change for readers, but in performance an actor can convey the meaning through the sound of the word.

37. Foakes, *King Lear,* 323.

38. Ibid., 346.

39. Act 1, scene 2, line 19.

40. *Othello,* ed. M. R. Ridley, Arden Shakespeare (London: Methuen, 1958), 9.

41. *Othello,* ed. E. A. J. Honigmann, Arden Shakespeare (London: Thomas Nelson and Sons, 1997; rpt., London: Thomson Learning, 2006), 138.

42. *Hamlet,* Act 2, scene 2, line 162.

43. *King John,* ed. John Dover Wilson, New Shakespeare (Cambridge: Cambridge University Press, 1936).

44. *King John*, ed. E. A. J. Honigmann, Arden Shakespeare (London: Methuen, 1954), 22. E. A. J. Honigmann has been criticized a great deal in this book, but in his defense (this example and the earlier comments on adding Hubert to the Angiers scene aside), Honigmann shows restraint in his Arden edition and mostly prints the First Folio.

45. *King John,* ed. R. L. Smallwood (Bungay, UK: New Penguin Shakespeare, 1974), 211.

46. Honigmann, *King John,* 77.

47. Smallwood, *King John,* 260.

48. Smallwood, Honigmann, *King John,* 84.

49. *King John,* 343–334.

50. *Venus and Adonis,* line 1004.

51. *Hamlet,* Act 4, scene 4, line 50. This speech is not included in the First Folio and is possibly a performance cut.

52. Act 5, scene 7, line 20.

53. The folio "Hamlet" is probably a Shakespearean rewrite; this is examined more closely in the next chapter.

54. *Hamlet,* ed. Harold Jenkins, Arden Shakespeare (London: Methuen, 1982; London: Routledge, 1989), 199.

55. Act 2, scene 1, line 25.

56. Act 3, scene 2, lines 218 and 223.

57. *Hamlet,* ed. T. J. B. Spencer (St. Ives, UK: New Penguin Shakespeare, 1980), 304–305.

58. Jenkins, *Hamlet,* 338.

59. Ibid., 413.

60. One of these quartos, published in 1619 but passed off as a 1604 "remainder," was issued by William Jaggard, who also printed the First Folio. "Table of green fields" is likely to be an inserted addition to the text and was obviously thought important since Jaggard took the trouble to add it.

61. *Twelfth Night,* Act 4, scene 2, line 100; *The Two Gentleman of Verona,* Act 1, scene 2, line 98; *Much Ado About Nothing,* Act 3, scene 3, line 35, *Richard III,* Act 5, scene 3, line 309, *Twelfth Night,* Act 1, scene 5, line 277, and Act 3, scene 4, line 364.

62. Act 1, scene 5, line 98.

63. *Henry IV, Part 2,* Act 3, scene 2, line 209.

64. John Southworth, *Shakespeare the Player* (Stroud, UK: Sutton, 2000), 331.

65. King James Bible.

66. Thomas Sternhold, John Hopkins, et al., *The Whole Book of Psalms Collected into English Metre* (Oxford: Clarendon Press, 1812). See also http://www.cgmusic.org/workshop/oldver_frame.htm.

67. *Hamlet,* Act 3, scene 2, line 16.

68. The Third Folio was published in 1663/4, forty years after the first, and added six plays that were not written by Shakespeare (at least not as single au-

thor), including *Pericles.* In 1685 the Fourth Folio appeared. There are some sensible adjustments made in both the Third and Fourth Folios, but neither has the authority of the first and second. Shakespeare's early editors used the Fourth Folio as their source text on the reasonable grounds, just as we would today, that it was the most up-to-date version available. And so the story of the divergence away from Heminge and Condell's original began.

69. Modern texts generally ignore this correction and, following quartos 2–4, print "a leven."

70. Not all of the plays printed in the First Folio used prompt books as their source, and it is likely that some were reprints (or near reprints) of earlier quarto copies.

Chapter 3

1. *Thomas Middleton: The Collected Works,* ed. Adrian Weiss (Oxford: Oxford University Press, 2010), 166. The editor alters "Pritter" to "Printer" even though the word "Printed" in the original is set correctly just a few lines earlier.

2. *Richard III,* Act 1, scene 3, line 6.

3. An alternative to consider is that all six quartos disagree with the Second Folio and assign these lines to the Frier rather than Romeo. Although modern texts follow the quarto in other areas, they generally agree with the Second Folio and have Romeo retain this passage. Another example of a lack of consistency among editor/adaptors and their "pick and mix" attitude—they refer to the quarto versions as authority only when it suits their ideas on a play.

4. It shouldn't be imagined that Leason was perfect in his work—he certainly wasn't. After all, he probably set the line "What? In a names that which we call a Rose" in *Romeo and Juliet.* Many of his mistakes simply come from inexperience in setting his type that resulted in broken words when letters and spaces fell out of the printing frame.

5. It's seductive to think that Peter would know Romeo from his jaunts with the Nurse and could direct him to the exact location of the Capel's Monument where Juliet lies. However, the lines and events point towards Romeo's "man" being Balthazar. For example, a letter is given to "Peter" in the folio but delivered by Balthazar who says it was him that brought news of Juliet's death to Romeo in Mantua. The person who does this, even in the First Folio, is named as Balthazar.

6. Leason isn't the only one who is blamed for irregularities in the folio printing. Alice Walker describes "the extraordinarily careless and high handed ways of Compositor B." This was a man who set about half the volume and as such played a major role in saving Shakespeare's plays. Alice Walker, *Textual Problems of the First Folio* (Cambridge: Cambridge University Press, 1953), 163.

7. *Love's Labour's Lost,* ed. John Kerrigan (St. Ives, UK: New Penguin Shakespeare, 1982), 206. For good measure Kerrigan cuts a folio passage between Berowne and Rosaline (also found in the quarto), at Act 5, scene 2, line 809. He makes the general comment, "To make the text coherent, the editor must move against what seems to be the thrust of authorial intention." Ibid., 246.

8. Don Weingust, *Acting from Shakespeare's First Folio* (New York: Routledge, 2006), 8.

9. None of the other folios make this "correction" and leave the name John.

10. *Henry V,* Act 3, scene 2, line 12.

11. Charlton Hinman, prep., *The First Folio of Shakespeare, The Norton Facsimile,* 2d ed. (New York: W. W. Norton, 1996).

12. Astonishingly, there is no modern collection of Beaumont and Fletcher's plays. Mosley's original words can be read online at http://ccnmtl.columbia.edu/projects/shakespeareandthebook/studyenv/pub00.html.

13. *Othello,* ed. Kenneth Muir (Bungay, UK: New Penguin Shakespeare, 1968), 219.

14. Introduction to *Othello,* ed. M. R. Ridley, Arden Shakespeare (London: Methuen, 1958), xliii.

15. *Measure for Measure,* ed. J. M. Nosworthy (St. Ives, UK: New Penguin Shakespeare, 1969), 186.

16. Chapter 4 in this book examines if the meter really is as "defective" as editor/adaptors claim.

17. Tom Stoppard, *Jumpers* (New York: Grove Press, 1972), Author's Note, ix.

18. The word "rehearse" for "repeat" is still in use today, particularly in Scotland.

19. Quince, like Shakespeare, was an actor in his own play. Whether Shakespeare, like Quince, was also the director, cannot be said with any certainty. However, he wrote for actors and seems to have placed acting notes in the body of his script, as will be seen in the next chapter.

20. *Hamlet,* Act 2, scene 2, line 534.

21. Ben Jonson, *Bartholomew Fair,* Induction, line 25. *Ben Jonson: Three Comedies,* ed. Michael Jamieson (Bungay, UK: Penguin, 1966), 331.

22. Act 3, scene 5, and at least parts of Act 4, scene 1, but possibly at other points too.

23. Compare Act 3, scene 5, of *The Two Noble Kinsman* with Beaumont's Masque: http://people.exeter.ac.uk/pellison/BF/masque/frameset.htm.

24. *Hamlet,* Act 3, scene 2, line 39.

25. *Twelfth Night,* Act 1, scene 5, line 235.

26. Hinman, *The First Folio.*

27. Ibid.

28. In fairness, Ben Jonson's other remark on the subject should also be noted: "I remember the players have often mentioned it as an honour to Shakespeare, that in his writing, whatsoever he penned, he never blotted out (a) line. My answer hath been, would he had blotted a thousand." *Timber, or, Discoveries* in *Ben Jonson: The Oxford Authors* (Oxford: Oxford University Press, 1985), 539. This doesn't contradict the theory that Shakespeare delivered a clean script *before* rehearsal, and Jonson's statement "blotted a thousand" seems to be less about theatrical cuts and more his acerbic wit in wishing whole plays consigned to the trash.

29. Jonson, *Timber,* 540.

30. *The Staple of News,* ed. Anthony Parr (Manchester: Manchester University Press, 1988), 66.

31. Beginning at Act 5, scene 2, line 81.
32. John Smethwick, part of the consortium that published the First Folio, had previously printed Quarto 3 of *Hamlet,* which is basically a reprinting of the Second Quarto that editors use for their adaptations of the play. If the folio setting is corrupt, he could easily have presented his partners with the "correct" copy—that is, Quarto 2, alias Quarto 3. But he didn't; he faithfully printed what he believed was Shakespeare's intention.
33. It should be remembered that Rowe was also the man responsible for uncorroborated stories (inventions?) about Shakespeare's early life such as leaving Stratford under a cloud after being caught poaching.
34. Hamlet has earlier told Laertes directly "I lov'd you ever." Act 5, scene 1, line 285.
35. Act 5, scene 2, line 313.
36. Stanley Wells, *Re-Editing Shakespeare for the Modern Reader* (Oxford: Clarendon Press, 1984), 57.
37. This is also another example of editorial inconsistency. If "defie" is correct, why not "my"? And if Quarto 1 has any authority, why not print lines from it such as the last act's "And young Benvolio is deceased too," which no modern editions do.
38. Act 3, scene 6, lines 16–55.
39. *King Lear,* ed. R. A. Foakes, Arden Shakespeare (London: Thomas Nelson and Sons, 1997; rpt., London: Thomson Learning, 2001), 261.
40. Introduction to *Love's Labour's Lost,* ed. R. W. David, Arden Shakespeare (London: Methuen, 1951), xx.
41. I am particularly indebted to three excellent books for information on Jaggard and the printing of the First Folio: Edwin Eliot Willoughby, *A Printer of Shakespeare: Biography of William Jaggard* (London: Philip Allan, 1934); Sonia Massai, *Shakespeare and the Rise of the Editor* (Cambridge: Cambridge University Press, 2007); Paul Collins, *The Book of William: How Shakespeare's First Folio Conquered the World* (New York: Bloomsbury, 2009).
42. The "King James" Bible, printed in 1611, bears comparison with the First Folio. Like the plays in the folio, it was written to be spoken and heard rather than privately read, was produced by collaborative hands, and contains printing errors.
43. It's interesting that, according to Patrick Tucker, when *West Side Story* was tried out in regional theaters before it hit Broadway, a version of the Prologue was included. It was later cut, possibly for the same reason Shakespeare's company omitted it too—it gave away the dramatic ending. Patrick Tucker, *Secrets of Acting Shakespeare: The Original Approach* (New York: Routledge, 2002), 223.
44. Ibid., 226.
45. Algernon Charles Swinburne, *Studies in Prose and Poetry* (London: Chatto & Windus, 1894), 90.
46. Thomas Heywood, *If you know not mee, you know no body* (online edition, Early English Drama and Theatre, EEBO Editions, ProQuest, 2010). Curiously, this prologue didn't appear until the 1639 printing of the play. One wonders why Heywood waited for so long and if his memory was defective or embittered by old age?
47. Thomas Heywood, *The Rape of Lucrece* (London: The Old English Drama, 1824).
48. Thomas Heywood, *An Apology for Actors* (Marston Gate: Elibron Classics, 2005), 62. Heywood's arguments against Jaggard might have more validity if Heywood wasn't also in the habit of literacy piracy. His poem that is a preface to *An Apology for Actors* begins with some familiar-sounding lines: "The world's a theatre, the earth a stage,/Which God and nature doth with actors fill:/Kings have their entrances in due equipage,/And some there parts play well, and others ill." Ibid., 13.
49. Hinman, *The First Folio*.
50. This volume is also sometimes called the "Pavier Quartos" after its publisher Thomas Pavier. He was dropped by the First Folio consortium, but not Jaggard.
51. William Stansby, printer of Ben Jonson's *Works* in 1616, was fined many times by the Stationers' Guild for various infractions. Editors make nowhere near as many changes to Ben Jonson's plays on the grounds of poor printing as they do with Shakespeare. It doesn't seem possible that Stansby was perfect and his rival Jaggard an incompetent. If that was the case, Heminge and Condell could have chosen Stansby as he had the experience of printing plays in folio.
52. Heywood, *An Apology,* 62.
53. Willoughby, *Printer of Shakespeare,* 92.
54. Ibid., 93.
55. Augustine Vincent is an interesting character in relation to the First Folio. A staunch Jaggard ally, he received what is believed to be a presentation copy of the book—dedicated to him in Jaggard's own handwriting—which is probably the *first* First Folio.
56. Willoughby, *Printer of Shakespeare,* 154.
57. Charles Nicholl, *The Reckoning: The Murder of Christopher Marlowe* (London: Picador, 1993), 69, 355.
58. *The Complete Works of Christopher Marlowe,* Vol. 2, ed. Fredson Bowers (Cambridge: Cambridge University Press, 2008), 430.
59. I directed a "performance with scripts" of this play at Shakespeare's Globe Theatre in London in 1998.
60. Carol A. Morley, *The Plays and Poems of William Heminge* (Madison, NJ: Fairleigh Dickinson University Press, 2005), 82.
61. William Heminge, *The Jewes Tragedy,* Act 3, scene 2, line 1. The text of the play can be found in Morley, *William Heminge,* 103.
62. Ibid., 18.
63. In 1619 Jonson visited Scotland and one of his hosts, William Drummond, noted down their one-sided conversations. Jonson comes across as someone with a scathing wit and an opinion on everything and everybody. It's difficult to believe that Jonson would have kept quiet, let alone contributed to the folio, if it was so inaccurate. Ben Jonson's own *Works* were first published in 1616 and he planned to add to his folio of plays in 1631 but canceled the project because he was unhappy with the printing quality. See Dewey Howard Brock, *A Ben Jonson Companion* (Bloomington: Indiana University Press, 1983).

64. Ben Jonson's words on *Julius Caesar* in *Timber* might be regarded as an exception.
65. John Jones, *Shakespeare at Work* (Oxford: Clarendon Press, 1995), 124.

Chapter 4

1. There is confusion in the folio as Montjoy is also referred to in speech prefixes as "Herald" and there's an English Herald in the same scene. So is it the English or French Herald? Most editor/adaptors choose to have the English Herald deliver the list, but Montjoy has arrived specifically to request he be allowed "to book" the French dead. Henry sends the English Herald off with him to gather information. Even if the English Herald on his return delivers the line when handing over the list, the captured Montjoy should surely still be with him and not allowed simply to wander off?
2. Any Third Arden Series text can be referred to, but since *Henry V* is under discussion see the General Editor's Preface to *King Henry V*, ed. T. W. Craik, Arden Shakespeare (London: Thomas Nelson and Sons, 1995; rpt., London: Thomson Learning, 2000), xv.
3. *The Two Gentlemen of Verona*, ed. Sir Arthur Quiller-Couch (Cambridge: Cambridge University Press, 1969), 10, 54, 61.
4. Samuel Schoenbaum, *William Shakespeare: A Compact Documentary Life* (Oxford: Oxford University Press, 1977), 142.
5. Gary Taylor and Stanley Wells remark on the language of *Love's Labour's Lost* that it "was written to be heard; the text is a score for several lost voices." *William Shakespeare: A Textual Companion,* eds. Gary Taylor and Stanley Wells (New York: W.W. Norton, 1997), 3.
6. Editor/adaptors generally set these two short verse lines as prose and add an exclamation point after "Ransome." They retain the folio mock Russian word spelling and often the italics.
7. The folio speech prefix denotes the type of role that the Lord in this scene is now playing; he is pretending to be an interpreter.
8. *All's Well That Ends Well*, Act 4, scene 1, line 19.
9. *Antony and Cleopatra*, ed. John Wilders, Arden Shakespeare (London: Routledge, Thomson Learning, 1995).
10. Act 2, scene 7, line 131.
11. *Much Ado About Nothing*, Act 2, scene 3, line 249.
12. Peter Hall, *Shakespeare's Advice to the Players* (London: Oberon Books, 2003), 14.
13. Act 1, scene 2, line 86.
14. Act 1, scene 2, line 108.
15. Act 5, scene 3, line 88.
16. *Othello*, Act 2, scene 3, line 356. The quartos print "Enmesh em" and modern editors generally follow this.
17. *Macbeth*, Act 5, scene 3, line 20.
18. Act 4, scene 3, line 99.
19. Lysander calls Hermia a "Minimus" in Act 3, scene 2, line 329, of *A Midsummer Night's Dream*.
20. John of Gaunt puns similarly on his name and physical condition—he is gaunt from illness—in Act 2, scene 1, lines 73–83 of *Richard II*.
21. Act 2, scene 3, line 23.
22. Act 4, scene 1, line 95.
23. Six lines near the beginning of the scene are very obviously assigned to the wrong characters in all of the folios, perhaps because the compositors were transcribing French? This is a good example, once again, that the folios can, in places, be flawed.
24. Craik, *King Henry V,* 224. The literal-minded Craik seems shy about the nick/vagina joke too: "It is arguable that Alice should pronounce *neck* correctly, since she can pronounce *chin."* Ibid., 223. Gary Taylor's comment is an appropriate response: "Criticism too often consists in filtering out pleasure in the pursuit of meaning." Gary Taylor, *Moment by Moment by Shakespeare* (London: Macmillan, 1985), 1. Taylor was making a general point and not writing about this particular passage.
25. *Twelfth Night,* Act 2, scene 5, line 35. Claudio in *Much Ado About Nothing* is referred to as a "count" in the scene where he wrongly accuses Hero of sex before her marriage. The Frier's first line to Hero, "Lady, you come hither to be married to this Count," Act 4, scene 1, line 8, foreshadows what is to follow. Beatrice is more forthright and sarcastically labels Claudio "a goodly Count," Act 4, scene 1, line 315. Benedick reveals himself to be of her mind when he refers to "Count Claudio" 12 lines later. Bertram in *All's Well That Ends Well,* some might say, very much lives up to his title of "count."
26. *Henry V,* Act 4, scene 1, line 48.
27. Act 1, scene 2, line 9.
28. Hotspur terms Bullingbrooke both "King of Smiles" and a "vile Politician." *Henry IV, Part 1,* Act 1, scene 3, lines 244, 239. Falstaff, in the folio, notices a resemblance between Bullingbrooke and his son, observing that Hal has "most unsavourey smiles." Modern editors change this to "similes." *Henry IV, Part 1,* Act 1, scene 2, line 76.
29. John Barton, *Playing Shakespeare* (London: Methuen, 1984), 3.
30. To balance this there's a good example of the folio probably getting a name wrong. *Cymbeline* was only published in the First Folio and the lead character is printed as "Imogen." Both Shakespeare's source and Simon Foreman, who saw the play in 1611, refer to her as "Innogen," and that is also the name of a "ghost character" (one that is mentioned in stage directions but never appears), in *Much Ado About Nothing*. A double "n" when written could easily appear to be an "m" and this is what Jaggard's workers printed.
31. Act 2, scene 3, line 84.
32. Charlton Hinman, prep., *The First Folio of Shakespeare, The Norton Facsimile,* 2d ed. (New York: W. W. Norton, 1996).
33. David Crystal, *Pronouncing Shakespeare: The Globe Experiment* (Cambridge: Cambridge University Press, 2005), and *"Think on My Words": Exploring Shakespeare's Language* (Cambridge: Cambridge Uni-

versity Press, 2008). In collaboration with his actor son Ben, David Crystal has recorded a CD of how Shakespeare's words might have been originally pronounced. This may be purchased online from the British Library: http://shop.bl.uk/mall/productpage.cfm/BritishLibrary/_ISBN_9780712351195%20/87294/Shakespeare%27s-Original-Pronunciation-%28audio-CD%29.

34. Act 3, scene 2, line 69.

35. Act 3, scene 4, line 43.

36. In the folio Seyton doesn't have an exit or reentry after Macbeth hears the "cry of women" so that he remains onstage apparently already knowing "The Queen is dead" (Act 5, scene 5, line 16). As with Marlowe's Mephistopheles and Faustus, his role at this point is as satanic tormentor. While Macbeth approaches his final battle calling on Satan, Mark Anthony goes to his calling for Eros, the Greek god of love.

37. *The Winter's Tale,* Act 1, scene 2, line 186.

38. Act 2, scene 2, line 64.

39. Act 1, scene 1, line 38.

40. *Romeo and Juliet,* Act 1, scene 3, line 11.

41. Crystal, *"Think on My Words,"* 128.

42. Crystal, *Pronouncing Shakespeare,* 88.

43. Original Pronunciation productions are swifter too. The Globe Theatre in London presented two versions of *Romeo and Juliet,* one using modern diction and the other Original Pronunciation. The OP version was 10 minutes shorter. Crystal, *Pronouncing Shakespeare,* 65.

44. Crystal, *"Think on My Words,"* 52.

45. Stanley Wells, *Re-Editing Shakespeare for the Modern Reader* (Oxford: Clarendon Press, 1984), 13.

46. Is the speech prefix "Hot," which he is given by the folio in this scene, fortuitous? In some other, less charged, scenes (such as Hotspurre considering Henry's offer of peace), the folio assigns him the prefix "Hotsp."

47. Act 1, scene 3, line 135.

48. An often used rehearsal exercise is "Letters and Cables," in which the actor is asked to reduce a speech—a letter—into a cable of 10 words or less in which each word has to be paid for. This helps the actor to discover important words and those that might go unnoticed (who would believe that "love" can be found in Hamlet's famous "To be, or not to be" speech?). The words chosen are nearly always the ones capitalized in the First Folio.

49. Even Neil Freeman's excellent Applause First Folio series doesn't print names in italics.

50. This is an example of the "y" *not* giving an "i" sound. "Buy," on the other hand, is spelled "Buie" in the First Folio printing of *Much Ado About Nothing.* Spellings are not always consistent but should always be considered.

51. The word "banish'd," it will be noticed, does *not* have a capital letter when it might be thought it should, since this is an important part of the plot. It is, but the key description and point of the speech is to establish the virtue of Posthumus and Innogen; they are the "good guys" in the story, the audience is told. The detail of the banishment is instead picked out clearly in parentheses by the folio use of brackets.

52. *Cymbeline,* ed. J. M. Nosworthy, Arden Shakespeare (London: Thomson Learning, 1995).

53. Crystal, *"Think on My Words,"* 91.

54. In Shakespeare's time the word "point" was used instead of the modern "punctuate." It's an apt choice in a theatrical context; if you point you give direction and to "point out" is to make something clear.

55. Sonia Massai, *Shakespeare and the Rise of the Editor* (Cambridge: Cambridge University Press, 2007), 12.

56. That is not to say Shakespeare's copy necessarily contained bad spelling and punctuation (although we know Hand D in *Thomas More* does), but we simply can't be certain one way or the other.

57. Act 1, scene 5.

58. Act 2, scene 1, line 138. Beatrice in *Much Ado About Nothing* is wrongly accused "that I had my good wit out of a hundred merry tales" (Act 2, scene 1, line 119). She's right to feel aggrieved. Her witticisms are not in italics and therefore indicate that they were not quoted from a book.

59. Act 2, scene 1, line 161.

60. Act 1, scene 3, line 366.

61. Act 2, scene 1, line 296.

62. The folio capital letter on "Soul" shows us how deep Iago's feelings are.

63. "Once" does not necessarily mean "a single occasion," and is used by Shakespeare in other plays with the sense of "at any time" or "at once."

64. *Richard III,* ed. E. A. J. Honigmann (London: New Penguin Shakespeare, 1968/2005), 233.

65. Humphrey could also be a pun on the sexual act, Richard's bawdy nickname for his mother's lover. Hump-free = freely having sex or sex with abandon.

66. *Richard III,* Act 3, scene 5, line 92.

67. *Henry VI, Part 3,* Act 3, scene 2, line 153.

68. Recent historical investigation has shown that Richard wasn't lying and his mother did have an affair (although not with Humphrey Stafford), that resulted in the birth of an illegitimate Edward IV.

69. Act 3, scene 5, line 94.

70. *King Henry IV, Part 1,* ed. P. H. Davison (Aylesbury, UK: New Penguin Shakespeare, 1968), 159.

71. "Phoebus" in the First and Second Folios is not set in italics. Another reminder that the folios are not always without fault. The Third Folio corrects this mistake.

72. *Romeo and Juliet,* Act 3, scene 5, line 149. There are numerous examples of the varied use of italics in the folio's *Henry IV, Part 1,* including letters, mimicking the speech of other characters, names, proverbs, and non–English phrases such as those in Latin.

73. Although Paris does refer to Capulet as "my Lord" (with a capital *L*), the phrase was used simply as a mark of respect. Capulet is never given the speech prefix "Lord Capulet."

74. Neil Freeman, *Shakespeare's First Texts* (Vancouver, BC: Folio Scripts, 1999), 8.

75. Act 1, Scene 3.

76. Introduction to *The Life and Death of King John,* prep. and ann. Neil Freeman (New York: Applause First Folio Edition, 2000), xlii.

77. Act 3, scene 2.
78. Act 5, scene 2, line 319.
79. Act 5, scene 1, line 195.
80. Act 5, scene 1, line 283.
81. Another word of warning. *The Comedy of Errors* was only published in the folio, more than 30 years after it was first written and performed. There are a number of corruptions, such as confusion in identifying the two Antipholuses and Dromios, and Luciana being referred to as "Juliana/Julia." Nonetheless, the points made still hold.
82. Act 5, scene 3, line 180, and Act 5, scene 3, line 209.
83. Act 1, scene 3, line 36.
84. Act 4, scene 1, line 202.
85. Act 4, scene 1, line 224.
86. Although one would hope their enthusiasm doesn't stretch to M. C. Bradbrook's views, who wrote: "The concentration camps of Nazi Germany bred many heroes and martyrs but also a few Shylocks." *Shakespeare and Elizabethan Poetry* (Harmondsworth: Penguin, 1964), 157.
87. Act 2, scene 1, line 307.
88. Neil Freeman points out that "the change comes in the middle of both Q1 column (C3), and an F1 column (Comedy R 106), and therefore cannot be attributed to compositor error." Introduction to *Much Adoe About Nothing*, prep. and ann. Neil Freeman (New York: Applause First Folio Edition, 2001), xliv.
89. Act 2, scene 1, line 326.
90. Act 5, scene 4, line 120.
91. Marjorie Garber, *Shakespeare and Modern Culture* (New York: Pantheon, 2008), 201.
92. Thomas Heywood, *An Apology for Actors* (Marston Gate: Elibron Classics, 2005, 29. Heywood ends this paragraph with "It instructs him to fit his phrases to his action, and his action to his phrase, and his pronunciation to them both." The phrase is familiar. Perhaps it was a similar case to that which Mr. Puff describes in Sheridan's *The Critic:* "All that can be said is, that two people happened to hit on the same thought—and Shakespeare made use of it first" (*The Critic,* Act 3, scene 1). Richard Brinsley Sheridan, *The School for Scandal and Other Plays,* ed. Eric Rump (St. Ives, UK: Penguin, 1988), 177.
93. David Edgar, *Nicholas Nickleby, Part 1,* Act 2, scene 12. *Edgar Plays: Two,* (London: Methuen Drama, 1990), 173, 174.
94. Patrick Tucker, *Secrets of Acting Shakespeare: The Original Approach* (New York: Routledge, 2002), 246.
95. Never one to miss an opportunity for a jibe against Shakespeare, Ben Jonson includes the heraldic motto "Not without mustard" in his play *Every Man Out of His Humour,* Act 3, scene 1, line 244.
96. Act 5, scene 2, line 42.
97. Act 1, scene 1, line 47.
98. "Full stop" is the British term for a period.
99. Many original manuscripts from famous authors have so many adjustments that their work is almost impossible to read.
100. Crane wrote about his work with the King's Men in the preface to his 1621 poem *The Works of Mercy:*

And some employment hath my useful Pen
Had 'mongst those civil, well-deserving men
That grace the stage with honour and delight
Of whose true honesties I much could write
But will comprise't (as in a Caske of Gold),
Under the Kingly Service they do hold
[Taylor and Wells, *Textual Companion,* 20].

101. Joseph Moxon, *Mechanick Exercises on the Whole Art of Printing,* Vol. 2, 197–198. Moxon seems to contradict himself and a few lines later also writes that it was "a task and duty incumbent on the Compositor ... to discern and amend the bad Spelling and Pointing of his Copy, if it be in English." However, it was the "carelessness" of some authors which has "forc'd Printers" to do this, Moxon states. Printing the copy faithfully was the overall objective but to allow badly misspelled volumes to be sold would obviously have a negative effect on the business and reputation of the printing house. Moxon's book can be read online at http://books.google.co.uk/books?id=BncsAAAAYAAJ&pg=PA401&lpg=PA401&dq=Moxon+the+Art+of+Printing&source=bl&ots=7Hqy_Xmovj&sig=-OdF87MfeiMX777HwXH_klOWRXY&hl=en&sa=X&ei=FVTtUpvbMseshQeAq4DwCg&ved=0CHUQ6AEwCTgK#v=onepage&q=Moxon%20the%20Art%20of%20Printing&f=false.
102. Tucker, *Secrets of Acting Shakespeare,* 240.
103. Act 3, scene 2, line 1.
104. Act 1, scene 1, line 41.
105. Act 1, scene 1, line 242.
106. Act 2, scene 1, line 25. Most modern editions print "there stand," only found in Quartos 2–4.
107. *Julius Caesar,* Act 3, scene 1, line 188. The most recent Arden printing follows the folio exactly, even down to spelling the conspirator name as Caska rather than the usual Casca, but it conforms to editorial tradition by placing a non-folio comma after each of the other names, thus reducing the impact of the special moment with Caska. *Julius Caesar,* ed. David Daniell, Arden Shakespeare (London: Thomson Learning, 1998).
108. *Othello,* Act 2, scene 3, line 306.
109. Act 1, scene 3, line 110.
110. When I directed the first modern production of Beaumont and Fletcher's *Love's Cure* the (excellent) editor Marea Mitchell missed a crucial moment in the play by removing a comma after "I will show strength in nothing," Act 4, scene 2, TLN 1594. The character Clara, who has been brought up as a man, discovers there can be equal strength in embracing her female birth gender—the whole point of the play. ("Nothing" or "No-thing" was a phrase used for a vagina/womanhood.) The comma brings this thought out. Beaumont and Fletcher, *Love's Cure,* ed. Maria Mitchell (Nottingham: Nottingham Drama Texts, 1992), 40.
111. Act 2, scene 2, line 13. *Macbeth,* ed. Kenneth Muir, Arden Shakespeare (London: Methuen, 1951). According to David Crystal (and remembering the First Folio has about 860,000 words), there are only

350 exclamation points in the whole volume. Crystal, "Think on My Words," 73.

112. Craik, *King Henry V.*

113. This is the Arden version, but almost every modern edition prints the same. *King Henry IV, Part 1*, 3d ed., ed. David Scott Kastan, Arden Shakespeare (London: Thomson Learning, 2002). Notice the addition of an extra "all" before the last word.

114. An example of a noncapital letter after a question mark, driving the words on.

115. Some readers might have spotted the inconsistent folio spelling of "hart/heart" that doesn't appear to have any significance. Another warning of paying too close attention to all things folio.

116. Dick the Butcher's vow, "The first thing we do, let's kill all the Lawyers," still raises a cheer from the audience whenever *Henry VI, Part 2*, is performed. Act 4, scene 2, line 73.

117. Welles wrote these words in *The Mercury*, a news sheet he issued to advertise his theater productions. John Ripley, *Julius Caesar on Stage in England and America* (New York: Cambridge University Press, 1980), 223.

118. Act 3, scene 2, line 74.

119. "Ermites" is spelled "hermits" in modern texts and removes a possible ironic play on words with ermine, the garb of monarchs.

120. Act 1, scene 4, line 13. The meter of this speech is very different from the First Folio in modern editions.

121. Act 2, scene 1, line 8.

122. Frank Kermode, *Shakespeare's Language* (London: Allen Lane/Penguin, 2000), 207.

123. Act 3, scene 3, line 147.

124. John Dover Wilson, *The Manuscript of Shakespeare's Hamlet ...* , Vol. 2 (Cambridge: Cambridge University Press, 1934), 197.

125. *Othello*, ed. M. R. Ridley, Arden Shakespeare (London: Methuen, 1958), 210.

126. Ibid., 212.

127. Ibid., 213.

128. This is a First Folio printing error, corrected to "the Censure" in the Second Folio.

129. The third Arden edition of *Othello* changes "lodging" back to "loading," although numerous other folio words aren't retained. This is another example of inconsistency and editor choices being made on personal taste. *Othello*, ed. E. A. J. Honigmann, Arden Shakespeare (London: Thomas Nelson and Sons, 1997; rpt., London: Thomson Learning, 2006).

130. Preface to *Antony and Cleopatra*, ed. M. R. Ridley, Arden Shakespeare (London: Thomson Learning, Thomas Nelson and Sons, 1989), xvi. Unusually, Ridley's version is an update of an enlightened edition from 1906 by R. H. Case. Case based his text entirely on the First Folio, only making emendations which demonstrate "that [it is] probability only short of certainty which alone justifies adoption. Certain changes countenanced by the best editions have, on the other hand, been rejected in favor of the original readings." Ridley, Introduction to *Antony and Cleopatra*, xxiii.

131. Tucker, *Secrets of Acting Shakespeare*, 243.

132. Honigmann, *Othello*, 362.

133. When I directed *Othello* for Fairbanks Shakespeare Theatre, Alaska, the actor playing Iago, Tom Robenolt, elected to use the folio "snipe" when offered the choice.

134. This is a very odd comment, given his enthusiasm for First Folio punctuation. If the folio punctuation isn't by Shakespeare, then why follow it? Honigmann, *Othello*, 326.

135. *Romeo and Juliet*, Act 2, scene 5, line 17.

136. Neil Freeman believes that a question mark followed by a capital letter in Elizabethan typography didn't necessarily indicate a new sentence. It's difficult to see the value of this for a performer—if it's not a new sentence it's certainly a separate thought. Freeman writes: "Any capitalized word after major punctuation demands double attention. First, the speaker, or listener, or both, is reminded to pay close attention to the next point: second, the point will be logically an important one." Isn't that what happens when we begin a new sentence? Freeman, *Shakespeare's First Texts*, 136.

137. Act 3, scene 2, line 2.

138. Don Weingust, *Acting from Shakespeare's First Folio* (New York: Routledge, 2006), 76.

139. As a simple illustration, think of how popular music from 1987 differs from that in 2014.

140. John Jones, *Shakespeare at Work* (Oxford: Clarendon Press, 1995), 88.

141. It should be remembered that the original Emilia was played by a boy, who may have needed coaching in his delivery of the lines.

142. Notice the excision of 3 question marks and the capital letters and the inclusion of an editor/director exclamation point.

143. Most modern editions follow the quarto and omit "you" even though the play in folio shows clear signs of being a Shakespearean rewrite.

144. The editor/adaptors remove the comma after "apt." This does not allow the audience to consider just how many of Iago's apparent lies were true.

145. Hall, *Shakespeare's Advice*, 26.

146. Peter Brook, *Evoking (and Forgetting!) Shakespeare* (London: Nick Hern Books, 2002), 14.

147. Tucker, *Secrets of Acting Shakespeare*, 230.

148. The Library of Congress displays a copy of the original speech on its website: http://www.loc.gov/exhibits/churchill/wc-hour.html.

149. *The Guardian*, July 31, 2004, http://www.theguardian.com/uk/2004/jul/31/arts.past.

150. The Nurse's long speech about Juliet's childhood in Act 1, scene 3, line 16, of *Romeo and Juliet* is also printed as prose in the folio but restructured into verse by editor/adaptors, thus raising the character's status. I once worked with an acting student in Australia who had followed the editor setting of this passage and diligently counted the syllables in each line and observed the punctuation. Despite all her hard work, she expressed the frustration that "it just doesn't make sense," completely unaware that the folio alternative existed.

151. *Romeo and Juliet*, ed. T. J. B. Spencer (St. Ives, UK: New Penguin Shakespeare, 1967).

152. Note that there's a period printed in the folio despite the speech being interrupted.

153. Even as notable a commentator as David Crystal can be seduced away from the folio's prose version of this speech, ignoring the evidence of the quartos: "Doubtless there was an error in the printing process. Page 58 must already have been typeset when the compositor working on page 57 realised that he had too much text to fit into the page. He rescued the situation by cramming thirty-eight lines of verse into thirty lines of tightly packed prose." For this to be true, exactly the same situation would have had to occur in five separate printings of the quarto over a period of 30 years. Crystal, *"Think on My Words,"* 216.

154. Barton, *Playing Shakespeare,* 68.

155. Ibid., 70. John Barton is not a particular advocate of the First Folio and he was not referring to the "Queen Mab" passage when he wrote this.

156. Comparing the two versions of the speech, notice how the editor/adaptor cannot resist tinkering with the minor punctuation, to no real effect.

157. Lear's moment of discovery, "I am old and foolish," is the perfect conclusion to the scene. Most modern texts print an exchange between Kent and a gentleman after this, which is found in the quarto and includes the unnecessary information that Cornwall is dead (the audience knows that), and the "red herring" that Kent is in Germany. The theatrical impact of King Lear's decline is thus lost.

158. The New Penguin edition places a period here, the second Arden a colon, and the third Arden a semicolon. None follow the folio's comma.

159. The folio sets Duncan's line in prose—he is eager for the dying man to conclude his story and anxious about the outcome of the fight. Attempting to reconstruct his line into verse makes the King more in control than events suggest.

160. Although editor/adaptors alter the meter of the speech, the character generally still retains the folio title "Captain."

161. See, for, example Muir, *Macbeth,* 8, "I suspect that a line or more is missing." The New Penguin editor/adaptor acknowledges that the meter is deliberate but provides a note that would be very unhelpful to a performer: "This short line, in the manner of Virgil, is used (like the epic simile) to mark the heroic technique of the messenger's speech." *Macbeth,* ed. G. K. Hunter (St. Ives, UK: New Penguin Shakespeare, 1967, 1995), 140.

162. Richard Flatter, *Shakespeare's Producing Hand: A Study of His Marks of Expression to Be Found in the First Folio* (1948; rpt., New York: Greenwood, 1969), 103.

163. Ibid., 24.

164. Ibid., 93.

165. *The Comedy of Errors,* ed. R. A. Foakes, Arden Shakespeare (London: Methuen, 1962), 77.

166. *Antony and Cleopatra,* 2d ed., ed. David Bevington, The New Cambridge Shakespeare (Cambridge: Cambridge University Press, 2005), 267. Quoted in the Introduction to *The Tragedie of Anthonie and Cleopatra,* prep. and ann. Neil Freeman (New York: Applause First Folio Edition, 1998), xl.

167. It was Ben Jonson, in his poem that is the opening introductory verse to the First Folio, who wrote of Shakespeare that he had "small Latine, and lesse Greeke." Hinman, *The First Folio.*

168. William Gaskill, *Words into Action: Finding the Life of the Play* (London: Nick Hern Books, 2010), 116.

169. A drawing of the bust in 1634 by William Dugdale in his book *Antiquities of Warwickshire* has Shakespeare leaning on what looks like a sack of grain or wool and there is no quill in his hand. This appears to fit with the image of respectability Shakespeare seemed anxious to project. However, Dugdale's drawing skills were not exact and the quill from the monument was stolen on a regular basis. The "anti–Stratfordian" claim that the bust was altered in 1748 to make it look like Shakespeare was a writer doesn't hold up under closer scrutiny. A drawing of the same monument by George Vertue in 1723 has Shakespeare with a quill.

Chapter 5

1. The most common reason a new play is rejected by a modern theater is that the author has worked in isolation and doesn't understand the mechanics of staging, working with actors, or writing convincing dialogue.

2. John Dover Wilson, *The Essential Shakespeare* (Cambridge: Cambridge University Press, 1932), 43.

3. It's naïve to think that Shakespeare simply turned up in London without a job. Traveling with no occupation incurred serious physical punishment in Elizabethan England. How would he get the money to travel? Any spare cash would be needed by his young family.

4. Peter Levi, *The Life and Times of William Shakespeare* (London: Macmillan, 1988), 61.

5. Christopher Marlowe, *The Complete Plays* (London: Penguin, 1969).

6. Ibid., Act 4, scene 4, line 6.

7. To be apprenticed didn't always require a formal and legally binding agreement as the word was also used to mean simply "trained."

8. As mentioned in Chapter 1, there is a theory that Shakespeare wrote an early version of *King John* called *The Troublesome Reign of King John.* The third quarto of the play cites him as the author. If this is true, then between 1588 and 1592 Shakespeare could have been writing and acting for both the Queen's Men and Pembroke's Men with no formal attachment to either.

9. *Julius Caesar,* Act 1, scene 2, line 202.

10. Quarto 2, and most modern editions, prints "warm'd" as "wann'd"—that is, wand.

11. The folio stage direction for part of the "Dumb Show" in Act 3, scene 2 (after line 133) of *Hamlet* is: "The Queene returns, findes the King dead, and makes passionate Action."

12. Richard Flecknoe, *A Short Discourse of the English Stage,* 1664. Reprinted in *Critical Essays of the Seventeenth Century,* Vol. 2, ed. J. E. Spingarn (Oxford: Clarendon Press, 1908), 95.

13. Anonymous, 1619. Reprinted in *English Professional Theatre, 1530–1660*, eds. Glynne Wickham, Herbert Berry, and William Ingram (Cambridge: Cambridge University Press, 2000), 181.

14. Jonathan Bate, *Soul of the Age* (London: Penguin, 2009), 394.

15. Act 2, scene 2, line 303. The Arden *Hamlet* prefers Quarto 2's version of this line, which omits the first "a" and reads "What piece of work is a man." It also excludes the sparingly used folio exclamation point, or "mark of wonder," as it was known. *Hamlet*, ed. Harold Jenkins, Arden Shakespeare (London: Methuen, 1982; rpt., London: Routledge, 1989).

16. This is not necessarily a leap of imagination. Young Edward in *Richard III*, Act 2, scene 2, line 13 remarks in the folio: "The King mine Unkle is too blame for it./God will revenge it, whom I will importune/With earnest prayers, all to that effect." Notice the second mention of the word is spelled "to" while the first "too" gives the sense that it is King Edward who is very much responsible for the death of Clarence.

17. "Conjuring" didn't have the same sense of performing a magic trick as it does today, but connoted raising spirits or the devil. Dr. Pinch in *The Comedy of Errors* is called a "conjurer."

18. Act 2, scene 2, line 2. Shakespeare had already written a scene of a "real" conjuration of the devil in *Henry VI, Part 2,* Act 1, scene 4.

19. Performances in Shakespeare's time took place in daylight, of course, but this might be imagined in the same way as Romeo paints a picture of moonlight on the fruit tree tops.

20. In the later scene, Act 3, scene 5, where Romeo leaves Juliet after their first, and only, night together, there is a stage direction in the folio: "Enter Romeo and Juliet aloft." They're certainly above the stage, but this doesn't necessarily mean they were on a balcony.

21. Notice that the folio speech prefix in this scene, where the Countess is bidding farewell to her son, is "Mother." In fact, she is never referred to as the Countess, but most often "Lady." In the scenes where she hears of the supposed death of Helena and the dishonorable conduct of Bertram, this changes to "Old Lady."

22. The great 20th century acting teacher Sanford Meisner wrote: "What you do doesn't depend on you; it depends on the other fellow." Sanford Meisner and Dennis Longwell, *Sanford Meisner on Acting* (New York: Vintage, 1987), 34.

23. Peter Hall, *Shakespeare's Advice to the Players* (London: Oberon, 2003), 12.

24. Ibid.

25. Many modern texts print "and when he shall die" even though this is only found in Quarto 4 and not in any of the folios or 5 other quartos.

26. William Gaskill, *Words into Action: Finding the Life of the Play* (London: Nick Hern Books, 2010), 85.

27. George Bernard Shaw, *Shaw on Shakespeare*, ed. Edwin Wilson (New York: Applause Theatre & Cinema Books, 1989), 48.

28. *Hamlet* Act 3, scene 2, line 247. Editor/adaptors do not print the folio "Pox"; a pity, since the lines that precede it are all sexual in nature.

29. Act 2, scene 2, line 462.

30. As the actor's part was on a roll, it made it very difficult to flip backwards and forwards to check what has happened and what is coming up as a modern actor might do. Shakespeare's players had no choice but to always be in the present.

31. It's also true that the boy playing Isabella in *Measure for Measure* would not know whether to take the Duke's hand in marriage at the end of the play. However, it's more than reasonable to suggest he would have just asked the author.

32. Tiffany Stern (Patrick Tucker's niece) points out that when cuts are made to the scripts by Shakespeare/the Playhouse, such as was done with the folio *Hamlet*, they are usually internal cuts within a speech that don't alter the actor's cue lines. Tiffany Stern, *Making Shakespeare, from Stage to Page* (Oxford: Routledge, 2004), 135.

33. Charles Marowitz, "Lear Log," *Encore* 10, no. 1 (January/February 1963), 23.

34. Patrick Tucker, *Secrets of Acting Shakespeare: The Original Approach* (New York: Routledge, 2002).

35. Don Weingust, *Acting from Shakespeare's First Folio* (New York: Routledge, 2006), 179.

36. *The Three Parnassus Plays*, ed. J. B. Leishman (London: Ivor Nicholson & Watson, 1949).

37. Francis Beaumont, *The Knight of the Burning Pestle*, ed. Michael Hattaway, New Mermaid Series (London: A & C Black, 1986).

Chapter 6

1. Philip Jacobson, "Sadistic Sergeant Tries to Escape Serial Killer Trial," *Daily Telegraph,* December 17, 2000, http://www.telegraph.co.uk/news/worldnews/africaandindianocean/reunionfrance/1378581/Sadistic-sergeant-tries-to-escape-serial-killer-trial.html.

2. *King Lear*, Act 1, scene 2, line 16.

3. Portia in *The Merchant of Venice* by comparison is blatantly racist and relieved that the dark-skinned Prince of Morocco makes the wrong choice of casket: "Let all of his complexion choose me so" (Act 2, scene 7, line 79). Iago's only racist remarks are in the first scene of *Othello*: "An old blacke Ram/Is tupping your white Ewe" and "You'le have your Daughter cover'd with a Barbary horse." They are spoken in the character of "a member of the general public" and obviously not as himself since he doesn't want to be revealed. The words are designed to provoke Brabantio's racism rather than reflect Iago's own views. Contrast this with Rodorigo, who calls Othello "the Thicks-lips" (Act 1, scene 1, line 65). Admittedly, Iago does propose a toast to "blacke Othello" (Act 2, scene 3, line 29). Perhaps he is testing Cassio, wondering whether he shares the opinion that Desdemona ought to marry someone "Of her owne Clime, Complexion, and Degree" (Act 3, scene 3, line 234); someone like Cassio, in fact?

4. Levin L. Schucking, *Character Problems in Shakespeare's Plays* (London: George G. Harrap, 1922), 203.

5. The Second Folio removes this extra metrical "a." There were no quarto printings of *The Comedy of Errors* before the First Folio.
6. Act 3, scene 11, line 7.
7. Act 3, scene 13, line 97.
8. Act 4, scene 14, line 14. This phrase is open to an alternative interpretation than is given here.
9. Act 5, scene 2, line 81.
10. *Twelfth Night*, Act 1, scene 5, line 176. The New Penguin editor alters the punctuation of this line to "by the very fangs of malice, I swear I am not that I play." This change is neither explained nor identified, not even under the usual "An Account of the Text." *Twelfth Night*, ed. M. M. Mahood (Bungay, UK: New Penguin Shakespeare, 1968).
11. *Twelfth Night*, Act 2, scene 2, line 24.
12. William Hazlitt, *On Actors and Acting*, published in *The Round Table* (London: Sampson Low, Son, & Marston, 1869). http://essays.quotidiana.org/hazlitt/actors_and_acting.
13. Notice that the folio speech prefix is "Richard" rather than "King."
14. Constantin Stanislavski, *An Actor Prepares*, trans. Elizabeth Reynolds Hapgood (New York: Routledge, 1989), 317.
15. Jean-Paul Sartre, *Being and Nothingness: An Essay on Phenomenological Ontology* (London: Routledge Classics, 2003).
16. *Richard II*, Act 5, scene 5, line 31. Quarto 1 prints "person" rather than "Prison," which is more appropriate to the argument here. However, the folios and Quartos 2–5 all print "Prison." Perhaps Richard is referring to the physical prison of his body as well as his cell?
17. Denis Diderot, *The Paradox of Acting* (London: Chatto & Windus, 1883), 53. https://archive.org/details/cu31924027175961.
18. Hazlitt, *On Actors and Acting*.
19. *King Lear*, Act 2, scene 3, line 21.
20. *Richard II*, Act 4, scene 1, line 200.
21. *Henry IV, Part 2*, Act 4, scene 5, line 197.
22. With this in mind, *Much Ado About Nothing* could be said to mean "Much Ado About Women" or—to give a cruder description—"Much Ado About Pussy."
23. *Coriolanus*, Act 5, scene 2, line 80.
24. *Coriolanus*, Act 5, scene 1, line 13.
25. *As You Like It*, Act 4, scene 1, line 145.
26. Act 3, scene 3, line 360.
27. Act 2, scene 1, line 295.
28. Notice how the folio punctuation and meter support the actor/character.
29. Act 5, scene 2, line 172.
30. Constantin Stanislavski, *My Life in Art*, trans. J. J. Robbins (London: Eyre Methuen, 1980), 466.
31. With dialogue it may be said that characters wish to *express* themselves with a speech or are *impressed* by the words of others.
32. Act 1, scene 2, line 67.
33. Act 3, scene 3, line 233.
34. Act 2, scene 1, line 289.
35. Act 2, scene 1, line 305.
36. Act 2, scene 3, line 309.
37. Constantin Stanislavski, *My Life in Art*, trans. Jean Beneditti (New York: Routledge, 2008), 261.
38. The First Folio sets "he's," which is probably a printing error, since the Second Folio corrects this to "ha's."
39. Act 2, scene 1, line 239.
40. *Richard III*, Act 1, scene 1, line 30.
41. The folio splitting of the word "myself" into "my self" is perhaps significant; if it isn't significant, it's certainly useful.
42. A *Midsummer Night's Dream*, Act 1, scene 2, line 60.
43. Stanislavski, *An Actor Prepares*, trans. Reynolds Hapgood, 177.
44. Act 3, scene 3, line 155.
45. Act 3, scene 3, line 70.
46. Act 2 of David Mamet, *Glengarry Glen Ross* (London: Methuen, 1984), 35.
47. A professional actor would recognize this as "text analysis," and about the first week of any rehearsal period is usually entirely devoted to "table work."
48. Iago is not onstage to witness Othello's speech to the Senators but is familiar with Othello's "bragging" and Desdemona's response to it, as he tells Rodorigo.
49. Notice the unusually high number of folio exclamation points; four in eight lines.
50. Act 5, scene 2, line 159.
51. Act 5, scene 2, line 187.
52. See, for example, Hermoine's innocent words in *The Winter's Tale*, which Leontes misreads as sexual: "The one, forever earn'd a Royall Husband/Th' other, for some while a Friend" (Act 1, scene 2, line 107).
53. Act 3, scene 4, line 181.
54. Act 2, scene 1, line 296.
55. As a comparison, the play title *Measure for Measure* has no comma.
56. Act 1, scene 3, line 369.
57. The sexual need of some men to be cuckolded (often by someone with a darker skin), is rarely spoken of or written about, but Google the word "Cuckold" and you'll be flooded with the addresses of thousands of pornographic websites that cater to this taste.
58. *Much Ado About Nothing*, ed. A. R. Humphreys, Arden Shakespeare (London: Methuen, 1981, 2003), 150. Editor/adaptors are not always unhelpful to actors, and Humphreys' note is something practical that a performer can use.
59. The Arden editor/adaptor does not see this as a possibility and brusquely comments, "He means the opposite." *Othello*, ed. E. A. J. Honigmann, Arden Shakespeare (London: Arden Shakespeare, Thomas Nelson and Sons, 1997; rpt., London: Thomson Learning, 2006), 240.
60. Meisner and Longwell, *Sanford Meisner on Acting*, 34.
61. Michael Chekhov, *To the Actor* (New York: Routledge, 2002).
62. Act 2, scene 3, line 173.
63. A possible mistake in the folio? The quartos print "conster" rather than "conserve," which makes more sense.

64. Despite the fact that, as we have seen, there were cuts and other adjustments made to the text of *Othello,* most modern editors insert some extra dialogue here from the quarto printing: "by this hand." The Arden editor/adaptor blames the scrivener Ralph Crane: "Probably omitted from F by Crane." Honigmann, *Othello,* 240. It seems odd that Crane would accidentally omit a complete phrase rather than single words, and the speech makes perfect sense without it.
65. Act 3, scene 3, line 222.
66. Stanislavski, *An Actor Prepares,* trans. Reynolds Hapgood, 267.
67. Stanislavski, *My Life in Art,* trans. Robbins, 184.
68. *Richard III,* Act 1, scene 3, line 47.
69. Act 1, scene 2, line 2.
70. Q1 and the folio have no stage direction that Iago stabs Rodorigo, although Q2 does and it comes *before* Rodorigo says "O damn'd Iago!" Even if directors and actors choose to follow Q2 the point is the same—Rodorigo dies to prevent him from revealing Iago rather than out of malice.
71. Since there is no exit signified for Iago, productions that wish to focus on his "villainy" might allow him meet Othello, who then addresses the following lines to Iago rather than as an aside: "O brave Iago, honest, and just,/That hast such Noble sense of thy Friends wrong,/Thou teachest me." Another performance choice.
72. There is a sense conveyed that Bianca is "aghast" at being discovered as a murderess. The quartos print "jeastures" rather than "agast" which, although it appears to have been discarded by Shakespeare, is a word more relevant to the argument.
73. Toby Cole and Helen Krich Chinoy, *Actors on Acting* (New York: Crown, 1970), 199.
74. Stanislavski, *An Actor Prepares,* trans. Reynolds Hapgood, 122.
75. Act 2, scene 2, line 535.
76. Act 1, scene 5, line 179.

Chapter 7

1. The term "comedy" doesn't necessarily mean that a play is humorous but rather one that has an affirmative resolution which is consistent with the plot. *All's Well That Ends Well* is how Shakespeare described his deeply ambiguous "comedy."
2. Richard Levin calls the latter practice "Fluellenism"—attempts to draw parallels on the flimsiest of evidence, as Fluellen in *Henry V* does with his comparisons between Henry and Alexander the Great. Richard Levin, *New Readings vs. Old Plays* (Chicago: University of Chicago Press, 1979), 209.
3. Michael Bogdanov, *Shakespeare: The Director's Cut* (Edinburgh: Capercaille Books, 2003), 82.
4. Act 5, scene 1, line 252.
5. Act 5, scene 1, line 276.
6. Act 4, scene 1, line 342.
7. This is another example of Shakespeare using the word "rehearsed" to mean "repeated."
8. A poem from 1566 by Isabella Whitney is a possible influence on this passage but has so far been unmentioned in editor/adaptor commentary. The structure of *The Copy of a Letter lately written by a gentlewoman in metre to her unconstant lover* has the same 4-line stanzas Shakespeare employs and the same characters—Dido, Medea, Jason. The poem may be read here: http://xtf.lib.virginia.edu/xtf/view?docId=chadwyck_ep/uvaGenText/tei/chep_1.0999.xml&chunk.id=d3&toc.id=d3&brand=default.
9. Act 3, scene 1, line 112. Jessica's betrayal occurs before Antonio's trial and is surely a mitigating factor in Shylock's later actions.
10. Act 5, scene 1, line 294.
11. Act 5, scene 1, line 30.
12. Act 2, scene 7, line 65. Perhaps significantly, Jessica carries a casket when she elopes with Lorenzo in the scene immediately before this.
13. Act 5, scene 1, line 69.
14. Act 5, scene 1, line 83.
15. Georg Brandes, *William Shakespeare: A Critical Study,* Vol. 2 (London: Heinemann, 1898), 218.
16. Prologue, line 10.
17. Thomas More, *The History of King Richard the Third* (1513), 73. http://www.thomasmorestudies.org/docs/Richard.pdf.
18. *Henry V,* based on the Caxton edition of *The Complete Works of William Shakespeare,* ed. Sidney Lee (but adapted by the United States government), Armed Services ed. (not for sale) (Mineola, NY: Dover, 2002), xi, xii, v.
19. William Hazlitt, *Characters of Shakespeare's Plays* (1817). http://www.library.utoronto.ca/utel/criticism/hazlittw_charsp/charsp_ch16.html.
20. Something similar occurs in the Epilogue to *Henry IV, Part 2.* There had been protests from the Oldcastle family at the depiction of their ancestor as Hal's boozy companion so the name of the character was changed to Falstaff. When the epilogue states, "Oldcastle died a martyr, and this is not the man," it merely increases speculation that it is.
21. Ben Jonson, *Every Man out of his Humour,* ed. Helen Ostovich, The Revels Plays (Manchester: Manchester University Press, 2001), Act 3, scene 6.
22. Act 3, scene 2, line 21. "Pressure" refers to an impression or likeness, as in wax.
23. The folios print "Abstracts," which means the same thing.
24. Act 2, scene 2, line 520.
25. Act 3, scene 1, line 111.
26. At the time of writing, struggles for regime change are happening throughout the Middle East.
27. Introduction to Thomas Fuller, *The History of the Holy War* (1639, reprinted 1840), vii. See https://archive.org/details/historyofholywar00fullrich.
28. Act 2, scene 1, line 248.
29. *Henry V* depicts the murder of boys and unarmed prisoners. In 1995 the notorious Bosnian Serb General Ratko Mladic allegedly rounded up and killed 7,500 boys and men at Srebrenica.
30. The numbers of English who died at Agincourt according to the text is surely propaganda and doesn't tally with historical records. Four are named

plus another 25, making 29 English dead, and 10,000 French. But the boys are not calculated nor the amount of English lost *before* the battle. There is no indication given in the play of the numbers of French killed while in custody. This is an obvious example of Shakespeare writing *Henry V* as heroic adventure.

31. Act 3, scene 1, line 1.
32. Act 3, scene 3, line 38.
33. Ralph Berry, *Changing Styles in Shakespeare* (Oxford: Routledge, 2011), 77.
34. The scene in production often highlights the comedy. This is a valid choice but one that won't be focused on, as the purpose of this section is to illustrate motivations behind thoughts, words, and actions rather than the comedic value of the text.
35. Some of the words of the Scottish and Irish captains, Jamy and MacMorris, are similarly spelled phonetically in order to suggest their accents.
36. In *King John* a military adventure in France leads to a (historically accurate) successful French counter-invasion. If Fluellen and Gower know about the wars of the Romans, they are also likely to know the history of England.
37. Some productions with large casts place Gower and Fluellen in these earlier scenes in order to establish a context for their later actions. It is likely that in the original presentation of the play the actors playing Gower and Fluellen doubled the role of a "traitor."
38. *Richard II*, Act 2, scene 1, line 65. This is a common theme in Shakespeare. The last speech in *King John* warns, "This England never did, nor never shall/Lye at the proud foote of a Conqueror,/But when it first did helpe to wound it selfe."
39. Even Henry V knows this was wrong and speaks of "the fault/My Father made, in compassing the Crown" (Act 4, scene 1, line 290).
40. *Henry IV, Part 1*, Act 5, scene 1, line 133.
41. Buckingham's revolt in *Richard III* is "backt with the hardy Welshmen" when it might have been thought they would support the Welsh-born Richmond (Act 4, scene 3, line 47). That said, Buckingham's family seat was at Brecon in Wales and it seems from later textual evidence that Buckingham's plan was to join forces with Richmond. Who Buckingham thought would rule after Richard's downfall is an open question.
42. Act 4, scene 1, line 73.
43. Some productions, imagining the Boy to be the Page whom Hal gives to Falstaff in *Henry IV, Part 2*, have the King find the dead Boy after he enters the scene—perhaps the reason for his rash emotional response in ordering his troops to slaughter prisoners? The Page is called Robin in *The Merry Wives of Windsor*, a play probably written before *Henry V*.
44. Act 4, scene 4, line 73.
45. Hamlet tells Rosencrantz and Guildenstern he knows they have been sent for by the King because he can see a "confession in your lookes." Act 2, scene 2, line 279.
46. In the latest Arden edition of the play—which, remember, claims to be a performance text—the editor/adaptor gives the note here: "an effectively serio-comic zeugma, as editors (none of whom have suggested a textual error), have recognized." *King Henry V*, ed. T. W. Craik. Arden Shakespeare (London: Thomas Nelson and Sons, 1995; reprint, London: Thomson Learning 2000), 309.
47. Act 3, scene 2, line 58.
48. Act 3, scene 2, line 82.
49. In the typography of the time, a question mark was sometimes interchangeable with an exclamation point. The folio setting of one of the Nurse's lines in *Romeo and Juliet* is, "Ah where's my man? Give me some Aqua-vitae?" (Act 3, scene 2, line 88). The first part of the sentence wonders where Peter is (a question), while the second calls for a strong drink (an exclamation). In other words, the actor's choice in speaking the line "In your Conscience now, is it not?" could either be an exclamation or a question; a rhetorical question, perhaps?
50. Act 4, scene 7, line 11. *King Edward III*, ed. Giorgio Melchiori, The New Cambridge Shakespeare (Cambridge: Cambridge University Press, 1998).
51. Act 3, scene 6, line 139.
52. Act 4, scene 6, line 36.
53. Act 4, scene 6, line 37.
54. Gary Taylor, editor/adaptor of the Oxford volume of *Henry V*, inserts his own directorial stage direction at this point: "The soldiers cut the throats of their prisoners." He believes it's important that the audience see this moment. *Henry V*, ed. Gary Taylor, The Oxford Shakespeare (Oxford: Oxford Paperbacks, 2008).
55. The "English Lesson" scene, although irrelevant here since the characters don't know it has taken place, has an interesting position in the narrative, coming immediately after the taking of Harfleur and after Henry has turned down the offer of marriage to Katharine. Why is the Princess learning English, then? It seems to suggest, certainly to the audience, that the French and English will eventually be united peacefully by a royal wedding and the Battle of Agincourt is a completely futile event with a huge waste of lives.
56. Act 4, scene 1, line 192.
57. Hamlet, in a letter to Claudius (Act 4, scene 7, line 42), refers to the King in sarcastic terms: "High and Mighty, you shall know I am set naked on your Kingdome. To morrow shall I begge leave to see your Kingly Eyes."
58. The second "borne" should be spelled "porne" to be consistent—another small folio printing error.
59. This statement, although often quoted as being by Wellington, was actually said about him by a rival—the Irish politician Daniel O'Connell.
60. Act 5, scene 1, line 76.
61. Act 4, scene 7, line 147.
62. Editor/adaptors usually change the folio accent spelling of Fluellen's "Orld" to the correct pronunciation, "world," even though the folio sets it that way twice, including the capital letter, so it's unlikely to have been a printing mistake. Other pronunciation-type spellings are retained.
63. Notice that although the folio places Monmouth in italics there are none on Wye. If it is used as a name, there ought to be.
64. Act 3, scene 6, line 53.

65. Act 3, scene 6, line 52.
66. Act 5, scene 5, line 47.
67. Act 2, scene 1, line 121.
68. Act 2, scene 2, line 97.
69. Act 3, scene 6, line 60.
70. Act 3, scene 6, line 66.
71. Davy Gam's birthplace is unknown.
72. Act 1, scene 2, line 187.
73. Act 3, scene 6, line 109.
74. Act 4, scene 7, line 54.
75. Act 3, scene 6, line 30.
76. The letters *G* and *E* in the folio are thought to refer to the actors who played these roles—Gough and Eccleston. Whether this is true or not, editor/adaptors raise the characters' status from "Captains" to "Lords."
77. Craik, *King Henry V*, 319.
78. Act 4, scene 7, line 115.
79. Letter from the field of Waterloo (June 1815). Edward Shepherd Creasy, *The Fifteen Decisive Battles of the World* (Safety Harbor, FL: Simon Publications, 2001), 396.
80. Robert Louis Stevenson, *The Works of Robert Louis Stevenson*, Vol. XXIV, 63. *Shakespeare in Production: Othello*, ed. Julie Hankey (Cambridge: Cambridge University Press, 2005), 195.
81. Katie Mitchell, *The Director's Craft* (Abingdon: Routledge, 2009), 125.

Chapter 8

1. In those days, 1983–87, women directors were a rarity at the RSC.
2. Most of the extracts and comments in this book concentrate on Shakespeare plays I have directed. Unless I've worked on a text in rehearsal, I don't feel I can write about it with a secure authority.
3. Keeping a rehearsal diary of his performance as King Lear in 1991, Brian Cox noted that it was nine days before director Deborah Warner put the play on its feet. Each line was paraphrased ("parrot-phrasing," Cox calls it), first by the actors in a group discussion. Cox's view was that "it's very boring, absolutely boring, but necessary, I suppose." Brian Cox, *The Lear Diaries* (London: Methuen, 1992), 23.
4. Cox, *Lear Diaries*, 21.
5. Act 3, scene 3, line 233.
6. Introduction to Mike Alfreds, *Different Every Night* (London: Nick Hern Books, 2007), xxii.
7. The current trend in productions of *Measure for Measure* is for Isabella to refuse to take the Duke's hand in marriage and exit alone. When I staged the couple walking off together, one review accused me of changing Shakespeare's ending.
8. I'd been preparing a production of *The Comedy of Errors* for more than eight months and suddenly discovered that the National Theatre of Great Britain was using the same idea of acting out Egeon's story at the beginning of the play. I'm sure this isn't original, but it worked for the German audience I was directing it for. Similarly, I'd undertaken a great deal of research into Welsh songs to include in *Henry IV, Part 1*, and came across one that I thought would be perfect. Much to my annoyance, I found that the song had been used in the BBC's video of the play, which I hadn't seen. It was "back to the drawing board," and I chose another song.
9. Cicely Berry, *From Word to Play* (London: Oberon, 2008), 75.
10. Ralph Berry, *On Directing Shakespeare* (London: Hamish Hamilton, 1989), 205. Ralph Berry and Cecily Berry are unrelated.
11. It is when Macbeth's Wife sleeps that she is confronted with the full horror of what she has done.
12. Another history play, *King John,* also starts with the word "Now." This supports Peter Brook's assertion that Shakespeare is always in the present. The last word in *King John*—"True"—implies that what the audience have watched is reality. Declan Donnellan's words are apt: "Nothing exists in the past because the past does not exist. Only the consequences of previous events can exist in the present." Declan Donnellan, *The Actor and the Target* (London: Nick Hern Books, 2002), 45.
13. Act 4, scene 3, line 97.
14. Act 4, scene 3, line 139.
15. Act 5, scene 1, line 73.
16. Act 1, scene 5, line 76.
17. Act 4, scene 1.
18. Act 2, scene 2.
19. Act 1, scene 3, line 180.
20. Notice Shakespeare's genius, which places the scenes at exactly the same point in each of the plays.
21. Act 3, scene 4, line 135.
22. Act 4, scene 2, line 63.
23. Act 3, scene 2, line 16.
24. Act 3, scene 2, line 50.
25. Act 3, scene 2, line 379.
26. Scene 6, line 146. *Sir Thomas More,* ed. John Jowett, Arden Shakespeare (London: Methuen, 2011). This edition dispenses with dividing the play into acts. It is generally agreed that Shakespeare only wrote parts of this play and it was not included in the First Folio.
27. It's advisable to use speeches from the Apocrypha with caution. There is an exchange between Audley and the Prince in *Edward III* (Act 4, scene 4, lines 1–60), that mirrors the Duke's views on death when he attempts to "comfort" Claudio in *Measure for Measure* (Act 3, scene 1, line 5). And the Mariner's description of the realities of war in the same play (Act 3, scene 1, line 142)—"there mangled arms and legs were tossed aloft" and so forth—is very similar to views expressed by Michael Williams in Act 4, scene 1, line 134, of *Henry V*: "The King him-selfe have a heavie Reckoning to make, when all those Legges, and Armes, and Heades, chopt off in Battaile." The difficulty with referring to the Apocrypha, as we saw with William Heminge's rewriting of "To be or not to be" in *The Jewes Tragedy,* is that some lines and scenes could be another author stealing from Shakespeare rather than Shakespeare repeating himself. The Apocrypha plays were probably composed in conjunction with other playwrights, and although it's possible to guess which parts Shakespeare wrote, it's impossible to do so with absolute authority. *Edward III,* however, was written

some time between 1590 and 1594, probably 1593, so it predates both *Henry V* and *Measure for Measure*.

28. Creating a back story for a character is vitally important for actors if their portrayal is to display truth but the modern editions don't help them. In Act 5, scene 4, line 162, of *Henry IV, Part 1*, Falstaff exclaims in the folio, "If I grow great again," which suggests that he was once great but has fallen. Editor/adaptors follow the quartos and remove the word "again" and along with it some important character information.

29. John Dryden, *All for Love*, New Mermaids Series (London: A & C Black, 2004), 97.

30. Jonson's parody doesn't call for a balcony.

31. Ben Jonson, *Poetaster* in *The Devil Is an Ass and Other Plays* (Oxford: Oxford University Press, 2000).

32. Cox, *Lear Diaries*, 47. Beginning work on the script too late in rehearsal is a constant complaint from actors about directors. David Weston's diary of, coincidentally, another production of *King Lear* with Sir Ian McKellen in the lead role notes, "Ian is getting restive because we haven't started blocking yet.... We've used up nearly two weeks rehearsal and with the two plays there's so much to do." David Weston, *Covering McKellen* (London: Rickshaw, 2011), 28.

33. L. C. Knights, *How Many Children Had Lady Macbeth? An Essay in the Theory and Practise of Shakespeare Criticism*, 1933. Reprinted in *Explorations: Essays in Criticism, Mainly on the Literature of the Seventeenth Century* (London: Chatto and Windus, 1946; rpt., Harmondsworth: Penguin, 1964), 30–33.

34. Act 1, scene 7, line 54.

35. Notice the capital letter on the second "All" and the uncommon folio use of an exclamation point.

36. Act 5, scene 4, line 14.

37. Act 5, scene 7, line 14.

38. Donnellan, *Actor and the Target*, 143.

39. It appears to have been a problem during Shakespeare's time too. Thomas Heywood urged players not to "stand like a stiff starcht man, but to qualify everything according to the nature of the person personated." Thomas Heywood, *An Apology for Actors* (Marston Gate: Elibron Classics, 2005), 29.

40. Dr. Albert Mehrabian, *Silent Messages: Implicit Communication of Emotions and Attitudes* (Belmont, CA: Wadsworth, 1972).

41. When I directed *Richard III*, I dropped the hump and cast a woman as Richard. The "half made up" king became someone with an intersex condition and created some interesting psychological relationships with the genetic women in the play, particularly Richard's mother.

42. Anthony Sher, *Year of the King* (London: Hogarth Press, Chatto & Windus, 1985), 98.

43. Ibid., 185.

44. Ibid., 122.

45. Sher later played the Fool in *King Lear* for the Royal Shakespeare Company and as part of his preparation for the role visited London Zoo to observe the movement and behavior of chimpanzees.

46. Clive Barker, *Theatre Games* (London: Eyre Methuen, 1977), 21.

47. Ibid., 177.

48. Cox, *Lear Diaries*, 23.

49. Charles Marowitz in "Lear Log," *Encore* 10, no. 1 (January/February 1963), 23.

50. This is a physical exercise. It should not be used to force the actors to stress the words marked in bold.

51. Possibly an example of the folio using a question mark in place of an exclamation point.

52. The folios are the only contemporary printing of *Timon of Athens* and there is no evidence that the play was ever performed, although there is equally no evidence to prove that it wasn't.

53. A probable folio punctuation mistake. The line should possibly read "To generall Filthes,/Convert o'th' Instant greene Virginity."

54. This is a First Folio printing error and should read "Sonne." The Second Folio prints "Sonne."

55. This should probably read "Sowe all."

56. Perhaps this is another example of the folio spelling of this word giving, as in *King Lear*, the double meaning of "bans"/"banes"—that is, religious announcements/poison?

57. *Timon of Athens*, ed. H. J. Oliver. Arden Shakespeare (London: Methuen, 1979).

58. *The Two Noble Kinsmen* was probably written in partnership with John Fletcher and is not included in any of the four published folios.

59. Donnellan, *Actor and the Target*, 143.

60. To satisfy the curious (and with thanks to Peter Hall), a trochee is an irregular inversion of the pronunciation of a word such as reVENue rather than the common use REvenue, a dactyl word has one hard stress followed by two soft, as in CANada, spondee describes a word that has two strong stresses, like PENKNIFE, an anapest word has two soft stresses and then one hard, an example being interCEDE, while an amphibrach word contains a strong stress in the middle of two soft ones, as in unCOMmon. Peter Hall, *Shakespeare's Advice to the Players* (London: Oberon, 2003). Now that you know this—forget it (if you are an actor or director)! The terms aren't important—it's often irrelevant anyway in parts of the world where the English pronunciation is different. *Why* the words were chosen is obviously something for the actor to consider as it can help to establish the character's state of mind.

61. Erving Goffman, *The Presentation of Self in Everyday Life* (London: Pelican, 1976).

62. Deborah Tannen, *You Just Don't Understand* (London: Virago Press, 1991).

63. Act 2, scene 2, line 110.

64. Alfreds, *Different Every Night*, 114.

65. Weston, *Covering McKellen*.

66. Alfreds, *Different Every Night*, 205.

Chapter 9

1. *Hamlet*, Act 2, scene 2, line 392.

2. The character name Escalus suggests scales and balance, although this may be intended as ironic. There are many lines that support the image of the scales of justice, perhaps the most memorable being

Angelo's declaration to Isabella in Act 2, scene 4, line 169, that "my false, ore-weighs your true."

3. Act 5, scene 1, line 65.
4. Act 3, scene 1, line 80.
5. Act 3, scene 2, line 274.
6. Act 4, scene 1, line 13.
7. Act 5, scene 1, line 202.
8. A "measure" is also a dance—another glance towards the play's classification as a comedy.
9. Act 1, scene 3, line 2.
10. In a similar archery image, Benedick has "challenged cupid at the flight" in Act 1, scene 1, line 35, of *Much Ado About Nothing*.
11. Act 3, scene 2, line 263.
12. Act 3, scene 1, line 137.
13. The idea of creating imagined back stories for characters is a commonly used rehearsal technique. When I directed *Much Ado About Nothing*, we supposed that Beatrice's father—who we dubbed Dai D'earlyio—was the oldest brother and Beatrice was brought up expecting to marry, have children, and inherit the estate. His sudden death passed the family succession to Leonato and Hero, helping to focus Beatrice's feelings of isolation.
14. Act 1, scene 3, line 46.
15. Act 1, scene 3, line 47.
16. Act 1, scene 3, line 8.
17. Act 3, scene 2, line 176.
18. Act 3, scene 1, line 36.
19. Act 4, scene 3, line 156.
20. The Provost recognizes the Duke's handwriting but not his face.
21. Act 1, scene 1, line 70.
22. Introduction to *Measure for Measure*, ed. J. W. Lever, Arden Shakespeare (London: Methuen, 1965), lxiv. Sometimes editor/adaptors break the trend and provide details that are extremely useful when producing the play.
23. *King John*, Act 3, scene 1, line 62.
24. See Malcolm in *Macbeth*, Act 4, scene 3, line 146.
25. Act 5, scene 1, line 367.
26. Act 2, scene 2, line 79.
27. Act 1, scene 2, line 24.
28. Act 5, scene 1, line 483.
29. Act 3, scene 2, line 270. It's fairly common in modern productions to see Barnadine spit at the Duke or laugh at him when he is freed. This is a cheap effect and has little value other than to undermine the Duke's authority. Lucio witnesses this inserted stage business and must surely think that if Barnadine is allowed to get away with this, then he and others can do the same.
30. Act 5, scene 1, line 382.
31. Act 5, scene 1, line 396.
32. Act 5, scene 1, line 532.
33. Act 2, scene 2, line 21.
34. Act 1, scene 2, line 167.
35. Act 3, scene 1, line 85.
36. Act 3, scene 1, line 140.
37. Both Angelo and Elbow are also accused of behavior similar to Claudio's.
38. Act 2, scene 1, line 6.
39. Act 2, scene 4, line 126.
40. Act 1, scene 4, line 4.
41. Act 2, scene 2, line 101.
42. Act 2, scene 4, line 77.
43. Olivia and Viola in *Twelfth Night* have also lost a father and a brother.
44. Act 2, scene 1, line 235.
45. Act 4, scene 3, line 111—"Good morning to you, faire, and gracious daughter."
46. Act 5, scene 1, line 490.
47. Act 5, scene 1, line 534.
48. Act 5, scene 1, line 535.
49. Thidias also uses the word "so" in the form of a conclusion in Act 3, scene 13, line 55 of *Anthony and Cleopatra*. Having established from Enobarbus that "If *Caesar* please, our Master/Will leape to be his Friend," he replies, "So. Thus then thou most renown'd, *Caesar* intreats,/Not to consider in what case thou stand'st/Further than he is *Caesar*" (F2). The modern equivalent of "so" in this context would be "OK, then."
50. Act 1, scene 1, line 3.
51. Act 2, scene 1, line 7.
52. Act 2, scene 1, line 192.
53. Act 2, scene 1, line 184.
54. Act 2, scene 1, line 281.
55. Act 5, scene 1, line 317.
56. Act 4, scene 2, line 133.
57. Act 5, scene 1, line 316.
58. Act 2, scene 2, line 176.
59. Act 3, scene 2, line 91.
60. Act 2, scene 2, lines 95–99.
61. Act 1, scene 4, line 68.
62. Act 2, scene 1, line 233.
63. Act 2, scene 1, line 282.
64. Act 3, scene 2, line 185.
65. Act 3, scene 2, line 189.
66. Act 5, scene 1, line 311.
67. Act 5, scene 1, line 471.
68. The plot doesn't need to include Barnadine since the Provost could simply skip to substituting Ragozine's head for Claudio's. Shakespeare must have intended the role to have a deeper significance than "light relief."
69. *Richard III*, Act 1, scene 1, line 30.
70. Act 5, scene 1, line 399.
71. Act 5, scene 1, line 449.
72. Modern editors more or less follow this and set 11 or 12 question marks, although not always where the folio places them. The Arden edition gets a little carried away and adds 4 exclamation points, whereas in the First Folio there are none. Lever, *Measure for Measure*.
73. *Othello,* Act 1, scene 3, line 402.
74. Act 4, scene 4, lines 26 and 30.
75. Act 5, scene 1, line 473.
76. Act 2, scene 4, line 88.
77. Act 2, scene 4, line 162.
78. Act 2, scene 4, line 159.
79. Act 2, scene 4, line 167.
80. Act 2, scene 2, line 179.
81. Act 1, scene 4, line 58.
82. Act 1, scene 4, line 60.
83. Act 2, scene 2, lines 138–140.

84. Act 2, scene 2, line 142.
85. Act 2, scene 4, line 140.
86. Act 2, scene 4, line 143.
87. Act 2, scene 4, line 146.
88. Shere Hite, *The Hite Report on Male Sexuality* (London: Macdonald, 1981), 137.
89. Joseph Swetnam, *The Arraignment of Women*, 1615 (BiblioBazaar, 2010).
90. Act 2, scene 2, line 180.
91. See Dostoyevsky's *Crime and Punishment*.
92. The word "nunnery" could be used during this period to mean either a house of religion or resort.
93. Act 1, scene 4, line 34.
94. Act 4, scene 3, line 171.
95. Act 5, scene 1, line 178. Notice how the First Folio employment of capital letters further dehumanizes women by giving them a narrow range of specific roles in life. The use of a question mark—sometimes in place of an exclamation point—provides the option of posing a question or making a statement.
96. Act 5, scene 1, line 180.
97. Act 2, scene 4, lines 133–137.
98. Act 5, scene 1, line 220.
99. Act 5, scene 1, line 524.
100. *Othello*, Act 3, scene 3, line 325.
101. Act 2, scene 2, line 183.
102. Act 4, scene 4, line 32.
103. Act 2, scene 1, line 242.
104. Act 4, scene 4, line 18.
105. *Macbeth*, Act 2, scene 2, line 72.
106. Act 2, scene 4, line 134.
107. *Macbeth*, Act 1, scene 7, line 47.
108. Act 4, scene 4, line 2.
109. Act 2, scene 1, line 239.
110. Act 2, scene 1, line 220.

Conclusion

1. Anthony Sher, *Year of the King* (London: Hogarth Press, Chatto & Windus, 1985), 156.
2. As the Arden/New Penguin texts are most commonly used in professional theater, they are the ones deliberately referred to throughout this book.
3. Sher, *Year of the King*, 180.
4. Alan Dessen, *The Director as Shakespeare Editor. Shakespeare Survey Volume 59, Editing Shakespeare*, ed. Peter Holland (Cambridge: Cambridge University Press, 2006).
5. Katie Mitchell, *The Director's Craft* (Abingdon: Routledge, 2009), 46.
6. David Mamet, *True and False: Heresy and Common Sense for the Actor* (London: Faber & Faber, 1998).
7. Brian Cox confessed that he used his son's copy of *Shakespeare Made Easy* when he played King Lear, which "caused a great deal of hilarity." Brian Cox, *The Lear Diaries* (London: Methuen, 1992), 21.
8. John Barton, *Playing Shakespeare* (London: Methuen, 1984), 10.
9. Declan Donnellan, *The Actor and the Target* (London: Nick Hern Books, 2002), 81.
10. Romeo's early line, "Here's much to do with hate, but more with love" (Act 1, scene 1, line 174), and the oxymorons in the speech that follows might be said to support this view.
11. Peter Brook, *Evoking (and Forgetting!) Shakespeare* (London: Nick Hern Books, 2002), 24.
12. Even the same production can be received differently when performed in a number of places. I was part of a tour of *Coriolanus* for the English Shakespeare Company during which the protagonist was perceived to be a fascist bully in Germany but a samurai warrior when played in Japan.
13. Peter Brook, *The Empty Space* (London: Pelican, 1972), 43.
14. Catholics in general might be said to have been a general target and audience pleaser, although in some plays such as *The Winter's Tale* there appears to be evidence of Shakespeare's Catholic sympathies.
15. This remark was recorded by Elizabeth's archivist William Lambarde in 1601.
16. *Twelfth Night*, Act 5, scene 1, line 376.
17. Bertolt Brecht, appendix #46 to *A Short Organum for the Theatre* (1949), republished in *Brecht on Theatre*, trans. John Willet (New York: Hill and Wang, 1964), 277.
18. Ralph Berry, *On Directing Shakespeare* (London: Hamish Hamilton, 1989), 190.
19. Brook, *Evoking (and Forgetting!) Shakespeare*, 39.
20. T. S. Eliot, *Selected Essays* (1951); new edition of revised 3rd publication (London: Faber & Faber, 1999), 203.
21. The National Theatre of Great Britain's production of *Richard III* in 1991 dispensed with using an editor/adaptor edition of the play. Brian Cox, who played Buckingham, commented: "It was nice to get a script that looks like a script and could be by anyone instead of one of those small Shakespeare books which are always so inhibiting." Cox, *Lear Diaries*, 32.

Bibliography

Shakespeare's Plays

All's Well That Ends Well

All's Well That Ends Well. Edited by G. K. Hunter. Arden Shakespeare. London: Methuen, 1959.

Antony and Cleopatra

Antony and Cleopatra. Edited by M. R. Ridley. Arden Shakespeare. London: Thomson Learning, Thomas Nelson and Sons, 1989.

Antony and Cleopatra. Edited by John Wilders. Arden Shakespeare. London: Routledge, Thomson Learning, 1995.

Antony and Cleopatra, 2d ed. Edited by David Bevington. The New Cambridge Shakespeare. Cambridge: Cambridge University Press, 2005.

The Tragedie of Anthonie and Cleopatra. Prepared and annotated by Neil Freeman. New York: Applause First Folio Edition, 1998.

As You Like It

As You Like It. Edited by Agnes Latham. Arden Shakespeare. Walton-on-Thames, UK: Methuen, Thomas Nelson and Sons, 1975.

The Comedy of Errors

The Comedie of Errors. Prepared and annotated by Neil Freeman. New York: Applause First Folio Edition, 1998.

The Comedy of Errors. Edited by R. A. Foakes. Arden Shakespeare. London: Methuen, 1962.

Cymbeline

Cymbeline. Edited by J. M. Nosworthy. Arden Shakespeare. London: Thomson Learning, 1995.

Hamlet

Hamlet. Edited by Philip Edwards. The New Cambridge Shakespeare. Cambridge: Cambridge University Press, 1985.

Hamlet. Edited by Harold Jenkins. Arden Shakespeare. London: Methuen, 1982. Reprint, London: Routledge, 1989.

Hamlet. Edited by T. J. B. Spencer. St. Ives, UK: New Penguin Shakespeare, 1980.

The Tragedie of Hamlet. Prepared and annotated by Neil Freeman. New York: Applause First Folio Edition, 1998, 2000.

Henry IV, Part 1

1 Henry IV. Edited by G. L. Kittredge. Boston: Ginn, 1940.

The First Part of Henry the Fourth. Prepared and annotated by Neil Freeman. New York: Applause First Folio Edition, 2000.

The First Part of Henry the Fourth. Edited by Frederic W. Moorman. The Warwick Shakespeare. London: Blackie & Son, no date.

Henry IV, Part 1. Edited by David Bevington. The Oxford Shakespeare. Oxford: Oxford University Press, 1987.

Henry IV, Part 1. Edited by Hebert Weil and Judith Weil. New Cambridge Shakespeare. Cambridge: Cambridge University Press, 1997.

Henry IV, Part 1. Edited by John Dover Wilson. New Cambridge Shakespeare. Cambridge: Cambridge University Press, 1968.

King Henry IV, Part 1, 2d ed. Edited by A. R. Humphreys. Arden Shakespeare. London: Methuen, 1960.

King Henry IV, Part 1, 3d ed. Edited by David Scott Kastan. Arden Shakespeare. London: Thomson Learning, 2002.

King Henry IV, Part One. Edited by P. H. Davison. Aylesbury, UK: New Penguin Shakespeare, 1968.

Henry V

Henry V. Based on the Caxton edition of *The Complete Works of William Shakespeare*. Edited by Sidney Lee (and adapted by the United States government). Armed Services edition (not for sale). Mineola, NY: Dover, 2002.

King Henry V. Edited by T. W. Craik. Arden Shakespeare. London: Thomas Nelson and Sons, 1995. Reprint, London: Thomson Learning, 2000.

King Henry V. Edited by A. R. Humphreys. Aylesbury: New Penguin Shakespeare, 1968.

Henry V. Edited by Gary Taylor. Oxford: The Oxford Shakespeare, Oxford Paperbacks, 2008.

King Henry V. Edited by J. H. Walter. Arden Shakespeare. London: Methuen, 1954.

The Life of Henry the Fifth. Prepared and annotated by Neil Freeman. New York: Applause First Folio Edition, 1998.

Julius Caesar

Julius Caesar. Edited by David Daniell. Arden Shakespeare. London: Thomson Learning, 1998.

The Tragedie of Julius Caesar. Prepared and annotated by Neil Freeman. New York: Applause First Folio Edition, 1998.

King Edward III

King Edward III. Edited by Giorgio Melchiori. The New Cambridge Shakespeare. Cambridge: Cambridge University Press, 1998.

King Henry VI, Part 3

King Henry VI, Part 3. Edited by Andrew S. Cairncross. Arden Shakespeare. London: Methuen, 1964.

King John

King John. Edited by E. A. J. Honigmann. London: Arden Shakespeare, Methuen, 1954.

King John. Edited by R. L. Smallwood. Bungay, Suffolk: New Penguin Shakespeare, 1974.

King John. Edited by John Dover Wilson. Cambridge: Cambridge University Press, 1936.

The Life and Death of King John. Prepared and annotated by Neil Freeman. New York: Applause First Folio Edition, 2000.

King Lear

King Lear. Edited by Nick de Somogyi. London: Nick Hern, 2004.

King Lear. Edited by R. A. Foakes. Arden Shakespeare. London: Thomas Nelson and Sons, 1997. Reprint, London: Thomson Learning, 2001.

King Lear. Edited by G. K. Hunter. Bungay, UK: New Penguin Shakespeare, 1972.

King Lear. Edited by Kenneth Muir. Arden Shakespeare. London: Methuen, 1972.

The Tragedie of King Lear. Prepared and annotated by Neil Freeman. New York: Applause First Folio Edition, 2000.

Love's Labour's Lost

Love's Labour's Lost. Edited by R. W. David. Arden Shakespeare. London: Methuen, 1951.

Love's Labour's Lost. Edited by John Kerrigan. St. Ives, UK: New Penguin Shakespeare, 1982.

Macbeth

Macbeth. Edited by Henry Cuningham. Arden Shakespeare. London: Methuen, 1912.

Macbeth. Edited by G. K. Hunter. St. Ives, UK: New Penguin Shakespeare, 1967/1995.

Macbeth. Edited by Kenneth Muir. Arden Shakespeare. London: Methuen, 1951.

The Tragedie of Macbeth. Prepared and annotated by Neil Freeman. New York: Applause First Folio Edition, 1998.

Measure for Measure

Measure for Measure. Edited by J. W. Lever. Arden Shakespeare. London: Methuen, 1965.

Measure for Measure. Edited by J. M. Nosworthy. St. Ives, UK: New Penguin Shakespeare, 1969.

Measure for Measure. Prepared and annotated by Neil Freeman. New York: Applause First Folio Edition, 1998.

The Merchant of Venice

The Merchant of Venice. Edited by John Russell Brown. Arden Shakespeare. London: Methuen, 1955.

A Midsummer Night's Dream

A Midsummer Night's Dream. Edited by Harold F. Brooks. Arden Shakespeare. London: Methuen, 1984.

Much Ado About Nothing

Much Ado About Nothing. Edited by A. R. Humphreys. Arden Shakespeare. London: Methuen, 1981/2003.

Much Adoe About Nothing. Prepared and annotated by Neil Freeman. New York: Applause First Folio Edition, 2001.

Othello

Othello. Edited by E. A. J. Honigmann. Arden Shakespeare. London: Thomas Nelson and Sons, 1997. Reprint, London: Thomson Learning, 2006.

Othello. Edited by Kenneth Muir. Bungay, UK: New Penguin Shakespeare, 1968.

Othello. Edited by M. R. Ridley. Arden Shakespeare. London: Methuen, 1958.

The Tragedie of Othello, The Moore of Venice. Prepared and annotated by Neil Freeman. New York: Applause First Folio Edition, 2001.

Richard III

Richard III. Edited by Anthony Hammond. Arden Shakespeare. London: Methuen, 1981. Reprint, London: Routledge, 1990.

Richard III. Edited by E. A. J. Honigmann. London: New Penguin Shakespeare, 1968/2005.

The Tragedy of King Richard III. Edited by John Jowett. Oxford: Oxford University Press, 2000.

The Tragedy of Richard the Third. Prepared and annotated by Neil Freeman. New York: Applause First Folio Edition, 2000.

Romeo and Juliet

Romeo and Juliet. Edited by Brian Gibbons. Arden Shakespeare. London: Methuen, 1980.

Romeo and Juliet. Edited by T. J. B. Spencer. St. Ives, UK: New Penguin Shakespeare, 1967.

The Tragedie of Romeo and Juliet. Prepared and annotated by Neil Freeman. New York: Applause First Folio Edition, 1998.

Sir Thomas More

Sir Thomas More. Edited by John Jowett. Arden Shakespeare. London: Methuen, 2011.

The Taming of the Shrew

The Taming of the Shrew. Edited by Brian Morris. Arden Shakespeare. London: Methuen, 1981.

Timon of Athens

Timon of Athens. Edited by H. J. Oliver. Arden Shakespeare. London: Methuen, 1979.

Troilus and Cressida

Troilus and Cressida. Edited by Kenneth Palmer. Arden Shakespeare. London: Methuen, 1982.

Twelfth Night

Twelfth Night. Edited by J. M. Lothian and T. W. Craik. Arden Shakespeare. London: Methuen, 1975.

Twelfth Night. Edited by M. M. Mahood. Bungay, UK: New Penguin Shakespeare, 1968.

The Winter's Tale

The Winter's Tale. Edited by J. H. P. Pafford. Arden Shakespeare. London: Methuen, 1963.

Other References

Adams, J. Q., ed. *The Dramatic Records of Sir Henry Herbert*. New Haven: Yale University Press, 1917.

Alfreds, Mike. *Different Every Night*. London: Nick Hern, 2007.

Astington, John H. *Actors and Acting in Shakespeare's Time*. Cambridge: Cambridge University Press, 2010.

Baldwin, Pat, and Tom Baldwin. *"King Richard III": Cambridge Student Guide*. Cambridge: Cambridge University Press, 2002.

Baldwin, Thomas Whitfield. *The Organization and Personnel of the Shakespearean Company*. Princeton: Princeton University Press, 1927.

Barker, Clive. *Theatre Games*. London: Eyre Methuen, 1977.

Barton, John. *Playing Shakespeare*. London: Methuen, 1984.

Bate, Jonathan. *The Genius of Shakespeare*. London: Picador, 1997.

_____. *Soul of the Age*. London: Penguin, 2009.

Bate, Jonathan, and Eric Rasmussen, eds. *RSC William Shakespeare Complete Works*. Basingstoke, UK: Macmillan, 2007.

Beaumont, Francis. *The Knight of the Burning Pestle*. Edited by Michael Hattaway. London: New Mermaids Series, A & C Black, 1986.

Beaumont, Francis, and John Fletcher. *Love's Cure*. Edited by Marea Mitchell. Nottingham: Nottingham Drama Texts, 1992.

Berry, Cicely. *From Word to Play*. London: Oberon, 2008.

Berry, Ralph. *Changing Styles in Shakespeare*. Oxford: Routledge, 2011.

_____. *On Directing Shakespeare*. London: Hamish Hamilton, 1989.

Blakemore Evans, G., ed. *The Riverside Shakespeare*, 2d ed. New York: Houghton Mifflin, 1997.

Bloom, Harold. *Shakespeare: The Invention of the Human*. London: Fourth Estate, 1999.

Blayney, Peter W. M. *The First Folio of Shakespeare*. Washington, D.C.: Folger Library Publications, 1991.

Bogdanov, Michael. *Shakespeare, the Director's Cut*. Edinburgh: Capercaille, 2003.

Brandes, George. *William Shakespeare: A Critical Study*, Vol. 2. London: Heinemann, 1898.

Brecht, Bertolt. *Brecht on Theatre*. Translated by John Willet. London: Eyre Methuen, 1978.

Brock, Dewey Howard. *A Ben Jonson Companion*. Bloomington: Indiana University Press, 1983.

Brook, Peter. *The Empty Space*. London: Pelican, 1972.

_____. *Evoking (and Forgetting!) Shakespeare*. London: Nick Hern, 2002.

_____. *The Shifting Point*. London: Methuen, 1988.

Brown, John Russell. *Free Shakespeare*. New York: Applause, 1997.

_____. *Shakespeare and the Theatrical Event*. Basingstoke, UK: Palgrave Macmillan, 2002.

_____. *Shakespeare Dancing: A Theatrical Study of the Plays*. Basingstoke, UK: Palgrave Macmillan, 2005.

Bryson, Bill. *Shakespeare*. London: Harper Press, 2007.

Caldarone, Marina, and Maggie Lloyd-Williams. *Actions: The Actors' Thesaurus*. London: Nick Hern, 2004.

Callow, Simon. *Being an Actor*. London: Methuen, 1984.

Cargill, Alexander. *Shakespeare the Player*. London: Constable, 1916.

Chambers, E. K. *William Shakespeare: A Study of Facts and Problems*. Oxford: Clarendon Press, 1930.
Chekhov, Michael. *To the Actor*. New York: Routledge, 2002.
Coghill, Nevill. *Shakespeare's Professional Skills*. Cambridge: Cambridge University Press, 1964.
Colby Sprague, Arthur. *The Doubling of Parts in Shakespeare's Plays*. London: Society for Theatre Research/Headley Brothers, 1966.
Collins, Paul. *The Book of William: How Shakespeare's First Folio Conquered the World*. New York: Bloomsbury, 2009.
Cox, Brian. *The Lear Diaries*. London: Methuen, 1992.
Coye, Dale. *Pronouncing Shakespeare's Words*. London: Routledge, 2002.
Craig, W. J., ed. *Oxford Shakespeare: Complete Works of William Shakespeare*. Oxford: Clarendon Press, 1914.
Crystal, David. *Pronouncing Shakespeare: The Globe Experiment*. Cambridge: Cambridge University Press, 2005.
_____. *"Think on My Words": Exploring Shakespeare's Language*. Cambridge: Cambridge University Press, 2008.
Dessen, Alan. *Recovering Shakespeare's Theatrical Vocabulary*. Cambridge: Cambridge University Press, 1995.
Diderot, Denis. *The Paradox of Acting*. London: Chatto & Windus, 1883.
Donnellan, Declan. *The Actor and the Target*. London: Nick Hern, 2002.
Edgar, David. *"Nicholas Nickleby"* in *Edgar Plays: Two*. London: Methuen Drama, 1990.
Egan, Gabriel. *The Struggle for Shakespeare's Text: Twentieth-Century Editorial Theory and Practice*. Cambridge: Cambridge University Press, 2010.
Escolme, Bridget. *Talking to the Audience*. London: Routledge, 2005.
Flatter, Richard. *Shakespeare's Producing Hand: A Study of His Marks of Expression to Be Found in the First Folio*. New York: Greenwood, 1969.
Freeman, Neil. *Shakespeare's First Texts*. Vancouver, BC: Folio Scripts, 1999.
Garber, Marjorie. *Shakespeare and Modern Culture*. New York: Pantheon, 2008.
Gaskill, William. *Words into Action: Finding the Life of the Play*. London: Nick Hern, 2010.
Goffman, Erving. *The Presentation of Self in Everyday Life*. London: Pelican, 1976.
Graham-White, Anthony. *Punctuation and Its Dramatic Value in Shakespearean Drama*. London: Associated University Presses, 1995.
Greenblatt, Stephen. *Will in the World*. London: Pimlico, 2005.
Greg, W. W. *The Shakespeare First Folio*. Oxford: Clarendon Press, 1955.
Gurr, Andrew. *Playgoing in Shakespeare's London*. Cambridge: Cambridge University Press, 2004.
_____. *The Shakespeare Company 1594–1642*. Cambridge: Cambridge University Press, 2004.
_____. *The Shakespearean Playing Companies*. Oxford: Clarendon Press, 1996.
_____. *The Shakespearean Stage 1574–1642*. Cambridge: Cambridge University Press, 1992.
Hall, Peter. *Shakespeare's Advice to the Players*. London: Oberon, 2003.
Halliday, F. E. *A Shakespeare Companion 1564–1964*. London: Penguin, 1969.
Hampton-Reeves, Stuart, and Bridget Escolme, eds. *Shakespeare and the Making of Theatre*. Basingstoke, UK: Palgrave Macmillan, 2012.
Harrison, G. B. *Shakespeare at Work: 1592–1603*. Ann Arbor: University of Michigan Press, 1958.
Hazlitt, William. *Characters of Shakespeare's Plays*. Oxford: Oxford World Classics, 1917.
_____. *On Actors and Acting*, published in *The Round Table*. London: Sampson Low, Son, & Marston, 1869.
Heywood, Thomas. *An Apology For Actors*. Marston Gate, UK: Elibron Classics, 2005.
Hinman, Charlton. *First Folio of Shakespeare: The Norton Facsimile*, 2d ed. New York: W. W. Norton, 1996.
Hite, Shere. *The Hite Report on Male Sexuality*. London: Macdonald, Optima, 1990.
Holinshed, Raphael. *Holinshed's Chronicle, as Used in Shakespeare's Plays*. Edited by Allardyce Nicholl and Josephine Nicholl. London: Everyman's Library, 1969.
Holland, Peter, ed. *Shakespeare Survey Volume 59: "Editing Shakespeare."* Cambridge: Cambridge University Press, 2006.
_____, and Stephen Orgel, eds. *From Performance to Print in Shakespeare's England (Redefining British Theatre History)*. Basingstoke, UK: Palgrave Macmillan, 2006.
Honigmann, E. A. J. *The Stability of Shakespeare's Text*. Lincoln: University of Nebraska Press, 1965.
Hyman, Stanley Edgar. *Iago: Some Approaches to the Illusion of His Characterization*. New York: Atheneum, 1970.
Jones, John. *Shakespeare at Work*. Oxford: Clarendon Press, 1995.
Jonson, Ben. *Ben Jonson—The Oxford Authors*. Oxford: Oxford University Press, 1985.
_____. *"Three Comedies."* Edited by Michael Jamieson. Bungay, UK: Penguin, 1966.
Kermode, Frank. *Shakespeare's Language*. London: Allen Lane/Penguin, 2000.
Kiernan, Pauline. *Filthy Shakespeare*. London: Ouercus, 2006.
King, T. J. *Casting Shakespeare's Plays*. Cambridge: Cambridge University Press, 1992.
Kirschbaum, Leo. *The True Text of "King Lear."* Baltimore: Johns Hopkins Press, 1945.

Kliman, Bernice W. "Introduction to *The Enfolded Hamlet*." http://triggs.djvu.org/global-language.com/enfolded/enfolded.intro.html.

Kokeritz, Helge. *Shakespeare's Pronunciation*. New Haven: Yale University Press, 1953.

Leishman, J. B., ed. *The Three Parnassus Plays*. London: Ivor Nicholson & Watson, 1949.

Levi, Peter. *The Life and Times of William Shakespeare*. London: Macmillan, 1988.

Levin, Richard. *New Readings vs. Old Plays*. Chicago: University of Chicago Press, 1979.

Lynch, Jack. *Becoming Shakespeare*. London: Constable & Robinson, 2008.

Mack, Maynard. *King Lear in Our Time*. London: Methuen, 1966.

Mamet, David. *True and False: Heresy and Common Sense for the Actor*. London: Faber & Faber, 1998.

Marlowe, Christopher. *The Complete Plays*. London: Penguin, 1969.

Marston, John, with additions by John Webster. *The Malcontent*. London: New Mermaids, A & C Black, 1998.

Massai, Sonia. *Shakespeare and the Rise of the Editor*. Cambridge: Cambridge University Press, 2007.

McMillin, Scott, and Sally-Beth MacLean. *The Queen's Men and Their Plays*. Cambridge: Cambridge University Press, 1998.

Meisner, Sanford, and Dennis Longwell. *Sandford Meisner on Acting*. New York: Vintage, 1987.

Miller, Jonathan. *Subsequent Performances*. London: Faber & Faber, 1986.

Mitchell, Katie. *The Director's Craft*. Abingdon: Routledge, 2009.

Morley, Carol A. *The Plays and Poems of William Heminge*. Madison, NJ: Fairleigh Dickinson University Press, 2005.

Mortimer, Ian. *The Time Traveller's Guide To Elizabethan England*. London: Vintage, 2013.

Muir, Kenneth, and Stanley Wells, eds. *Aspects of Shakespeare's "Problem Plays."* Cambridge: Cambridge University Press, 1982.

Nicholl, Charles. *The Lodger: Shakespeare on Silver Street*. London: Penguin/Allen Lane, 2007.

_____. *The Reckoning: The Murder of Christopher Marlowe*. London: Picador, 1993.

Nuttall, A. D. *Shakespeare the Thinker*. New Haven: Yale University Press, 2007.

Onions, C. T. *A Shakespeare Glossary*. Oxford: Clarendon Press, 1911. 2d ed. 1919 revised. 1980 with enlarged addenda.

Orgel, Stephen. *The Authentic Shakespeare: And Other Problems of the Early Modern Stage*. New York: Routledge, 2002.

Palfrey, Simon, and Tiffany Stern. *Shakespeare in Parts*. Oxford: Oxford University Press, 2007.

Partridge, Eric. *Shakespeare's Bawdy*. Abingdon, UK: Routledge Classics, 2001.

Pasternak-Slater, Ann. *Shakespeare the Director*. Brighton: Harvester Press, 1982.

Pope, Alexander. *The Works of Alexander Pope*, Vol. 9. London: J. F. Dove, 1822.

Porter, Charlotte, and Helen A. Clarke, eds. *Shakespeare's Complete Works*. London: George G. Harrap, 1903.

Rabkin, Norman. *Shakespeare and the Problem of Meaning*. Chicago: University of Chicago Press, 1981.

Sartre, Jean-Paul. *Being and Nothingness: An Essay on Phenomenological Ontology*. London: Routledge Classics, 2003.

Schoenbaum, Samuel. *William Shakespeare: A Compact Documentary Life*. Oxford: Oxford University Press, 1977.

Schucking, Levin L. *Character Problems in Shakespeare's Plays*. London: George G. Harrap, 1922.

Shapiro, James. *1599: A Year in the Life of William Shakespeare*. London: Faber & Faber, 2005.

Shaw, George Bernard. *Shaw on Shakespeare*. Edited by Edwin Wilson. New York: Applause Theatre & Cinema, 1989.

Sher, Anthony. *Year of the King*. London: Chatto & Windus, Hogarth Press, 1985.

Skura, Meredith Anne. *Shakespeare the Actor and the Purposes of Playing*. Chicago: University of Chicago Press, 1993.

Southworth, John. *Shakespeare the Player*. Stroud, UK: Sutton, 2000.

Spingarn, J. E., ed. *Critical Essays of the Seventeenth Century*. Vol. 2. Oxford: Clarendon Press, 1908.

Stanislavski, Constantin. *An Actor Prepares*. Translated by Elizabeth Reynolds Hapgood. New York: Routledge, A Theatre Arts Book, 1989.

_____. *Building a Character*. Translated by Elizabeth Reynolds Hapgood. London: Eyre Methuen, 1979.

_____. *Creating a Role*. Translated by Elizabeth Reynolds Hapgood. London: Methuen, 1980.

_____. *My Life in Art*. Translated by Jean Benediti. New York: Routledge, 2008.

_____. *My Life in Art*. Translated by J. J. Robbins. London: Eyre Methuen, 1980.

Stern, Tiffany. *Making Shakespeare, From Stage to Page*. Oxford: Routledge, 2004.

_____. *Rehearsal from Shakespeare to Sheridan*. Oxford: Clarendon Press, 2000.

Stevenson, Robert Louis. *The Works of Robert Louis Stevenson*, Vol. XXIV.1922–23.

Swetnam, Joseph. *The Arraignment of Women*. BiblioBazaar, 2010.

Tannen, Deborah. *You Just Don't Understand*. London: Virago Press, 1991.

Taylor, Gary. *Moment by Moment by Shakespeare*. London: Macmillan, 1985.

Taylor, Gary, and John Jowett. *Shakespeare Reshaped 1606–1623*. Oxford: Oxford Shakespeare Studies/Clarendon Press, 1993.

Taylor, Gary, and Stanley Wells. *William Shakespeare: A Textual Companion.* New York/London: W. W. Norton, 1997. Oxford: Oxford University Press, 1987.

_____, ed., with John Jowett. *William Shakespeare: The Complete Works.* Oxford: Oxford Shakespeare, Clarendon Press, 1988.

Thompson, Ann, and Gordon McMullan, eds. *In Arden: Editing Shakespeare: Essays in Honour of Richard Proudfoot.* London: Arden Shakespeare Library/Thomson Learning, 2003.

Trevis, Di. *Being a Director.* Abingdon, UK: Routledge, 2012.

Tucker, Patrick. *Secrets of Acting Shakespeare: The Original Approach.* New York: Routledge, 2002.

Walker, Alice. *Textual Problems of the First Folio.* Cambridge: Cambridge University Press, 1953. Reprint, London: Norwood Editions, 1977.

Weingust, Don. *Acting From Shakespeare's First Folio.* New York: Routledge, 2006.

Wells, Stanley. *Re-Editing Shakespeare for the Modern Reader.* Oxford: Clarendon Press, 1984.

_____. *Shakespeare & Co.* London: Penguin, 2007.

Weston, David. *Covering McKellan.* London: Rickshaw, 2011.

Wickham, Glynne, Herbert Berry, and William Ingram, eds. *English Professional Theatre, 1530–1660.* Cambridge: Cambridge University Press, 2000.

Willoughby, Edwin Eliot. *A Printer of Shakespeare: Biography of William Jaggard.* London: Philip, 1934.

Wilson, John Dover. *The Essential Shakespeare.* Cambridge: Cambridge University Press, 1932.

Wood, Michael. *In Search of Shakespeare.* London: BBC, 2003.

Worthen, W. B. *Shakespeare and the Authority of Performance.* Cambridge: Cambridge University Press, 1997.

Online Resources

David Crystal and Ben Crystal's website: www.shakespeareswords.com (packed with information, including a comprehensive glossary).

Folios 1–4: www.internetshakespeare.uvic.ca/Library/facsimilie/bookplay/SLNSW_F2.

Shakespeare's Quartos: www.bl.uk/treasures/shakespeare.

Index

Act to Restrain the Abuses of Players 62
acting exercises 175–198, 228n48
actioning the text 111–114, 129, 141, 158
additions to the scripts in the First Folio 59
Alfreds, Mike 174, 197
All for Love 186
All's Well That Ends Well 27, 69, 114, 170, 180, 185
animal study acting exercise 191–192
Anthony and Cleopatra 5, 69–70, 106, 124, 146, 176, 178–179, 185, 217
Apley, William 64
Arden, John 153, 159
Arden Shakespeare 4, 7, 8, 12–13, 15, 17, 21, 23, 24, 25, 26, 27, 28, 30, 31, 32, 33, 36, 41, 44, 46, 55, 68, 69, 71, 78, 79, 89, 90, 93–97, 106, 113, 136, 170, 189, 196, 213
As You Like It 31, 32, 73, 126, 141, 193–194

Barker, Clive 192
Barton, John 72, 102, 215
Bate, Jonathan 10, 111
Beaumont and Fletcher 54–55, 56, 136
Berry, Cicely 175
Bevington, David 106
Blount, Edward 63–65
Bogdanov, Michael 147, 175
Bradley, A. C. 189
Brecht, Bertolt 152, 217
Brook, Peter 6, 26, 99, 118, 193, 216, 217, 221n54
Brooks, Harold F. 21–22
Brown, John Russell 24
Burbage, Richard 110–111, 119

Callow, Simon 28
Cambridge New Shakespeare 68
capital letters 73–77, 78, 91, 94, 95, 112, 203, 205, 228n48
censorship 8–9
Chambers, E. K. 26
character changes by editors 15–18
Chekhov, Michael 138
Churchill, Winston 99
Clarke, Helen 10; *see also* Porter, Charlotte
cliché 6, 174–175, 202, 208

The Comedy of Errors 11, 31, 83, 106, 123–124, 178, 183–184, 185, 187–189, 196
Compositor E 52–53, 225n4; *see also* Leason, John
Coquelin 145
Coriolanus 45, 126
Cotes, Thomas 64
Cox, Brian 174, 187, 192, 236n3, 239n21
Craig, W. J. 4, 9
Craik, T. W. 71, 170, 227n24
Crane, Ralph 55, 86, 229n100
Crystal, David 17, 72, 73, 78
cue scripts 117–119, 161
Cunningham, Henry 26–27, 189
cuts to the text in the First Folio 54–55, 58–59, 61, 232n32
Cymbeline 28, 77–78

Daniell, David 13
David, R. W. 61
Davison, P. H. 81
De Monchaux, Paul 99
Dessen, Alan 214
Diderot, Denis 126
Donnellan, Declan 175, 191, 196, 215, 217, 236n12
Duke of Wellington (soldier) 161–162, 172

Edgar, David 85
Edward III 158, 236n27
Edwards, Philip 6
Eliot, T. S. 218
"explanations" of words and phrases by editors 27–29, 223n58

false folio 63
Field, Richard 63, 78
first and last lines 176–178
First Folio mistakes 15, 35, 45, 47–48, 51–52, 87, 107, 227n23, 228n71, 229n81, 235n58
Flatter, Richard 104–105
Foakes, R. A. 12, 31–32, 38, 61, 106
foul papers 8–9, 86, 220n30
Fourth Folio 42, 224n68
Freeman, Neil 1, 82–83, 228n49, 230n136

247

Freudian Slips 52, 54
Fuller, Thomas 152

Garber, Marjorie 84, 173
Gaskill, William 107, 116
ghost characters 51
Gibbons, Brian 113
Goffman, Erving 196
Gorboduc 186
Greene, Robert 56
Greg, W. W. 219n18

Hall, Peter 70, 99, 114–116
Hamlet 11–12, 15, 35, 41, 43–46, 47, 56, 58–60, 85–86, 87, 88–89, 110, 111–112, 113–114, 152, 176, 183
Hazlitt, William 124, 126, 130, 151
Heminge, William 65
Heminge and Condell 6–9, 20, 54–55, 57, 63, 72, 73, 78, 85, 108, 117, 160, 181, 218, 221n63
Henry IV Part 1 3–4, 11, 17–18, 23–24, 27–28, 31, 56–57, 58, 71–72, 74–75, 81–82, 106, 164, 171
Henry IV Part 2 47, 151, 156, 166
Henry V 11, 26, 47–48, 51, 54, 67–68, 71, 83, 89–90, 150–172, 176, 184–185, 194, 235n55
Henry VI Part 1 71
Henry VI Part 2 57
Henry VI Part 3 57, 121, 124, 190
Herbert, Henry 9, 219n22
Heywood, Thomas 62–63, 84–85, 226n48, 229n92
Hite, Shere 209
Holinshed, Raphael 16, 160
Honigmann, E. A. J. 15, 17, 23, 26, 27, 35, 42, 43, 80, 95–97
Humphreys, A. R. 28, 136, 160, 170
Hunter, G. K. 25, 27

improvisation 181–182, 186
italics 77–82, 91, 129, 228n49, 228n58

Jaggard, William 21, 52, 61–66, 72, 85
Jenkins, Harold 8, 44, 46
Jones, John 66, 97, 221n3
Jonson, Ben 7, 56, 57–58, 64, 106–107, 151, 186, 217, 225n28, 226n63, 229n95
Joyce, James *Ulysses* 27
Julius Caesar 11, 13, 58, 67, 75–76, 88, 91–92, 176–177, 194, 217, 220n36

Kastan, David Scott 4, 12, 17–18, 24
Kermode, Frank 10, 12, 92, 173
Kerrigan, John 18, 26, 54, 225n7
King, T. J. 16
King John 15–17, 27, 41–44, 70, 82–83, 89, 176, 182
King Lear 18–19, 25, 31–32, 38–39, 60–61, 70, 87, 103, 121, 126, 180–181, 182, 186, 216
Kirschbaum, Leo 8
Kittredge, G. L. 11
Kliman, Bernice W. 6
Knight, Edward 8
Knights, L. C. 189

Laughton, Charles 73–74
Leason, John 52–53, 225n4; *see also* Compositor E
Lever, J. W. 27, 33, 36, 37
Levi, Peter 109

Levin, Richard 5, 11–12
line re-assignments by editors 18–24
lineation 80, 97–107, 133, 204; *see also* meter
Love's Labour's Lost 18, 25–26, 35, 53–54, 63, 72, 82, 87–88, 173, 178

Macbeth 26–27, 30–31, 33, 56, 70, 73, 79, 81, 89, 92, 103–105, 175, 177–178, 183, 189–190, 211, 216, 228n36
Mack, Maynard 34
Mahood, M. M. 34
Mamet, David 133, 140, 214
Marlowe, Christopher 64, 109
Massai, Sonia 78–79
Master of the Revels 8–9
Measure for Measure 6, 27, 32–33, 35–37, 55, 62, 70, 102, 199–211
Meisner, Sandford 137, 232n22
The Merchant of Venice 26, 83–84, 86, 147–150, 176, 182, 184
meter 80, 97–107, 133, 204; *see also* lineation
Middleton, Thomas 51, 55
A Midsummer Night's Dream 20–23, 56, 85, 86, 119
Miller, Jonathan 6
mirror scenes 129, 131, 182–186
Mitchell, Katie 172, 181, 214
More, Thomas (politician) 151
Morley, Carol A. 65
Morris, Brian 28
Mosley, Humphrey 54–55
Moxon, Joseph 79, 86–87, 229n101
Much Ado About Nothing 15, 35, 47, 51, 73, 84, 90–91, 136, 174, 176, 178, 228n58
Muir, Kenneth 23, 30, 55, 89, 189

New Cambridge Shakespeare 4, 6, 106
New Penguin Shakespeare 15, 18, 23, 24, 25–26, 33, 34, 35, 36, 42, 44, 54, 55, 80, 81, 100, 160, 170, 213
Nicholl, Charles 64
Nosworthy, J. M. 28, 33, 35, 36, 37, 55
Nuttall, A. D. 5, 173

Oliver, H. J. 196
"omitted" quarto lines re-introduced by editors 54
original pronunciation 72–73, 76, 80, 227n33, 228n43
Othello 8, 12, 23, 26, 34, 35, 39–41, 51, 52, 55, 73, 79, 88, 93–97, 97–99, 102–103, 121–146, 174, 176, 181, 182, 184, 185–186, 222n38; Iago's motivation 121–123
Oxford Shakespeare 4, 18, 29, 169

Palmer, Kenneth 28
The Passionate Pilgrim 63
Poetaster 186
pointing acting exercise 193–194
Pope, Alexander 10
Porter, Charlotte 10; *see also* Clarke, Helen
Priestley, Clive 3
Psalm 23 47–48
punctuation 84–97, 133, 204, 207, 208, 229n111, 230n136

The Rape of Lucrece 181
repeated text in the First Folio 51–52, 53–54

re-writes by Shakespeare 20–23, 60–61
Richard II 58, 71–72, 126, 171, 216, 227n20
Richard III 10–13, 29, 47, 50, 51, 79–81, 83, 118, 124–125, 176, 183, 191–192
Ridley, M. R. 5, 7, 23, 40, 55, 93–95
Riverside Shakespeare 16, 25, 54, 64, 65
Robenolt, Tom 174, 230n133
Romeo and Juliet 11, 19–20, 42, 52, 53, 60, 62, 68, 72, 73, 82, 88, 99–102, 109, 111, 112–113, 115, 118–119, 176, 177, 181, 185, 204
Rowe, Nicholas 60, 226n33
Royal Shakespeare Company 3, 16, 70, 72, 146, 173, 175, 191, 215

Salvini 141, 172
Sartre, Jean-Paul 125–126
Schoenbaum, Samuel 68
Schucking, Levin L. 123
Second Folio 32, 33, 45, 48–49, 52, 53, 64, 65, 221n1
Shakespeare as actor 108–109
Shaw, George Bernard 14, 35, 117
Sher, Anthony 191–192, 213–214
Sir Thomas More (play) 86, 184
Smallwood, R. L. 15, 42, 43
Smethwick, John 64–65, 226n32
Sonnets 78, 109, 136, 178–181, 211
Southworth, John 47
speech prefixes 18, 82–84
spellings 69–73, 76, 155, 162
Spencer, T. J. B. 46, 100
Stanislavski, Constantin 125, 127, 132, 141; creative/magic if 129–130, 132; emotion memory 110, 132, 134; given circumstances 129, 138, 141, 200; justification 145–146
Stern, Tiffany 117
Stevenson, Robert Louis 172
Stoppard, Tom 55–56
Strasberg, Lee 110, 133
swapping roles acting exercise 187
Swetnam, Joseph 209–210

The Taming of the Shrew 28, 56, 111, 176, 184, 185, 202

Tannen, Deborah 196
Taylor, Gary 61, 227n24, 235n54
The Tempest 26, 38, 57
theatre games 192–193
Theobald, Lewis 19, 28, 39, 47, 143
Third Folio 42, 224n68, 228n71
thought change acting exercise 194–196
Tilney, Edmund 9
Timon of Athens 26, 39, 54, 57, 86, 195–196
Titus Andronicus 16, 207
Troilus and Cressida 28, 62, 73
The Troublesome Reign of King John 16
Tucker, Patrick 1, 33, 60, 62, 78, 85, 87, 94, 99, 117, 118
Twelfth Night 33–34, 47, 71, 111, 124, 125, 183–184, 185–186, 216
The Two Gentlemen of Verona 47, 56, 68, 141
The Two Noble Kinsmen 56, 196

unexplained by editors 27, 80, 223n59, 224n15
untranslated Latin in edited volumes 27–28

Venus and Adonis 43, 181
verse fossils 99
verse speaking 114–117
Vincent, Augustine 63, 226n55

Walker, Alice 225n6
Warner, Deborah 186–187, 192
The Warwick Shakespeare 4
Weingust, Don 54, 64, 65–66, 96, 117
Welles, Orson 92
Wells, Stanley 4, 60, 61, 73–74, 221n63
Wilders, John 69
Williams, George Walton 12–14
Wilson, John Dover 17, 41, 44, 93, 108
Wilson, Thomas 63
The Winter's Tale 35, 70, 73, 116, 141, 176, 179–180, 183
word changes by editors 29–50
word frequency 175–176, 199